Legitimate Targets?

Based on an innovative theory of international law, Janina Dill's book investigates the effectiveness of international humanitarian law (IHL) in regulating the conduct of warfare. Through a comprehensive examination of the IHL defining a legitimate target of attack, Dill reveals a controversy among legal and military professionals about the 'logic' according to which belligerents ought to balance humanitarian and military imperatives: the logics of sufficiency or efficiency. Law prescribes the former, but increased recourse to international law in US air warfare has led to targeting in accordance with the logic of efficiency. The logic of sufficiency is morally less problematic, yet neither logic satisfies contemporary expectations of effective IHL or legitimate warfare. Those expectations demand that hostilities follow a logic of liability, which proves impracticable. This book proposes changes to international law, but concludes that according to widely shared normative beliefs, on the twenty-first-century battlefield there are no truly legitimate targets.

JANINA DILL is a Lecturer in the Department of Politics and International Relations at the University of Oxford.

CAMBRIDGE
UNIVERSITY PRESS

University Printing House, Cambridge CB2 8BS, United Kingdom

Cambridge University Press is part of the University of Cambridge.

It furthers the University's mission by disseminating knowledge in the pursuit of education, learning and research at the highest international levels of excellence.

www.cambridge.org
Information on this title: www.cambridge.org/9781107694866

© Janina Dill 2015

First published 2015

A catalogue record for this publication is available from the British Library

Library of Congress Cataloguing in Publication data
Dill, Janina, 1983– author.
Legitimate targets? : social construction, international law and US bombing / Janina Dill.
    pages   cm – (Cambridge studies in international relations ; 133)
ISBN 978-1-107-05675-6 (hardback)
1. Air warfare (International law)   2. Humanitarian law.
3. War (International law)   4. Air warfare – United States – History.
5. United States. Air Force – History.   I. Title.
KZ6695.D55   2014
341.6'3–dc23
                                                    2014012739

ISBN 978-1-107-05675-6 Hardback
ISBN 978-1-107-69486-6 Paperback

For my parents Ulrike and Harald G. Dill

Contents

Acknowledgements

This book originated with a doctoral thesis completed at the Department of Politics and International Relations at the University of Oxford. I am deeply grateful to my adviser, Henry Shue. With his wisdom, enthusiasm and immeasurable perseverance he has encouraged and supported me above and beyond his obligations. He continues to provide invaluable guidance and is a source of inspiration in my academic work as well as in my life generally.

For reading parts of the book and providing helpful comments, I would like to thank Charles Beitz, Martha Finnemore, Andrew Hurrell, Peter J. Katzenstein, Robert O. Keohane, David Luban, Jeff McMahan, Chris Reus-Smit, Adam Roberts, Kathryn Sikkink, Benjamin Valentino, Jeremy Waldron, Jennifer Welsh, two anonymous reviewers at Cambridge University Press and four anonymous reviewers at Oxford University Press. For sparking my interest in ethics and for reading several chapters, I am indebted to the members of the Oxford War Workshop: Zahler Bryan, C. A. J. Coady, Ned Dobos, Cécile Fabre, Michael Gibb, Chrisantha Hermanson, Per Ilsaas, Seth Lazar, Alexander Leveringhaus, Marco Meyer, Jonathan Parry, David Rodin, Cheney Ryan, Klem Ryan, Serena Sharma, Henry Shue and Saul Smilanski. I have also benefited greatly from discussions with Dapo Akande, Jutta Brunnée, Stephanie Carvin, Mark Clodfelter, Neta Crawford, Tami Davis Biddle, Matthew Evangelista, Charles Garraway, Isabel V. Hull, David E. Johnson, Walter Ladwig III, Nicolas Lamp, Nicholas Lees, Cetta Mainwaring, Robin Markwica, Nicholas Onuf, Hays Parks, Sarah Percy, Mary Perry, Nina Silove, Hugo Slim, Victor Tadros and Stephen Toope. All remaining errors or inconsistencies in the book are, of course, solely my own responsibility.

This book would not have been possible without the insight and candour of the forty members of the United States armed forces who agreed to be interviewed. For their patience and for their kind willingness to share their expertise on the record I am particularly grateful to David A. Deptula, Charles Dunlap Jr, Leon A. Edney, Marc Garlasco and John A. Warden III. I am also indebted to Jeff Davies and his family, who welcomed me into their home, giving me the opportunity to learn first-hand not only about the Navy's approach to air power, but also about life on a Navy post. Although I did not use the material gathered in this book, I learned a great deal from fifteen interviews with members of the Royal Air Force.

For lively discussions, I would like to thank Michael O'Hanlon and the members of the fall 2009 class on defence analysis at the Woodrow Wilson School of Public and International Affairs. Furthermore, I have benefited enormously from the Summer Workshop for Analysis of Military Operations and Strategy (SWAMOS) in 2008 and have been inspired by its participants as well as its conveners, Richard K. Betts and Stephen Biddle. For opportunities to present parts of this work and receive valuable feedback, I would like to thank among others the members of the Oxford Changing Character of War (CCW) Programme, the Oxford Institute for Ethics, Law and Armed Conflict (ELAC), Oxford University's Centre for Socio-Legal Studies, the Law Faculty at Warwick University, the Mario Einaudi Center for International Studies at Cornell University and the Institut für Theologie und Frieden Cologne. The following organisations kindly provided the resources necessary to collect data and to write this book: the Studienstiftung des Deutschen Volkes, the Deutscher Akademischer Austauschdienst, Merton College (Domus Scholarship), the Cyril Foster and Norman Chester Funds, Oxford University's Faculty of Law, Wolfson College Oxford and the Woodrow Wilson School of Public and International Affairs at Princeton University.

For their unfailing support I am grateful, more than words can express, to my family in Hanover and Selbitz and to my additional family in Munich and Oxford.

Table of treaties under international law

Table of cases

Other courts

Acronyms

API	First Additional Protocol
C3	command, control and communication
CAS	close air support
DMPI	desired mean point of impact
EBOs	effects-based operations
GC I	First Geneva Convention
GC II	Second Geneva Convention
GC III	Third Geneva Convention
GC IV	Fourth Geneva Convention
ICJ	International Court of Justice
ICL	international criminal law
ICRC	International Committee of the Red Cross
ICTY	International Criminal Tribunal for the Former Yugoslavia
IHL	international humanitarian law
IL	international law
IR	international relations (the discipline)
JAG	Judge Advocate General
NATO	North Atlantic Treaty Organization
ODS	Operation Desert Storm
OIF	Operation Iraqi Freedom
OLB I	Operation Linebacker I
OLB II	Operation Linebacker II
ORDC	*Official Records of the Diplomatic Conference*
ORT	Operation Rolling Thunder
UAV	unmanned aerial vehicle
UN	United Nations
UNC	United Nations Charter

Introduction

Tales of 'dropping artillery on people's homes',[1] of 'shooting down [fleeing] men and women',[2] of intimidation and looting[3] and mutilated children's bodies[4] have emerged from US military operations in Iraq. These accounts of brutality refer to a military that only twelve years earlier conducted what was then hailed as 'the most legalistic war ... ever fought'.[5] They describe a war that prominent military commentator Michael Schmitt called 'undoubtedly the most precise in the history of warfare',[6] during which US forces 'went to great pains to comply with the applicable norms of international humanitarian law';[7] US forces that the famous investigative journalist Seymour Hersh denounced as more 'violent and murderous'[8] than any American military before them.

Two themes dominate the popular and academic discussion of US military operations: criticism that US military practices inflict unacceptable harm on civilians, on the one hand,[9] and praise for the subjection of

---

[1] Massing (2007) 20; also Wright (2005). [2] Farrell (2008); also Fick (2005).
[3] Bellavia with Bruning (2008).
[4] Wright (2005); also Zoepf and Dagher (2008).
[5] Colonel Raymond Rupert, staff judge advocate to General H. Normand Schwarzkopf, quoted in Keeva (1991) 77; similar Jochnick and Normand (1994) 49: 'the cleanest and most legal war in history'; Schmitt (1997/98) 255: 'the most discriminate and controlled air campaign in history'; also Parks (1991/92) 393.
[6] Schmitt (2008) 36.
[7] Schmitt (2003) 108; similar Farrell (2005) 179; Kahl (2006) 12; Shaw (2005) 15.
[8] Quoted in Lukacs (2006).
[9] Research that criticises the human costs imposed by contemporary US military practices includes Bothe (2001); Conetta (2002); Cordesman (2003); Dougherty and Quénivet (2003); Gardam (1993); Heintschel v. Heinegg (2003) 284; Human Rights Watch (1991); Human Rights Watch (2003); Jochnick and Normand (1994); Ratner (2002) 913; Sassòli (2005); Shue (2011); Shue and Wippman (2002). For non-academic accounts of the 2003 war against Iraq that highlight civilian suffering see Bellavia and Bruning (2008); Fick (2005); Massing (2007); Raski and West (2008); Wright (2005).

every aspect of combat operations to legal review, on the other hand.[10] The criticism is reinforced by media reports of widespread outrage about US military operations among the populations under attack.[11] The praise seems vindicated by a closer examination of the military's institutional set-up and organisational culture. An increasing number of professional lawyers have seen their involvement in decision-making grow, and legal terminology has gradually infused military discourse.[12] Where once the law was considered to be silent – on the battlefield of war – today its voice, or at least its vocabulary, is omnipresent. Some commentators consider this an indication of the effectiveness of international humanitarian law (IHL), and indeed the normative acceptability of US warfare, notwithstanding the vigorous reprobation of just that warfare by their colleagues.

Of course, different professional angles generate distinct emphases in the assessment of war. None the less, the coincidence of these two themes – widespread condemnation for the harm inflicted during hostilities and commendation for war's comprehensive subjection to regulation by international law (IL) – is puzzling. The thought that the subjection of US warfare to IL may have gone hand in hand with its brutalisation appears counterintuitive. We tend to associate law with order and restraint. We would therefore expect the penetration of war

---

[10] Studies of the US military that stress the importance of legalism in its organisational culture and the crucial role played by lawyers in recent wars include Blum (2001); Coe and Schmitt (1997); Dunlap (2001a); Dunlap (2001b) 15; Dunlap (2008); Kahl (2006); Kahl (2007); Keeva (1991); Kramer and Schmitt (2008); Lewis (2003); Parks (1990); Parks (1991/2); Roberts (1994); Rogers (2004); Schmitt (1992); Schmitt (1998); Schmitt (2003); Schmitt (2004); Schmitt (2010).

[11] For media reports about public protests against civilian suffering allegedly inflicted by coalition forces in Iraq and Afghanistan see among others Faiez (2012); Farrell (2008); Raski and West (2008). The coverage of US targeted killings in Pakistan features a similar theme. Bergen and Tiedemann argue that the perception that air strikes kill innocent civilians accounts for the fact that 'nearly two-thirds of those polled in Pakistan's tribal areas said that suicide attacks against US military targets are justified'. Bergen and Tiedemann (2011); similar McClatchy (2010); Rohde (2012); Salopek (2012); Shanker (2008); Tavernise and Lehren (2010) A1.

[12] Bowman (2003); Centre for Law and Military Operations (2004) 5f.; Fontenot (2005); for a detailed account of the gradual increase in the importance of legal considerations in US military decision-making see also Chapter 5. For observations of this trend in modern militaries in general, consider, among others, Kennedy (2006); Kennedy (2012) 160; Mégret (2011).

by IL to result in fewer deaths and less destruction. That combat operations subjected to law are widely considered worthy of intense criticism or even moral reprehension betrays these expectations.[13]

There are two ready ways of explaining this puzzle. One option is to point to individual instances in which it appears that the US has broken the law and to argue that, its legalistic façade notwithstanding, the US military in fact disregards IL whenever it contradicts its interests. The problem would then lie in the unlawful behaviour of the US military. An alternative hypothesis would draw attention to the fact that states are not only the addressees of international legal regulation but also its creators. Any betrayal of our expectations could be explained not by a lack of respect for the law, but by the fact that the law itself is seriously at odds with our normative standards. In this scenario states have created IL which, rather than constraining their behaviour in war, accommodates military imperatives and permits conduct that public opinion deems problematic.

These two possibilities raise a crucial question: what does it mean for warfare to be subject to legal regulation? 'War is about killing people and breaking things.'[14] Or in other words, it inevitably jeopardises individual rights on a large scale. War often marks a breakdown of international order and stability. Yet the current international system is anarchic in the sense that it lacks an overarching authority. As a result, the use of force by states against states is sometimes the only available means to maintain order or protect human life. IL seems to offer a way out of this dilemma. How can states reconcile non-pacifist foreign policies with their identity as benevolent members of an international society that undeniably has liberal human rights-affirming tendencies? They count on IL to render warfare, at least in a basic sense, normatively acceptable. Should they not?

The strikingly dichotomous commentary on US military operations gives us reason to investigate more closely what is ultimately one of the

---

[13] This work by no means rests on the ready assumption that US conduct in war is in fact normatively problematic, or for that matter, that the US military always duly adheres to its obligations under IL. The commentary, both popular and academic, on US military practices is highlighted because it presents the conundrum that initially inspired this project. Both questions, whether the US adheres to the laws of war as well as whether and according to what criteria contemporary US combat operations are condemnable, are addressed in the chapters to come.

[14] Roat (2000) xi.

most fundamental questions in the study of international relations: can war, the seemingly endemic phenomenon in which international relations temporarily take the form of a confrontation involving the use of force, be effectively regulated by IL? This book is not primarily concerned with the equally important issue of whether war is indeed an inevitable occurrence in interstate relations. Nor does it explore the possibility of overcoming the use of force through a legalisation[15] or 'constitutionalisation' of these relations.[16] The focus is on the question of whether, once states have resorted to the use of armed force, IL can be effective in regulating their conduct.[17]

International armed conflict, the purposeful use of force between states for the achievement of political goals,[18] is a hard case for testing IL's capacity to influence state behaviour. The stakes for the belligerent states will generally be high. The fact that a conflict has escalated to the point of an armed confrontation furthermore suggests that common ground is hard to come by. States at war seek relative gains over each other so that the interaction of belligerents necessarily takes the form of a zero-sum game. Indeed, armed conflict most resembles the realist 'ideal type'[19] of international relations, where the very survival of states is on the line.[20] As a result, adages such as *Kriegsraison geht vor Kriegsmanier*[21] or *inter arma silent leges*[22] strike many as compelling truths.

Yet since the end of the Second World War the development of the law of armed conflict, IHL or *jus in bello*[23] seems to have defied these

---

[15] I use the term legalisation as shorthand for the subjection of an activity to regulation by IL. The term does not imply a judgement on the legality of the activity in question.

[16] The debate about a possible constitutionalisation of IL is addressed in section 8.2; for the most widely cited works see Bogdandy (2006); Bryde (2003); Cohen (2010); Kumm (2004); Schilling (2005); Slaughter and Burke-White (2002).

[17] Although the primary intellectual interest of this book is the regulation of the *conduct* of war by IHL, some chapters necessarily touch on questions of resort.

[18] Kagan (2006) xvi; also Gray (2006) 30.   [19] Weber (1949) 90.

[20] Grieco (1988a) 487; for outlines of the realist conception of international relations see also Donelly (2010); Mearsheimer (1995); Waltz (1979); Wohlforth (2010).

[21] 'The necessities of war take precedence over the rules of war.' Commentary to the Protocol Additional to the Geneva Conventions of 12 August 1949, Relating to the Protection of Victims of International Armed Conflicts, adopted 8 June 1977 (API), 390, §1368.

[22] 'When weapons speak the law is silent.' For the origins of the quotation that is usually attributed to Cicero see Roberts and Guelff (2002) 31.

[23] I use these three terms interchangeably despite their slightly different evocations.

assumptions about its inevitably limited role.[24] Though one of the oldest areas of IL, it was only with its codification in the four Geneva Conventions of 1949 (GC I–IV)[25] that IHL developed into a coherent regime dealing with important issues on the periphery of war, such as prisoners, civilians, soldiers *hors de combat* and belligerent occupation. It took the API of 1977[26] for IHL to reach states' behaviour during actual combat with detailed positive regulation.[27] IHL now proscribes and prescribes states' conduct in hostilities in a number of legal instruments. Participation in these treaties has spread and their reception into customary law has been consolidated. Today most states in the international system are bound by a relatively uncontested set of core legal norms regarding their conduct in war.[28] Moreover, the last decades have seen a dramatically raised profile of law in international relations in general.[29] As a result, legal terminology has

[24] This book discusses warfare between states only. Unfortunately, this is largely untrue for non-international armed conflicts.

[25] First Geneva Convention for the Amelioration of the Condition of the Wounded and Sick Armed Forces in the Field, first adopted in 1864, last revision in 1949 (GC I); Second Geneva Convention for the Amelioration of the Condition of Wounded, Sick and Shipwrecked Members of Armed Forces at Sea, first adopted in 1906, last revision in 1949 (GC II); Third Geneva Convention Relative to the Treatment of Prisoners of War, first adopted in 1929, last revision in 1949 (GC III); Fourth Geneva Convention Relative to the Protection of Civilian Persons in Time of War, first adopted in 1949 (GC IV).

[26] See note 21.

[27] Earlier treaties contain provisions on means and methods of injuring the enemy. However, these legal instruments merely stipulate general principles that proscribe certain methods of combat, such as the bombardment of undefended towns. In contrast to the API, they do not prescribe courses of action for engaging the enemy. See the Convention on the Laws and Customs of War on Land of 29 July 1899 (The Hague II), revised in The Hague IV of 18 October 1907; the Convention of the Bombardment by Naval Forces in Time of War of 18 October 1907 (The Hague IX); and the Declaration on the Launching of Projectiles and Explosives from Balloons of 29 July 1899.

[28] There are important caveats to this statement both regarding the unambiguousness of these rules as well as their universality. Particularly relevant in the context of this work is the fact that the US has to this day not ratified API. This issue is further discussed in section 4.2. Here it deserves emphasis that in less than sixty years arguably the most essential rule regulating conduct in war, the legal norm of noncombatant immunity, understood as a prohibition against directly targeting civilians, has reached a level of internalisation at which it is rarely openly contested.

[29] Similar Abbott *et al.* (2000) 408; Byers (2010) 976; Crawford and Koskenniemi (2012) 15; Keohane (2012a) 128; Reus-Smit (2004a); Sloane (2010) 561.

gradually permeated military discourse. The battlefield set-up of inter-state wars has started to reflect this 'move to law'.[30] In David Kennedy's words, '[l]aw now shapes the institutional, logistical and physical landscape of war and the battlespace has become as legally saturated as the rest of modern life'.[31]

As adumbrated, the development of warfare into 'a legal institution'[32] has led many commentators to the conclusion that IL in war is after all effective, that indeed IHL is one of few branches of IL that can claim victory over anarchy in its area of regulation.[33] The observation that IL has penetrated warfare, in turn, serves as a forceful argument against the realist dogma of the eternally unchanging nature of international relations.[34] If IL can regulate war, where social and moral norms against the use of violence have broken down, surely no part of international relations is beyond its grasp. In parallel to its increased importance in reality, IHL has thus evolved from a neglected and seemingly invidious field of IL to one of the most prominent issues on the academy's research agenda.[35]

US military practices present the most striking example of radical change. Not five years before the entry into force of the API, the US waged war against North Vietnam (from 1965 to 1972) largely without considering IHL in military decision-making. In contrast, during the war against Iraq in 1991, legal considerations did play a role in shaping combat operations. Twelve years later, the invasion into Iraq to topple Saddam Hussein was thoroughly and comprehensively subjected to law. If IL can successfully regulate the conduct of war, this ability will most probably be manifest in contemporary US combat operations. In

---

[30] Goldstein *et al.* (2000) 385.   [31] Kennedy (2012) 161.   [32] *Ibid.*, 162.

[33] For instance, Belt (2000) 136; Canestaro (2004) 431; Dunlap (1999) 28; Kahl (2007) 36; Kennedy (2006) 7.

[34] For a dismissal of this realist premise of the impossibility of fundamental change in international relations see Keohane (2012a) 127.

[35] Hersch Lauterpacht famously said that 'if international law is, in some ways, at the vanishing point of law, the law of war is, perhaps even more conspicuously, at the vanishing point of international law' (Lauterpacht (1952) 382). This verdict and the implied scepticism regarding IHL's qualification as law used to mean that any scholar studying IHL had to overcome an even higher threshold of doubt about her subject than other international lawyers before her research could hope to meet with the interest of peers. This is the case no longer. Scholars of IHL are like other international lawyers, as Thomas Franck observed, largely 'emancipated from the constraints of defensive ontology ... [and] now free to undertake a critical assessment of its [IL's] content' (Franck (1995) 6).

2003, the air war was arguably the most exhaustively legalised part of the invasion. A comparison of earlier US bombing campaigns that were not subjected in the same way to IL with the air war of 2003 is a researcher's best bet to shed light on whether IL makes a difference in war. This book's theoretical propositions are therefore tested with a comparative study of US air warfare from 1965 to 2003.[36]

Against the backdrop of the traditional, deeply rooted scepticism towards the ability of IL to regulate interstate war and the recent hailing of its triumph in precisely this endeavour, the academic stakes in showing whether IHL is effective appear high. Of course, much higher are the stakes that parties to an actual armed conflict have in IL's ability to regulate it. The vital importance of IL's restraining capacity for the populations under attack is immediately obvious. However, whether IHL effectively constrains state behaviour during combat operations is also crucial for the legitimacy of the attacking powers' use of military force. It is thus relevant in humanitarian as well as in political terms. For the fulfilment of IHL's humanitarian and political purposes the ability to delimit *that* part of a state and society at war that may be engaged in combat operations is particularly important. Indeed the determination of what is fair game for and what is immune from attack is the litmus test of effectiveness for IL in war. The book hence focuses not just on the role of IHL in US air warfare generally, but specifically on the influence of the legal definition of a legitimate target of attack on what the US chooses to bomb.

To sum up, the subject of enquiry of this book – the effectiveness of IHL in defining a legitimate target of attack in US air warfare – is the result of three deliberate choices. First, IL is studied with a hard, possibly the hardest, case for showing its ability to be effective in international relations: interstate war, in particular the conduct of hostilities. If the analysis could show that IL makes a difference in combat operations, then that would bode well for IL's ability to regulate international relations in general. This ability is in international relations scholarship (references to the discipline herein IR) as well as popular perception still often in doubt. Second, IHL is studied with, as war goes, the easiest specific case for showing its ability to effectively regulate war: comprehensively legalised US air warfare. If IL can render war an acceptable policy choice at all, that capacity should be on display

---

[36] For a more detailed explanation of the case selection see Chapter 5.

in contemporary US combat operations from the air. Third, IHL's effectiveness is studied in the light of the task that in humanitarian and political terms is its most important: to define a legitimate target of attack.

What does effectiveness mean when it comes to IL? That states rarely defy the largely non-enforceable rules of IL tends to surprise jurists and scholars of IR. These low expectations explain the standard account that equates effectiveness of IL with recourse to it: a rule of IL that is widely drawn upon in decision-making is deemed effective.[37] The dichotomous assessment of current US military practices, illustrated at the beginning, however, suggests that we should demand more of IL before we call it effective. A concept of legal effectiveness needs to take account of IL's ability to actually make a difference for behaviour and of the normative implications of adherence to a legal rule.[38]

The book therefore first explores whether international legal norms can have an impact of their own on behaviour. States presumably create law that reflects their interests. Moreover, non-legal social or moral norms may well influence state action. In order to be able to call IL effective, we have to establish that the law has *some* impact on behaviour that is not merely attributable to a state's interests or shaped by other (non-legal) norms. When an actor recurs to law in decision-making, does she behave differently compared with how she would have behaved according to her interests and pre-legal normative beliefs alone? The book endeavours to determine whether the subjection of interstate armed conflict to IHL can make a distinguishable difference for behaviour. Does recourse to the legal definition of a legitimate target of attack have what I call 'an impact of its own' on what the US attacks?[39]

We generally believe that law guides behaviour in the direction of what is right. Yet we cannot simply assume that recourse to IL leads to normatively acceptable behaviour. After all, congruence between IL

---

[37] For instance, Alter (2000); Byers (1999); Chayes (1974); Chayes and Chayes (1995); Franck (1992); Koh (1997); Young (1979).

[38] Chapter 1 provides a detailed discussion of the relevant debates between scholars of law and IR. It finds that both disciplines lack enquiries into IL's effectiveness understood in this way.

[39] This is not meant to suggest that IL can be independent of underlying interests or norms. The next two chapters elaborate on what IL having 'an impact of its own' or 'a counterfactual added value' or law 'making a distinguishable difference' means.

and non-legal – for instance, moral – prescriptions for proper conduct cannot be taken for granted. While many laws can be traced back to a higher principle, other considerations, such as military imperatives in the case of IHL, also shape a legal regime.[40] This then raises the question of whether the behaviour that results from resort to IHL in decision-making accords with our pre-legal normative expectations regarding warfare. In other words, it is insufficient to show that IHL has *some* impact of its own on behaviour. We also need to know whether the difference that it makes leads to normatively acceptable behaviour, in this case combat operations that are perceived as legitimate. Whether an attack in war is legitimate is a matter of perception. Determining the effectiveness of IL hence requires the identification of a relevant audience and the extra-legal normative standard this audience brings to bear when judging behaviour and by implication when evaluating IL.

To recapitulate, assessing the effectiveness of IL in a given issue area comprises two tasks: first, showing that the law has an effect on behaviour beyond what interests and non-legal normative beliefs would have led an actor to do anyway; second, enquiring whether this counterfactual difference leads to normatively acceptable behaviour. I refer to these two aspects of legal effectiveness as IL's behavioural relevance and its normative success respectively.[41] Behavioural relevance concerns the relationship between the legal definition of a legitimate target of attack and what the US in fact attacks. Normative success concerns the relationship between what the US targets (to the extent that this is determined by law) and what is a legitimate target of attack according to an audience yet to be identified and the extra-legal normative standard guiding expectations of what IHL should accomplish in war. Behavioural relevance describes a causal mechanism;[42] normative success judges the mechanism's result. Together they are necessary and sufficient conditions for calling IHL effective in regulating the conduct of hostilities.

---

[40] Moreover, the notion that law can have an effect that is distinguishable from the effects of an actor's other normative beliefs (and her interests) presupposes conceptual separateness of law from other normative codes.

[41] This book develops various innovative concepts that do not occur in the existing literature. While these concepts are carefully introduced and discussed in detail over the course of the book, they are also defined in the appendix for easy reference.

[42] I discuss the notion of causality underlying this analysis in detail in section 7.4.

Do we really need two new terms in order to study the role of IL in international relations? How do the behavioural relevance and normative success of IL relate to 'compliance', the most commonly used concept to judge the performance of IL? The answer to this question depends on what exactly one means by compliance, which is not at all self-evident. The following paragraphs relate different ways of understanding compliance to the notions of behavioural relevance and normative success respectively and define compliance for the purposes of this book. They show that an enquiry into the effectiveness of IL, as undertaken here, differs fundamentally from a study of compliance.[43]

Compliance can mean conformity of behaviour with a legal rule. Conformity as such, of course, says little about the actual role that law plays in bringing it about. This is why scholars have pitted compliance against convergence: behaviour that happens to conform to law for reasons other than recourse to law is considered to be due to convergence. In this view, compliance only describes behaviour that would not have occurred had it not been for IL. This in turn means that any claim that states comply with IL already contains the assumption that recourse to IL makes a difference for behaviour, because compliance signals an adjustment of behaviour due to law rather than other factors. However, I suggest that we do not yet know whether and how IL can make a difference for behaviour. The concept of compliance as 'conformity of behaviour that does not count as convergence' does not purport or imply a particular theory about the 'whether' or the 'how'. An enquiry into IL's behavioural relevance affords both.

The other assumption made by the understanding of compliance as conformity of behaviour with law is that the putative difference that law makes corresponds to the content of the law. However, it is a problematic notion that a legal rule has 'one content' and a certain corresponding behaviour that can be expected to result from recourse to it. The meaning of a legal provision arises partly in its interpretation, during which an actor's prior normative beliefs and interest-driven considerations play a role. It follows that we can only theorise in the abstract about whether and how IL can make a difference (behavioural relevance), not what kind of difference a specific legal rule will in fact make (normative success).

---

[43] For discussions of the various partly diverging conceptions of compliance in IR literature and legal scholarship see, among others, Downs, Rocke and Barsoom (1996); Guzman (2002); Kingsbury (1997/8); Simmons (1998).

In order to know the latter we have to actually observe behaviour and investigate to what extent it is due to the behavioural relevance of law. This in turn allows us to appraise the kind of difference that a specific rule of IL in a certain context makes. A normative evaluation of the kind of behaviour that follows recourse to law – and by implication of the law as well as of the interpreting actor – is what an enquiry into IL's normative success accomplishes. To the contrary, compliance alone implies an assessment of the observed behaviour only to the extent that we consider conformity with law a normative end in itself. It does not imply a normative evaluation of the law at all.

Besides denoting conformity of behaviour with law, compliance can also allude to an actor's agreement with, acceptance or approbation of a law. We can interpret this to indicate solely an acquiescent mental state or a favourable position regarding a legal rule. Alternatively compliance as approbation could imply a behavioural effort in action to adjust one's behaviour to accord with the law. If we assume that it implies a mental state only, compliance is not a concept conducive to explaining behaviour because instrumental considerations or competing normative beliefs might prevent an actor from translating approbation of law into action. Even if we think that approbation necessarily generates an attempt at norm-conforming behaviour, compliance still does not tell us whether and how that makes a difference. After all, actors may approve of law because it accords with their pre-legal normative beliefs or because it furthers their instrumental goals. In other words, they might have behaved in the same way had it not been for IL.

What approbation actually describes is one among many possible reasons why an actor might recur to IL in the first place. It denotes a source of an actor's intent to draw on law in decision-making. It is a potential source of a sense of legal obligation.[44] This is what most scholars actually investigate when they study compliance with IL: why do states adhere to IL? Is it because of their agreement with the content of the law, their general perception of IL as legitimate or due to some instrumental consideration such as fear of reputational costs

---

[44] The concept of legal obligation presents its own definitional challenges. In line with Reus-Smit, I understand obligation to provide one of many possible explanations for compliance, just like approbation or coercion (Reus-Smit (2003) 5). However, unlike approval of a rule or the fear of sanctions, a sense of obligation requires further explanation. I touch on attempts to account for the obligatory nature of IL in section 1.3.

or even sanctions? The question arises, of course, because IL, contrary to municipal law, is not systematically enforced. I discuss this literature in Chapter 1. Here it is crucial to stress that throughout this book the word 'compliance' (or the synonyms recurrence and adherence) denotes the initial act of drawing on a legal rule when faced with the task of making a decision, and nothing else. Effectiveness asks what happens after this initial recourse, after compliance: does it make a difference (behavioural relevance) and, if so, of what kind (normative success)? In this reading compliance is a precondition for IL to potentially be effective. Compliance is a necessary but not a sufficient condition of IL's effectiveness.

In order to shed light on the effectiveness of IL in war the book will successively answer four different questions. A positive answer to each question is a precondition to asking the next. First, *can* IL make a distinguishable difference for behaviour in international relations where actors create laws that reflect their normative beliefs and interests and no central authority enforces those that do not? Second, can IHL make a difference specifically in war? The answers to these two questions are theoretical in nature. While the former concerns social science, specifically IR theory, the latter also requires a close investigation of IHL, in particular the law defining a legitimate target of attack. Third, *does* IHL in fact make a difference in US air warfare? This question calls for an empirical answer. And fourth, if so, *what kind* of difference does recourse to IL make in war? The answer to this last question depends on identifying an appropriate normative standard to hold IHL to. The analysis of the effectiveness of IL in the regulation of warfare thus has a twofold theoretical, an empirical and a normative, aspect, reflected in the four-part structure of the book.

Part I explicates how theoretically recourse to law in international relations can make a difference for behaviour. Based on the proposed theory of how IL works, I adopt an account of what IL is. In particular, I establish which features allow a legal rule to potentially have an impact on behaviour beyond the influence of an actor's interests and normative beliefs. Against this backdrop, Part II thoroughly analyses those rules that together define a legitimate target of attack according to IHL. In the process, I address various interpretative debates in IHL and explain them in terms of two competing visions of how hostilities ought to be conducted. I refer to them as the logic of sufficiency and the logic of efficiency.[45] Part I thus draws on methods of social scientific theory building and Part II on legal exegesis. The aim is to contribute to both: an IR theory of IL and a consensus on the legal definition of a legitimate target of attack.

Part III tests the propositions of Parts I and II with an investigation of US practices in selected air campaigns from the first bombing campaign against North Vietnam in 1965 to the air war against Iraq in 2003. A comparison of targets over this period of time leads to the finding that increased recourse to law coincides with a change in the logic that hostilities follow: initially warfare largely accords with the logic of sufficiency, but as legal input grows targeting follows more and more the logic of efficiency. I explain the connection between the subjection of warfare to IHL and the logic hostilities accord with by drawing on interviews with US military personnel. They shed light on how the legal provisions on targeting become constitutive of the definition of a legitimate target; specifically how US decision-makers come to believe that the legitimacy of a target hinges on how efficiently an attack contributes to a war's overall political goals. Part III thus follows an exercise of empirical theory testing with a renewed effort in theory building. I conclude that recourse to IHL makes a distinguishable difference in US air warfare. IHL is, in fact, behaviourally relevant.

Part IV assesses the normative success of IHL in US air warfare. What kind of behaviour follows behavioural relevance of IHL in US air warfare? Crucially, showing that law influences the choice of targets by the US military does not mean that we have a clear picture of how contemporary warfare would look if the US did *not* recur to IL. Specifically the humanitarian implications of combat operations, such as civilian casualties or lives lost in general, are also determined by other factors. As it is not possible to establish whether legalised contemporary US air warfare causes less human suffering or fewer civilian casualties than non-legalised combat operations under the same circumstances, I evaluate *how* IHL distributes the harm involved in conducting hostilities.

I present an argument, based on moral criteria as well as public perception, for why it is preferable to distribute harm according to the

---

[45] The logics are introduced in sections 3.4 (sufficiency) and 4.3 (efficiency) respectively. Section 6.2 discusses the kind of targets the two logics each define as fair game and the extent to which they underlie US air targeting. Their respective normative merits are compared in section 8.1. For a definition see the appendix.

logic of sufficiency rather than in accordance with the logic of efficiency. This explains to some extent the initial observation that targets in contemporary US air warfare, which are, as it turns out, chosen under the guidance of IHL and in accordance with the logic of efficiency, do not generally meet with public approval. The US definition of a legitimate target of attack diverges from the way 'the international public' seems to define a legitimate target of attack.[46] Would the logic of sufficiency do better? If IHL were changed so that recourse to law would largely guarantee that combat operations followed the logic of sufficiency, because a good faith interpretation would exclude target selection according to efficiency considerations, would conforming air strikes be perceived as legitimate?

I show that IHL that imposes the logic of sufficiency would still fall short of rendering combat operations acceptable by commonly held moral standards. In international relations increasingly those standards have come to be premised on the preservation of individual rights.[47] Of course, common perceptions of legitimacy are not based only on a society's shared moral beliefs. Most people allow for instrumental considerations to play a role when judging the legitimacy of conduct, specifically in war. However, I argue that IHL that endorses the large-scale violation of individual rights as a legally privileged course of action – both logics imply just that – is unlikely to be perceived as legitimate by the international public of the twenty-first century. I further demonstrate that a law that seems to ensure that the infringements of individual rights that occur during the conduct of hostilities could be morally justified – by imposing what I refer to as the logic of liability[48] – cannot in reality be coherently applied and bears the potential to make things worse. The best IL can do in war – impose the logic of sufficiency – is to generate air strikes widely perceived as illegitimate.

The book draws three main conclusions. First, IL can make a difference for behaviour when it is recurred to in decision-making, and it does so even in war: in US air warfare IL proves constitutive of the definition of a legitimate target according to the logic of efficiency. Second, IHL is not normatively successful in regulating US bombing. Third, even if IL

---

[46] Sections 7.3 and 8.2 discuss the extent to which there is such a thing as 'an international public' or 'a global public opinion' with identifiable shared normative beliefs and common expectations of IHL.

[47] There is a growing literature on the subject; see most recently Reus-Smit (2013).

[48] For a definition of the logic see the appendix.

did the best it could to regulate warfare, it could not vouchsafe the legitimacy of warfare according to popular perception. To the extent that widely shared moral standards in international relations increasingly centre on the protection of individual rights, IL cannot possibly afford the normative acceptability of combat operations. Together these findings explain the original puzzle that comprehensively legalised warfare meets with widespread academic criticism and popular outrage. In the twenty-first century, normative beliefs widely shared across the international society suggest that in war there is no such thing as legitimate targets.

PART I

A constructivist theory of international law

1 | *The challenge*

IL is ubiquitous in modern life. Its significance for international relations is beyond doubt.[1] Accordingly, IR scholarship has come a long way since dismissing IL as irrelevant;[2] as long a way as legal theory has come since rejecting it as not law.[3] Yet our theoretical grasp of the phenomenon is neither comprehensive nor secure. There is a lacuna where there should be an account of, or at least a debate about, the effectiveness of IL.[4] Specifically the question of how IL relates to interests and non-legal norms remains largely unanswered. How can law make a difference in international relations, where states create legal rules that accord with their interests and normative beliefs, while no central authority enforces those legal rules that do not?

This first chapter does not specifically discuss the regulation of war. Rather it systematises scholarship about IL in IR and in legal theory. I ask three questions that scholars of IR, faced with the phenomenon of IL, have posed: why do states create IL, why do states comply with IL and what is distinctive about the norms of IL? In addition, I discuss a

---

[1] For discussions of the role of IL in international relations see, among others, Abbott *et al.* (2000) 408; Byers (2000); Byers (2010) 612; Crawford and Koskenniemi (2012) 15; Keohane (2012a) 128; Reus-Smit (2004a); Sloane (2010) 561.

[2] Famously Morgenthau (1948) 211.

[3] John Austin defined law as commands issued by a sovereign and backed by a threat of sanctions, which meant that IL did not qualify (Austin (1832); Austin (1897/ 2002) 141f.). Hans Kelsen in a variation suggested that law is the authorisation of an official to deliver sanctions (Kelsen (1967) 110; see also Koskenniemi (2005) 25). Though H. L. A. Hart used this command theory of law as a foil for his own putatively less reductionist concept of law, he likewise dismissed IL as not truly law. Later his most conciliatory assessment of IL was that its analogy with municipal law was one 'of function and content not of form' (Hart (1997) 237). For criticism of the focus on sanctions in legal theory see O'Connell (2008); Shapiro (2006). For the most recent claim that IL is not really law see Goldsmith and Posner (2005) 202.

[4] Similar Dunoff and Pollack (2012a); Martin (2002); Raustiala and Slaughter (2002); Simmons (1998); Stein (2012); for the definition of effectiveness and its relationship to compliance, consult the introduction, pp. 8ff.

question mostly addressed by legal scholars: what does IL mean? Or rather, to what extent does the meaning of IL arise during its interpretation? The aim is to show that the answers to these four questions provided by the major theories of IR and by legal theory prejudicially pre-judge the notion that IL can make a counterfactual difference for behaviour. I conclude that existing scholarship, in law as well as IR, casts considerable doubt on IL's ability to be what I call 'behaviourally relevant'.[5]

1.1 The causal dependence of international law

Why do states create international law?

The first question IR theory ever asked when faced with IL was why states create it at all.[6] The adoption of supposedly binding, yet largely non-enforceable, rules for state conduct clashes with two fundamental assumptions underlying mainstream IR theory about structure and agency: international relations are conducted under conditions of anarchy,[7] and states are rational utility-maximising actors. Realism's answer to why states nevertheless resort to international law-making is, of course, that it can occasionally be in their interest to do so: '[I]nternational law serves largely to rationalise the policies of powerful states, which exploit its symbols to manage international affairs for their own purposes.'[8] Interests, according to the realist understanding, centre on obtaining power and/or security. Both are measured in terms of relative gains in material capabilities. As law-making follows states' interests, IL reflects the distribution of (material) power in the international system.

   However, contrary to what this conception of law would imply, resort to IL is not a rare phenomenon, but a regular occurrence in

---

[5] For a definition of the concept see the appendix. This chapter is not meant to provide a chronological overview of IR's engagement with IL. Several comprehensive accounts already exist. See Byers (2010); Dunoff and Pollack (2012a); Koh (1997); Reus-Smit (2004a).

[6] Similar Goldstein *et al.* (2000) 386.

[7] Ayson (2011) 563; Barnett and Sikkink (2010) 63; Battistella (2008) 3; Bull (1995) 77; Bull (1977) *passim*; Buzan (2007) 148; Donelly (2010) 154; Hurd (2010) 304; Waltz (1979) 88; Wendt (1992) *passim*; Wohlforth (2010) 133.

[8] Nardin (2008) 387; see also Aaken (2006); Goldsmith and Posner (2005); Thompson (2012).

international relations. Since the end of the Second World War, international legal regulation has become significantly more prevalent. Regime theory, which developed into liberal institutionalism, better accounts for this reality. While agreeing with realism's premise of utility-maximising actors seeking material gain, institutionalism provides a more sophisticated answer to the question of '[w]hy and when ... states choose legalised institutional forms when their autonomy would be less constrained by avoiding legalisation'.[9] It does so by drawing attention to the functional benefits of law-making.[10]

In the institutionalist's view, accepting a legal obligation, specifically in the context of an institution, signals a credible commitment. Repeated rule-governed interaction then puts a premium on maintaining actors' reputation and it allows for positive-sum cooperation.[11] Such a pursuit of absolute rather than relative gains is an option for rational actors in those areas of international relations where interaction with others does not directly affect their security, for instance international commerce.[12] While liberal institutionalists are thus much more optimistic than realists that states will, in fact, have an interest in international law-making, like the latter, they hold firm to the belief that 'law always rests on power and interests'.[13]

Constructivists have provided an alternative explanation for why states regularly create IL. Their account focuses on norms, which are defined as shared ideas containing 'standards of "appropriate" or "proper" behaviour'.[14] As shared beliefs about right and wrong are the basis of law-making,[15] explaining the creation of IL amounts to exploring 'why actors sometimes prefer to reinforce normative consensus with legalised institutions'.[16] Answers centre on the translation of norms into law as a by-product of norm-internalisation or as a means of

---

[9] Goldstein *et al.* (2000) 391.

[10] The pioneering works in this area are Keohane (1989); Krasner (1983); Young (1989).

[11] Abbott and Snidal (2000); also Abbott (1989); Fehl (2004) 357; Kahler (2000); Keohane (1997); Keohane (2002); Keohane (2009a) 204; Klabbers (2004/05); Slaughter-Burley (1993); Slaughter, Tuliumello and Wood (1998); Trubek, Cottrell and Nance (2005) 8.

[12] Stein (2010) 206.   [13] Keohane (2012a) 133.

[14] Lutz and Sikkink (2000); I use the terms 'norm', 'normative belief' and 'principled belief' interchangeably. They all refer to a shared idea that contains a supposition of appropriateness or an 'ought'.

[15] Sikkink (1998) 518; likewise Lutz and Sikkink (2001).

[16] Goldstein *et al.* (2000) 9.

norm-dissemination.[17] Many constructivists recognise the possibility that both normative beliefs as well as interests feed into IL. At the same time, liberal institutionalism has developed towards including norms, or 'principled beliefs', besides interests as possible building blocks of IL.[18] Some scholars in both camps now combine insights from different theoretical paradigms in order to understand the 'underlying motivations for legalisation'.[19]

In sum, IR theory conceives of international law-making as an expression of actors' interests (realists and liberal institutionalists),[20] normative beliefs (constructivists) or a combination of both. Scholars across theoretical orientations agree that IL is infused with political considerations, be those instrumental or principled.[21] In the words of E. H. Carr, 'the law is not an abstraction. It cannot be understood independently of the political foundation on which it rests.'[22] All this suggests that IL is a product of pre-existing interests and normative beliefs – which I refer to as reasons for action or motivational forces – and that its role in international relations is best understood by investigating these component variables.

Why do states comply with international law?

Ultimately the true explanatory challenge for IR is not that states create and enter into legal contracts, but that they then do not simply flout their obligations when it suits their interests to do so. In the absence of the coercive power of an enforcing sovereign, rational actors are predicted to routinely defect from their legal commitments. It is hence a

---

[17] For instance, Finnemore and Sikkink (1998); Franck (1992); Kratochwil (1989); Lutz and Sikkink (2000).

[18] Abbott (2004/5); Keohane (2009a); Keohane (2009b); Keohane (2012a); in fact even before the 'constructivist turn' in IR, some major works by liberal institutionalists considered the role of ideas. Famously Goldstein and Keohane (1993).

[19] Abbott and Snidal (2002) S143; Abbott and Snidal (2012); Abbott (2004/5).

[20] In a slight variation from liberal institutionalists, new liberals, such as Andrew Moravcsik, emphasise not interests, but preferences, specifically those of domestic pressure groups. Moravcsik (2012) 23.

[21] Explicitly Byers (2005); Byers (2010); Chayes and Handler Chayes (1993) 175; Colgan, Keohane, Van de Graaf *et al.* (2012); Goldsmith and Posner (2005); Keohane (2012a); Keohane (2012b); Nardin (2008); Reus-Smit and Clark (2007); Reus-Smit (2003); Reus-Smit (2004a); Reus-Smit (2004b).

[22] Carr (1946) 179.

widespread assumption that IL 'when confronted with the actions of determined states ... is weak and ineffectual'.[23] However, in the famous words of Louis Henkin, 'almost all nations observe almost all principles of international law and almost all of their obligations almost all the time'.[24] IR theory has taken on the task of explaining Henkin's observation by exploring the question of why states comply with IL.

High levels of adherence to legal norms pose a fundamental challenge to a theory of agency widely associated with neorealism. It conceives of states with reference to the concept of the *homo oeconomicus*, whose understanding of the world is 'complete and fixed'.[25] Based on the material structure of the international system, namely the distribution of power, he formulates interests that he pursues in a utility-maximising fashion. The coupling of materialism and rationalism in this concept of agency closes off two avenues for explaining widespread adherence to IL: first, the possibility that interests are formed and changed in an iterative process rather than arising from material circumstances and remaining fixed henceforth; and second, the possibility that states follow norms for their own sake.

To this materialist understanding of agency constructivism's ideational concept provides a natural counterpoint. In this view interests are endogenous, established and changed in social processes of interaction and identity formation. Since it is through ideas that actors attribute meaning to the material reality, their beliefs (including those about appropriateness) are constitutive of the world as they perceive it.[26] It follows that norms (shared ideas about what ought to be) not only potentially make a causal difference, they also help constitute actors' identities and hence their interests.[27] Actors may follow a norm of IL not only because they have an interest in adherence, such as fear of reputational costs or demonstrating credible commitment, but also because they have internalised a norm,

---

[23] Reus-Smit (2004a) 16 (paraphrasing the realist position on IL).
[24] Henkin (1979) 47; similar Mégret (2012) 76; Sloane (2010) 552.
[25] For the concept see Kydd (2010); also Farrell and Finnemore (2009) 59.
[26] Wendt (1999) 313.
[27] Hathaway and Koh (2005) 111; Legro (2005) 4; also Reus-Smit (2003); Reus-Smit and Clark (2007); Wendt (1992); Wendt (1995) 397; section 7.4 discusses the connection between causation and constitution.

or they conceive of themselves as good citizens of an international society based on certain norms.[28]

It is crucial to stress that this ideational concept of agency does not rule out rationality; it just implies a different understanding of it. In the constructivist view, an actor's understanding of the world can be neither fixed nor complete; it necessarily involves an open-ended process of discovery and interpretation. Yet many constructivists would agree that the social construction of actors can create 'instrumental, goal-seeking agents who pursue their goals in part by comparing costs and benefits [italics omitted]'.[29] Only what those actors perceive as costs and benefits, and hence what they deem to be in their interest, is a function of the ideas they hold about the world. Fearon and Wendt even argue that rationalism's 'point of departure has long been the explanation of action by reference to optimality in light of beliefs and desires'.[30] This includes beliefs and desires about how international relations *ought* to be, in other words, norms.

Between the ideational and the materialist concepts resides the liberal institutionalist understanding of agency, which Chris Reus-Smit and Duncan Snidal refer to as 'rationalist institutional'.[31] In this view, ideational factors 'mediat[e] the relationship between material or other interests and political outcomes'.[32] However, ideas are not constitutive of the structures of international interaction or actors' identities. Many constructivists would without hesitation designate ideational forces as more important than material forces, as in their view the material

---

[28] For instance, Finnemore and Sikkink (1998) 902.

[29] Hurd (2010) 311; also Ashley (1986); Farrell and Finnemore (2009) 60; Finnemore and Sikkink (1998) 910; Kydd (2010) 426f.

[30] Fearon and Wendt (2002) 8.

[31] Reus-Smit and Snidal (2010) 21; many proponents of classical and new liberalism likewise embrace a middle position rejecting both materialism and constructivism. It is difficult to adequately describe the concept of agency of classical realists, such as Hans Morgenthau, because their works tend to be less theoretically aware. Neoclassical realism is a label that is used for radically differing approaches to the study of international relations. One possible common denominator is a materialist approach to power and interests combined with a preoccupation with perceptions (see, for instance, Rose (1998); Schweller (1998)). This combination places neoclassical realists in opposition to neorealism as well as constructivism. To the extent that this scholarship rests on a coherent conception of agency it is closest to the liberal institutionalist middle position.

[32] Reus-Smit and Snidal (2010) 21.

reality has no intrinsic meaning and enjoys causal powers 'only in virtue of the contingent social relations in which [it is] embedded'.[33] To the contrary, liberal institutionalists dismiss deciding whether material or ideational factors are 'fundamental' as not 'a sensible enterprise'.[34] What about norms then? If they are neither constitutive of an inter-subjectively constructed reality nor epiphenomena of a material reality, what exactly is the role of shared ideas containing an 'ought' according to this third understanding of agency?

The position that 'ideas are not just "hooks" for interests, [but] have independent impact'[35] seems to allow for the possibility that norms are followed for their own sake due to the specific ideas an actor holds, as the ideational concept of agency suggests.[36] Yet the assertion that (normative) ideas matter tends to be overlaid with the caveat that they only do so to the extent that an actor has an interest in promoting them.[37] Robert Keohane's work, for instance, is permeated with insinuations that instrumental somehow trumps principled behaviour: norms 'are significant for strategy but not determinative of actions'[38] because in international relations 'norm-following behaviour is challenged by the logics of strategic interaction and instrumental rationality'.[39] This is first and foremost a substantive assumption, but one that has implications for and is revealing of an ontological premise. If both interests and norms are subject to ideas, it is unclear why the former should be prior to the latter in this way. The notion that interests confront actors in a different way from norms is plausible only if interests are connected to the material

---

[33] Wendt (2000) 169; also Hopf (1998); Hurd (2010); Kratochwil (2010); Kratochwil (2000).

[34] Keohane (2000) 129; similar Moravcsik (2010); Nye (2010); Richardson (2010); Simpson (2010); Stein (2010).

[35] Keohane (2009c) 38.

[36] Some liberal institutionalists acknowledge a resemblance between their propositions and constructivism (for instance, Abbott (2004/5); Abbott and Snidal (2000); Abbott and Snidal (2002); Keohane (2009c) 38). Ian Hurd considers this convergence an indication for the fact that constructivism's main claims have 'been largely internalized by the discipline'. He maintains that 'while the shift from a materialist to a socially constructed view of international relations was controversial in the early 1990s, it has now been broadly accepted' (Hurd (2010) 311).

[37] Keohane (2009c) 38.

[38] Keohane (2009b) 5; similar Keohane (2012a) 133; Keohane (2012b) 2f.

[39] Keohane (2009b) 5; similar Coglan *et al.* (2012) 120f.; Keohane (2009a) 204; Keohane (2012a) 129.

reality in a different way from norms. Do liberal institutionalists embrace neorealism's material concept of agency, according to which actors follow material interests, after all?[40]

Liberal institutionalists tend to deny that they conceive of interests as material.[41] Ultimately, the liberal institutionalist concept of agency is thus somewhat unstable – making overtures to constructivism when recognising the influence of ideas in general while inexorably drifting towards materialism when curtailing the importance of particular shared (often normative) beliefs.[42] While institutionalists' take on norms, as a result, remains ambivalent,[43] it is safe to say that this

---

[40] It is common practice among constructivists to bring their paradigm's surplus value into sharper relief by denouncing liberal institutionalism as materialist. Among others, Fearon and Wendt (2002) 13; Hurd (2010) 300; Wendt (2000) 169.

[41] Keohane (2000) 162, 128; Keohane (2009c) 38; Moravcsik (2012) 16.

[42] This suggests that the crucial axis of debate in IR theory runs between the materialist and the ideational concept of agency, hence between materialist theories and constructivism (similar Finnemore and Sikkink (2001); Hurd (2010)). In opposition, the more widespread view in the literature is that the most important dividing line in IR theory is situated between the rationalist and constructivist approaches (Dunoff and Pollack (2012a); Fearon and Wendt (2002); Reus-Smit (1996)). Yet, as mentioned earlier, some constructivists conceive of actors as rational just like liberal institutionalists and realists. Differences between their respective conceptions of rationality are chiefly determined by the role that various theories attribute to ideational forces. As a result, I believe that formulating the controversy in terms of materialism versus constructivism expresses what remains truly contested among different strands of IR theory: how material and ideational forces interact so that actors come to have certain interests and/or normative beliefs and what it means to be rational.

[43] In contradiction to his assertion that norms 'are significant for strategy but not determinative of actions', quoted above, in his earlier work with Judith Goldstein Keohane allows for the possibility that '[p]rincipled ideas can shift the focus of attention to moral issues and away from purely instrumental ones focussed on power and interest' (Goldstein and Keohane (1993) 17). Indeed, one argument of their influential book *Ideas in Foreign Policy* is that 'normative ideas that specify criteria for distinguishing right from wrong and just from unjust' can have an 'independent impact' (9, 21). Yet in his recent work Keohane comes very close to admitting to a material basis of interests in his conception of world politics. He criticises his colleagues for 'forgetting that law always rests on power and interests' (Keohane (2012a) 133). While he affirms IL's ability to 'reinforce and extend order', Keohane limits that possibility to circumstances when a 'sufficiently favourable structure of power and interests' underlies legalisation (133). He closes with the clarion call that 'a core lesson of Realism needs to be learned and relearned: Institutions rest on power and changes in power generate changes in institutions' (135, italics omitted). Similarly, Keohane's work with Colgan and Van de Graaf argues that IL changes when 'the underlying structures

concept of agency explores one of the two mentioned avenues for explaining widespread adherence to IL – it is conceivable that interests change. This can happen through the influence of ideas.[44] Regularly, however, interests develop because instrumental calculations change in the face of institutionalisation and the establishment of regimes, which create the functional benefits of norm compliance. Liberal institutionalists mostly discount the option that agents might follow norms for their own sake. For this limitation to be fully plausible we would require an explanation of the precise interaction of material and ideational factors according to this concept of agency – an explanation that liberal institutionalists still owe.[45]

Constructivists, to the contrary, conceive of the international system as 'a historically created and evolving structure of common understandings, rules, norms and mutual expectations'.[46] That structure is constituted and reproduced in agents' practice.[47] Concepts such as epistemic communities,[48] the norm lifecycle theory[49] or communities of practice[50] are well equipped to account not only for the prominent role of shared ideas about appropriateness in the interaction of states, but also for high levels of (at least partly non-instrumental) norm-conforming behaviour.

Despite their fundamental differences, all three concepts of agency – neorealist/materialist, constructivist/ideational and liberal institutionalist – converge on the notion that it is exogenous motivational forces that provide the reasons for adherence to IL: interests and/or shared normative beliefs.[51] As making and following IL amounts to an actualisation of prior interests and/or normative beliefs, behaviour

of power and interests no longer conform to institutional arrangements' (Colgan *et al.* (2012) 120). In the same work the benefits of and satisfaction with the legal regime under investigation are conceived in purely material terms (121) as is the 'importance' of states in the area of regulation (123).

[44] Goldstein and Keohane (1993) 16; also Keohane (2000) 129.

[45] The same can be said about many moderate constructivists, such as Alexander Wendt, who believes that a 'rump' material reality has its own causal impact that is not subject to perception (Wendt (1999) 96).

[46] Hurrell (2002) 142.   [47] Adler and Pouliot (2011) 6; Mattern (2011) 75.

[48] Adler (1997); Haas (1992).

[49] Finnemore and Sikkink (1998) 896; also Sandholtz and Stone Sweet (2004); Sikkink (2011).

[50] Wenger (1998).

[51] Similar Abbott *et al.* (2000); Moravcsik likewise identifies the exogenous motivation for adherence to IL as the common denominator of most IR research on IL regardless of its theoretical leanings (Moravcsik (2012) 33). For criticism

seemingly inspired by law is really either instrumental or principled. In this reading IL does not provide an independent reason for action. It is not a motivational force in its own right, but one whose creation and application are 'entirely conditioned by the vicissitudes of politics'.[52] IL is what I call 'causally dependent'.[53]

1.2 The epistemic dependence of international law

What does international law mean?

A reason why an agent acts in a certain way also sets a standard for the appraisal of that action. Evaluating behaviour in the light of its accordance with an actor's interests means enquiring into its 'utility'.[54] Assessing behaviour with a view to its correspondence to shared normative beliefs amounts to a judgement of its 'appropriateness'.[55] The basic reasons for action – interests and normative beliefs – hence correspond to two alternative normative standards or codes – utility and appropriateness.[56] What about IL? Does it provide a third standard for guiding and evaluating behaviour? In order to know the answer to this question we need to explore the extent to which IL embraces or constrains actors' quests for utility or appropriateness.[57] The standard

of the one-sided treatment of IL as a dependent variable see Adler (2005); Byers (2010) 615; Warner (1998) 322.

[52] Crawford and Koskenniemi (2012) 5.

[53] The concept of IL's causal dependence and the two later designations of IL as epistemically and ontologically dependent are not used in the IR literature discussing IL or by any scholar whose work I quote. They are defined in the appendix.

[54] I refer to arguments about utility as 'strategic' and behaviour guided by interest as 'instrumental'.

[55] Throughout the book arguments about appropriateness that advocate compliance with a norm are referred to as 'aspirational' and behaviour guided by norms is called 'principled'. While social norms set a standard of 'appropriateness', moral norms purport a standard better understood as 'justness'. For reasons of simplicity, and given that the following analysis only exceptionally differentiates between moral and social norms, I refer to the standard set by all norms simply as appropriateness.

[56] It might be counterintuitive to think of interests as providing a *normative* standard. However, interests prescribe how an actor ought to decide between different courses of action given certain utilities. Similar Mercer (2005) 80f.

[57] Likewise Dunoff and Pollack (2012b) 17; Nardin (2008). I have largely focused on bona fide IR scholars so far. While legal scholars have, with few exceptions, left the exploration of states' reasons for making or complying with IL to their colleagues in IR, they have naturally enquired more systematically into the

IL purports is obviously legality. Investigating the meaning of IHL means determining how legality relates to utility and appropriateness.

Martti Koskenniemi's influential explication of international legal argument *From Apology to Utopia* draws attention to the role of interests and normative beliefs not only in the creation of and adherence to IL, but also as the forces that govern IL's interpretation and thus determine its meaning. In Koskenniemi's view, IL is conceptually torn between being rooted in state consent, on the one hand, and needing to embody higher principles (non-legal norms), on the other hand. Because IL must be both deferential to interests and faithful to norms, two alternative forms of legal argument are possible.[58] An 'ascending' pattern of justification takes what states explicitly consent to as the starting point for an interpretation of IL. The alternative is a 'descending' pattern of justification, which emphasises the binding character of the law as a function of its intrinsic normativity.[59] This takes the norm or principle from which the law's content is derived as the starting point for the determination of a law's meaning.[60]

Koskenniemi then argues that to the extent that a legal interpretation fails to take account of actual state consent (descending argument), the

interpretation of IL. The next section introduces some legal theorists' takes on the reasons for compliance with IL.

[58] Koskenniemi (2005) 16; Koskenniemi (2012a) 12; Koskenniemi (2012b) 16.

[59] In fact, among international lawyers a divide persists about which element is ultimately more important for a rule of IL to emerge: state consent or the authority or importance of the underlying norm. On one side are international jurists mindful of preserving the 'traditional' strictly consensual international order, which 'starts from a position of complete freedom of states that it then attempts to curtail, rather than from a position of obligation from which zones of liberty might emerge' (Mégret (2012) 66; see also *France* v. *Turkey, SS Lotus* Permanent Court of International Justice, Judgment of 7 September 1927, File E.c. Docket XI Judgment no.11). On the other side are advocates of concepts such as general IL, objective regimes or *jus cogens*, which presuppose that in certain instances a state can be bound by virtue of the importance of the content of a law, without explicit consent. Scholars of IL who recognise concepts that qualify the indispensability of explicit state consent are, among others, Allott (2001); Simma (1994); Simma and Paulus (1998); Tomuschat (1993). See also section 8.2.

[60] Koskenniemi (2005) 58ff.; not all laws rest on a normative principle, some have a purely pragmatic character. However, the descending pattern of justification works only if a law expresses a shared normative belief that certain behaviour is required by principle. That does not have to be a moral principle, but could derive from religion, natural law or a social norm. Laws that simply respond to a need to regulate behaviour in one way rather than another naturally rely for their compliance pull more on actors' consent to behave in the chosen way.

meaning of law will approximate that of the underlying principle. In so far as an interpretation follows state consent and neglects those underlying principles (ascending argument), law is nothing more than an expression of states' interests.[61] As the determination of legal content always rests on one or the other line of argument, an interpretation of IL is always either strategic (furthering an interest) or aspirational (advocating a principle or norm).[62] In turn, IL readily lends itself to justifying purely instrumental actions or (less problematically) behaviour that is really guided by extra-legal normative beliefs.

As in this view the meaning of any given legal rule arises during its interpretation, rather than being fixed in the text, a rule readily accommodates an actor's prior interests or pre-legal normative beliefs. Martti Koskenniemi has elaborated this concern in the greatest detail and has gone furthest with his conclusion that 'international law is singularly useless as a means for justifying or criticizing international behaviour'[63] because it can always be interpreted to back up strategic or aspirational arguments. Other legal scholars have raised similar concerns.[64] They reject the essentialism underlying the traditional approach to interpretation according to which every law is assumed to have not only a penumbra of uncertainty in which its application is unclear, but also one incontestable core meaning.[65]

The conception of IL as a product of prior reasons for action in IR theory hence corresponds with a conception in legal theory of IL as a way of expressing the normative standards implied by those reasons for action. Just as the creation of IL and later compliance merely bring prior interests and normative beliefs to bear, the interpretation of IL is

[61] Koskenniemi (2005) 58ff.
[62] Koskenniemi uses the terms 'apologetic' and 'utopian' instead of 'strategic' and 'aspirational'. In his view, IL that justifies its claim to validity with state consent rests on 'an apologetic subjectivism that gives precedence to states' sovereign will and interests over the objective normative code' (Koskenniemi (2005) 59). On the other hand, rooting legal justification in the normative content of the law amounts to a 'utopian subjectivism [that] rests on an aprioristic assumption about what is right' (Rasulov (2006) 587, paraphrasing Koskenniemi). I prefer the terms 'strategic' and 'aspirational', to signal that I do not share Koskenniemi's assumption that normative beliefs and interests are always inherently subjective. They are subject to perception, but matter most in international relations when they are intersubjectively held, when they are shared.
[63] Koskenniemi (2005) 67.
[64] Dunoff (2011) 327; Henkin *et al.* (1993) 17; Kennedy (2012); Mégret (2012).
[65] Most famously, Hart (1958) 614; also Hart (1997) 12.

always either strategic or aspirational. The resulting contention is that legality is not its own autonomous normative code for proper behaviour.[66] Rather when guiding or judging behaviour IL feeds off pre-existing normativities, off utility and appropriateness. IL is what I call 'epistemically dependent'.[67]

1.3 The ontological dependence of international law

The two previous sections suggest that IL vanishes between the motivational forces on which it depends for its creation and compliance (interests and normative beliefs) and between the corresponding normative codes on which it depends for its meaning (utility and appropriateness). This twofold dependency raises a question: what *is* IL? Is it anything besides its component variables? Or are the rules of IL merely stipulated instrumental considerations or congealed beliefs about appropriateness? Thomas Franck declared the age of 'defensive ontology' for IL to be over.[68] However, the scholarship discussed so far implies considerable uncertainty regarding the purport and contours of IL's existence. In Koskenniemi's view, for instance, epistemic dependence certainly connotes that IL does not occupy an 'identifiable intellectual realm'.[69] IR scholars of different theoretical leanings insist on calling IL an 'epiphenomenon'.[70] Can we draw a boundary between IL and the variables on which it depends? Or is IL completely reducible to norms or interests?

Legality, like appropriateness and utility, pronounces an 'ought'. However, IR literature often forgets that interests like norms imply a normative standard. The way IR theory has therefore explored the question 'what is IL' is by enquiring into the distinctiveness of international legal norms compared to other norms. There are three ways in which one could attempt to set apart legal norms: by their form (the

---

[66] Koskenniemi (2011) 319; Koskenniemi (2012b) 61; similar Mégret (2012) 69.
[67] For a definition see the appendix.
[68] Franck (1995) 6; for the opposing view that IL needs to perpetually defend its own existence see Bederman (2006) 6.
[69] Koskenniemi (2005) 16.
[70] Carr (1946) 170; Bork (1989/90); Goldsmith and Posner (2005); Grieco (1988b); Krasner (1983); Krasner (1999); Morgenthau (1948) 249; Waltz (1979) 88ff.; for critiques of this conceptualisation of IL see Berman (2005); Byers (1999) 22; Guzman (2002).

formal features or characteristics that only legal norms have), by their mode of operation (how legal norms elicit compliance) and by their effects on behaviour. Of course the form, mode of operation and effects of a (legal) norm are interrelated. Investigations of them can work together to draw out the distinctiveness of IL. Over the following paragraphs, I discuss IR scholars' attempts to distinguish IL along these three dimensions.

What is distinctive about norms of international law – their form?

Positivism reigns supreme among theories of the nature of law as far as municipal law is concerned. The core tenet of legal positivism is that the validity of a rule as law does not depend on the rule's content, merit or relationship to justice, but on whether it derives from a recognised source.[71] It follows that laws can be identified by such features as having been promulgated by a legislature, or triggering sanctions determined by judicial decision and imposed by an executive. In other words, legal norms are recognisable by their form.[72] Not surprisingly, the first systematic contemporary engagements of IR theory with IL relied on the formal features of municipal law to identify their subject of enquiry, affirming IL to the extent that it resembled 'proper' law.[73]

If we recall jurists' initial dismissal of IL as not really law, the limits of this approach are immediately evident. Whichever characteristic of municipal law we use as the point of departure, the implied concept of IL is either over- or under-inclusive (often both at the same time) with regard to what we know to be IL. For instance, a trait widely considered to characterise law in the domestic realm is promulgation, meaning the fact that legal norms are posited.[74] However, drawing a line accordingly excludes non-codified norms of customary IL and

---

[71] Gardner (2001) 199.

[72] See Green (2003); Hart (1997); Raz (1979); the relationship between positivism and legal formalism is more complex. However, it is beyond the scope and demands of this chapter to explore it further.

[73] Similar Abbott (1989) 338; Keohane (1997); Slaughter-Burley (1993).

[74] Sanctions or state consent are also sometimes considered markers of legality. However, in the international realm enforcement is uneven and often non-existent. State consent, in turn, is often hardly more than a fiction, belied by concepts such as general IL or objective regimes.

might include, among others, non-binding resolutions.[75] The limited usefulness of the positivist framework for grasping IL goes some way towards explaining the relative neglect of the nature or concept of IL as objects of enquiry by legal scholars.[76]

The liberal institutionalist notion of 'legalisation'[77] likewise hinges the distinctiveness of legal norms on their form. However, it uses three 'identifiable dimensions of variation'[78] that are chosen not with municipal law in mind, but in the light of developments observed in international relations: the precision of norms, the delegation of their interpretation and the obligation pull they exert.[79] Proponents of this approach deem obligation to be the most important among the defining traits of IL.[80] Yet, it is unclear whether this criterion is meant to hint at a specific mode of operation of law (law inspires a sense of obligation) or whether it merely describes objective degrees of bindingness. Even more importantly, the underlying reasons why states should either perceive an obligation or consider themselves bound where IL is concerned remain largely unexplored.[81]

Defining legal norms by their form leaves open the question of whether the difference between legal and other norms matters, whether 'being "legal" add[s] any kind of weight to a norm'.[82] In order to be a useful first step in elucidating the distinctiveness of IL, an approach that attempts to grasp IL by describing its formal features would therefore ideally afford at least two things: first, a definite boundary, i.e. certainty about where IL begins and ends and, second, a plausible boundary that defines IL in accordance with common understandings of it. Specifically, a definite boundary would make it much easier to then explore whether being legal makes a difference for compliance

---

[75] Those are also often subsumed under the heading of soft law. For an introduction to the concept see Chinkin (1989); also Abbott and Snidal (2000).

[76] Similar Abbott (1989) 338; exceptions include Bederman (2006); Crawford and Koskenniemi (2012); Fichtelberg (2008); Henkin *et al.* (1993); Koskenniemi (2000); Mégret (2012).

[77] I use inverted commas to distinguish the specific theoretical approach to grasping the legality of norms introduced in a special issue of *International Organisation* in 2000 from the general phenomenon that is the subjection of an activity to regulation by law. I never use legalisation to denote the legality of an activity.

[78] Abbott *et al.* (2000) 403.   [79] *Ibid.*, 401

[80] *Ibid.*; also Goldstein *et al.* (2000); Kahler (2000).

[81] For similar criticisms see Finnemore and Toope (2001) 748; Reus-Smit (2008).

[82] Finnemore (1999/00) 701.

(mode of operation) or, alternatively, whether compliance with a law makes a difference for behaviour (effect).[83]

However, besides its mentioned weaknesses, the neoliberal concept of 'legalisation' falls short of providing a definite boundary. Norms of IL vary widely in their determinacy. It is unclear at what degree of imprecision the 'legalisation' approach means to exclude these norms from the body of IL. The same holds true for obligation. Whether we define it as a discrete objective category that measures bindingness or as a continuous subjective variable referring to a sense of obligation, it remains a matter of degree. Like positivism, 'legalisation' moreover fails to erect a fully plausible boundary that delineates IL in accordance with what we already know about it. Legal norms that are not enshrined in a treaty or embedded in a regime necessarily leave the criterion of delegation unfulfilled. 'Legalisation' hence grasps only those norms of IL that are institutionalised.

What is distinctive about norms of international law – their mode of operation?

An alternative to describing the form of some norms that we know to be laws is describing the way those norms operate in international relations, namely the way they elicit compliance. Compliance theories, associated with but not limited to constructivists and a number of prominent legal theorists,[84] attempt to tease out IL's distinctiveness by investigating how IL gets states to adhere to it. The implication is not that laws can only be those norms that are complied with, but rather that the rules of IL exert a specific compliance pull, be it weak or strong. The assumption of a specific mode of operation, of course, runs counter to the above contention that actors recur to legal norms for exogenous

---

[83] One could very reasonably interject that it is too demanding to ask for a definite boundary between norms and laws. It is only as a means of determining what is distinctive about IL that a description of legal norms would ideally be clear cut. If we could get at IL's distinctiveness by another way, for instance, by describing its specific mode of operation or by showing that it has distinguishable effects on behaviour, we could, of course, tolerate that a description of norms alone does not afford a definite judgement on whether or not a norm is also a law.

[84] The most important works are Chayes and Handler Chayes (1995); Franck (1990); Franck (1992); Franck (2006); Goodman and Jinks (2005); Guzman (2002); Koh (1997); Reus-Smit (2011); Simmons (1998).

reasons (prior interests or extra-legal normative beliefs) rather than because of the norms' legal status. If a specific compliance pull of IL were to be identified, we would not only be able to answer the question of what IL is, we could also reject the charge of causal dependence.

So why do states comply with IL if not because of pre-legal normative beliefs or the expectation of material gain? Ryan Goodman and Derek Jinks argue that besides coercion and persuasion there is a third 'conceptually distinct social mechanism'[85] by which states come to comply with legal regimes. Coercion means that instrumental considerations account for compliance, and instilling an actor with the normative belief that compliance is appropriate amounts to persuasion. A third mechanism that is specific to certain regimes is acculturation.[86] Goodman and Jinks define this process as the 'identification with a reference group which generates varying degrees of intellectual and social pressures to conform with the behavioural expectations of a wider culture'.[87]

Abram and Antonia Chayes's so-called managerial theory starts with the forum for repeated interaction that legal institutions provide. This is reminiscent of an institutionalist explanation for compliance in which states' instrumental considerations about the benefits of repeated, predictable interaction account for compliance. Yet, the Chayeses argue that it is not only the 'social mechanism' that generates IL's compliance pull, but also law's ability to set clear boundaries for a 'justificatory discourse'. The fact that within this discourse 'good legal argument can be generally distinguished from bad'[88] puts a premium on compliant behaviour. Of course, this is more often true for legal rules that are enshrined in an institution which plays the role of manager of compliance.[89]

The premise and contention of these approaches that focus on institutionalised interaction or legal discourse is that '[l]egal rules constitute a distinct communicatively constituted strata [sic] of this world'.[90] The distinctiveness of legal compared to aspirational or strategic deliberation is often seen to lie in the greater determinacy of

---

[85] Goodman and Jinks (2008) 726.   [86] Goodman and Jinks (2009) 2.

[87] Goodman and Jinks (2008) 726; also Goodman and Jinks (2004); Goodman and Jinks (2005).

[88] Chayes and Handler Chayes (1995) 25ff.

[89] For a similar criticism see Koh (1997) 2637.   [90] Reus-Smit (2008) 603.

IL. In Kratochwil's words, legal rules 'provide relatively firm guidance not only with respect to ends but also to the means to be adopted'.[91] In a slight variation, Thomas Franck argues that determinacy generates legitimacy and therefore compliance.[92] In his view determinacy is one among four intrinsic qualities of legal norms that make them appear legitimate and thus account for states' compliance with law: the other three are symbolic validation, coherence and adherence.

However, the criticism levelled against the institutionalist 'legalisation' approach can likewise be brought forward against these explanations of compliance: they rely on a sense of legal obligation to grasp the distinctiveness of legal norms, a sense of legal obligation that remains unaccounted for. Whether an actor advances a good or bad legal argument only matters if states, given their interests or normative beliefs, already attach value to conformity with law in international relations. Only a shared normative belief in the values of coherence or determinacy, in turn, means that the latter generate compliance. Ultimately it makes little difference which characteristics of laws or of legal deliberation we rely on. In order for them to serve as sources for IL's compliance pull, we invariably have to presuppose that 'a legitimating norm that must of necessity lie outside of the international legal system'[93] already purports their appropriateness or utility and hence desirability. What elicit compliance are hence actors' extra-legal or prior normative beliefs or interests, not the legal norms themselves.

Has the attempt to grasp what IL is by exploring its mode of operation failed? Christian Reus-Smit suggests that the sense of legal obligation, which has proved so elusive to the reviewed theoretical approaches, is a reason for compliance that unlike interests and normative beliefs does not lie outside IL.[94] Reus-Smit maintains that a theory of obligation – an explanation for why states feel they need to comply with IL beyond interests or extra-legal normative beliefs – 'must ultimately be historical-sociological in nature'.[95] It is thus contingent

---

[91] Kratochwil (1989) 206; also Onuf (1989) 136; Reus-Smit (2008) 603.
[92] Franck (1995) 30.   [93] Reus-Smit (2008) 600.
[94] Reus-Smit (2011) 339; likewise Brunnée and Toope (2010) 55; Brunnée and Toope (2011a) 6, 115; Franck (1995) 44.
[95] Reus-Smit (2003) 594.

on the social context within which law-abiding actors form their identities.[96] Jutta Brunnée and Stephen Toope, to the contrary, aim to offer an explanation for why law inspires a specific sense of obligation that they present as stable across time and different social contexts. In the following I show that despite its many merits, their so-called 'interactional theory' of IL in its very attempt to elucidate the specific mode of operation of legal norms casts further doubt on the possibility that legal norms are systematically different.

In Brunnée and Toope's view, legal obligation is the product of three elements: first, a norm is based on shared understandings; second, a norm meets eight criteria of legality; and third, the norm is sustained in practice. The basis of shared understandings and the mutual reinforcement between criteria of legality and legal practice is 'crucial to generating distinctive legal legitimacy and a sense of commitment among those to whom law is addressed'.[97] The eight criteria of legality are borrowed from Lon Fuller: the norm must be clear, general, promulgated or accessible, non-retroactive, realistic, non-contradictory, constant and there must be congruence between the norm and official behaviour. While 'the failure to live up to the requirements of legality is likely to erode whatever commitment to the law citizens might have',[98] the criteria are not a sufficient condition for a norm to be law.[99] The congruence criterion foreshadows the additional requirement that a norm be reflected in practice in order to count as interactional IL.[100] Only then, according to Brunnée and Toope, does a norm inspire a sense of legal obligation or what Fuller refers to as 'fidelity'.[101]

---

[96] In other words, Reus-Smit believes that the sense of obligation that legal rules inspire is irreducible to underlying normative beliefs or interests. He nevertheless considers obligation dependent, or contingent, on prevailing notions of utility and appropriateness. This resembles the understanding of IL introduced in chapter 2.

[97] Brunnée and Toope (2011b) 307. Brunnée and Toope are adamant that shared understandings do not have to amount to a Habermasian common life world as a precondition for law to emerge. The recognition of a need for regulation in a certain issue area, rather than agreement on values or substantive goals, is enough as a basis for interactional IL. It is therefore perfectly possible that interactional IL emerges in a pluralist international society.

[98] *Ibid.* 68.   [99] *Ibid.* 86.

[100] Brunnée and Toope (2011a) 114; also Fuller (1969) 39, 46ff.; the difference between the congruence criterion and the practice of legality is that the latter 'requires a sustained and continuous effort to realize *all* the criteria of legality [italics mine]' (Brunnée and Toope (2010) 283f.).

[101] Fuller (1969) 39.

Is the generation of fidelity the specific mode of operation that sets IL apart from other norms and that sheds light on what IL is beyond congealed norms or stipulated interests? Norms that fulfil the eight criteria of legality and are reflected in practice have probably developed beyond the initial shared understandings that form their basis, being internalised or institutionalised. Yet they are ultimately still merely norms. The plausibility of Brunnée and Toope's contention that the eight mentioned characteristics inspire the kind of sense of obligation they call fidelity is afforded by our awareness that actors already value these traits in a norm. As Reus-Smit has pointed out, the eight criteria are bound up with the liberal concept of individual security under the rule of law.[102] The only reason why meeting those criteria should usher a norm towards fidelity are prior shared normative beliefs that accord with liberal values. The sense of obligation that amounts to fidelity and that Brunnée and Toope put so much weight on as the key to IL's distinctiveness again depends on normative beliefs that lie outside IL. It seems that we have come full circle to IL's causal dependence.

But is there not a difference between having a prior normative belief or interest that accords with the *content* of a law and therefore behaving in accordance with it, on the one hand, and having prior normative beliefs that value the form of legal norms (meeting the eight criteria), on the other hand? IR theory's story is that if neither an instrumental consideration nor a normative belief points towards compliance, an actor will fail to adhere to a rule of IL. Imagine a scenario then in which neither principled nor instrumental considerations suggest that an actor adheres to IL, but because he attaches value to the features of the norm that qualify it as law according to Brunnée and Toope, he nevertheless complies. It would, of course, be the prior normative belief in the value of the eight criteria that would account for compliance. But if those are the criteria that render norms legal is it not then their legality to which we attribute compliance? If the eight characteristics could *produce* compliance where there would otherwise have been disregard of a norm, Fuller's features would have an effect on compliance, legality would have the 'added

---

[102] In response to a review by Reus-Smit, Brunnée and Toope have admitted to the liberal premise of their theory. The ultimate source of legal obligation in the interactional account is historically contingent after all (Brunnée and Toope (2011c); Reus-Smit (2011)).

value' Brunnée and Toope claim law has.[103] But, the question is moot because the congruence criterion and the requirement that a norm be sustained in practice guarantee that only those norms are laws that are carried by either instrumental considerations or normative beliefs in the first place. Legality in the interactional account does not produce or even explain compliance, it follows it. The circular element in Brunnée and Toope's conception of obligation (and hence in their explanation of compliance) leads any attempt to grasp the distinctiveness of IL by its effects on compliance *ad absurdum*.

What if we used the interactional theory not to elucidate the specific mode of operation of IL, but as a means of describing the form that legal norms take? The congruence criterion and the requirement for a norm to be sustained in practice mean that a law is defined here as a norm that is complied with, one that inspires fidelity-like obligation. That is implausible as we know some (though admittedly few) rules of IL that are widely broken.[104] We should dispense with the practice requirement and the congruence criterion then and use Fuller's remaining seven criteria to distinguish legal norms from others. Do the seven remaining criteria systematically distinguish legal norms? No, the norms grasped by those criteria are not coextensive with what we conventionally consider to be IL.[105] Some bona fide norms of IL do not fulfil the remaining seven criteria of legality. For instance, the provisions regarding reservations in the Vienna Convention on the Law of Treaties of 1969, one of the most central, almost universally ratified treaties under IL, are contradictory.[106] Moreover, the criterion of promulgation seems to exclude non-codified customary IL. Like positivism and 'legalisation', the interactional approach neither as a whole nor reduced to seven of Fuller's criteria affords a plausible boundary. It does not grasp the entirety of the phenomenon we know to be IL.

Do the criteria at least draw a definite line between norms and laws – even if that line is not where we would conventionally draw it? With the exception of clarity and congruence, the eight criteria of legality at

---

[103] Brunnée and Toope (2011b) 307.

[104] For instance, the prohibition on child labour and the related norm of *jus cogens* against slavery.

[105] The authors admit as much (Brunnée and Toope (2010) 69).

[106] Brunnée and Toope themselves mention this as an example of a rule of IL that does not also count as interactional law.

first appear to be binary. However, in reality generality, feasibility and constancy are matters of degree. Non-contradiction is a question of interpretation, specifically in norms that are not posited.[107] If we understand accessibility to denote promulgation, as the authors seem to do,[108] it is a binary condition. Otherwise it is likewise a matter of degree. The difference between any norm and a legal rule in the interactional account is hence one of degree – the extent to which a norm meets the criteria of legality and the robustness of its reflection in practice. We arguably do not know the precise point at which a successful norm counts as interactional law. Nor do we know when exactly a perception of being bound amounts to a sense of legal obligation or fidelity. It follows that the boundary between extra-legal and legal norms set by Brunnée and Toope is neither plausible nor definite. We arrive again at the previous section's conclusion: seems that there is no set of characteristics that plausibly and definitively distinguishes legal from non-legal norms.

What is distinctive about norms of international law – their effects?

What about the third route to grasping the distinctiveness of IL by its effects? There are two possible ways of understanding 'the effects of IL': first, the effects of legality on compliance, and, second, the effects of compliance (specifically with law) on behaviour. Martha Finnemore, who first drew attention to the fact that '[w]hat distinguishes legal norms from other norms is simply not clear',[109] framed the question in terms of whether legal norms 'command more compliance than other kinds of norms' (effects *on* compliance). She did not consider the possibility that compliance with legal norms could have systematically different effects from adherence to other norms (effects *of* compliance). However, I have already ruled out that legality has distinctive effects on compliance when I showed that IL lacks a distinctive mode of operation because it is causally dependent on prior interests or normative beliefs.

---

[107] The only truly binary criterion out of the seven is non-retroactivity, which only really matters if a legal norm is subject to adjudication.
[108] Brunnée and Toope (2011b) 310.   [109] Finnemore (1999/2000) 703.

IR scholarship has largely neglected the investigation of IL's effects on behaviour, i.e. the effects *of* compliance, as a means of drawing out its distinctiveness. This is not surprising given that much of the research discussed so far casts considerable doubt on the possibility that IL could have a distinguishable impact on states' behaviour in international relations. To recapitulate, scholarship on IL maintains that actors create and comply with IL due to prior instrumental or principled considerations, and that legal interpretations are strategic or aspirational arguments in disguise. Legal norms are not systematically distinguishable by their form (which could then produce compliance) and nor do they have a specific mode of operation. It seems to naturally follow that it makes no difference whether actors pursue their interests and follow their normative beliefs directly or via recourse to IL.

Scholars who leave open the possibility that adherence to IL could afford an added value for behaviour consider the exercise of identifying those net effects 'daunting'.[110] They do not contemplate undertaking the implied task of theorising *how* IL could make a difference, i.e. theorising what I call 'behavioural relevance'. A number of scholars have recently called for a distinction between the issues of, on the one hand, compliance with, and, on the other hand, effectiveness of IL.[111] However, they merely tend to ask whether IL, when it is complied with, is also 'effective in addressing problems of international cooperation'.[112] Their understanding of effectiveness hence denotes what I call 'normative success'. They largely fail to enquire into whether recourse to IL, i.e. compliance specifically with legal norms, has distinguishable effects on behaviour in the first place.[113] If IL can make a counterfactual difference for behaviour, we do not have a theory as to how.

Where does this leave us regarding the question what IL is? IL is clearly ontologically dependent[114] in the sense that there would be no IL

---

[110] Goldstein *et al.* (2000); similar Abbott *et al.* (2000) 409.
[111] Dunoff and Pollack (2012a); Martin (2002); Raustiala and Slaughter (2002); Simmons (1998); Simmons (2009); von Stein (2012).
[112] Dunoff and Pollack (2012a) 23; also Ratner (1999/00).
[113] In other words, these enquiries into IL's effectiveness cover only one of the two necessary conditions for calling IL effective, normative success. They neglect IL's behavioural relevance. For definitions of behavioural relevance and normative success see the appendix.
[114] Ontological dependence is also defined in the appendix.

were it not for shared normative beliefs and states' interests in making and adhering to IL. This is almost a truism. Yet I submit that depending on prior variables for its existence is not the same as being reducible to them. In turn, there is no reason why ontological dependence should mean that there is nothing distinctive about those norms that count as IL. 'Things, says Hegel, exist in and through the boundaries which delimit them from other things.'[115] Granted, we have not yet found the boundaries between legal norms and the reasons for actions (prior interests and extra-legal normative beliefs) on which they depend for compliance. Nor do we know where to draw the line between legality and the normative codes on which it depends for its meaning (utility and appropriateness). But we have not yet tried to find those boundaries by way of investigating the effects of compliance with IL on behaviour either. As long as the search for the distinctiveness of IL is not over, there is no reason to answer the question 'what is IL?' with Koskenniemi's laconic conclusion that it is 'impossible to find [the] "essence" for international law'.[116]

This chapter has told the story of two disciplines, IR and legal theory, wrestling with a phenomenon that conflicts with their most fundamental premises. The international system possesses no sovereign to issue commands and impose sanctions, ingredients eminent legal theorists consider essential to law.[117] Relations between states are anarchic, or so IR scholarship of all orientations tells us. Both disciplines have made some headway in grasping IL partly by taking steps to overcome their mutual 'estrangement'.[118] Yet, while few scholars of either discipline would explicitly challenge the notion that IL exists, it is residual uncertainty about the contours and purport of IL's existence that accounts for the holes in our theoretical understanding of it. In the next chapter I show that, IL's dependence

---

[115] Koskenniemi (2005) 16.   [116] *Ibid.*, 8.
[117] Austin (1832/1995); Kelsen (1967).
[118] Koh (1997) 18; it is widely acknowledged that the exchange between legal scholarship and IR over the last twenty years has been somewhat 'unidirectional' with IR providing most of the terminology and concepts for the theorisation of IL (Dunoff and Pollack (2012a) 3). The persistent neglect of theoretical questions by mainstream scholars of IL and the relative neglect of IL by legal theorists also accounts for the predominance of IR theorists in this chapter.

notwithstanding, recourse to legal norms can make a counterfactual difference. The effects of compliance with IL on behaviour, meaning IL's potential behavioural relevance, in turn, hold the key to unlocking IL's distinctiveness. In other words, finding out how IL works sheds light on what IL is.

2 | *The theory*

IR scholarship fails to entertain the possibility that recourse to IL in the process of actualising interests and normative beliefs could have a distinguishable effect on behaviour, or so the previous chapter showed. However, I submit that from IL's causal dependence[1] on prior interests or non-legal norms it does not follow that it makes no difference for behaviour whether or not actors' instrumental or principled considerations are subject to law. By the same token, epistemic dependence[2] does not mean that drawing on IL to make a strategic or aspirational argument has no distinguishable effect. Since the effects of compliance with IL on behaviour have so far not been an object of investigation in IR theory, this chapter undertakes the task of providing a theoretical account of how recourse to law can afford a counterfactual added value. It introduces a theory of IL's behavioural relevance[3] and discusses its implications for the distinctiveness of legal norms. The chapter concludes that IL is indeed ontologically dependent.[4] It is dependent, yet separate.

---

[1] In the international realm, actors create IL and comply with it if this serves their prior interests and/or accords with their extra-legal normative beliefs. IL does not provide an independent reason for action. See also the appendix.

[2] In the international realm, actors draw on IL in order to make strategic arguments (based on their prior interests or their conception of utility) or aspirational arguments (based on their extra-legal normative beliefs or their conception of appropriateness). IL does not provide a normative code for guiding action or an objective standard for evaluating behaviour that is independent of appropriateness or utility. See also the appendix.

[3] IL is behaviourally relevant when recourse to law makes a counterfactual difference for behaviour. This means that adherence to IL has an effect on behaviour beyond what prior interests and extra-legal normative beliefs would have led an actor to do anyway. The agent in question would have acted differently had she merely followed her normative beliefs and/or interests without considering IL. See also the appendix.

[4] Norms of IL do not exist independently of interests and shared normative beliefs. See also the appendix.

2.1 How international law works: intellectual and motivational effects

Chapter 1 outlined Martti Koskenniemi's influential explication of the structure of international legal argument and his contention that IL does not provide an independent standard for evaluating action. Koskenniemi's view is exemplary for the position, implicit in much of IR scholarship on IL: IL's dependence means that recourse to law makes no difference for behaviour. An actor might as well have followed her interests or normative beliefs directly.[5] From his observation that IL has 'no meaning that can be determined independently from power and or morality',[6] Koskenniemi infers that IL is merely 'a means to articulate particular preferences or positions in a formal fashion'.[7] This, in turn, grounds his conclusion that 'legal arguments do not *produce* substantive outcomes but seek to *justify* them [italics in original]'.[8] Over the following paragraphs I uncover and dispute the assumptions that lead to this equation of IL's dependence with a lack of behavioural relevance. The aim is to show that, in spite of its threefold dependence, IL can have a distinguishable effect on behaviour – an effect that makes norms of IL distinctive.

Defining interests and norms

Koskenniemi holds that IL is 'a unified structure of argument [which] reveals a particular conception about the relationship' between instrumental and principled considerations.[9] Why does having such a unified structure not make a difference for behaviour? Koskenniemi assumes that both interests and norms are given, exogenous to international interaction, and therefore static.[10] Moreover, he draws a sharp line between what he refers to as states' 'behaviour, will and interest',[11] on

---

[5] Likewise Abbott *et al.* (2000) 409; Goldsmith and Posner (2005); Goldstein *et al.* (2000); Morgenthau (1948) 229; Raustiala and Slaughter (2002).

[6] Koskenniemi (2005) 26f.   [7] *Ibid.*, 570.   [8] *Ibid.*

[9] *Ibid.*, 4; similar Mégret (2012) 78.

[10] According to the previous chapter interests and normative beliefs are reasons for action that correspond to the normative codes of utility and appropriateness respectively.

[11] Koskenniemi (1990) 7; Koskenniemi (2005) 16; Koskenniemi (2012b) 60.

the one hand, and in his terminology 'moral principles',[12] on the other hand. Koskenniemi implicitly assumes that what an actor wants and does as a result of instrumental considerations is naturally antagonistic to what an actor should want and do in the light of moral principles. The conflict an actor faces can be seen as between two different normativities: utility, given interests, and appropriateness, given principles (or norms).[13]

The combination of these two assumptions, first, that a stable divide separates interests and norms, and, second, that the normative imperatives they respectively imply (utility and appropriateness) are 'mutually exclusive'[14] is the necessary condition for Koskenniemi's equation of IL's dependence on interests and normative beliefs with lack of behavioural relevance. Only if instrumental and principled considerations always differ is any legal argument that uses a point of reference outside itself compromised, as this point of reference is *either* a principle *or* derived from a matter of fact (creating an interest). Arguments based on descriptive observations (which in Koskenniemi's view always reflect instrumental considerations or interests) and those based on normative beliefs are, in this reading, an exhaustive disjunction, with no overlap and no middle ground.[15] As a result, IL can at one moment only be used in the service of one or the other: it can advocate either utility or appropriateness, expressing either a strategic or an aspirational argument. But it can add nothing of its own.

Interests have to be understood as material if they are always to be stable and exogenous to interaction. In IR scholarship, only the neorealist conception of agency, as outlined in section 1.1, is firmly committed to this assumption and hence accepts that interests and norms are made of fundamentally different cloths. Even hardened neorealists, however, would allow for the possibility that states sometimes have a material

---

[12] Principled considerations can derive from a number of coherent sets of normative prescriptions that are widely recognised to have authority, such as religion, natural law or social mores. In contrast to Koskenniemi, when I speak of 'principled considerations', 'normative beliefs' or 'norms', no reference and limitation specifically to morality is implied.

[13] Koskenniemi refers to 'power' and 'morality' as the two poles of the dichotomy. His equation of instrumental considerations with power reveals that his is a materialist conception of interests. A state's 'will, interest and behaviour', i.e. what instrumental considerations suggest an actor ought to do, are a function of material circumstances.

[14] Koskenniemi (2005) 59.   [15] *Ibid.*; also Koskenniemi (2012b) 61.

interest in following a norm. It is conceivable that utility and appropriateness overlap rather than inevitably being mutually exclusive.[16] Of course, from this neorealist point of view, it is the interest that provides the true reason for norm-conforming behaviour. In other words, instrumental considerations account for actions that accord with normative prescriptions. But in contrast to Koskenniemi, neorealists do not think that following interests or norms is always an either/or.

Neoliberal institutionalism has demonstrated that such a convergence of interests and norms is a regular occurrence. Many norms in international relations have arisen from instrumental considerations. Moreover, whenever adherence to norms provides functional benefits, utility and appropriateness point in the same direction. In addition, according to most liberal institutionalist scholars, two different actors in the same material circumstances may well have different interests, because those are subject to ideas.[17] It is hence perfectly possible not only that states happen to have an interest in following a norm, but also that ideas about appropriateness (norms) may change what is in an actor's interest. Norms are not followed for their own sake, but neither norms nor interests are exogenously given or stable.[18]

If one dispenses with materialism wholeheartedly, as most constructivists do, there is no reason to consider interests to be prior to, or confronting an actor more immediately than, norms.[19] Interests are constructed in the same way as normative beliefs – in a process that is subject to perceptions. Interests arise from and inform actors' interaction and the formation of their identities. From the constructivist standpoint adopted here, motivational forces or reasons for action are hence socially constructed and changeable. Norms can be endogenous to interests; interests can be endogenous to norms. There is neither a pre-ordained canon of interests (material or otherwise) on behalf of which a strategic legal argument could be made, nor a separate universe of normative beliefs that could be brought forward disguised as an aspirational interpretation of law.

---

[16] For instance, Mearsheimer (2001) 58.

[17] Goldstein and Keohane (1993) 9ff.; also Keohane (2000).

[18] See Moravcsik (2010); Nye (2010); Richardson (2010); Simpson (2010); Stein (2010).

[19] Section 1.1 suggested that liberal institutionalists deny that interests are necessarily material. They nevertheless prioritise interests over norms without providing a fully convincing account as to why.

This then raises the question of whether it makes sense to distinguish so sharply between interests and normative beliefs in the first place. If they are both subject to the same processes of social construction and there is no stable contradiction between the normative imperatives they imply, what is the difference between those reasons for action that we call interests and those we call norms? What else does utility denote except one way of thinking about what is appropriate and vice versa? However, I maintain that categorising motivational forces as normative beliefs or interests is a useful tool to describe the fact that in the perception of an actor not all reasons for action are cast from the same mould. Some of those emerge as the immediate requirements of a situation. Following them seems opportune or expedient. Other reasons for action exist in spite of these immediate requirements. For instance, reasons for action that are connected to an actor's self-perception, future interactions, expected developments of the situation, or an actor's ideas about how a society works seem indicated by appropriateness. In other words, in most situations an actor faces not just one, but various reasons for action. We can imagine them to lie on a continuum with immediate imperatives at one end and more remote and abstract reasons for action at the other end.[20] Courses of action that satisfy immediate imperatives are perceived as in the actor's interest; they are indicated by instrumental considerations. Arguments to justify them would appropriately be called strategic. Courses of action that do justice to more distant requirements can be considered to follow considerations of principle, or norms. Arguments for why they ought to be followed would appear more aspirational. Crucially, the latter kind of reason for action seems more removed, abstract or less immediate than the former only from the point of view of the actor in that situation. From the perspective of a neutral observer they might be equally or more pressing than situational requirements. Whether reasons for action fall under the heading of interest or norm is thus a matter of individual perception.[21]

Based on this understanding, my categorisation of motivational forces as instrumental versus principled almost amounts to a sleight of hand.

---

[20] I make no assumption that these always necessarily diverge or that every actor perceives these motivational forces similarly.

[21] For this somewhat idiosyncratic definition of interests and normative beliefs consult the appendix.

I use terms that connote abstract sources of motivation with an infinite
variety of possible content (interests and norms/principles) to describe
what is a very concrete substantive way of differentiating reasons for
action (immediate/situational and long-term/abstract imperatives).[22]
However, in performing this sleight of hand I am in good company. As
Michael Byers points out, scholars who consider actors as largely making
instrumental calculations so as to follow their interests tend to assume
that those are 'selfish decision-makers. They expect – and manifest – no
concern for the welfare of people in other countries.'[23] In this reading,
utility (accordance with interests) is a normative standard that contains
very concrete assumptions about the content of the interests pursued:
they are non-altruistic. The identification of interest with egoism or even
hedonism is, of course, to be rejected. The widespread association of
instrumental considerations with immediacy and instant gratification is
nevertheless useful. I draw on it to sort reasons for action, but not into
egoism versus altruism or hedonism versus asceticism. As mentioned,
instead I distinguish between urgent imperatives that arise from the
present situation or on-going action and promise relatively immediate
gratification (interests), on the one hand, and reasons for action that exist
in spite of the situation, stemming from an actor's perception of self, of
how the system works and how it ought to work, on the other hand
(norms).[24]

---

[22] Moreover, the terms instrumental and principled echo an ontological distinction
between material and ideational sources of motivation. However, it is important
to stress that in the constructivist framework of this book interests are also
ideational. It is the ascription of meaning to something as a currently pressing
imperative that puts it into the category of interests.

[23] Byers (2010) 618; likewise Koskenniemi (2012a) 17.

[24] A scenario seems possible in which it appears that a normative belief makes an
immediate demand: for instance when someone comes to the rescue of a
drowning child at some foreseeable cost to herself. Kant describes us as feeling an
Achtung in the face of a fully understood categorical imperative (Kant (1956)
140). I am grateful to Henry Shue for drawing my attention to Kant's elaboration.
However, the theory proposed here relies on a moment of deliberation, however
fleeting (see section 7.1). Via socialisation and internalisation law can also
change the subconscious, but the processes described below are part of an
exercise that involves weighing alternatives for action. In the *Achtung* scenario,
whether or not the actor rescues the child is based on upbringing, instinct
reactions, socialisation and character. Of course, it is entirely possible that an
actor who does deliberate in this situation perceives rescuing the child as in his
interest. The desires to be perceived as heroic, to perceive oneself as doing the
right thing or to avoid feelings of guilt can all count as interests. In general, in this

Interests, norms and recourse to law

Differentiating between motivational forces in this way makes it easier to grasp the role of law in determining behaviour. Indeed, if we define interests and normative beliefs in this way, we find that law often prescribes a compromise between the two. It does so out of necessity. If law consistently prevented actors from acting on immediate situational imperatives, it would be an ultimately irrational institution. Law would also probably be systematically disregarded, as scholarship suggests that even adherence to municipal law is often unconnected to the threat of sanctions.[25] Of course, the necessity for law to allow actors to follow what tend to be immediate situational imperatives in its area of regulation is even more acute in the international realm, where those sanctions are often completely absent. At the same time, law cannot simply express what actors tend to 'want' to do in any given situation. Its purpose is, after all, to regulate behaviour in such a way that a society can continue to exist. In addition, law is a society's instrument to express an ideal of how its members would ultimately like to live together. For those reasons, law needs to prescribe behaviour also in the light of long-term or systemic imperatives that are connected to the ideas of a society as to how it wishes to order and maintain itself.[26] IL is torn between 'concreteness' and

framework altruism can be in an actor's interest if its results will manifest immediately.

The scenario in which an actor does something blatantly egoistic, but with delayed gratification, is more of a challenge to the taxonomy proposed here. Given our intuitive association of (self) interest with egoism, we would probably flinch at such an action being described as following a normative belief. However, if gratification is very remote, the demands of egoism are indeed aspirational. Understanding such an egoistic act with delayed gratification as following a moral principle would, of course, be incoherent, because we commonly understand morality to purport some degree of altruism. An actor may hence follow a normative belief or a perceived requirement of appropriateness without his necessarily striving to conform to a *moral* principle. In the following, when I use the term 'moral' instead of 'normative' before belief or principle, this signals that the motivational force in question not only stems from a systemic, abstract, removed imperative, but also from the established set of substantive values that are considered to be backed by higher authority and generally associated with the term morality. The category of normative belief/principle is thus broader than the category of moral belief/principle.

[25] See for instance Friedland (1989); Scholz (1984); Tyler (2006).

[26] Section 4.1 enquires into the creation of positive IL. It demonstrates that during the negotiation of treaties states indeed take into account both, ideas about how they anticipate 'wanting' to behave in certain situations, but also what they

'oughtness',[27] as Koskenniemi holds. But that does not mean it has to decide between what I refer to as utility and appropriateness; it integrates them. IL is at heart a compromise between diverging reasons for actions.

In this reading, law construes motivational forces, meaning the reasons for action that agents tend to encounter in certain situations, as possible to anticipate. They can be grasped and categorised as interests and norms respectively. Law then presents the actor with a ready compromise between what is assumed to be the instrumental course of action and the demands of shared normative beliefs in a certain situation. Legal regulation thereby allows a society to agree on how far an actor may follow immediate imperatives and what outcome is still considered normatively acceptable in the light of principled considerations. The legislator defines *ex ante* what that compromise is and prescribes a way to get there; judges review *ex post* whether an actor has made a good faith effort to get there (abide by the law). Law hence rests on a division of labour between the legislature, the judiciary and the individual.

What about the individual? What difference does law then make for how an individual in a given situation perceives interests and norms and how those are translated into action? Law, contrary to more abstract normative codes such as much of morality, utility and social mores, tends not merely to proscribe certain types of action or stipulate wrong states of mind. Law also specifies in detail *which* behaviour is required in order to attain an acceptable outcome that reflects what a society considers an adequate compromise between utility and appropriateness.[28] As law gives detailed guidance about how this compromise between immediate

think behaviour ought to be like with a view to maintaining orderly international relations. Section 4.3 shows that the emergence of customary law, to the contrary, does not rest on a compromise between immediate situational imperatives and long-term, systemic considerations.

[27] Koskenniemi (2012b) 60.

[28] This is, of course, a simplification. Different moral prescriptions display varying degrees of specificity and legal rules diverge significantly in their determinacy, as the following chapters elucidate. In addition, for morality the touchstone of correctness differs depending on the kind of moral code put forward. Consequentialist approaches specify acceptable outcomes, often in abstract ways. Deontological morality hinges correctness on the intention of the actor. One could argue that right intent necessarily implies a corresponding effort in action. Even if this were the case, however, deontological specifications of right intent rarely include concrete instructions for a course of action to bear out this intent. In general it is true that legal rules 'commonly contain much specific detail, and draw arbitrary distinctions, which would be unintelligible as elements in moral rules or principles' (Hart (1997) 237). In turn, moral principles are often very

and abstract, systemic imperatives is achieved, it to some degree relieves the individual of the intellectual burden of having to find her own compromise between interests and norms as defined here and to figure out how to act in order for her causal intervention into the world to reflect this compromise. Law makes it easier to align right intent (comply with law) with an acceptable compromise between appropriateness and utility. This is what I call the 'intellectual effect' of IL.[29]

Actors may presume that adhering to law takes care of acting rightly. If compliance with law were guaranteed to produce an acceptable compromise outcome, then anything *but* that outcome would betray an agent's failure to adhere to the law. Of course, adherence to IL does not guarantee an acceptable outcome, because even action guided by law can have unintended consequences. In addition, all law is subject to interpretation, a point to which I will return later. But insofar as the intellectual effect of law helps an actor match right intent with right action, it makes an acceptable outcome more likely. It follows that an actor's intent to abide by or defy the law is more clearly expressed in the outcome of an action guided by law than is an actor's intent to act rightly or inappropriately in the outcome of an action not guided by law. This, in turn, has an effect on how an actor perceives various reasons for action. The pertinence of a legal rule to behaviour in a certain situation puts acting appropriately, which then amounts to following the law, on the perceived continuum of motivational forces closer to the end where imperatives for action appear as immediate. Following the law is more of an interest (rather than 'merely' a norm) than acting appropriately is in the absence of law. This shift of compliance with IL towards the immediate end of the spectrum of reasons for action is the 'motivational effect' of IL.[30]

It is important to emphasise again that given the intricacies of the international system, IL does not on its own instil the individual actor with the intent to adhere to it. If an actor merely follows her interests (or less probably her normative beliefs) without consideration of IL, the intellectual and motivational effects of IL do not ensue.[31] As the

---

abstract and therefore not 'sufficiently selective to tell us how we should organise our coexistence' (Habermas (1998) 193; similar Habermas (1996) 114f.).

[29] For a definition consult the appendix.

[30] For a definition consult the appendix.

[31] As the introduction clarified, compliance is the precondition for the possibility of IL to be effective. In order for IL to make a difference an actor must first recur to it.

introduction clarified, compliance is not a sufficient, but a necessary condition for IL to be effective. Once actors do recur to IL, it can have an intellectual and motivational effect that other norms would not have; it can thus make a counterfactual difference for behaviour.

2.2 What international law is: dependent, but separate

The previous section does not contradict the conclusion of Chapter 1 that IL does not exist independently of interests and norms. Yet it gives us a clearer idea what the ontological dependence of IL does or does not imply. IL can have (intellectual and motivational) effects on behaviour that are not imputable to its component variables. As it has separate effects IL can certainly be differentiated from those variables. It exists separately from utility and appropriateness. By separate I mean 'different or distinguishable from', 'added or irreducible' to, but not 'independent of' or 'possible on its own'.[32] What does the theorisation of behavioural relevance then tell us about the boundaries and purport of IL's separate existence? What do the intellectual and motivational effects of compliance with legal norms suggest is distinctive about those norms?

Action guidance and justiciability

Two features of legal rules ground their abilities, first, to align action with a compromise between utility and appropriateness (intellectual effect) and second, to make acting rightly be perceived as an immediately required instrumental course of action (motivational effect). The first of these features is often referred to as the law's 'action guidance'. As mentioned above, next to more abstract normative codes for behaviour that tend to prescribe either right states of mind or acceptable outcomes, but often stop short of specifying required action, such as utility or appropriateness, law prescribes behaviour. In Jeremy Waldron's words, 'guiding action (or guiding conduct or guiding behaviour) is the mode of governance distinctive to law [italics omitted]'.[33] Second, that law allows the outcome of behaviour to be more easily subjected to retroactive

---

[32] Interestingly, in his very recent work Koskenniemi argues very similarly: 'Although law is embedded in social behaviour it is also irreducible to it' (Koskenniemi (2011) 319).

[33] Waldron (2010a) 5; similar Kratochwil (1989) 206; Onuf (1989) 136; Reus-Smit (2008) 603.

assessment, thereby making the consequences of acting wrongly manifest and complying with the law more immediately relevant, is referred to as the 'justiciability' of conduct that legal regulation affords.

Justiciability does not necessarily mean that behaviour is subjected to institutionalised legal review by adjudicative bodies. Such review is often not available on the international stage. The motivational effect of law can ensue based on other forms of 'retroactive review', such as public scrutiny or self-assessment. A crucial way in which IL can change an actor's perception of the motivational imperatives she faces is by providing her with a measure to perceive her own actions as falling short. Justiciability, as understood here, produces the motivational effect of recourse to law by providing intersubjective tools for the easy and certain recognition of non-compliance *ex post facto* by any observer. Of course, if an international legal regime came with a blanket review mechanism and comprehensive and reliable enforcement, the motivational effect would be much strengthened. In that case, however, the questions of IL's added value or separate existence would be easily answered in the first place. After all, '[t]he most obvious reason why legal norms might exert unique influence is the connection between law and the coercive powers of the state' in the domestic realm.[34]

The justiciability of conduct that IL affords evokes various theories of compliance reviewed in section 1.3. The Chayeses, for instance, hold that legal discourse, as opposed to instrumental or principled deliberations, provides that 'good legal argument can be generally distinguished from bad', which puts a premium on compliance.[35] In their view, actors anticipate that IL will make it easier to recognise deviant behaviour in the outcome of actions. The Chayeses would thus argue that what I call justiciability of conduct is an explanation and a reason for why states adhere to IL in the first place. In this reading, anticipated justiciability means that what I call a motivational effect produces compliance rather than being a result of it. Accordingly, IL would be a motivational force in its own right and not causally dependent.

In opposition, I differentiate reasons for the initial decision to adhere to law from the motivational effect that occurs as a result of compliance. Why? In the previous chapter I argued that the reasons for the initial compliance decision are always exogenous to IL. Prior interests or extra-legal normative beliefs account for recurrence to IL

---

[34] Finnemore (1999/2000) 703.   [35] Chayes and Handler Chayes (1995) 25.

in decision-making.[36] This chapter has shown that the motivational effect, to the contrary, is endogenous to legal compliance; it is attributable to IL itself. Only once an actor has recurred to IL does the latter's action guidance produce the intellectual effect which, in turn, provides the basis for justiciability and thus produces the motivational effect. As the interplay between action guidance and justiciability is endogenous to legal compliance, the motivational effect is attributable to IL.

The difference between exogenous reasons for the initial decision to comply and the endogenous motivational effect of compliance with IL becomes clearer if we take a look at domestic law. Domestic law, which is systematically and comprehensively enforced, provides actors with an initial interest in compliance that stems from a feature of the law: the fact that it is issued by a sovereign and backed by a threat of sanctions. One could argue that municipal law likewise relies for compliance on the prior interests of actors in not facing the state's enforcement power. However, if law in the domestic realm is defined as sovereign commands backed by a threat of sanctions, if 'being enforced' is an attribute of law, then that interest is created by law; it is endogenous. In the domestic realm law is co-original with the coercive power of the state. It is therefore not merely separate, but also independent of a specific agent's motivations in any given situation. That actors in fact often comply with domestic law for reasons other than a conscious consideration of sanctions does not undermine the fact that municipal law is theoretically causally independent.

This distinction between a hypothetical 'initial' recurrence to law for which IL does not itself give reasons and every following recurrence to IL, which is influenced by the motivational effect and thus at least partly attributable to IL, might strike the reader as an exercise in academic hair-splitting. However, the distinction is crucial for our theoretical grasp of IL. Scholars studying IL tend to either deny that IL is dependent on prior reasons for action, arguing that it can make a difference, or they recognise the dependence of IL and deny that it is a variable in its own right. The differentiation between initial compliance with IL and every

---

[36] The constructivist literature on IL has provided plausible accounts for the origins of such a wish to abide by IL in the absence of enforcement and immediate material benefits from compliance. Among others, Fichtelberg (2008); Franck (1990); Franck (1992); Franck (1995); Reus-Smit (2003).

subsequent recurrence to IL (influenced by the motivational effect) allows me to draw out that IL is a variable in its own right, its dependence notwithstanding.

Structural and contingent indeterminacy

Action guidance and justiciability are two sides of the same coin: determinacy. Is determinacy what distinguishes legal from other norms? It plays a role in several of the theorisations of IL reviewed in Chapter 1.[37] Contrary to these theories, I distinguish between two different types of indeterminacy. All IL is indeterminate in a very fundamental sense. The previous chapter explained at some length that IL is epistemically dependent. It does not offer an independent normative standard for judging behaviour, but one that is a product of – the previous section actually suggested a compromise between – utility and appropriateness. The determination of a legal norm's content therefore depends on prevailing understandings of utility and appropriateness. Actors can approach IL looking for strategic as well as aspirational justifications precisely because utility and appropriateness make up the deep structure of IL. This is the kind of indeterminacy that Koskenniemi means when he calls it 'a structural property'[38] of IL. I therefore call this 'structural indeterminacy'.[39]

The other kind of indeterminacy varies dramatically across legal rules. All law exists in language. It follows that legal arguments are of necessity open ended to some extent because 'general propositions do not decide concrete cases'.[40] No matter how specific a legal prescription is, there are always cases for which it is unclear whether a legal rule applies. However, *how* indeterminate a legal rule in fact is, is contingent on the architecture of a regime – how individual provisions relate to

---

[37] For instance, Brunnée and Toope (2010); Franck (1992); Kratochwil (2000).

[38] Koskenniemi (2005) 62; similar Gordon (1982); Kennedy (1987).

[39] For a definition of structural indeterminacy see the appendix. Interestingly Habermas believes that it is this compromise character of law that makes it *more* determinate compared to moral prescriptions: 'Because motivations and value orientations are interwoven with each other in law as an action system, legal norms have the immediate effectiveness for action that moral judgements as such lack' (Habermas (1996) 114). What Habermas refers to as motivations and value orientations are concreteness and oughtness in Koskenniemi's terminology and utility and appropriateness in mine.

[40] Hart (1958) 614.

each other, the ambivalence of particular language, the contestability of concepts to name just a few. I therefore call this type 'contingent indeterminacy'.[41]

Crucially, structural indeterminacy does not mean, as Koskenniemi alleges, that IL regularly fully yields to actors' prior motivations.[42] A compromise between two normative codes, while not providing an independent standard for judging behaviour, puts forward a third separate standard (legality) that cannot simply be reduced to either appropriateness or utility. How far a rule of IL can, in fact, be bent to accommodate an actor's underlying instrumental considerations or principled beliefs, depends on its *contingent* indeterminacy. The law's intellectual effect aligns the outcome of an actor's causal intervention into the world with a compromise between immediate situational imperatives (interests) and long-term, systemic considerations (shared normative beliefs). If the law leaves too much room for interpretation as to what that compromise is or how to get there, the kind of difference that recourse to law will make may depend more fully on what (a normative belief or an interest) guided compliance and the interpretation of law in the first place. By the same token, the wider the range of results that can pass for legal, the easier it is to claim legality for an action that follows interests or normative beliefs.

That very (contingently) indeterminate law is hence unlikely to have a consistent set of predictable effects means that contingent indeterminacy affects the normative success of a legal rule. If we recall the introduction, normative success is the second necessary condition for calling IL effective besides behavioural relevance.[43] The kind of difference law makes should lead to behaviour that is normatively acceptable or perceived as legitimate. The normative success of IL, unlike behavioural relevance, cannot be defined in the abstract. It depends on the kind of law under investigation. For instance, we require a different standard to measure the normative success of IL in regulating diplomatic relations than for international environmental or human rights law. The extra-legal normative expectations of a society regarding what an adequate compromise between utility and appropriateness in any of these areas looks like naturally vary. We can nevertheless generalise that a high

---

[41] For a definition see the appendix.
[42] Koskenniemi (2005) 8; Koskenniemi (2012a) 19.
[43] For a definition of normative success and behavioural relevance consult the appendix.

degree of contingent indeterminacy means that recourse to the rule is less likely to 'guarantee'[44] a specific outcome. As a result, adherence to contingently indeterminate law more probably leads to results that diverge from what a society would consider an acceptable compromise between utility and appropriateness and thus legitimate behaviour in that area of regulation.

Past a certain point contingent indeterminacy may also negate IL's behavioural relevance. Contingent determinacy is a measure for a rule's ability to resist interpretation on behalf of *only* either instrumental or principled considerations. If ever a legal rule yielded fully to one side, it would no longer add anything of its own. It is then that IL becomes a ready disguise for behaviour that simply follows either an actor's interests or extra-legal normative beliefs. Only in that case does IL lend itself to making fully strategic or utterly aspirational arguments. Such an extraordinarily contingently determinate law would indeed jusify any 'arbitrary aggregation of preferred solutions',[45] which is what Koskenniemi suspects *all* legal rules do due to their structural indeterminacy.

Contingent indeterminacy, like the criteria of legality advanced by Brunnée and Toope (of which determinacy is, in fact, one), is a matter of degree. It comes with all the attending pitfalls of using a non-binary category as a means of delineating legal from other norms. Namely, it does not provide a definite boundary between norms and laws. If we were arbitrarily to establish a cut-off point of vagueness beyond which international norms no longer qualified as law, we would probably end up excluding many norms as not being part of IL that common sense and common usage would consider to fall into that very category. As I pointed out regarding the interactional theory of IL in section 1.3, a significant divergence of an analytical category from its real-world counterpart is undesirable. A theory based around such an implausible category fails to grasp the entirety of the phenomenon it purports to explain. The degree of IL's contingent indeterminacy is therefore better thought of as distinguishing bad IL from good (behaviourally relevant and more likely normatively successful) IL, rather than non-legal from

---

[44] Even extremely determinate law still requires interpretation. By the same token, law cannot rule out that some actions have unintended consequences. So an actual guarantee is impossible.

[45] Koskenniemi (2005) 68.

legal norms. Contingent determinacy is indicative of a legal rule's effectiveness; it is not the touchstone of its distinctiveness.

I contend that it is the *way* in which IL was shown to be able to make a difference – the intellectual and motivational effects of recourse to law – that yields a theory about what it means to be a legal as opposed to any other norm. The generation of both kinds of effect centres on mediation between prior motivational forces. IL makes a difference because it is a unifying prescription, telling us what to do in the light of interests *and* norms, utility *and* appropriateness. IL's purport is accommodating situational *and* long-term or systemic imperatives, concreteness *and* oughtness. The answer to the question of what distinguishes law from other norms and interests is as compelling as it is simple: that it encompasses both interests and norms. Laws are neither merely stipulated instrumental considerations nor congealed beliefs about appropriateness because every legal rule is both.[46]

I need to stress that unlike Franck, and Brunnée and Toope, I do not propose to erect the boundary 'between law and its neighbouring discourses'[47] at the maximum degree of contingent indeterminacy past which law in fact no longer makes a difference. IL's distinctiveness lies in its *structural* indeterminacy and the resulting possibility of making a counterfactual difference for behaviour. Structural indeterminacy accounts for IL's epistemic dependence and vice versa.[48] IL brings to bear instrumental considerations and principled beliefs, but unless it is too contingently indeterminate, it never brings to bear only one of the two. Its distinctiveness lies in the possible intellectual and motivational effects of its mediation between the diverging motivational forces on which it simultaneously depends.

IL is defined here as offering a compromise between motivational forces and the normative standards they imply. If that is what we look for in law and what we understand the category of IL to stand for, the question arises of whether a lopsided rule that gives too much weight to interests or norms in an issue area does not qualify as legal. No, a rule that is perceived to unduly privilege either reason for action might meet with less compliance. In addition, even compliance with IL might not

---

[46] Section 1.1 summarised IR scholarship as defining IL as a product of interests and/or norms. It turns out, that the conjunction is crucial. It is because IL is an expression of instrumental considerations *and* principled beliefs that it can make a difference.

[47] Koskenniemi (2005) 13.   [48] Both concepts are also defined in the appendix.

lead to behaviour considered legitimate. Such a rule would thus fail to be normatively successful for a reason other than too much contingent indeterminacy. Yet it would still be part of IL. It is the scope of law as providing a compromise between diverging motivational imperatives that distinguishes it from prior reasons for action. There is no assumption about the concrete shape this compromise takes; nor must it necessarily be a balanced one. After all, it is the prerogative of international society to give priority to immediate considerations in one issue area and to put forward more aspirational prescriptions in another.

Another question raised by this conception of IL's distinctiveness is whether any norm that purports to take interests into account hence qualifies as law. The question is moot since both interests and norms are subject to perception. If an actor does not perceive an alternative imperative for action besides what is indicated by her normative beliefs, or alternatively if what she considers appropriate in certain circumstances accords with the immediate demands of that situation, whether or not the actor follows a norm or an interest is impossible to say. Is that reason for action not automatically a law? It is not because convergence and compromise are different things. Where there is only one reason for action or all motivational forces point in the same direction, a law that expresses a corresponding compromise makes no difference.

In this scenario – a rule of IL does not actually have separate effects because underlying motivational forces converge – is that rule not a law? No! A need for regulation and hence law-making mostly arises where alternative diverging imperatives for action are widely perceived. However, that does not mean that every actor perceives these alternatives and that recourse to law makes a counterfactual difference every single time an actor makes a decision informed by IL. If in a specific situation an actor would have acted in the way law prescribes even without taking it into consideration because her interests and principled beliefs converge where law draws the compromise between utility and appropriateness, law does not have distinguishable effects. For another actor recourse to IL might make a difference in that same situation, because she perceives the prevailing reasons for action differently. The *possibility* of behavioural relevance depends on law's unifying scope (which also makes it distinctive); actual behavioural relevance also depends on circumstances and on the actor. It is the most significant problem of the interactional theory that it makes the success of a norm (inspiration of fidelity) the condition of its qualification as law. The *way* in which IL can make a difference is indicative of what is distinctive about it; a legal rule does not depend on actually being behaviourally relevant in order to count as law.

As determinants of behaviour, interests and normative beliefs are prior to law. They are original reasons for action, whereas law is a secondary motivational force, deliberately constructed within the ideational structure of the international system. Interests and normative beliefs hence serve as the medium for IL's creation.[49] Of course, norms and interests are not purely structural but likewise require agency to be actualised. They are products of the intricate process of mutual constitution and thus endogenous to interaction. The difference is that law is at least theoretically always at the disposition of actors to be changed. In a hypothetical static picture instrumental imperatives and shared normative beliefs are beyond the reach of immediate intentional change by actors, while IL in theory is not.[50] This element of deliberate, theoretically instant malleability is why IL can emerge from the motivational forces on which it depends and put forward a compromise between their implied normative standards if those diverge.

If deliberate malleability differentiates IL from imperatives of action that are 'original' motivational forces, customary IL presents a challenge. The emergence, change and demise of customary law are never instant. The ability of states to deliberately influence these processes is limited. In addition, customary law is *per definitionem* a convergence not a compromise between two elements, state practice and opinio juris,[51] that will often track instrumental and principled considerations respectively. Indeed, rules of customary law are a set of specific normative beliefs that are reflected in practice presumably because they also accord with interests. Customary law hence only comes about if instrumental and principled considerations actually regularly converge and no compromise is necessary.[52]

According to the interactional theory, IL is not deliberately malleable either. Brunnée and Toope do not rule out that IL is used strategically or that a norm entrepreneur attempts to deliberately push a norm towards

---

[49] For an explanation of this structurationist assumption see Giddens (1984) 25.

[50] Similar Chayes and Handler Chayes (1993) 184.

[51] An *opinio juris* is defined as the belief that certain behaviour is required as a matter of IL.

[52] Chapter 4 provides an in-depth discussion of customary IL regulating warfare.

reaching the stage of interactional law.[53] However, before the norm reaches the stage of legality, it needs to be taken up in practice. Accordingly, the act of positing law does not create law. Interactional law, like customary law, is not instantly malleable because it is endogenous to actors' interaction. Like customary law, it depends for its existence on its reflection in practice. As a result, the precise point at which a norm reaches the quality of interactional law is as contestable as the emergence of a rule of customary law. The concept of fidelity to law is as elusive as that of *opinio juris*.

I argue that IL can make a difference because it is a compromise between motivational forces that can only be distinguished if they diverge. Do I argue that customary law does not emerge from underlying motivational forces; that it cannot be behaviourally relevant because it rests on a convergence of, rather than a compromise between, interests and normative beliefs? Though customary law has widely been criticised as incoherent, difficult to establish and possibly a fiction,[54] convincingly showing that it therefore is not part of IL is beyond the scope of this chapter. I will return to the issue in Chapter 4. Here it is noteworthy that Brunnée and Toope provide an intuitively compelling theory of customary IL. As it fails to grasp the distinctiveness of treaty law, it is implausible when drawn on to grasp IL as whole.[55] The theory of IL presented here, to the contrary, is challenged by customary law.

This chapter introduced the differentiation between independent and separate. IL is ontologically dependent, yet separate. This raises questions with regard to the other two dependencies introduced in Chapter 1. I have already put on record that IL provides a separate normative standard for guiding and evaluating action, its epistemic dependence notwithstanding. What about causal dependence? One might argue that just as the compromise that IL brings forward is

---

[53] Brunnée and Toope (2011a); Reus-Smit (2011).

[54] Among others, Akehurst (1977); D'Amato (1971); Fidler (1996); Kelly (2000); Swaine (2002); Trimble (1986).

[55] Interestingly, one of the eight criteria that a norm has to fulfil in order to count as interactional IL is accessibility, which the authors concretise to mean promulgation. This would seem to exclude customary law from interactional law. I will argue later that with very few exceptions customary law in the contemporary world matters – it can be established beyond major controversy and we roughly know what it means – if and only if it is also codified in treaty law, hence when it is promulgated. This indeed suggests that promulgation is the only way in which a norm of IL can become truly accessible.

separate because it is a mixture of appropriateness and utility, so law's compliance pull presents a separate reason for action because IL appeals to a mixture of strategic and principled considerations. Yet the latter is not a defining feature of IL. IL regularly meets with compliance purely for its accord with *either* the interests *or* the normative beliefs of an actor. To the contrary, IL that accommodates only either utility or appropriateness, and ignores a countervailing reason for action in a certain situation, is not a regular occurrence. As related above, it is a specificity of IL that, contrary to municipal law, its mere existence does not induce actors' initial decision to adhere to it. IL is causally dependent *and* fails to provide a separate reason for action, i.e. for the first compliance.

As IR literature focuses on the reasons why states comply with IL in the quest to establish the distinctiveness of legal norms, it tends to arrive at just that conclusion: IL is not an independent, not even a separate motivational force besides interests and normative beliefs. The focus on IL's mode of operation hence accounts for what the previous chapter discovered: the residual uncertainty in IR literature about what IL is. That it does not give actors a separate reason for action is a distinctive characteristic of IL, a challenge to its effectiveness and the reason why we are having this discussion about how IL works and what it is, in the first place. In turn, it is the enquiry into the intellectual and motivational effects of recourse to IL here that unlocks the distinctiveness of norms of IL and gives an answer to the question of what IL is. It is a compromise between pre-existing motivational forces and normative codes.[56] IL is dependent, but separate.

---

[56] Reus-Smit likewise believes that the sense of obligation that legal rules inspire is separate from underlying normative beliefs or interests; legal obligation is irreducible to principled or instrumental considerations (Reus-Smit (2003) 594).

PART II

The definition of a legitimate target of attack in international law

3 | Positive law

In the midst of war, combatants are at every turn confronted with the overwhelming demands of military necessity. Not following them will most definitely give the enemy an advantage in the struggle for victory and can *in extremis* put an immediate end to a combatant's life. The social, legal and emotional consequences of killing or maiming another human being in war, to the contrary, are uncertain and remote.[1] In the presence of a threatening enemy combatant, an actor's commitment to the notion that all human life is worthy may appear abstract, his self-conception as a compassionate person fanciful. Yet few actors will fail altogether to perceive imperatives for action arising from humanitarian concerns, even though those imperatives may interfere with the pursuit of victory or survival.

IL can make a difference for behaviour by providing an actor faced with the task of making a decision with an acceptable compromise between his normative beliefs and instrumental considerations in a certain situation.[2] When it comes to warfare, norms and interests as defined here tend to present directly opposite imperatives for action. Urgent requirements of the situation at hand (interests) in war will often centre on self-preservation and defeat of the adversary. Principled beliefs about war tend to revolve around concerns for the protection of human life beyond one's own. This chapter introduces the definition of a legitimate target of attack according to international treaty law.[3]

---

[1] In the sense that, if they materialise, they only do so fully once the war is over.

[2] Interests are defined as imperatives for action that appear to arise from the immediate requirements of a situation. Norms are imperatives that exist in spite of those situational requirements, related, for instance, to an actor's self-perception, anticipated interactions or expected future developments. See Chapter 2, pp. 46ff.

[3] This analysis focuses on legitimate targets as far as objects are concerned. The increase in targeted killings of suspected terrorists with unmanned aerial vehicles (UAVs) by the Obama administration has drawn attention to the question of which persons can legitimately be attacked. Without entering into the debate on

The definition's complicated architecture and considerable contingent indeterminacy[4] bear testimony to the difficulty of balancing utility and appropriateness during the conduct of hostilities.

3.1 The definition of a legitimate target of attack

Modern IL pertaining to conduct in war was conceived in the late nineteenth and twentieth centuries in The Hague when war was still a regular tool of statecraft and a legal means of resolving conflicts in the international system.[5] Mindful not to 'unduly limit the military's discretion or curtail its ability to win victory',[6] law creation and codification was guided by instrumental considerations and a good dose of pragmatism regarding the realities of warfare. The subjection of war to treaty law was mainly meant to afford combatants protection against certain degrees and types of suffering that conflicted with notions of chivalry or were considered so cruel that they would undermine combatants' will to fight.[7] The Hague Conventions' major achievement was the definitive establishment of the rule that in 'any armed conflict the right of the Parties to the conflict to choose methods or means of warfare is not unlimited'.[8] The treaties' humanitarian ends are by current standards modest.

whether the 'battlefield' in the war on terror extends to Pakistan, Yemen or Somalia, it is safe to say that what are colloquially referred to as drone strikes differ from regular all-out war from the air. During the latter, specifically in the course of the initial air assault on a country, targeting of individual persons, mostly in the form of decapitation strikes, is dwarfed by attacks on objects considered military. As a result, defining a legitimate target of attack is in reality first and foremost a matter of categorising objects. Of course, the designation of persons as either combatants or civilians arises during the application of the principle of proportionality, when decision-makers calculate the so-called 'collateral damage' to be expected from an air strike on an object.

[4] For the introduction of the concept of contingent indeterminacy see section 2.2. For a definition consult the appendix. In the following chapters of the book I mostly drop the word contingent before indeterminacy though that is what I discuss.

[5] Reus-Smit (1999) 140ff.; also Best (1997); this chapter does not provide a comprehensive overview of the historical development of the laws of war. For the most widely referenced such accounts see Best (1983); Neff (2005).

[6] Meron (2006) 61.

[7] Guirola (2012a) 324; US Department of Defense (1957/1976) 2; Walzer (2006a) 34.

[8] Article 22 The Hague II; also Article 35(1) API.

The second wave of international treaty-making in the area of warfare coincided with the prohibition on the use of force in international relations after the Second World War.[9] The adoption of the Geneva Conventions in 1949 marks a shift towards more ambitious humanitarian goals, though without turning away from military pragmatism.[10] The four treaties carve out space for humanitarian considerations during an armed confrontation between states by identifying four groups of persons not directly involved in the fight: the wounded and sick armed forces in the field, the sick and shipwrecked members of armed forces at sea, prisoners of war and civilian persons. It is possible to protect those groups from the harmful effects of war at least to a certain extent, without making warfare prohibitively difficult. 'Geneva law', contrary to 'Hague law', does not deal with the actual conduct of hostilities.[11] Its relevance for the legal definition of a legitimate target of attack is hence indirect.

It took the amalgamation of Geneva law and Hague law in the API of 1977 for IHL to explicitly spell out prescriptions for the conduct of hostilities that strive to accommodate military imperatives as well as humanitarian concerns. It is in the API that we find the positive definition of a legitimate target of attack. Unfortunately the law does not

---

[9] I use the terms treaty-making or positivisation rather than law-making because many of the provisions found in the Geneva Conventions are based on pre-existing customary rules for the conduct of war. Of course, both the status as well as the precise content of these rules was uncertain prior to their translation into positive law. For a detailed discussion of the customary definition of a legitimate target of attack see Chapter 4.

[10] This shift is visible in the different parameters of applicability of the two sets of conventions. The Hague Conventions impose constraints on belligerents' freedom of action only to the extent that those are reciprocal. The so-called *si omnes* clause stipulates that the treaty only applies during an armed conflict, if *all* belligerent states involved are also parties to it (for instance, Article 2 The Hague IV). To the contrary, the Geneva Conventions apply between those parties to an armed conflict that have ratified them, regardless of whether that includes all belligerents involved (Common Article 2 GC I–IV). Geneva law displays what Theodor Meron refers to as a 'homocentric' impetus; its ultimate beneficiary is the individual who requires protection from the harmful effects of war (Meron (2006) 6, 9). The Geneva Conventions hence impose obligations on belligerents 'out of respect for the human person as such' (Pictet (1952) 28f.). These obligations are unconditional and non-reciprocal. Violations by the adversary do not absolve a belligerent from the duty to observe them.

[11] Dinstein defines 'hostilities' as comprising all operations designed to directly hurt the enemy, including non-kinetic ones, such as computer network attacks (Dinstein (2010) 1f.).

simply spell out this definition in one straightforward provision. Several legal principles seem to be relevant for the question of what is fair game in war. The precise content, scope and even denomination of these principles are subject to considerable disagreement. Moreover, as they operate at different levels of abstraction, they relate to each other in complicated ways. Over the following paragraphs, I introduce these legal principles one by one and discuss what they add to and where they merely illustrate or concretise each other. I argue that ultimately two principles exhaustively define a legitimate target according to treaty law: distinction and proportionality.[12]

Distinction and proportionality

Article 48 API lays down the obligation 'to distinguish [at all times] between the civilian population and combatants and between civilian objects and military objectives' and to 'direct ... operations only against military objectives'. The understanding that all persons and objects can and must be attributed either to a civilian sphere that is immune from direct attack or to a sphere of legitimate military engagement is what 'the whole idea of a law of war absolutely depends on'.[13] The proposition that it is possible to delimit military confrontations from the societies within which they occur by way of distinction is at the heart of IL's attempt to regulate warfare. The International Court of Justice (ICJ) considers distinction a 'cardinal' and 'intransgressible' principle, which 'constitut[es] the fabric of humanitarian law'.[14]

A legitimate target of attack under IL is thus first and foremost military. A 'military objective', in the terminology of the API, can be

---

[12] As mentioned, this book is primarily concerned with objects as legitimate targets. If the scope of the investigation were broadened to include persons as legitimate targets, three principles would be relevant: the principle of unnecessary suffering besides proportionality and distinction.

[13] Best (1983) 265; the principle of distinction is as old as the laws of war themselves. The Lieber Code in Article 22 required 'the distinction between the private individual belonging to a hostile country and the hostile country itself with its men in arms'. Instructions for the Government of Armies of the United States in the Field, General Order no. 100 of 1863 (Lieber Code).

[14] *Legality of the Threat or Use of Nuclear Weapons*, ICJ, Advisory Opinion of 8 July 1996, ICJ Reports 1996, §§78ff.

an object or a person.[15] The class of military objectives is delimited by the provisions protecting the civilian population (Article 51)[16] and civilian objects (Article 52). Neither may ever be directly attacked. Moreover, several provisions establish categories of specifically protected persons[17] and objects, such as cultural objects and places of worship (Article 53), objects indispensable for the survival of the civilian population (Article 54), the natural environment (Article 55) and works and installations containing dangerous forces (Article 56). They may be attacked never or only under very limited conditions.

Besides this description *ex negativo* of a military objective as neither civilian nor specifically protected, Article 52(2) API contains a positive definition of a military objective as far as objects are concerned. The provision holds that military objectives are only 'those objects which by their nature, location, purpose or use make an effective contribution to the military action and whose partial or total destruction, capture or neutralisation in the circumstances ruling at the time offers a definite military advantage'. In reality the two criteria – an 'effective contribution to military action' and a 'definite military advantage' – mostly presuppose each other.[18]

An object identified as a military objective according to Article 52(2) API is not automatically also a legitimate target. From an exclusively humanitarian point of view it is unimaginable that law should allow any

---

[15] Military persons are combatants. They can be targeted individually or as a group. A separate detailed analysis of the legal provisions defining combatants and the parameters of direct participation in hostilities is bracketed in this chapter. For a comprehensive discussion of the current IL on targeting persons see Altman (2012); Guirola (2012a); Guirola (2012b); Maxwell (2012); Ohlin (2012). For enquiries into the concept of direct participation in hostilities see Akande (2010); Melzer (2009). For a comparison of the law defining non-immune persons and the law qualifying objects as military objectives see section 9.2.

[16] The civilian population prima facie comprises every person that is not a combatant in accordance with Article 43 API.

[17] For instance, Article 15 API affords religious and medical personnel immunity from attack.

[18] In other words, it is impossible that the engagement of an object that makes an effective contribution to the adversary's military action would not yield a military advantage. By the same token, the most likely reason why an attack on an object should be militarily advantageous is that it contributes to enemy military action. Similarly Dinstein (2002) 4; Sassòli (1990) 363; for an opposing view see McCormack and Durham (2009) 222; Pilloud *et al.* (1987) 635 §2018. Pilloud *et al.* stress that the two criteria have to be met cumulatively, which presupposes that they can come apart.

harming of civilians in war even as a side effect of attacks on military objectives. Yet a requirement of absolute civilian immunity from harm would render the goal of sufficiently weakening the enemy for military victory virtually unachievable, which would contradict the pragmatism that IHL is infused with. Even though an attack on a military objective is hence not illegal merely because it will cause harm to civilians or damage to civilian objects as a side effect, the harm done to the civilian sphere has to be taken into account. This is the role of the principle of proportionality.

Though the provision does not use the term, Article 51(5)b contains the principle of proportionality. The only military objectives that are not legitimate targets on the basis of proportionality are those against which the '[l]aunching [of] an attack … may be expected to cause incidental loss of civilian life, injury to civilian objects, or a combination thereof, which would be excessive in relation to the concrete and direct military advantage anticipated'. Belligerents are hence required to strike a compromise between the military gain they envisage to result from an attack and the harm to civilians the latter is expected to cause. The harm in question must be foreseen – genuine accidents are not covered by the principle – but not intended. An attack that is *meant* to harm civilians is prohibited already under the principle of distinction.

The principle of proportionality is the most condensed expression of the Protocol's difficult mission to accommodate humanitarian concerns as well as military imperatives during the conduct of war. Affirming the principle's compromise character, one commentary to the API acknowledges that with proportionality the drafters of the treaty settled for 'a limited rule' the 'advantage of which was that it would be observed'.[19] Proportionality's role in the regulation of war is nevertheless extremely controversial. Some critics argue that the principle furthers belligerents' apathy towards the harmful consequences of combat operations since it ostensibly 'set[s] a seal of approval on incidental civilian casualties'.[20] Others hold that having to take into account the side effects of military operations can constitute an obstacle to military victory.[21] The principle

---

[19] Bothe, Partsch and Solf (1982) 361; similar Abi-Saab (1984).

[20] Meron (2006) 61 relating other scholars' views; for exponents of this view see Crawford (2007); Herol (2009); Owens (2003) 597; Rockel (2009); Shaw (2005).

[21] Most recently Gross (2009); Fitzgerald (2003) 26; similar Dunlap (1999); Dunlap (2000a); Dunlap (2000b); Meyer (2001); Ricks (2002) 111.

is hence criticised both for being too lenient, given humanitarian considerations, and too stringent in the light of military imperatives.

Constant care and discrimination

A legitimate target is also characterised by the process of preparing and carrying out an attack. Article 57 API requires that belligerents take 'constant care ... to spare the civilian population'.[22] This means that individuals 'who plan or decide upon an attack shall do everything feasible to verify that the objectives to be attacked are ... military objectives'[23] and 'take all feasible precautions in the choice of means and methods of attack'.[24] These prescriptions are sometimes considered to express a third so-called 'precautionary principle'.[25] I argue that most of Article 57's paragraphs do not add substantively new obligations that would not already be implied by the principles of distinction or proportionality themselves. Paragraph 2, for instance, enjoins belligerents to cancel or suspend an attack 'if it becomes apparent that the objective is not a military one ... or that the attack may be expected to cause' excessive harm to civilians. Of course, if probably disproportionate attacks or those that are not geared towards a military objective are illegal, it is necessarily prohibited to launch one or to refrain from cancelling one.

What about the obligation put forward in paragraph 3? It demands that 'when a choice is possible between several military objectives for obtaining a similar military advantage, the objective to be selected shall be that the attack on which may be expected to cause the least danger to civilian lives and to civilian objects'. In other words, an attack is not legal if an opportunity to further reduce expected collateral damage was missed. Paragraph 3 alludes to a condition of necessity in target selection: in order to be legal a specific attack has to have been the only way to proceed without inflicting even more incidental harm. I suggest that this condition is already contained in the principle of proportionality. As far as war is concerned, proportionality implies an absolute obligation to minimise expected collateral damage as much as possible. This minimisation effort in turn comprises the task of making sure that there

[22] Article 57(1) API. [23] Article 57(2)a(i) API. [24] Article 57(2)a(ii) API.
[25] Melzer (2012) 508.

would not have been an alternative militarily equivalent target with a more favourable proportionality calculus.

The reason why proportionality in war contains a necessity condition is that proportionality between incidental civilian harm and military advantage is not a fixed state that can be defined *in abstractum*. For a natural state of balance to exist between two values one has to be able to be expressed in terms of the other or they have to be translatable into a common metric. If such an objective state, where the loss of life was proportionate to military advantage, were conceivable – for instance, ten expected civilian casualties are worth and therefore proportionate to a medium-sized anticipated military advantage – one could argue that, once the prognosis of an attack accorded with that state, the principle of proportionality imposed no further obligation to reduce the expected collateral damage by looking for alternative targets.

It is precisely because there is no such abstract state, where loss of human life and military gain are, as it were, in balance, that the expectation about an attack can only even aspire to satisfying the principle of proportionality once all means to further reduce collateral damage have been exhausted and milder alternatives have been ruled out. Paragraph (2)a(ii) corroborates that necessity is a condition of proportionality, demanding that belligerents minimise expected collateral damage. Of course, the exhaustion of milder means to achieve the same military advantage, and hence the knowledge that it was, in fact, necessary to proceed with an attack and cause collateral damage, does not on its own satisfy the principle of proportionality. Though logically necessary, military necessity is not a sufficient condition of proportionality.

The only paragraph of Article 57 that does create a new obligation for belligerents is Article 57(2)c API which requires belligerents to issue 'effective advance warning[s]' of impending attacks 'unless circumstances do not permit'. The bulk of Article 57, rather than purporting a third principle for the legal definition of a legitimate target of attack, has the very important function of outlining what it means to do justice to distinction and proportionality. The provision prescribing precautionary measures in attack to some extent concretises the implications for action of the two 'cardinal principles'.[26]

---

[26] It warrants emphasis that the rejection of a separate precautionary principle here does not imply a dismissal of Article 57. In the light of the indeterminacy of the

Like precautions in attack, the prohibition on indiscriminate attacks enshrined in Article 51(4) API is also sometimes mentioned besides distinction and proportionality as a third principle contributing to the legal definition of a legitimate target of attack. From a purely semantic point of view, an attack that is indiscriminate is not necessarily either directed against civilians/civilian objects (violating distinction) or resulting in excessive collateral damage (violating proportionality). For instance, target area bombing of several sparsely populated industrial sights, some civilian and some military, is indiscriminate but does not perforce violate either proportionality or the prohibition on targeting civilians. This suggests that discrimination is indeed a separate legal principle.

However, Article 48 (the basic rule incarnating the principle of distinction) imposes a positive obligation to direct attacks against military objectives, rather than merely a prohibition on aiming at civilian objects or persons. Failure to have a specific military objective in mind and to direct one's weapon against it, as in the case of target area bombing, is hence already a violation of the principle of distinction. Of course, while every indiscriminate attack violates distinction, not every violation of distinction stems from an indiscriminate attack. A deliberate, precise attack on a civilian hospital is highly discriminating, but still a violation of the principle of distinction. Indiscriminate attacks according to Article 51(4) are a subspecies of attacks prohibited under the principle of distinction.

That distinction and proportionality hence exhaustively describe attacks on objects prohibited under IHL does not, however, resolve all questions around discrimination. The provision introducing the prohibition, Article 51(5)b, contains the principle of proportionality. In fact the latter is introduced as one possible example of an indiscriminate attack. The prominent legal commentator Yoram Dinstein therefore argues that because the Protocol 'brings the prohibition of disproportionate collateral damage under the heading of indiscriminate attacks, it follows that an attack giving rise to proportionate collateral damage

principles of distinction and proportionality, discussed in the next section, the importance of Article 57 can hardly be overstated and will be highlighted below. The differentiation between legal principles that contain substantive obligations, on the one hand, and provisions that spell out the latter's implications, on the other hand, is crucial for an analytically clear grasp of the positive definition of a legitimate target of attack.

can never be regarded as indiscriminate'.[27] I disagree. The scenario sketched at the beginning of this discussion of discrimination illustrates the possibility of an indiscriminate attack not resulting in disproportionate civilian casualties.[28] The architecture of the provision in fact suggests that an attack violating the principle of proportionality is *always* also an indiscriminate attack, not vice versa.

So every indiscriminate attack violates the principle of distinction and some indiscriminate attacks also violate the principle of proportionality. Article 51 concerns the connection between, on the one hand, distinction, which hinges on the intention and effort in action of an attacker and, on the other hand, proportionality, which regulates the expected results of an attack. The function of the prohibition on indiscriminate attack is illustrative; it draws attention to the fact that a lack of effort in distinction probably leads to disproportionate results. Specifically the kind of violation of distinction that also violates discrimination (rather than a violation of distinction with an intentional attack of civilians or civilian objects) is likely to violate the principle of proportionality.

Humanity and military necessity

Even scholars who would agree that discrimination and precautionary measures respectively illustrate and concretise the principles of distinction and proportionality sometimes describe the legal regulation of warfare as based on four principles: distinction, proportionality, military necessity and humanity.[29] However, humanity (I prefer the less ambitious term humanitarianism) describes IHL on a different level from distinction and proportionality. The latter are the two rules that together represent the *way* in which IHL proposes to reach its regulative goals. Humanitarianism is one such goal.[30] Is military necessity the other goal that IHL acknowledges? No, necessity is not a substantive goal like humanitarianism because the implications of necessity

---

[27] Dinstein (2010) 130, 121.   [28] Likewise Sassòli (1990) 404.

[29] Among others, Rogers (2004); Schmitt (1997/8); Melzer in a curious variation considers the four principles to be '(i) necessity; (ii) proportionality; (iii) precaution; and (iv) humanity', which raises the question of the whereabouts of distinction (Melzer (2012) 508). Canestaro drops distinction in favour of discrimination (Canestaro (2004) 483).

[30] Similar Best (1983); Bothe *et al.* (1982) 305.

themselves depend on a substantive goal. After all, an action has to be necessary *for* something. I contend that the other substantive goal of IHL is military pragmatism; not making warfare militarily impossible. If we recall the brief historical outline above, military pragmatism in combination with chivalry was the 'original' regulative purpose of the laws of war. When it comes to the API, besides rendering warfare as humane as possible, the impetus of the treaties' drafters was to allow combat operations to actually proceed. Current IHL strives to honour its commitment to humanitarianism and military pragmatism at the same time through, first, distinction – the absolute imperative to make only military objectives the intended target of an attack – and, second, proportionality – an attempt to compromise between the military and humanitarian stakes in war.

What about necessity then?[31] Appeals to military necessity regarding the use of force are inherently ambivalent. Historically military necessity 'admit[ed] of all direct destruction [that was] incidentally unavoidable in the armed contests of the war'.[32] In this sense necessity was often used as a licence for violence: all force that proved necessary for military victory had to be permissible. For much of the history of warfare arguments about necessity hence served to override prima facie limits on warfare. In stark contrast to the resulting connotations of military necessity as promoting brutality,[33] the Hague Conventions ordered belligerents to 'abstain from destruction not imperatively demanded by the necessities of war'.[34] In this reading, military necessity restricts violence: only force that is necessary can even come into the realm of what is permitted. Necessity is 'the limit of legality'.[35] That appeals to necessity no longer justify violations of acknowledged rules is supported by a wide consensus.[36]

---

[31] For a detailed discussion of the literature on military necessity see Schmitt (2012).

[32] Canestaro (2004) 454.

[33] For a discussion of the historic use of military necessity as a justificatory basis for violence see Canestaro (2004) 454ff.; Hull (2005) 123f.

[34] Article 23(g) The Hague IV.   [35] Pilloud *et al.* (1987) 396.

[36] This was the *ratio decidendi* of the Nuremberg Military Tribunal in the *Hostage Case* (*USA* v. *List et al.*, Hostage Case, American Military Tribunal Nuremberg, 1948, 11 NMT, 1230 at 1253ff. and 1256). The British Manual on the laws of war is likewise unequivocal that 'necessity cannot excuse a departure from that law' (UK Ministry of Defence (2005) §2.2.1(b)); see also Carnahan (1998) 230;

The uncontroversial status of necessity as a limit on the use of force notwithstanding, its place in the legal regulation of the conduct of hostilities remains contentious. Necessity is certainly semantically unfit to denote a substantive goal of legal regulation, such as military pragmatism or humanitarianism. But is it a third principle, determining the legitimacy of a target together with distinction and proportionality?[37]

Above, I identified necessity as a condition of proportionality. It hence plays a crucial role in the protection of civilians. When it comes to the limited protection afforded to combatants, IHL does not rely on proportionality.[38] Yet it still draws on necessity. While combatants are legitimate targets of attack, they may not be subjected to unnecessary suffering or superfluous, meaning unnecessary, injury. In Article 35(2) the API echoes one of the oldest norms of warfare already expressed in Article 16(2) of the Lieber Code of 1863: '[M]ilitary necessity does not admit of cruelty – that is, the infliction of suffering for the sake of suffering.'[39] Even combatants are protected against harm that does not grow out of the purposeful competition between militaries. It seems that necessity is a *Leitmotiv* in the regulation of war. It is discernible in two major legal principles regulating the conduct of hostilities, though it appears in different variations and at different levels of abstraction.[40]

How does necessity relate to the principle of distinction? The line IHL draws between the military and the civilian sphere of a society at war cannot be coherently explained in terms of the actual threat that an object poses to the adversary.[41] Rather, it is the 'reasonable connection between the destruction of [certain objects] and the overcoming of the

---

Dinstein (2010) 7; International Institute of Humanitarian Law (2006) 8; Jackson (2010) 233.

[37] For this view see Melzer (2012); Rogers (2004); Schmitt (1997/8) 257; Schmitt (2010) 40; UK Ministry of Defence (2005) §2(1).

[38] For the minority view that considers the deaths of combatants to also be subject to a proportionality requirement see Melzer (2012) 513.

[39] Instructions for the Government of Armies of the United States in the Field, General Order no. 100 of 1863 (Lieber Code).

[40] Proponents of somewhat similar views include Abi-Saab (1984) 265; Bothe *et al.* (1982); Dinstein (2010); Meron (2006); Meyrowitz (1994); Pilloud *et al.* (1987) 396.

[41] Objects can be military objectives solely by nature, meaning that even a weapons cache far behind the front lines and unlikely to be of actual use for on-going combat operations or to pose a threat to opposing troops is a legitimate target of attack.

enemy forces'[42] that places them into the category of military objectives. An object that 'makes an effective contribution to [enemy] military action' stands in the way of military victory, while an object that has no role in combat operations is unnecessary to engage.[43] Distinction is based on the understanding that it is necessary to disable some objects during war while others can be put off limits.[44] Necessity in this incarnation gives meaning to the principle of distinction. It explains rather than determines what is distinguished as military and why. Situation-specific necessity judgements therefore do not alter what counts as a military objective. So if it turned out that in order to continue the fight a belligerent would have to attack civilian schools, distinction would not permit that. As mentioned above, an appeal to necessity never serves as a justification for otherwise prohibited actions. The role of necessity here is one of drawing a definitive bottom line. That which is in principle not necessary to engage for overcoming an enemy military can never be a legitimate target of attack according to the principle of distinction. Necessity is built into the principle of distinction and its concretisation in the definition of a military objective according to Article 52(2).

I propose the following taxonomy: necessity is a concrete condition for or an element of proportionality (necessity 1); it denotes the way IHL demarcates the sphere of legitimate direct attack (necessity 2); and

---

[42] *USA* v. *List et al.*, American Military Tribunal Nuremberg, 1948, 11 NMT, 1230, §1253.

[43] Something similar holds true for the application of distinction to persons. A combatant can be attacked while asleep or when he is too frightened or incompetent to actually pose a threat. Nor for that matter is it a person's responsibility or guilt that explains whether she is a legitimate target of attack (section 8.2). Combatants with their right to take part in hostilities and those civilians that do participate in hostilities without legal permission potentially stand in the way of military victory. An engagement of all other civilians, who are not directly contributing to fighting, to the contrary, can be assumed not to be necessary. For a more detailed discussion of potential justifications for IHL's differentiation between combatants and civilians and for an elaboration on the role of necessity in distinction see Chapter 9; also Dill and Shue (2012).

[44] This is a potentially controversial take on the principle of distinction that I will defend at length in the next section (see also Dill and Shue (2012); Dill (2013)). Emily Crawford brings military necessity under the heading of distinction in a similar way. However, she unexpectedly concludes that necessity means 'the aim of distinction should be the weakening of the military potential of the enemy, not their outright destruction'. She fails to explain her apparent assumption that the complete destruction of an enemy's military forces is never necessary to overcome them (Crawford (2010) 35).

it undergirds the prohibition on superfluous combatant suffering (necessity 3). Though in all three incarnations necessity serves as a limit on the use of force, they differ regarding the strictness of the standard they impose and regarding the aim with regard to which indispensability has to obtain. Combatants' suffering is considered unnecessary only if it is completely wanton or senselessly cruel. The force used must be necessary for killing or disabling combatants, but the attack *per se* does not have to be indispensable. Necessity 3 is the least demanding. Necessity 2 permits the attack of only those objects whose engagement is theoretically necessary for the competition between two militaries to proceed. Proportionality contains the strictest understanding of necessity. Necessity 1 is satisfied only if in any concrete situation alternative courses of action that would have been less destructive ways of achieving the same advantage are unavailable. The attack has to be necessary for the achievement of a particular independently legitimate military advantage.

Recent attempts to make necessity 1 in certain circumstances also a condition for direct attack have met with severe criticism.[45] One such attempt is the interpretative guidance issued by the International Committee of the Red Cross (ICRC) with regard to the notion of direct participation in hostilities. It stipulates that 'the kind and degree of force which is permissible against persons not entitled to protection against direct attack must not exceed what is actually necessary to accomplish a legitimate military purpose in the prevailing circumstances'.[46] While highly controversial in the context of attacking combatants and civilians directly participating in hostilities, it has to be noted that necessity 1 is already a requirement for direct attacks on a number of specifically protected objects. Because these objects are prima facie immune from attack, necessity 1 operates here exceptionally as a criterion overriding a prohibition.[47]

In spite of the clarification afforded by the proposed taxonomy, necessity continues to pose three distinct problems. The first is evidentiary: it is arguably impossible to ever satisfactorily prove that an attack

---

[45] Schmitt (2010) 14, 40; also Cohen and Shany (2007) 8f.
[46] Melzer (2009) 77ff.; see also Blum (2010).
[47] For instance, Article 56(2) API describes under which conditions the prohibition on destroying works and installations that contain dangerous forces is suspended: when an 'attack is the only feasible way' to terminate their support to the enemy's military effort. See also Article 54(5) API.

is really the *only* way to achieve a certain aim. This poses a challenge specifically for the application of the concept's strictest incarnation (necessity 1). While one could address this problem with a standard of reasonableness as to the length any actor can be expected to go to in order to rule out alternatives, necessity also raises two substantive questions. First, it is open to debate whether the availability of an alternative B with a somewhat lower probability of success, but the same anticipated military advantage and fewer expected collateral casualties, means that alternative A is no longer necessary. The API treats expectations as binary. Either collateral damage may be expected or not. The treaty specifies neither at what probability of emergence a military advantage may be anticipated nor how likely collateral damage has to be in order to be expected. Finally, the coexistence of three different incarnations of necessity points towards a certain opaqueness of the concept in the first place.

The next two sections address challenges in the interpretation and application of the provisions just introduced. This first enquiry into the complicated web of legal provisions that regulate the conduct of hostilities leaves us with the following conclusions. Variations on the *Leitmotiv* of 'necessity as the limit of legality' appear in all three relevant legal principles. Necessity would seem to be the basis 'on which all law relating to the conduct of hostilities is ultimately founded'.[48] Humanitarianism and military pragmatism are the two acknowledged substantive goals of the legal regulation of warfare. The prohibition on indiscriminate attack and the prescription of precautionary measures in attack illustrate and concretise what it means to do justice to IL in war. Avoiding all redundancy, IHL relies on three legal principles to regulate the conduct of hostilities: distinction between civilian and military objects and persons, proportionality of incidental civilian harm, and the prohibition on unnecessary combatant suffering/injury. The latter is mostly a question of means and methods of attack rather than of target selection. I will therefore focus on proportionality and distinction; together they define a legitimate target of attack under positive IL.

---

[48] Pilloud *et al.* (1987) 396; similar Abi-Saab (1984) 265; Bothe *et al.* (1982); Dinstein (2010); Meron (2006).

3.2 A purposive and textual interpretation

Can this legal definition of a legitimate target make a difference for what is attacked in war? In applying and interpreting proportionality and distinction an actor, of course, relies on her interests and extra-legal normative beliefs. However, as section 2.2 explained, recourse to IL only fails to make a difference if legal rules yield completely to an actor's instrumental or principled considerations, which in war often align with military pragmatism and humanitarianism respectively. Whether adherence to IHL simply accommodates an actor's prior commitment to military and humanitarian concerns, or whether distinction and proportionality impose a compromise between these often conflicting imperatives for action, depends on the degree of indeterminacy of the provisions under investigation. Can we identify the boundaries of a proper interpretation of the positive definition of a legitimate target just outlined?

The object and purpose of defining a legitimate target

According to legal doctrine, the object and purpose of a legal rule provides an important benchmark for distinguishing bona fide inter-pretations from deviations. It delimits the range of admissible interpre-tations because an interpretation *contra legem*, i.e. against the object and purpose of the law, is always invalid.[49] What is the object and purpose of the regime defining a legitimate target of attack? The gist of the previous section is that the API acknowledges two goals: it is founded on an 'uneasy compromise'[50] between military pragmatism and humanitarianism. If these two imperatives are really recognised as of equal importance, neither one of them alone can occupy the position of the object and purpose of IHL. Or does one ultimately override the other?

Some scholars argue that the object and purpose of all rules of IL for the conduct of war is humanitarian.[51] The reasoning behind this posi-tion is the assumption that belligerents follow military imperatives anyway. The task of law in war is then to add weight to humanitarian considerations. This take on the law regulating warfare is subject to

---

[49] Fuller (1958) 614.   [50] Shue and Wippman (2002) 559.
[51] Among others, Fenrick (2009) 271; Uhler and Coursier (1958) 21.

disagreement, which is manifest in the persistent survival of alternative names for the branch of IL concerned with warfare. Yoram Dinstein, for instance, rejects the term 'international humanitarian law' for creating 'the false impression that all rules governing hostilities are – and have to be – truly humanitarian in nature, whereas in fact not a few of them reflect the countervailing constraints of military necessity'.[52] The ICRC is the strongest promoter of the label IHL. Military practitioners to the contrary tend to use the designation 'laws of armed conflict'.

Naming preferences aside, the conclusion is inescapable that the object and purpose of the regime defining a legitimate target of attack is not simply humanitarian. It may have been the impetus of the Geneva Conventions to promote humanitarian considerations at the margins of war against belligerents' natural tendencies to follow military impera-tives. Yet prescriptions for the conduct of hostilities whose sole purpose was to let humanitarian concerns trump military pragmatism would probably be widely disregarded. Depending on what we consider the standard of humanitarianism to be, such a law might also render combat operations prohibitively difficult. Accordingly, the API displays clear signs of a split purpose. For instance, the principle of proportion-ality would be absurd if humanitarianism presented the sole or over-riding regulative purpose of IHL. In that case, law could simply specify a maximum of acceptable incidental civilian harm beyond which an attack would be prohibited regardless of the military advantage at stake.[53]

Of course, allowing the competition between two militaries to be carried out regardless of the humanitarian costs – military pragmatism pure and simple – is not the goal of IHL either. Is the purpose of IHL to render war as humane as possible given the requirements of warfare? Or is it to allow for the competition between two militaries to proceed as unencumbered as possible given humanitarian standards? It is both. The object and purpose of the law regulating warfare is to offer a compromise between humanitarianism and military pragmatism. This

---

[52] Dinstein (2010) 19; likewise Canestaro (2004); Dunlap (2001b); Garraway (2004); Jochnick and Normand (1994); Kahl (2007); Meyer (2001); Schmitt (2007).

[53] If the object and purpose was to render warfare 'humane', IHL might even have to outlaw any incidental harming of civilians and impose a zero collateral damage rule. Chapters 8 and 9 enquire into what we can reasonably expect IHL to accomplish in war if one goal is also to not render warfare impossible.

compromise is what every interpretation should be geared towards. What does this mean in practice? Is an interpretation *contra legem* then one that privileges either aim? What does a balanced compromise between humanitarianism and military pragmatism look like? To recall, the previous section suggested that human life and military gain cannot be expressed or determined in terms of each other, and nor can both be translated into a common metric. Whenever two such incommensurable imperatives are contradictory in that a gain in one implies a loss in the other – which for military and humanitarian considerations is often though not always the case – it is prima facie subjective where they are in 'balance'.[54] The split purpose of IHL is a source of indeterminacy.

How important the object and purpose is for the interpretation of a legal rule, of course, depends on the inconclusiveness of a textual interpretation. For a clearly worded provision an exegesis of the text on its own might definitively set the boundaries between a legitimate interpretation and a deviation. The split purpose of IHL hence urgently raises the question of *how* the legal rules actually prescribe the equal accommodation of humanitarian and military considerations. A closer look reveals that the request to strike a balance between the demands of combat and the protection of human life is restated in the principle of proportionality. Instead of resolving the tension underlying IHL, the provision embodying the principle of proportionality seems merely to reproduce it in the text. Article 51(5)b just repeats the request to 'compare ... dissimilar values',[55] without any further guidance as to how to do so or what such a balance might look like.

Proportionality is a common standard in law; surely jurists have ways to operationalise it? Three criteria are often drawn upon to determine proportionality: first, the means chosen must be adequate, i.e. suitable to achieving the desired outcome; second, they must be necessary to attain this outcome, i.e. no less destructive means are available to achieve the same result; and third, the advantages must be commensurate with the disadvantages resulting from the action.[56] The first

---

[54] For the argument that the image of 'balancing' is used in law to cover up unjustified, unexplained choices see Waldron (2010b) 22.

[55] Schmitt (2002) 8.

[56] The High Court of Justice of Israel has taken a similar approach, asking for (a) a rational link between an action and the advantage sought, (b) the fact that the chosen course of action was the 'least injurious alternative', and (c) 'proportionality *strictu sensu*'. *Beit Sourik Village Council* v. *The*

criterion restates the requirement that in order to be justifiable destruction in war has to have a reasonable connection to the goal of overcoming the enemy. This is also a requirement of distinction. An attack that is not expected to generate a military advantage is illegal even if the attacker anticipates zero civilian casualties.[57] The second criterion evidently expresses necessity 1. The third requirement, however, presents the same recurring problem of purposive indeterminacy.

As mentioned above, the state where a loss of human life is not excessive because it is meaningfully tied to a certain expected progress in war cannot be defined *in abstractum*. We can further concretise this assertion now. It is the adequacy and the necessity aspects of proportionality – the questions of whether an attack in fact yields an advantage and by how much expected collateral damage can be reduced or milder alternatives found – that depend on the situation. The third dimension of proportionality, commensurability, is also ultimately subjective. While reasonable observers may agree in their assessment of extremely easy cases, we in fact observe widely diverging reactions to most attacks that cause *some* collateral damage and yield *some* military advantage.[58] A prescription to balance often diametrically opposed imperatives representing fundamentally dissimilar values resists translation into either a workable *ex ante* guideline or a watertight *ex post* test.

The previous section related scholars' and practitioners' criticisms of the principle of proportionality as not lenient enough from a military point of view, or not stringent enough to satisfy humanitarian imperatives. It seems the principle's true failing is to not provide any clearly defined substantive standard at all. The provision embodying the principle of proportionality is no more concrete than the statement that in war belligerents ought to give equal weight to military and humanitarian concerns. IHL fails to provide us with an actual guideline of how to do so. Section 2.2 identified guiding action as an important part of how legal rules make a difference and safeguard normative success. The rule of proportionality fails to tell the individual how to bring her actions into line with a compromise between humanitarian and military

---

Government of Israel, Israel High Court of Justice, Judgment of 30 May 2004, HCJ 2056/04, §41.

[57] This dimension of proportionality also suggests that the rules for conduct in war contain an echo of the 'reasonable chance of success' criterion that is part of the requirement for justified resort to war as defined by just-war theory.

[58] Similar Dunlap (2001b)17; Dunlap (2008); Fenrick (2004) 189.

considerations. The law does most definitely not relieve the individual of the intellectual burden of forming her own judgments on whether a military objective is also a legitimate target of attack.

The assessment of the consequences of an attack

What about the consequences of an attack? Will they not reveal whether an actor has given too much weight to military imperatives? Is the outcome of an attack not indicative of whether an actor can claim to have acted lawfully or whether she just relied on a legal argument to justify what her interests suggested she do anyway? What do the consequences of a legal attack look like? Distinction is primarily a matter of intent – having a military objective in mind when launching an attack. In terms of action Article 48, the prescription to 'direct' an attack against a military objective demands having a weapon delivery system home in on an actual military objective. In fact, Article 57(2)a(i) API asks for even more action, namely that belligerents 'do everything feasible to verify that the objectives to be attacked are neither civilians nor civilian objects and are not subject to special protection but are military objectives'. Does the outcome of doing everything feasible bear on whether an individual has done justice to distinction?

Directing an attack against a military objective does not guarantee that the objective is hit. The military objective might have moved, or it may not have been where it was assumed to be in the first place. The weapon could have gone astray or been diverted, or another object turned out to block and thereby protect the military objective. The requirement of distinction – to direct all military operations towards military objectives – may well have been fulfilled in spite of an attack's failure to yield any military advantage at all. By equating distinction with the *direction* of military operations, not the destruction they cause, the principle of distinction demands that a combatant assume responsibility for her state of mind – the intent to destroy a military objective – and for behaviour that matches that intent, but not for the consequences of that action.

What about proportionality? Again Article 57 is crucial for shedding light on what exactly proportionality requires. The provision stipulates that doing justice to proportionality means that a belligerent takes 'constant care to spare the civilian population, civilians and civilian objects'.[59] Moreover, proportionality contains an obligation to minimise expected collateral damage and explore alternative courses of action. These prescriptions definitely require action, but does the outcome of an attack have to meet a certain standard? In theory the requirement of proportionality of incidental harm is meant 'to hold the agent responsible, to some degree, for the unintended effects as well as the intended effects' of action.[60] In other words, after (1) belligerents have identified a military objective, (2) verified its status as such, (3) carefully chosen the weapons and method of attack in order to ensure that they cause the least possible incidental damage to civilians and civilian structures in the process, and (4) after discounting genuinely unforeseeable consequences, the standard brought forward by the principle of proportionality to assess the consequences of that attack should be the arbiter of whether belligerents did justice to the law or just followed their interests and privileged military imperatives.

However, in the API the provisions that embody the principle of proportionality concern expectations. According to Article 51(5)b an attack is prohibited and needs to be cancelled or aborted if it 'may be *expected* to cause incidental loss of civilian life, injury to civilians, damage to civilian objects, or a combination thereof, which would be excessive in relation to the concrete and direct military advantage *anticipated* [italics mine]'. Rather than giving us a standard to evaluate outcomes, the principle of proportionality merely adds a requirement to what it means to have the right state of mind in war: right intent in war not only means fixing one's thoughts on a military objective (distinction). The right state of mind includes the desire to 'balance' the pursuit of military progress against the imperative of protecting civilians (proportionality). Commentators are adamant that '[t]he actual results of an attack are irrelevant to the reasonableness of the assessment of the military advantage at the time when the attack was planned or executed'.[61]

But even only in order for there to be a standard of reasonableness regarding the *expectations* a belligerent has about the humanitarian and military consequences of his actions, we first need an intersubjective

---

[59] Article 57(1) API.   [60] Shue (2003) 756.
[61] International Humanitarian Law Research Initiative (2010) 44; similar Dinstein: 'The linchpin [determining whether an actor has done justice to the principle of proportionality] is what is mentally visualized before the attack' (Dinstein (2010) 132).

understanding of what it means for collateral damage not to be excessive in relation to a military advantage. Yet, as argued above, disagreement subsists even about easy cases so that an actor's expectations about an attack 'remain... subjective and fact-specific'.[62] IHL clearly does not provide a standard for evaluating the consequences of an attack. No specific outcome in war is conclusive evidence that the principles of proportionality and distinction were not interpreted and applied in good faith, but were instead used merely as an apology for behaviour that really followed belligerents' interests (or less probably their normative beliefs).

Section 2.2 suggested that legal rules are behaviourally relevant and normatively successful in part by affording justiciability of conduct. This analysis suggests that drawing on distinction and proportionality, observers will have difficulties recognising wrongful behaviour based on the consequences of an attack.

The connection between objects and military operations

Do we at least know with reasonable certainty on what to fix our thoughts and where to direct our weapons in order to do justice to distinction? According to Article 52(2) API a military object is defined by two criteria – an 'effective contribution to military action' and a 'definite military advantage'. They are closely linked. In reality, it is inconceivable that the engagement of an object that makes an effective contribution to the enemy's military action would *not* yield a military advantage. In turn, the main, though not the only possible, reason why an attack on an object should be militarily advantageous is that the object contributes to the enemy's military action.

We can think of exceptional cases in which the two criteria come apart. For instance, destroying two bridges over a river so that the enemy is forced to use the one that best lends itself to being ambushed provides a military advantage and arguably renders the first bridge a military objective. The latter, however, might not yet, and possibly never would, contribute to the enemy's military action. It follows that objects which make an effective contribution are only a subclass, though arguably by far the largest, of objects whose engagement will provide a military advantage. The criterion of military advantage has

---

[62] Dunlap (2001b) 7.

the final say over where IL draws the line between immune civilian objects and military objectives.

It is the connections of an object to the conduct of combat operations, those of the enemy belligerent (effective contribution) and one's own (military advantage), that put an object into the category of military objectives. But how close must that connection be? And what is the right degree of nexus between an attack and the military advantage? The text says that the advantage has to be 'definite', which could mean 'tangible', 'visible', 'palpable', or alternatively 'precise', 'determinate', 'distinct', 'unequivocal'. These words describe the quality of the advantage to be achieved – the first group alludes to the fact of the existence, possibly the likelihood, of its emergence; the second group refers to, as it were, the sharpness of the contours of the advantage. These synonyms of 'definite' do not describe the connection that an advantage has to have to the attack in order for it to be legal. Designations such as direct, immediate, prompt or instant would do so.

One commentary to the API interprets the word 'definite' to mean that the military advantage must be 'concrete and perceptible ... rather than ... hypothetical'.[63] Perceptible belongs in the category of words that describe the quality of the required advantage. 'Concrete' and 'hypothetical' could refer either to the latter or to the connection between the attack and the military advantage. If we consider them to imply a reference to the connection between the attack and the advantage, the words would suggest that a high degree of nexus between them is required. Another commentary requires the advantage not to be 'potential or indeterminate',[64] which rules out too low a degree of nexus, but stops short of requiring a direct advantage. Scholars in general disagree on whether an indirect military advantage arising from an attack renders the object in question fair game.[65]

Not surprisingly, the degree of nexus between an attack and the military advantage arising from it is often a function of the degree of nexus between an object and the adversary's military action. However, a similar interpretative controversy besets the other criterion in the definition of a military objective. What is the minimum degree of nexus between an object and the enemy's war effort for the object to

---

[63] Bothe *et al.* (1982) 326.   [64] Pilloud *et al.* (1987) 636 §2024.
[65] For discussions of this issue see Dinstein (2002) 3; Dinstein (2010); Schmitt (2002) 4.

qualify as a military objective based on the 'effective contribution' the latter makes to the enemy's military action? Some scholars interpret Article 52(2) to allow the engagement of only those objects that contribute to the enemy's *military* effort; others consider a connection to the *war* effort more broadly sufficient.[66]

An example of a class of objectives whose contribution to the military effort is vital yet indirect is the food processing and supplying industry of a belligerent. Since soldiers need to eat, this quite literally sustains the adversary's war effort. Yet it is two causal steps removed from the enemy's *military* effort, meaning the engagement of the enemy belligerent in hostilities. By the same token its engagement ultimately generates a military advantage because hungry forces are less effective. Moreover, complicating the enemy's food procurement ties up manpower and resources that otherwise could be used in support of the fighting. However, these military advantages are not a direct result of the attack. They are two steps rather than one causal step away from the destruction of the object in question. The result of the attacks is that the industry is in ruins and food supplies decrease; first causal step – soldiers get hungry; second causal step – military effectiveness declines.

Compare this to an attack on an object more directly related to combat operations, for instance, a power plant producing the energy supply for the opposing armed forces. Unlike food production, power plants generate an output which provides something soldiers need to fight rather than 'merely' to live. As a result, the decrease in military effectiveness directly follows from the destruction of the object. It is widely accepted that power plants that are used by armed forces, among others, are military objectives. Whether food suppliers that service the military should also be off limits is controversial.

Many other objects in a modern society yield potentially significant military advantages when engaged. Yet they do so only two or more causal steps down the line from the attack. Two causal steps separate the attack and physical destruction from a decrease in military effectiveness when it comes to any production facility or industrial plant supporting the non-combat related logistics of the armed forces. Similarly, attacks on import/export businesses or, in general, any object used for a taxable economic activity decrease in step one the financial resources of the state and in step two the state's capacity to procure weapons

---

[66] For instance, Rogers (2004); Schmitt (2006a); Schmitt (2007) 443.

and hence military effectiveness. Considering production and trade facilities that only indirectly support the fighting military objectives is controversial.

Even further removed from the initial attack is the military advantage arising from a neutralisation of certain media installations. The attack causes a decrease in information and/or propaganda. This in turn may lower civilian morale (step two); civilians, as a result, may contribute less to the war effort (step three). Alternatively such attacks might sow doubt in or cause worry to the relatives at the front (step three) or even cause civilians to rise up against the government (step three). It is hence only in step three or even further down the causal chain that a decrease in military effectiveness ensues. Another example is the engagement of public infrastructure that is of no current or future use to the military, but whose destruction interferes with the lives of civilians, including regime cronies, or the political leadership – for instance, power plants, communication links, transportation, bridges or roads. Attacks on these structures likewise require at least three causal steps before they affect military effectiveness.

What about civilian schools that enhance the intellectual and physical abilities of boys and young men, who will be a source of manpower that is better suited for military service as a result of their education? This example illustrates that the more causal steps separate the military advantage sought from the initial attack, the less certain it is whether that military advantage will materialise at all. Any extra causal step increases the chances that the initial effects of the attack are mitigated by intervening agency. For instance, a belligerent government deprived of the ability to broadcast information/propaganda could hand out leaflets instead or put up signs saying 'keep calm and carry on'. While every step makes the military advantage anticipated from the attack slightly less certain and less definite, at some point it becomes plainly 'hypothetical' and thus insufficient to make an attack legal according to the commentary quoted above.

Section 3.1 showed that the concept of military advantage not only defines the objects that may be attacked deliberately. It also determines what can outweigh unintended, but foreseen, harmful side effects of an attack. Here the advantage is required to be 'concrete and direct'. One commentary interprets this to mean 'substantial and relatively close'.[67]

---

[67] Pilloud *et al.* (1987) §2209.

These specifications suggest that in the context of proportionality the military advantage has to emerge as an immediate (direct) result of an attack. Does this mean that the interpreter should extrapolate to the military advantage necessary to qualify an object as military objective as likewise requiring a high degree of nexus to military operations? Or, in opposition, should the inference be that the use of different attributes indicates that the drafters of the Protocol meant to stipulate that a specific connection of a military advantage to a given attack on an object could be sufficient to reckon this object a military objective for the purposes of distinction, but at the same time, that the connection would not be close enough to outweigh any projected incidental harm of this attack?[68] This would in effect mean that there was a class of military objectives that could only be attacked with an expectation of zero collateral damage. The textual interpretation alone suggests as much.

The definition of progress in war

Closely related to the question about the minimally required connection between an object and combat operations is the question of how we define progress during hostilities. The point of reference used to determine a military advantage could alternatively be the destruction of one object, the thwarting of one of the enemy's operational objectives, a discrete step in the process of overcoming the adversary's military forces – such as the capture of a designated area of enemy territory or the destruction of the opponent's air defence system – or victory as such. Most commentators agree that it does not have to be a single air strike or artillery barrage that provides the advantage. Progress may be the result of several attacks taken together. But what is the most general point of reference for the understanding of progress in combat? Is it overall victory? Does any contribution to victory constitute a definite military advantage?

The issue is contested. The interpretative statement on Article 52(2) API introduced by the UK during the negotiations to the API argues that

---

[68] Hampson suggests that the different wording implies a difference in required magnitude and quality rather than directness. She argues that 'more is required of the claimed advantage for it to constitute a military advantage for the purposes of the proportionality requirement' (Hampson (2010) 10).

definite military advantage 'is intended to refer to the advantage anticipated from the attack considered as a whole and not only from isolated
or particular parts of the attack'.[69] The UK's position has been often
reproduced and is widely endorsed.[70] The US interpretation that military advantage 'is not restricted to tactical gains, but is linked to the full
context of one's war strategy'[71] goes only a little further. However, it is
on the verge of challenging the notion that 'an attack as a whole is a
finite event, not to be confused with an entire war'.[72]

If it were victory that provided the point of reference for the definition
of a military advantage, the question would arise whether we mean
victory on the battlefield or achieving one's desired political end-state. If
the political goals of a war served as the point of reference for defining
progress, targeting choices might no longer follow strictly military
imperatives. Imagine, for instance, a war whose ultimate political goal
is regime change for the purpose of democratisation. Political victory is
achieved when the adversary's current government is no longer in
power and the structures of the current regime are dismantled to make
way for elections. Military victory to the contrary would mean overcoming the enemy military until it could no longer resist and the government had to step down or enter into negotiations. The question of which
is the adequate point of reference for the definition of a military advantage would determine whether objects such as party headquarters, civilian leadership bureaux or information links between the government
and the public were considered military objectives. Engagement of these
objects would allow the attacker to directly oust the political regime by
killing/capturing its leaders or rendering them unable to govern the
state, i.e. achieving political victory with force.

Alternatively some just-war theorists wish to define military advantage
not in accordance with a war's political goals, but in the light of its just
causes. They have elaborated this with regard to the principle of proportionality which requires weighing the anticipated military advantage
against expected civilian harm: 'a war has certain just aims … the
goods involved in achieving those aims count toward its proportionality'.[73] In this reading the reference point for the determination of progress

---

[69] UK Ministry of Defence (2005) 56.
[70] For instance, Dinstein (2002) 6; Hampson (1993) 94; also Primoratz (2007).
[71] US Department of Defense (2010c) 12.   [72] Pilloud *et al.* (1987) §2209.
[73] Most prominently Hurka (2005) 40; also Coady (2008); Hurka (2008);
McMahan (2009); Rodin (2008); Rodin (2012).

in war would be the achievement of a morally just cause rather than overcoming the enemy militarily. If we recognised forcible democratisation as a just cause (which IL does not), the above case would provide an example of defining progress in war and hence a legitimate target of attack with reference to the just cause of a war, rather than in the light of the goal of military victory.

The text of course suggests that an attack has to generate *military* progress: a military, not a moral, political, psychological, or economic advantage makes for a military objective. However, this merely brings us back to the question of the right degree of nexus between an attack and a decrease in the enemy's military effectiveness, i.e. a genuine military advantage. As elaborated earlier, virtually every attack ultimately generates a genuinely military advantage. The question that the text leaves open is what the point of reference is for the qualification of the first-order effects of an attack as progress. The more flexible the definition of progress in war and the looser the required connection between an object and the military confrontation, the more likely the law is to authorise the kind of action required to deliver what a war is ultimately meant to achieve, which is often a political goal, sometimes a supposedly just cause.

The degree of nexus between an object and military action (and hence between an attack and the military advantage) and the point of reference for the qualification of the first-order effects of an attack as advantageous are two closely related issues about which a controversy abounds concerning the adequate delimitation of the sphere of deliberate military engagement according to positive IHL. Specifically, the indeterminate point of reference for the definition of progress in war illustrates Koskenniemi's argument introduced in section 1.2. He holds that the meaning of IL arises during its interpretation rather than lying in the text itself. What kind of behaviour law prescribes and justifies therefore depends entirely on the interpreting actor's prior interests and normative beliefs. Using the political goal of a war as point of reference for the determination of an advantage would push the law along the lines of its indeterminacy further towards where it accommodates the interests a belligerent pursues with the use of force. Defining military advantage according to a morally just cause, as some just-war theorists demand we do, would lead to an interpretation of

IHL that sanctions the use of force on behalf of belligerents' normative beliefs.[74]

To conclude, this textual and purposive interpretation of the provisions that embody distinction and proportionality in the API has uncovered three types of indeterminacy. First, given IHL's split purpose a purposive interpretation of any IHL rule relating to combat operations depends upon a situational and largely subjective decision about what a compromise between military pragmatism and humanitarianism looks like. The principle of proportionality merely restates the request to compromise between the expected loss of human life and anticipated military progress without specifying how to do so (purposive indeterminacy). The second type of indeterminacy stems from the absence of a standard for assessing the consequences of an attack (consequential indeterminacy). Proportionality merely asks for an intellectual balancing effort, and an effort in action to minimise *expected* collateral damage, but not for specific outcomes. Interpretations of IHL that give undue weight to either interests or normative beliefs are hence not exposed as deviations after an attack. The purposive and consequential indeterminacy are primarily rooted in the 'architecture' of the principle of proportionality. However, the principle of distinction fails to mitigate these two types of indeterminacy as it merely asks for the direction of an attack towards a military objective, not for the destruction of specific objects.

The third type of indeterminacy is semantic. The imperative of distinction hinges on targeting only that which achieves a military advantage. However, the point of reference for determining progress in war is subject to controversy. The application of distinction is hence chiefly a function of the goal that a belligerent has in mind when determining whether an attack would be advantageous. The required degree of nexus between an object and the military confrontation that warrants an attack on the former is equally contested. Proportionality likewise relies on the concept of a military advantage. However, a purely textual exegesis suggests that here the degree of nexus has to be high because Article 51(5)b demands a military advantage that is

---

[74] As section 2.1 argued, utility and appropriateness are matters of perception. One government could perceive a goal like regime change for the purposes of democratisation as in its interests; another could consider it a matter of principle. Nothing suggests that a belligerent could not also consider it both a matter of utility and appropriateness at the same time.

'direct'.[75] The semantic indeterminacy of the concept of a military advantage seems to primarily befall the principle of distinction.[76]

What does this mean for IHL's effectiveness, its ability to make a difference in the conduct of hostilities? A purposive and textual interpretation leaves us with a legal definition of a legitimate target that readily bends to endorse the targets an actor might choose purely on the basis of her interests or (less likely) normative beliefs. Before we conclude, however, that IHL cannot therefore be behaviourally relevant, we need to explore whether a historical or a contextual approach results in clearer boundaries for the legal definition of a legitimate target of attack. Do these interpretations reduce IHL's considerable indeterminacy?

3.3 A historical interpretation

One way to look for clearer delimitations of a valid interpretation of distinction and proportionality is to enquire into the intentions of the API's drafters. This section supplements the purposive and textual interpretation undertaken in the previous section with a historical approach to the treaty. When the delegations came together for the Diplomatic Conference on the Reaffirmation and Development of International Humanitarian Law Applicable in Armed Conflicts (hereafter diplomatic conference) in 1971, did they deliberately create legal rules that appear to yield so readily to an actor's interests or did they envisage definitive boundaries for the legal definition of a legitimate target?

The previous section concluded that three types of indeterminacy render the legal definition of a legitimate target under IHL vague: purposive, consequential and semantic. This finding raises four specific questions for a historical interpretation of the Protocol. First, did the

---

[75] This solves the question of the point of reference. If the first-order effects of an attack have to be military in order to outweigh any projected collateral damage, then the point of reference for the determination of the advantage has to be at maximum generic military rather than political victory.

[76] The principle of proportionality contains other semantically indeterminate concepts, i.e. concepts whose meaning is subject to interpretation and contestation, such as 'incidental loss of civilian life', which I bracket here. The meaning and the implications for action of feasibility are discussed as part of a more detailed interpretation of Article 57 API in sections 7.1 and 7.2.

drafters intend to merely repeat the split purpose of IHL, the aspiration to compromise between military and humanitarian imperatives, in the principle of proportionality? Or does an agreement on what it means to not excessively harm civilians in the pursuit of victory underlie this rule? Second, did they mean for IHL not to spell out a substantive standard for outcomes in war? Why did they seemingly hinge the permissibility of conduct largely on the attacker's intent and to a certain extent on his effort in action, but not on the consequences of an attack? Third, what degree of nexus between an attack and the military advantage were they envisaging would provide for an object to count as a military objective? Closely related is the fourth question: what point of reference for the determination of a military advantage did they have in mind? A review of the negotiation records of the API should provide answers to these questions.[77]

Purposive indeterminacy

Many delegations initially objected to a codification of the principle of proportionality on the grounds that it 'amounted to legal acceptance of the fact that one part of the civilian population was to be deliberately sacrificed to real or assumed military advantages'.[78] The objections against proportionality were not all centred on the permissibility of collateral damage, however. Even more delegations expressed concern about the principle's vagueness, criticising it as 'too ambiguous',[79] 'too complicated',[80] 'subjective',[81] 'open to different interpretations'[82] or 'lead[ing] to confusion'.[83] Most such statements reasoned that proportionality therefore undermined IHL's goal of protecting civilian

---

[77] The full reference of the records is International Committee of the Red Cross, *Official Records of the Diplomatic Conference on the Reaffirmation and Development of International Humanitarian Law Applicable in Armed Conflicts (1974–1977)/Conférence diplomatique sur la réaffirmation et le développement du droit international humanitaire applicable dans les conflits armés* (1974–1977), www.loc.gov/rr/frd/Military_Law/RC-dipl-conference-records.html (last accessed 30 January 2012). In the following I use the abbreviation ORDC for official records of the diplomatic conference.

[78] ORDC vol. XV, 241; Ivory Coast: ORDC vol. IX, 308; Romania: ORDC vol. IX, 236 and vol. VI, 305; Syrian Arab Republic: ORDC vol. IX, 48.

[79] Czechoslovakia: ORDC vol. IX, 69.   [80] Colombia: ORDC vol. VI, 212.

[81] India: ORDC vol. IX, 69.   [82] Turkey: ORDC vol. VI, 167.

[83] Colombia: *ibid.*, 168.

populations. Some also warned that the rule's indeterminacy could 'give rise to serious [unintended] violations' of IHL.[84] The root of the problem was identified to be that the principle 'called for a comparison between things that were not comparable and thus precluded objective judgment'.[85] The Democratic Republic of Vietnam called the principle of proportionality 'dangerous'[86] and proposed an amendment according to which it was 'strictly forbidden to base an attack on the principle of proportionality'.[87]

At the same time, several delegations presented proportionality as without alternative, upholding that an absolute prohibition on inflicting civilian casualties as a side effect of military operations was impossible to honour and unlikely to be obeyed.[88] The US was one of the principle's greatest advocates.[89] The delegation emphasised that 'collateral damage to civilians and civilian objects was often unavoidable and it was unrealistic to attempt to make all such damage unlawful: the rule of proportionality was as far as the law could reasonably go'.[90] It is the limited ambition of the provision that appears to have appealed to the US. The delegation was adamant that '[t]he task of the Conference was not to prevent the consequences of war, but to moderate them as much as possible. The rules should be capable of acceptance by Governments and of practical application . . . [Proportionality] set out the maximum protection that could be provided.'[91] Many delegations agreed. The flexibility of the principle was considered an asset.[92]

---

[84] Turkey: *ibid.*, 167.   [85] Hungary: ORDC vol. IX, 49; similar Iraq: *ibid.*, 54.

[86] The Democratic Republic of Vietnam pronounced the same verdict on the concepts of unnecessary suffering and military necessity. ORDC vol. IV, 180.

[87] Republic of Vietnam: *ibid.*, 185; other delegations merely called for the deletion of the provisions in question. Norway: ORDC vol. IX, 59; Philippines: ORDC vol. III, 206.

[88] Canada: ORDC vol. IX, 55; Finland: *ibid.*, 66; France: *ibid.*, 65; Hungary: *ibid.*, 68; UK: *ibid.*, 64; US: *ibid.*, 67.

[89] ORDC vol. IV, 162.   [90] ORDC vol. XIV, 67, 138.

[91] *Ibid.*; also ORDC vol. VII, 294.

[92] ORDC vol. IX, 63; several delegations, among them the US, argued that the principle was too vague specifically and only for the purposes of constituting the basis of a grave breach (Austria: *ibid.*, 307; Mexico: ORDC *ibid.*, 318; Switzerland: *ibid.*, 279; US: *ibid.*, 19). Otherwise the principle's staunchest defender, the US delegation warned that it provided 'a standard so imprecise as to create the risk that any soldier involved in the conduct of warfare, would without intentional violation of the Protocol's provisions, be open to charges of war crimes' (US: *ibid.*, 19). While indeterminacy was hence overlooked, even appreciated when it diminished the rule's action guidance, it was perceived as

Between these two extremes of vehement disapproval and enthusiastic approbation middle positions were rare.[93] The ICRC granted that 'the idea of proportionality called for the exercise of judgement on the part of combatants'[94] and acknowledged that 'combatants would have to strike a balance between civilian losses and military advantage', two values that 'were not commensurate'.[95] It still sided with the proponents of proportionality.[96] Ultimately, the term 'proportionality' did not make it into the treaty, though. Its omission bears testimony to the continued apprehensions of many delegations.[97] Nevertheless, Article 51(5)b was meant to express the principle of proportionality, even though it stands to reason that the terms 'excessive' and 'disproportionate' describe different levels of collateral damage. It is noteworthy that serious discussions of possible alternatives to proportionality short of an absolute prohibition of collateral damage are completely absent from the records.[98]

In the deliberations about Article 57 and precautions in attack delegations debated the length to which a belligerent could be expected to go in order to obtain the information necessary to make a proportionality judgement.[99] They did not, however, discuss instructions for the actual balancing. Nor did they address possible examples of such a judgement. How many expected civilian casualties a commander could reasonably consider 'not excessive' in relation to a certain military advantage remained unexplored. It follows that the final provision does not stand on a shared understanding about what it means for

---

problematic in the light of potentially enhancing the justiciability of conduct in war.

[93] The exception was Yugoslavia. The delegation acknowledged both the principle's inherent flaws and its central role in a workable legal regime, embracing the conclusion that proportionality 'should stand until a better formula could be found'. Yugoslavia did not, however, make any suggestions for such an alternative formula (*ibid.*, 51).

[94] *Ibid.*, 182.   [95] *Ibid.*

[96] The ICRC also expressed and registered assurances that the rule of proportionality was not meant to 'be construed as authorisation for attacks against civilians' (ORDC vol. XV, 285).

[97] The draft Protocol of 1973 still contained the term disproportionate in the provisions on the protection of the civilian population and on precautionary measures in attack (ORDC vol. I, 16).

[98] Uruguay proposed to focus on risk to civilians rather than expected collateral damage, but did not address the thorny issue of a comparison between risk to civilians and military advantage (ORDC vol. IX, 60).

[99] *Ibid.*, 185ff.

anticipated collateral damage to be proportionate. The historical interpretation does not deliver a concretisation of the prescription to find a
compromise between the often contradictory imperatives of achieving a
military advantage and protecting the civilian population. The purposive indeterminacy of proportionality and thus of the legal definition of
a legitimate target was universally acknowledged and either condemned
or welcomed, but never remedied.

Consequential indeterminacy

What about the fact that the wording of the above provisions embodying the principle of proportionality means that IHL does not require
certain results from attacks, but merely asks for proportionality
between *anticipated* advantage and *expected* collateral damage?
Several delegations registered their concern that it was difficult to
establish intent,[100] and that the phrasing of the principle of proportionality as hinging on an intellectual effort provided a loophole for belligerents not to take collateral damage into account at all.[101] Mauretania
called for the replacement of 'the concept of intention ... by more
objective terms'[102] and Austria suggested weighing expected civilian
harm against the military 'advantage sought' not the one 'anticipated'.[103] While this represents an attempt at objectifying one side of
the proportionality calculus, it does not amount to attaching legal
significance to the military advantage ultimately 'achieved'. Ghana's
proposition to consider the civilian casualties 'caused' by an attack in
the proportionality calculus was rejected outright.[104] Even Austria's
less ambitious proposal did not ultimately meet with the approval of a
majority.[105]

The US championed the delegations embracing the provisions' focus
on intentions.[106] It argued against spelling out a standard for results,
cautioning that '[i]f the element of intent was omitted, the provision
might be used to justify trials for accidents or for unavoidable damage'.[107] In general, many delegations were concerned about the epistemic burden on combatants, expressing that a proportionality calculus

---

[100] Hungary: *ibid.*, 49; Iraq: *ibid.*, 54; Mauretania: *ibid.*, 62; Mongolia: *ibid.*, 53;
       Sweden: *ibid.*, 60.
[101] Mongolia: *ibid.*, 53.   [102] Mauretania: *ibid.*, 62.
[103] Austria: ORDC vol. III, 204.   [104] *Ibid.*, 208.   [105] ORDC vol. IX, 62.
[106] Dinstein (2010) 139ff.   [107] ORDC vol. XIV, 67.

was to be judged in light of the 'sources [of information] available to [military personnel] at the relevant time',[108] not with hindsight. The words 'may be expected to cause' excessive incidental harm won with forty-seven votes to fifteen and two abstentions against the alternative phrase 'create a risk of causing' excessive collateral damage. A majority of delegations did not wish to impose a duty on their military personnel to assess risk, but opted to keep the proportionality judgement in the realm of prima facie subjective expectations.

The same reluctance to establish objective standards that could be used to judge the consequences of an attack, and hence pin its illegality on its outcome, is visible in the negotiations for precautionary measures in attack. That Article 57 was meant to concretise the implications of the obligations to distinguish and to observe proportionality should have created a strong case for formulating the provision as clearly and precisely as possible.[109] Yet the ICRC went on record to state that it had 'deliberately proposed a flexible wording . . . as . . . it was for the parties concerned to make it more precise, in terms of the organisation of their armed forces and of the kind of troops engaged'.[110] The negotiations revolved around the extent of belligerents' duty of care. Most delegations ultimately preferred the prescription to do everything 'feasible' in order to do justice to proportionality and distinction to an obligation to do everything 'reasonable'.[111] Of course, both terms acknowledge situational contingency, but reasonableness is a legal category generally used to judge behaviour with hindsight.

The historical interpretation so far suggests that two of the positive targeting regime's sources of indeterminacy are the result of deliberate drafting. Purposive indeterminacy, specifically the mere restatement of the goal to find a compromise between military and humanitarian imperatives in the principle of proportionality, remained a source of contention. Consequential indeterminacy, the absence of a standard for results in war afforded by the focus on expectations, was more unequivocally welcomed.[112] Nevertheless, when the US applauded Article 51(5) b for providing 'military commanders [with] uniformly recognised guidance',[113] it probably overstated not only the provision's ability to guide action, but also delegations' support for it.

---

[108] UK: ORDC vol. VI, 164; *ibid.*, 226.
[109] Similarly only Mauretania: *ibid.*, 187.   [110] ICRC: *ibid.*, 182.
[111] ORDC vol. XV, 285.   [112] ORDC vol. XIV, 300.   [113] ORDC vol. IV, 241.

Semantic indeterminacy

What about the semantic indeterminacy of the term military advantage? The concept denotes the positive side of the proportionality calculus and is prominently featured in the provision defining a military objective (Article 52(2) API), which concerns the principle of distinction. During the diplomatic conference, three major axes of debate emerged around the codification of distinction: first, whether to positively define military or civilian objects, second, whether to define them in the abstract or concretely with a list, and third, what criteria should be used for an abstract definition.[114] As we know, delegations settled on an abstract definition of military, not civilian objects. It is thus in the context of, on the one hand, the determination of criteria for this definition and, on the other hand, the dispute over proportionality, that the intended meaning of 'military advantage' must be investigated.

As outlined in the previous section, the Protocol in Article 52(2) API features two criteria for defining a military objective: an effective contribution to military action and a definite military advantage resulting from its destruction, seizure or neutralisation.[115] Unfortunately, the record does not provide a compelling narrative of why or how delegations made up their mind in favour of these two criteria. A myriad of alternatives were on the table, including 'recognised to be of military interest',[116] 'serving military ends',[117] 'used mainly in support of the military effort',[118] 'contributing to the military potential of the adverse Party',[119] 'offering a distinct military interest',[120] 'of military character or nature'[121] and 'serving military ends'.[122] The record shows that the criteria containing terms like 'interest' or 'recognised' were rejected mostly for their subjective connotations.[123] Yet criticism did not halt before the criterion of military advantage either. Some delegations demurred that 'when interpreted and applied by the combatants, the concept … advantage would almost inevitably be given a wide meaning'.[124]

---

[114] ORDC vol. IX, 113ff.; *ibid.*, 130ff.   [115] ORDC vol. XIV, 132, 128.

[116] ORDC vol. I, 16; ORDC vol. III, 211.   [117] ORDC vol. XIV, 130.

[118] Amendment by Finland and Sweden: ORDC vol. IV, 82.

[119] France: ORDC vol. IX, 121.   [120] *Ibid.*, 128.   [121] Poland: *ibid.*, 129.

[122] Republic of Vietnam: *ibid.*, 130.   [123] *Ibid.*, 112.

[124] *Ibid.*, 182; for instance, Albania: *ibid.*, 70; Federal Republic of Germany: *ibid.*, 56; Hungary: *ibid.*, 69.

The specification of the required military advantage as 'definite' remains equally hard to account for. Alternative adjectives under consideration were 'clear',[125] 'immediate',[126] 'obvious',[127] 'specific',[128] 'distinct',[129] 'distinct and substantial',[130] 'direct'[131] or 'direct and substantial'.[132] At times the record shows no specification at all.[133] Many commentators have since tried to find meaning in the chosen phrasing. The most widely quoted interpretation for 'definite' is that it connotes 'a concrete and perceptible military advantage rather than a hypothetical and speculative one'.[134] As discussed in the previous section, this could be understood to suggest that the drafters wished to impose a limit on how low the degree of nexus between the attack and the military advantage and hence the object and the enemy's military action might be. Was this the intent?

The record states that delegations urged that '[g]reat care should be taken to avoid formulating too narrow a ban on attacks on civilian objects which were used in support of the military effort'.[135] They were hence concerned with the opposite danger: the possibility of too stringent a requirement for the connection between an object and the competition between enemy militaries. Delegations rejected the notion that an object had to be mainly military in order to qualify as a military objective.[136] Nothing suggests that they meant to exclude the anticipation of an indirect military advantage as grounds for legitimate attack.

Ultimately, the record creates the strong suspicion that the choice of the word 'definite' from among its many alternatives did not reflect a substantive agreement on what an adequate degree of nexus between an object and the enemy's military action and hence between an attack and the ensuing military advantage would actually consist of. The Rapporteur of the Third Committee to the Plenary, when asked, was indeed 'unable to draw any clear significance from this choice'.[137] The

---

[125] ORDC vol. XV, 332.   [126] *Ibid.*   [127] *Ibid.*   [128] *Ibid.*
[129] ORDC vol. III, 47.   [130] ORDC vol. XV, 332.   [131] *Ibid.*
[132] ORDC vol. I, 16; ORDC vol. III, 209ff.
[133] Joint amendment by Brazil, Canada, the Federal Republic of Germany and Nicaragua: ORDC vol. III, 202.
[134] Bothe *et al.* (1982) 326.   [135] ORDC vol. XIV, 119.
[136] ORDC vol. IX, 117; the UK maintained that no object could 'be subject to absolute protection at all times' (*ibid.*, 119f.). The Democratic Republic of Germany in contrast proposed to simply agree on which objects should never be attacked and assemble them in a list (ORDC vol. IX, 78).
[137] ORDC vol. XV, 332.

categories of location, nature, purpose and use were not meant to flesh out what 'effective contribution' might mean. The four terms were originally preceded by the word 'namely', signalling that they did not exhaustively define the ways in which an object could be connected to an enemy's war effort, but merely served illustrative purposes.[138]

What about the use of 'military advantage' in the context of proportionality? The previous section hypothesised that the use of the terms 'concrete and direct' meant that a higher degree of nexus was required between the attack and the claimed advantage if it was meant to outweigh incidental civilian casualties and that a lower degree would suffice for qualifying an object as a military objective. After all, no specification of 'directness' is implied by the word 'definite'. The investigation of the negotiation records does not support this interpretation. The ICRC draft protocol used the same specification in both contexts: 'distinct and substantial'.[139] The negotiations then indicate that the specification of the required advantage as direct did not represent a deliberate choice. The adjectives 'concrete and direct', just like the word 'definite', do not reflect a common understanding of the required directness of an advantage. The principle of proportionality cannot be excluded from the semantic indeterminacy of the definition of a legitimate target of attack, even though the text is clearer.

What about the other dimension of indeterminacy of the definition of a military objective, the point of reference for the determination of a military advantage? During the negotiations on Article 52(2) several delegations stated that the advantage that would justify targeting an object was to be 'anticipated from the attack considered as a whole and not only from isolated or particular parts of that attack'.[140] This shows that delegations were aware that the point of reference for the assessment of an attack's effects as advantageous or not needed to be defined for the provision to be workable. Yet they seem to have been mostly concerned with ruling out an interpretation of Article 52(2) that would have required a determination of military advantages in smaller operational steps. Did they consider what the most general allowable conception of progress in war and hence of military advantage was?

---

[138] ORDC vol. III, 208ff.   [139] Pilloud *et al.* (1987) §2027.

[140] ORDC vol. IV, 241; Canada: ORDC vol. VI, 179; Federal Republic of Germany: *ibid.*, 188; Italy: *ibid.*, 231; Netherlands: *ibid.*, 168; UK: *ibid.*, 164; US: *ibid.*, 241.

The adjective 'military' before advantage appears to serve that purpose by drawing attention to the fact that the advantage anticipated should not be a political, economic or psychological one. By implication the point of reference for its determination cannot be the desired political end-state, but as a maximum the goal of military victory. But given the controversy around the degree of nexus, we do not know whether the military advantage was meant to come about as part of the first-order effects of an attack or whether those might put the belligerent ahead in psychological, political or economic terms which also had ultimately to have military implications. The negotiation history shows no evidence of the word's intentional utilisation as a means to forestall targeting directly for political, economic or psychological effect in the hope of achieving a military advantage later.

To sum up, a historical interpretation does not significantly reduce the law's indeterminacy. The principle of proportionality was adopted by many delegations in spite of, by some because of, its failure to put flesh on the bones of the prescription to balance humanitarian and military concerns (purposive indeterminacy). Most delegations hedged against IL imposing a standard for legally acceptable outcomes of an attack (consequential indeterminacy). And the drafters seem to have chosen the criterion of a military advantage without substantively agreeing on a necessary degree of nexus between an object and military action for the advantage to count as a military objective or for it to outweigh incidental civilian harm. Nor did the delegations clearly state the point of reference they envisaged would determine what counted as a military advantage in the first place (semantic indeterminacy). In Martti Koskenniemi's language, it seems that the diplomatic conference made sure that IHL would be flexible enough to serve as a ready apology for the pursuit of states' interests in war.

3.4 The logic warfare ought to follow: sufficiency

A contextual interpretation

Though the intent of the drafters is not made explicit in the records, I contend that a contextual or systematic interpretation of Article 52(2) within the API necessarily leads to the conclusion that the most general permissible point of reference for the determination of progress in war is *military* victory. The following paragraphs show why.

The API ended the virtual silence of twentieth-century IL on the conduct of combat operations by proposing a way to regulate warfare that supposedly accommodated both humanitarianism and military considerations. The latter created the imperative for law not to make warfare impossible. The former created the imperative for law not to allow more destruction than necessary for warfare to be possible. It follows that IHL must allow no more and no less violence than is sufficient. Sufficient for what exactly? It is commonplace that belligerents ultimately seek political goals when fighting each other. Does the law permit exactly that violence which is sufficient for belligerents to achieve their specific political goals? Are objects whose engagement is necessary for the attainment of the latter hence military objectives and legitimate targets of attack?

No, a belligerent's political, moral or other goals cannot determine what violence is sufficient and hence permissible. The API as the first treaty to propose rules for the conduct of hostilities in the light of the prohibition on the use of force in the United Nations Charter (UNC) does not recognise the notion of a just cause or a legal political goal of armed conflict. IHL is independent of the reasons for resort to force and their legality. Law that does not allow any appeal to the causes or goals for which a war is fought in guiding the conduct of hostilities must work from the assumption that there is a stable (if very abstract) concept of military victory, what I call 'generic military victory',[141] that is valid across most wars, notwithstanding their different moral and political contexts (independence of IHL).[142] As IHL is blind before the legality, appropriateness or utility of belligerents' resort to force, it does not distinguish between belligerents on different sides in a war either. It is a widely acknowledged characteristic of IHL that it is the same for both sides in a war (symmetry of IHL). Often adversaries in war will have different goals, for instance, regime change/finding weapons of mass destruction (US) and defence of the country (Iraq) in 2003. If sufficiency of violence were determined with regard to belligerents' political, economic or other goals, opposing belligerents would be permitted different courses of action.

---

[141] For a definition see the appendix.

[142] Is there a meaningful concept of generic military victory independent of the political context of a war? I further discuss practical and normative problems associated with the concept in section 9.2.

Of course, only one side can win each war, i.e. actually achieve generic military victory. It follows that IHL does not allow that amount of violence that is actually sufficient for the achievement of generic military victory. Sufficiency means enough for a competition among militaries to proceed – a competition in which both sides strive for generic military victory. Such a generic military victory then represents the most general permissible point of reference for the determination of progress in war. Belligerents' goals have to be achieved via advantages that appeal to this concept of generic military victory only, rather than directly to the political or moral reasons for which they are ultimately fighting.

In turn, without generic military victory as the broadest possible point of reference for the definition of progress in war, it would be impossible to draw a line between acceptable reasons for action in war (conduct) and the legal, political and moral reasons for which a state is using force (resort). But, as mentioned, it is uncontroversial that the API is premised on the separation of IHL from the question of whether or not a resort to force is legally permissible, morally just or politically opportune. Its preamble unequivocally spells out that the Protocol's provisions must be applied 'without any adverse distinction based on the nature or origin of the armed conflict or on the causes espoused by or attributed to the Parties to the conflict'.[143]

If the first-order effects of an attack have to be advantageous in the light of generic military victory, nothing else, the required degree of nexus between an attack and a (genuinely) military advantage can be no more than one causal step. By the same token the connection between an object and the competition between two militaries has to be immediate, instant or direct. That is what a contextual interpretation suggests

---

[143] Moreover, the negotiation records are replete with affirmations that the justice or legality of a war has no bearing on the rules for the conduct of hostilities (among others, ICRC: ORDC vol. V, 11; Israel: *ibid.*, 58; Switzerland: ORDC vol. VII 298; US: ORDC vol. V, 110). The US maintained that '[t]he introduction into international humanitarian law of "Just war" concepts would inevitably result in a lowering of the standards of protection accorded to war victims. Rare [is] the man who [thinks] his enemy right' (US: *ibid.*, 110). Nevertheless, a minority of delegations expressed unease about the possibility that the independence of IHL from questions of resort created the impression that an aggressor would be exonerated by observing the rules of IHL (Nigeria: ORDC vol. VI, 312), a concern that still plagues some scholars working on IHL. For instance, Epping (2007) 7.

the word 'effective' before 'contribution to military action' denotes. The above discussion showed that almost every object in a belligerent society somehow contributes to the war effort. A contextual interpretation draws a definitive line around the confrontation among militaries – only objects contributing to the goal of generic military victory directly, in one causal step, are military objectives. A contextual interpretation of Article 52(2) thus avoids the slippery slope of a textual exegesis, illustrated in section 3.2. By the same token, the projected military advantage that renders an object fair game for attack is the same as the military advantage that attackers may weigh against the expected incidental civilian harm.

The logic of sufficiency

Based on the two identified features of IHL – it regulates warfare, first, while attempting to equally accommodate military and humanitarian concerns and, second, regardless of belligerents' reasons for resort to force (independence) and thus similarly for belligerents within and across different wars (symmetry) – we can discern a logic according to which the treaty envisages that combat operations ought to be conducted.

The logic the API proposes rests on two commands addressed to belligerents: first, sharply distinguish the use of force from the pursuit of political or other goals. While hostilities are on-going, belligerents have to bracket their larger political goals or moral aspirations when devising how to act, namely what to attack and who to injure incidentally. I call that 'sequencing'.[144] Belligerents are commanded to observe a strict sequence of the use of force now and politics later. Second, sharply distinguish objects and persons directly connected to the competition among enemy militaries from everything else, which is immune from direct attack. I call this 'containment'.[145]

Two assumptions about sufficiency underlie this vision of how war ought to be waged, which is why I call it a 'logic of sufficiency'.[146] The

---

[144] The term sequencing to grasp the regulative implications of the prohibition on the use of force and the separation of IHL from questions of resort is an original contribution of this analysis and should be read as such. For a definition of the sequencing command see the appendix.

[145] For a definition of the containment command consult the appendix.

[146] For a definition consult the appendix.

command of containment relies on the understanding that it is sufficient to engage those objects that are directly connected to the competition between two militaries and thus count as military objectives for this competition to be carried out.[147] In turn, being allowed to attack those objects and persons whose engagement provides a genuinely military advantage in one causal step is necessary for the competition between two militaries to proceed. This corroborates the argument tentatively introduced in the first section of this chapter that necessity gives meaning to the principle of distinction. For example, if it is deemed sufficient to engage objects directly connected to the military effort, it is by implication unnecessary to attack privately owned media facilities or infrastructure not used by the military.

The command of sequencing premises that military victory is sufficient to allow states to subsequently achieve their legitimate political or other goals. If states had a right to use force as a regular expression of sovereign statecraft, we would have to test whether this sufficiency assumption actually held empirically. We would need to know whether generic military victory was in fact sufficient for the achievement of those goals that IL recognises as legally pursuable with force. However, the current international legal order rests on a presumption against the use of force as a continuation of politics by other means. That the command of sequencing probably rules war out as a suitable instrument for the achievement of a wide range of political or other goals – all those that are unlikely to be achieved based on a generic military victory – is therefore unproblematic.[148]

Does this contextual interpretation not contradict a purposive interpretation because it curtails the permissibility of attacks and prioritises humanitarian concerns? To recall, IHL has two often diametrically opposed regulative goals. As a result, an interpretation *contra legem* is one that gives too much weight to either concern over the other and a purposive interpretation chiefly depends on where we consider military and humanitarian considerations to be 'in balance'. While the previous section suggested that there was no ready intersubjective standard for what a compromise between military imperatives and humanitarian

---

[147] Note that sufficiency does not obtain with regard to military victory as such. At least one side loses every war.

[148] Section 9.2 addresses the implications of the second sufficiency assumption for cases of self-defence, the exception that gives states a right to use force under IL.

considerations would look like, we would probably recognise if a legal interpretation endorsed a stark imbalance between the two aims. I hold that such an imbalance would arise if the point of reference for the definition of progress in war were *not* specified and an advantage with a view to any goal a belligerent might set for herself could turn an object into a military objective and outweigh collateral damage. In other words, without the commands of containment and sequencing and their attending assumptions of sufficiency the legal definition of a legitimate target would endorse almost all imaginable attacks that in truth follow a belligerent's prior motivations. IHL would yield to a belligerent's instrumental considerations and probably end up sanctioning a prioritisation of military imperatives.[149]

The logic of sufficiency actually proposes a compromise between humanitarianism and military pragmatism in that neither part of IHL's split purpose is fully accommodated. Rather than rendering war humane, the logic leaves room for the incidental harming of civilians and sanctions direct attacks on a wide range of objects that may be essential to civilian life but also have a direct causal link to the competition between enemy militaries. At the same time, rather than giving in to military imperatives, the logic of sufficiency makes winning wars difficult, both in the military and the political sense. It renders immune many objects whose attack would be extremely helpful in the pursuit of military victory, because their connection to the military competition is not direct. Moreover, it stands to reason that an ultimately political confrontation that descends into the use of force would often be resolved much more quickly if all those objects were fair game that are connected to the specific political issue of contention, not merely those objects connected to generic military victory. As mentioned above, for the resolution of many political or moral disputes the outcome of a military competition, generic military victory, is in fact not

---

[149] It is unlikely that a belligerent would ever give undue weight to principled beliefs over her interests. However, if the point of reference remained unspecified an outside observer could interpret IHL with a view to shared normative beliefs alone, thereby prioritising humanitarian imperatives, for instance by demanding that a genuinely military advantage arises with regard to a small operational step rather than generic military victory. Such a legal argument could be used to inflict reputational costs on a belligerent attempting in good faith to balance military and humanitarian concerns.

sufficient. For those conflicts IHL renders war an altogether unsuitable means of resolution.

In conclusion, a contextual interpretation shows that IHL is not so indeterminate after all. To recapitulate, we found that the point of reference for progress in war is generic military victory. The assumption that it is sufficient to engage objects closely connected to the competition between two militaries in turn implies that IHL requires a high degree of nexus between an object and the military confrontation and hence between an attack and a genuine advantage in that confrontation. I argue that it requires a military advantage, often a decrease in the enemy's military capabilities, to arise in one causal step from the attack – the point of reference for the qualification of an attack's first-order effects is generic military victory. This knowledge helps us (1) to concretise one side of the proportionality calculus and thus ease the implications of semantic indeterminacy for the principle of proportionality, (2) to largely cancel the semantic indeterminacy of the principle of distinction, and (3) to mitigate the implications of purposive indeterminacy for the principle of distinction. Article 52(2) bears up against the most singularly strategic or utterly aspirational interpretations. The consequential and purposive indeterminacy of the principle of proportionality remain without remedy.

4 | Customary law

The US has not ratified the API. The next task is hence to establish the customary definition of a legitimate target of attack. Customary law is defined as a 'general practice accepted as law'.[1] The 168 ratifications of the API bear testimony to the fact that the definition of a legitimate target that was hammered out during the diplomatic conference and adopted on 8 June 1977 is widely accepted as law.[2] A universally ratified treaty provides a strong presumption that customary law is congruent with its positive counterpart.[3] Yet the API, contrary to the Geneva Conventions, is not universally ratified. Among other countries, Afghanistan, Azerbaijan, Egypt, Eritrea, India, Iran, Iraq, Israel, Pakistan and the former Federal Republic of Yugoslavia, like the US, are not parties to the treaty, suggesting they do not accept it as binding IL. While not a large group, it includes the states that have most often been involved in interstate armed conflict in the recent past.[4] In fact, with one exception there has never been an international armed conflict in which the Protocol was applicable among parties on different sides in the war since its entry into force in 1979.[5] The practice of warfare is

---

[1] Article 38(1)b Statute of the ICJ (1945).
[2] Of the 192 UN member states 87.5 per cent are party to the API. *Parties to the First Additional Protocol*, www.cicr.org/ihl.nsf/WebSign?ReadForm&id=470&ps=P; *Member States of the United Nations* www.un.org/en/members/index.shtml.
[3] Sassòli (1990) 502.
[4] Only sixteen states have ever taken part in an armed conflict while at the same time being bound by the API. These are Kuwait, the Russian Federation, Armenia, Bosnia Herzegovina, Croatia, Cameroon, Nigeria, Ecuador, Peru, Belgium, Canada, Ethiopia, the UK, Australia, Djibouti and Lebanon. In addition, the API is only relevant when at least one state party on each side has ratified or agreed to apply the treaty (Article 96(2) API). That has happened only once; see the following footnote.
[5] The exception is the 2008 confrontation between the Russian Federation and Georgia which the ICRC called a 'full-scale international armed conflict' (ICRC (2009) 9). Both countries were parties to the API while conducting hostilities. To the contrary, the low-level border clashes between Cameroon and Nigeria in 1994

hence dominated by states that are not bound by the positive definition of a legitimate target of attack. Do these states disagree with the way in which the principles of proportionality and distinction are enshrined in the treaty? If they do and their practice hence diverges from positive law, what is the customary definition of a legitimate target of attack?

4.1 The definition of a legitimate target of attack

The first step in attempting to establish the customary definition of a legitimate target of attack is an investigation of the status of proportionality and distinction pre-positivisation, meaning before the diplomatic conference was convened in 1971. To that end I will briefly sketch the principles' respective histories. This endeavour prepares the ground for an assessment of how the API may have influenced the customary definition of a legitimate target of attack.

Distinction and proportionality in history

The principle of proportionality expresses the doctrine of double effect according to which an action can be permissible even though it brings about a negative effect, if that effect is unintended and outweighed by a positive intended effect. Although double effect is an ancient proposition originally developed to justify self-defence,[6] the status of the principle of proportionality in the regulation of war was for a long time highly obscure. Some early just-war theorists understood the requirement of a just cause for resort to war to contain a prudential element. In this view the overall harm expected to result from a war had to be proportionate in relation to the cause pursued.[7] Francisco de Vitoria allowed for an echo of this prescription to also bear on behaviour *in bello*. He held: 'it does not seem to me permissible to kill a large number of innocent people ... in order to defeat a small number of enemy combatants'.[8] Many theorists, however, disregarded or

---

and Ecuador and Peru in 1995 are generally considered not to have risen to the level of international armed conflicts.

[6] The doctrine is attributed to St Thomas Aquinas's thirteenth-century work *Summa Theologica*. See, among others, Davies (1984); McMahan (1994).

[7] Neff (2005) 51.

[8] Vitoria (1995) 315, 317; note that he does not specify whether the killing of innocent men is intentional or whether it is a side effect of killing combatants. He merely prescribes a reasonable relationship between means and ends.

rejected the possibility that the harm done as a side effect of military action could be subject to any restrictions.[9]

At the time of the emergence of Hague law, proportionality was accepted as a feature of self-defence and of its remedial counterpart, reprisals.[10] These two legal institutions are relevant in both spheres, the resort to force as well as the conduct of war. Moreover, if 'resort proportionality' were defined as the relation of the expected over-all harm to the just cause, it would depend on the proportionality of individual acts within it.[11] Yet no treaty before the API ever gave expression to proportionality, either as a prescription for the conduct of war or, for that matter, as a requirement for justified resort.[12] On the other hand, although proportionality was not featured in positive IL and civilian casualties were numerous in both world wars, no belligerent ever asserted a right to disproportionately or excessively harm

---

[9] For instance, Pufendorf (1991) 171; for a more elaborate historical account of just-war theory see Engle (2009) 2.

[10] Neff (2005) 129, 227; also Obradovic (1997).

[11] The ICJ has affirmed the customary requirement that resort to force in self-defence has to be proportionate (*Islamic Republic of Iran* v. *United States of America, Case concerning Oil Platforms*, ICJ, Judgment on the Merits of 6 November 2003, ICJ Reports 2003, §§73ff.; *Legality of the Threat or Use of Nuclear Weapons*, ICJ, Advisory Opinion of 8 July 1996, ICJ Reports 1996, §§37ff.; also Fletcher and Ohlin (2008) 72ff.). However, the precise implications of this injunction are unclear. Proportionality of resort can hardly hinge on the overall harm probably caused during a defensive war since assessing this would pose monumental evidentiary problems. Proportionality of resort can only be a rough evaluation of commensurability between the initial threat and an armed response. It seems that once the former rises to the level of an armed attack, responding with force is presumed to be proportionate under positive IL. After all, it would be highly controversial to ever deny a right to self-defence in the case of an armed attack because the response would probably cause excessive harm. Such a limitation would potentially conflict with the conception of self-defence as an 'inherent' right in Article 51 of the UNC. This important provision is conspicuously silent on the matter of proportionality.

[12] It has been argued that as far as the *conduct* of war is concerned, GC IV embodies the principle of proportionality in Article 147. The provision qualifies as a grave breach 'extensive destruction and appropriation of property, not justified by military necessity and carried out unlawfully and wantonly'. 'Extensive' in contrast to 'excessive' is an absolute measure. It refers to the magnitude of destruction not its relation to military gain. The principle of proportionality allows for extensive destruction if the military advantage sought is appropriately weighty. Article 147 GC IV spells out when a violation of the principle of distinction is also a grave breach. It does not allude to incidental harm in the pursuit of military advantage as proportionality does.

civilians.[13] At the time of the diplomatic conference, proportionality was hence a principle with an unclear scope of application whose status under customary IL was highly contestable.

What about distinction? Just-war theory has always recognised an imperative to spare the innocent in war. However, rather than taking the form of a prescription to actively target only certain categories of objects and persons, the principle of distinction was long folded into military necessity.[14] *Jus in bello* identified certain groups of people as harmless, literally innocent and by implication unnecessary to attack.[15] Of course, as discussed in section 3.1, if it turned out that harming presumptively innocent persons was in fact necessary, for instance, during siege warfare, military necessity would provide the justification for doing just that.

The principle of distinction began to graduate from a general imperative to, if possible, spare the innocent to a more detailed legal prescription only in the late nineteenth century. Early Hague law dealt with means of injuring the enemy, sieges and bombardments[16] and required a distinction between defended and undefended towns and places.[17] The first provision to explicitly require distinction at the level of individual objects was Article 24 of the 1923 Hague Rules of Aerial Warfare.[18] The document featured a list of military objectives, which was framed as exhaustive. The formidable constraining force of a closed list of objects open to attack may have contributed to the legal instrument's failure to ever enter into force. The obligation to distinguish as such was not contested.

---

[13] Canestaro (2004) 454; Sassòli (1990) 404.

[14] Hartigan (1982); McKeogh (2002); Neff (2005) 51, 64.

[15] Vitoria (1995) 314; also Neff (2005) 65.

[16] The Hague II of 29 July 1899, revised in The Hague IV of 18 October 1907; The Hague IX of 18 October 1907; Declaration on the Launching of Projectiles and Explosives from Balloons of 29 July 1899.

[17] Gasser (1993) 61; this prescription presupposes a degree of separation between the battlefield and the rest of society that, even at the time of the treaty's adoption, was largely aspirational. In the light of the availability of air power, it is arguably impossible to determine the implications of the prohibition on attacking undefended places. On the relationship between legal norms and the conception of the battlefield see also Mégret (2011) 4.

[18] Their full name is Rules Concerning the Control of Wireless Telegraphy in Time of War and Air Warfare, drafted by a Commission of Jurists at The Hague, December 1922–February 1923.

Some scholars argue that after its frequent violation during the Second World War distinction as enshrined in Hague law was on the verge of falling into desuetude.[19] However, even during the carpet bombing of inner cities by the Luftwaffe and allied air forces, civilian casualties, particularly among workers on industrial sites, were often cast as the deaths of 'quasi-combatants'. The destruction of infrastructure was framed as, in fact, contributing to the war effort or as an unavoidable by-product of war rather than as legally sanctioned attacks on civilian objects.[20] These justifications demonstrate that the prohibition on deliberately attacking what was then considered civilian was an accepted rule of customary law. The Geneva Conventions furthered the solidification of the principle of distinction in the negative by establishing groups of persons who were immune from direct attack. Furthermore, by clearly defining combatants as 'members of the armed forces ... as well as members of militias or volunteer corps'[21] GC III implicitly rejected the idea of quasi-combatants. However, when the diplomatic conference was convened distinction was not yet attached to an established definition of military objectives as far as objects were concerned.

The impact of promulgation

The stated goal of the diplomatic conference was to 'reaffirm and develop' IHL. It was thus acknowledged that many provisions of the Protocol would be based on already existing customary law. Indeed multilateral conventions often have as their goal to 'give customary IL the imprimatur of *lex scripta* without altering its substance'.[22] This process is usually referred to as codification. Of course, a treaty can also alter existing rules of customary law or lay down new obligations that only bind its parties. These new or altered rules may later come to

---

[19] Sassòli (1990) 510ff.

[20] Sherry (2009) 31; given the very widespread bombing of uncontroversial civilian objects, such as apartment blocks, during the Second World War, it is likely that these justifications were to a certain extent non-genuine. However, the perceived necessity to frame these operations as militarily relevant suggests that there was an *opinio juris* purporting that the direct attack on civilians and civilian objects was unacceptable as a matter of law. Similar Parks (1983) 2, 6ff.; Sassòli (2005) 368ff., 457.

[21] Articles 4(A) 1 GC III.   [22] Dinstein (2010) 12; Sassòli (1990) 508.

attain customary status as a result of their reflection in practice and *opinio juris* (aspirational progressive development of custom). The practice of states not party to the treaty is crucial in this respect because the state parties' subsequent practice is first and foremost attributed to their obligations under positive IL. In addition, a treaty can allegedly immediately, 'in its own impact', create customary law.[23] This process of crystallisation whereby promulgation itself confers customary status, usually on an emerging rule, is controversial. It implies that a 'multilateral codification convention may simultaneously produce both treaty and customary rules'.[24]

In which of these categories – codification, progressive development or crystallisation – does Article 51(3)b belong, the provision embodying the principle of proportionality? At the time, delegations disagreed about whether proportionality was new or whether the provision merely codified an existing constraint on the side effects of military operations.[25] The extremely controversial discussion of Article 51 and the fact that it was not adopted by consensus[26] rule it out as a candidate for crystallisation. Whether or not the principle already had customary status in 1971, it clearly has it now. The US, one of the most prominent states not to ratify the Protocol, integrated the rule verbatim into its military manuals and has never questioned the principle's applicability or customary standing since.[27] The ICRC likewise considers Article 51(3)b API a rule of customary law.[28] More recently proportionality has also become an essential term in public debates about the legitimacy of military operations.[29]

That the precise implications of the obligation to strive for proportionality are unclear has in all likelihood helped states overcome their initial reluctance towards the principle. The theory of IL outlined in section 2.2 suggests that a very high degree of contingent

---

[23] *North Sea Continental Shelf Cases*, ICJ, Judgment on the Merits of 20 February 1969, ICJ Reports 1969, 42, §72; also International Law Commission (2000) 20f.

[24] Danilenko (1993) 155. [25] ORDC vol. XIV, 67. [26] ORDC vol. VI, 163.

[27] US Department of Defense (1957/1976) §41; the following recent *Operational Law Handbooks* issued by the US Department of Defense, Army Judge Advocate General's Legal Center and School, International and Operational Law Department also feature the principle of proportionality in the wording of the API: (2002a) 9; (2004) 14; (2007a) 229; (2011a) 12; (2012) 13; see also US Department of Defense (2006a) 614; (2008a) 13.

[28] Henckaerts and Doswald-Beck (2005) 46. [29] Kennedy (2012).

indeterminacy is problematic because it can undermine the normative success of a rule and ultimately even prevent it from being behaviourally relevant.[30] Some scholars also argue that indeterminacy is correlated with higher levels of treaty violation.[31] Yet the widespread endorsement of Article 51(3) API, even though several states fought tooth and nail against its inclusion in the Protocol, brings into sharp relief that indeterminacy also serves an important purpose: it significantly increases the acceptability of IL.[32]

In the light of the history of the principle of distinction, it is safe to say that Article 48 API was a codification of customary law. However, the development of the principle of distinction sketched above also revealed that as far as objects were concerned the exact way of delimiting military objectives, which is different from the general point that the military must somehow be distinguished from the civilian sphere, was not yet a matter of custom. A customary obligation to distinguish of course already presumes that there is some meaningful difference not only between civilians and combatants but also between military and civilian objects. The lengthy negotiations to Article 52(2) API and the many alternatives to the chosen formula that were contemplated, however, corroborate the interpretation that the modus of distinction among objects was not yet a matter of general agreement. The API hence added a positive definition of objects that are military objectives to the customary obligation to distinguish.

This raises the question of whether or to what extent this addition altered the customary obligation to distinguish during the conduct of hostilities. A systematic interpretation in Chapter 3 demonstrated that it is Article 52(2) API that bears out the logic of sufficiency.[33] It does so by setting two crucial parameters for warfare. First, generic military victory is the most general point of reference for the determination of a military advantage and, second, a high degree of nexus (one causal step) has to connect an object to the confrontation between enemy militaries for the object to count as a military objective. The provision proscribes targeting objects whose engagement directly furthers belligerents'

---

[30] See section 2.2 for the argument and the appendix for definitions of behavioural relevance and normative success.

[31] Chayes and Handler Chayes (1993) 14; also Goldstein and Martin (2000) 604; Moravcsik (2012) 19.

[32] Likewise Kennedy (2012) 169; Koskenniemi (2005) 591.

[33] For a definition of the logic of sufficiency see the appendix.

political or other goals. The two commands underlying this logic for waging war – target objects directly contributing to a military confrontation for this confrontation to proceed (containment) and seek a political victory only after achieving generic military victory (sequencing) – are not implied by the prescription to distinguish as such or by Article 48 API alone.

The logic of sufficiency may have nevertheless been part of customary law independent of an explicit agreement on a definition of military objectives and hence before Article 52(2) was drafted. One indication would be that before the diplomatic conference states already refrained from attacks not directly creating a genuinely military advantage. However, during the Second World War both sides regularly used air power to target civilian morale, i.e. they attacked residential areas and transport used by civilians with a view to creating psychological effects.[34] Like the above-mentioned attacks on what we now consider a society's civilian workforce, the strategy of creating disaffection among terrorised civilians was pursued openly and considered not to violate the principle of distinction.[35] This belies Marco Sassòli's claim that an *opinio juris* rejecting targeting for what we would consider psychological or political rather than military advantage prevailed at the time.[36] Belligerents made an effort at distinction, but considered objects and persons with a low degree of nexus to the military confrontation, whose engagement would not immediately create a genuinely military advantage, 'not civilian' and thus presumptive legitimate targets of attack.[37]

What about the point of reference for military progress? Already in 1868 the preamble to the St Petersburg Declaration had stated that: 'the only legitimate object which States should endeavour to accomplish during war is to weaken the military forces of the enemy ... for this purpose it is sufficient to disable the greatest possible number of men' – a clear expression of the command to sequence the use of force and the pursuit of politics. Yet the Declaration had not settled the matter. Even during the

---

[34] For instance, Biddle (2002); Schaffer (2009); Sherry (1987); Sherry (2009).

[35] The British bomber command used terms such as 'de-housing' and 'morale lowering' to describe this strategy. See Biddle (2002); Grayling (2006).

[36] Sassòli (1990) 369. [37] Likewise Sherry (2009) 31.

negotiations to the Protocol, on the occasion of an eleven-day US air campaign against North Vietnam around Christmas 1972 the question was raised: '[c]an air attacks ever be justified when the proclaimed purpose of the raid is political and when political not military, advantages are the immediate end sought by the specific attack?'[38] Answers ranged from a resounding 'no'[39] to 'this presses the distinction between military and political acts too far for practical significance'.[40] These divergent positions on sequencing, like the mentioned state practice of targeting for other than narrowly defined military advantage, suggest that the logic of sufficiency was not a matter of customary law before the API was drafted.

As Article 52(2) API and the logic of sufficiency represented a change to the existing customary obligation to distinguish at the time, we have to investigate what status promulgation conferred on it. Article 52 was adopted without any nay votes, but not by consensus.[41] It is hence implausible that a new customary standard of distinction crystallised right there and then. Did the definition of military objectives in accordance with the logic of sufficiency acquire customary status after the diplomatic conference? As mentioned, the litmus test for whether a new treaty rule becomes general IL subsequent to promulgation is its reception by states that are not party to the treaty. I will focus on the role of Article 52(2) API in the US vision for the conduct of hostilities because the US is a dominant actor in contemporary armed conflict and undertakes much real-world targeting from the air. Moreover, the US is the focus of enquiry of the empirical study in Part III.

---

[38] DeSaussure and Glasser (1975).

[39] Dinstein (2010) 93; Pilloud *et al.* likewise take the position that a 'military advantage can only consist in ground gained and in annihilating or weakening the enemy armed forces' (Pilloud *et al.* (1987) §2218). The International Humanitarian Law Research Initiative concurs: 'Military advantage refers only to advantage which is directly related to military operations and does not refer to other forms of advantage which may in some way relate to the conflict more generally. Military advantage does not refer to advantage which is solely political, psychological, economic, financial, social, or moral in nature. Thus, forcing a change in the negotiating position of the enemy only by affecting civilian morale does not qualify as military advantage.' International Humanitarian Law Research Initiative (2010) 45; see also *ibid.* (2009).

[40] Carnahan (1998) 219.   [41] ORDC vol. IV, 168.

4.2 The United States and the First Additional Protocol

The US expressed its support for Article 52(2) API calling the provision a 'significant and important development in the humanitarian law of armed conflict'.[42] 'The distinction between civilian objects and military objectives will be made easier to identify and recognize.'[43] While these statements indicate that the US considered parts of the definition a progressive development of custom rather than a mere codification, they also show that the US endorsed the formulation. The US Field Manual 27–10 of 1956 was changed in 1976 to reflect the language of Article 52(2) API.[44] An Air Force pamphlet of the same year likewise features the Protocol's definition of military objectives.[45] All in all, the US signalled that it considered its forces to be bound by Article 52(2).[46]

Yet, over the following paragraphs, I will demonstrate that US legal doctrine and military strategy have evolved towards implicitly rejecting the logic of sufficiency with its commands of containment and sequencing. Two examples evidence that the US envisages a diverging framework for the interpretation of the concept 'military advantage' and an alternative logic for the conduct of hostilities. First, a subtle change in the wording of the definition of military objectives indicates that US doctrine in operational law allows a lower degree of nexus between an object and military operations than the logic of sufficiency. Second, several currents in military strategy cast doubt over the US commitment to the logic's injunction that belligerents' desired political end-state is not a permissible point of reference for the definition of progress in war.

The connection between objects and military operations

As mentioned above, the US adopted the language of Article 52(2) into its operational law manuals, signalling that it accepted the Protocol's addition to the customary obligation to distinguish as binding general IL.[47] Yet two decades later legal doctrine started to feature a change in

---

[42] *Ibid.*, 163.   [43] *Ibid.*, 204.   [44] US Department of Defense (1957/1976).
[45] US Department of Defense (1976) 5.
[46] Likewise Henckaerts and Doswald-Beck (2005) 187; Matheson (1987) 426.
[47] The following recent *Operational Law Handbooks* issued by the US Department of Defense, Army Judge Advocate General's Legal Center and School, International and Operational Law Department contain the formulation of Article 52(2) API:

the wording of the definition of military objectives. In the 1997 Field Manual on the Joint Targeting Process the attribute 'war-sustaining'[48] emerged as a criterion for mission assessment.[49] The Joint Doctrine for Targeting of 2002 used the term to explain the definition of military objective.[50] The term has entered this definition in Military Commission Instruction no. 2 of 2003. The document defines military objectives as those objects which 'effectively contribute to the opposing force's war-fighting or war-sustaining capability', as opposed to the original criterion of 'an effective contribution to military action'.[51] According to the new formulation a link to military action properly so-called is no longer the only way an object can become a military objective. Another way is to contribute to an enemy's 'war-sustaining capability'. The *military* advantage that may ultimately arise from attacks on objects that can conceivably be construed as sustaining a belligerent's capabilities to wage war can have a very low degree of nexus to the attack.[52] Section 3.2 showed that anything from the

(2002a) 16; (2003a) 8; (2004) 12, 20; (2007a) 21, 446; (2008c) 19, 614; (2010c) 12; (2011a) 20; (2012) 22; see also US Department of Defense (2008a) 19f.

[48] The position that objects that are 'war-sustaining' are legitimate targets of attack originated with naval warfare. The US Navy traditionally considers legitimate '[e]conomic targets of the enemy that indirectly but effectively support and sustain the enemy's war-fighting capability' (for instance, US Department of Defense, (1995 403). The term appeared for the first time in *The Commander's Handbook* of 1989, namely in the annotated supplement. It was there accompanied by the explicit qualification that it was not intended to alter the meaning of Article 52(2) API (Robertson (1997/8) 46). For the original meaning and purpose of the term in naval warfare see Melson (2009) 44.

[49] US Department of Defense (1997) I-10.

[50] US Department of Defense (2002b) A-2.

[51] US Department of Defense (2003c) Article 5(d).

[52] The 2007 *Joint Doctrine for Targeting* brings back the link between sustaining and war-*fighting*. However, compared to its predecessor of 2002, it introduces another change. The document reads: 'Civilian populations and civilian/ protected objects, as a rule, may not be intentionally targeted, although there are exceptions to this rule' (US Department of Defense (2007d/2011) 91). According to the API the prohibition on targeting the civilian sphere is certainly without exception. It has been suggested that the sentence refers to civilians that are directly participating in hostilities. However, given the status of 'direct participation' as a hard-won and intensely debated legal category, the term would likely be mentioned if that was what the provision referred to. The provision goes on to ignore the consensus established during the diplomatic conference that, as the presumably smaller category military objectives not civilian objects, are defined in law. It states that '[c]ivilian objects consist of all civilian property and activities other than those used to support or sustain the adversary's war fighting capability' (*ibid.*, E2).

(civilian) political apparatus, manufacturing and food-processing industries to civilian morale sustains the war in some way.

The shift towards a lower degree of nexus is also visible in the yearly *Operational Law Handbook* issued by the Judge Advocate General School. Since 2004 the *Handbook* has started the definition of military objectives with a verbatim repetition of Article 52(2) API and then elaborates:

> The connection of some objects to an enemy's war fighting or *war-sustaining effort* may be direct, indirect, or even discrete. A decision as to classification of an object as a military objective ... is dependent upon its value to an enemy nation's war fighting or *war-sustaining effort* (including its ability to be converted to a more direct connection), and not solely to its overt or present connection or use [italics mine].[53]

The criterion of having value to an enemy's war-sustaining effort is thereby framed as an interpretation of the uncontroversial formulation defining a military objective according to Article 52(2). But is it?

The matter is controversial. Prominent military expert Hays Parks, in a lecture at Chatham House, referred to the issue as 'more of an intellectual argument between various semantic alternatives which does not make a real practical difference'.[54] Michael Schmitt likewise maintains that the use of the attribute 'war-sustaining' as a feature defining military objectives has not led to problematic targeting choices.[55] The International Humanitarian Law Research Initiative abstained from using the term in its 2009 *Manual on Air and Missile Warfare*. The commentary describes it as 'a matter of dispute' whether 'the definition includes objects which indirectly yet effectively support military operations'. The Initiative goes on to reject the argument that objects that merely sustain the war should fall under the definition contained in Article 52(2).[56] Yoram Dinstein considers 'war-fighting'

---

[53] Among others, US Department of Defense (2007a) 22; (2010c) 19f. 21; (2011a) 21; (2012) 23; it is unclear what a 'discrete' connection between an object and the adversary's war-sustaining effort might mean: an isolated, volatile, separate or abstract connection?

[54] Chatham House (2011) 21.   [55] Schmitt (2002) 70; Schmitt (2006b) 281.

[56] International Humanitarian Law Research Initiative (2010) 50; the *Manual on Air and Missile Warfare* contains the *Operational Law Handbooks'* contention that '[t]he connection between a military objective and military action may be direct or indirect'. However, the commentary to the Manual specifies that this

capability largely synonymous with military action, but like Frits
Kalshoven he rejects 'war-sustaining' as too broad.[57]

Admiral Robertson argues that the change in language is a deliberate
signal that the US changed its position: '[T]he inference that one may
draw from this change in wording is that the United States ... has
rejected the presumptively narrower definition contained in Article 52
of Protocol Additional I in favour of one that, at least arguably, encompasses a broader range of objects and products.'[58] Corroborating the
view that the criterion 'sustaining a war effort' creates a more inclusive
category of military objectives, the *Operational Law Handbooks* of
2006 to 2008 list, without qualification, '(1) Power (2), Industry (war
supporting manufacturing/export/import), (3) Transportation'[59] as
military objectives. However, objects that fall in any of these categories
are not military objectives by nature. The API requires that a link to
military action via their location, purpose or use be established
before they can legally be attacked.[60]

The broadest conception of military objectives in US doctrine yet is
implied by the permission to intentionally attack 'objects that
contribute to an opposing state's ability to wage war', which has
featured in *Operational Law Handbooks* since 2010.[61] Ultimately the
entire civilian infrastructure can be considered to contribute to a
state's ability to wage war. The statement includes no specification of
the required nexus between an object and the actual military effort. The
same operational law manuals acknowledge that the US defines
'"definite military advantage" very broadly'.[62] A preventive argument

---

makes military objectives of objects such as 'enemy military storage depots or
barracks far from the battlefield because such assets constitute reserves for further
military action by the enemy' (International Humanitarian Law Research
Initiative (2009) rule 24). The latter is rather uncontroversial.

[57] Dinstein (2002)146; Fenrick (2004) 172; also Fenrick (2009) 275; Kalshoven
(1991) 300; Roscini (2005) 422; Watkin (2004).

[58] Robertson (1997/98).

[59] US Department of Defense (2006b) 20; (2007a) 21; (2008c) 19.

[60] The most recent *Operational Law Handbooks* from 2010 onwards do not
contain this list.

[61] US Department of Defense (2010c) 20; (2011a) 20; (2012) 22; previous
Handbooks bore the slightly more specific formulation 'military objectives that
enable an opposing state and its military forces to wage war'. Among others, US
Department of Defense (2006b) 20.

[62] US Department of Defense (2010c) 146; (2011a) 132; (2012) 134.

against critics is implicit in the statement that '[s]tates may come to different conclusions regarding whether certain objects are military objectives in accordance' with Article 52(2).[63] It is certainly safe to conclude that US operational law doctrine allows for a lower degree of nexus between an object and the enemy's military action and hence between an attack and the resulting military advantage than the API, which commands containment of military operations.

The definition of progress in war

Military strategy likewise challenges the logic of sufficiency. The military doctrine of effects-based operations (EBOs) has three closely related implications that place it in opposition to the logic of sufficiency. First, and most importantly, in defiance of the command of sequencing, the premise of EBOs is that achieving one's ultimate political goals while *not* having to destroy the enemy's military forces is the height of successful warfare.[64] In the operationalisation of distinction the doctrine recommends that those targets are to be selected which 'contribute *directly* to the achievement of strategic objectives [emphasis in original]'.[65] 'Strategic' is defined as 'the highest level of an enemy system that, if affected, will contribute most directly to the achievement of our national security objectives.'[66] The doctrine hence advocates choosing objects as targets that are linked not to generic military victory, but to the specific strategic, read political, goals of a war. Accordingly, 'offensive action [is allowed and welcomed] against a target – whether [it is] military, political, economic, or other'.[67] Manuals contrast effects-based targeting with attrition or interdiction, which are shunned for their lack of effectiveness.[68] Rather than limiting combat operations as much as possible to the competition between enemy militaries as the logic of sufficiency does, EBOs as much as possible avoid this competition.

Second, the doctrine urges commanders to 'consider *all* possible types of effects [emphasis added]'[69] when selecting targets. It advocates

---

[63] US Department of Defense (2010c) 552; (2011a) 132; (2012) 5261.
[64] US Department of Defense (2004) 464.
[65] US Department of Defense (2007b) 2.   [66] *Ibid.*, 3.
[67] US Department of Defense (2007c) III-20.
[68] US Department of Defense (2003d) 18.
[69] US Department of Defense (2006c/2011) 14.

producing 'political effects beyond the mere destruction of those tar-gets'[70] because those indirect effects are often considered to be more important than the immediate kinetic results of an attack.[71] In other words, an effects-based approach does not follow the sharp distinction between military objectives narrowly defined and the rest of a belliger-ent society as prescribed by the logic of sufficiency, specifically the command of containment. Military manuals explicitly credit effects-based thinking for inspiring the engagement of objects other than '"traditional" wartime targets'.[72] The prescriptions to avoid the engagement of enemy military forces and to strive for other than kinetic effects are taken even further by the doctrine of achieving rapid dominance, colloquially known as 'shock and awe'. The latter explicitly identifies the civilian population as the most promising object of psychological warfare.[73]

The third problematic recommendation of EBOs is that targets should be chosen in the light of their usefulness for the achievement of the desired political end-state, but also with a view to doing so efficiently. The prescription is that mission accomplishment should be 'sought while minimizing cost in lives, treasure, time, and/or opportu-nities',[74] seeking 'to achieve objectives most effectively, then most efficiently'.[75] But is this instruction even in conflict with the logic of sufficiency? Surely, the latter does not forbid the minimisation of time, blood and treasure in the attempt to win a war. It does not, but seeking efficiency in accordance with the logic of sufficiency is only possible within clearly defined boundaries. I will briefly elaborate on the three ways in which the API is what I call 'efficiency defying'.

First, the goal over which other factors can be minimised is military progress narrowly defined. What the logic of sufficiency thus precludes is the efficient (direct, quick and cheap) pursuit of the belligerents' ultimate political goals. Second, even military victory may only be achieved with the engagement of objects that in one causal step contribute to the competition among opposing militaries. That remains true even if the engagement of other objects promises to contribute to

---

[70] *Ibid.*, 11.   [71] *Ibid.*, 19.   [72] US Department of Defense (2011b) 27.
[73] Ullman and Wade (1996); I will return to the role of shock and awe in US combat operations in sections 6.1 and 7.3.
[74] US Department of Defense (2006c/2011) 14.   [75] *Ibid.*

ending the war more quickly by generating a political or psychological advantage, but only an indirect military advantage (ending the war). The logic that the Protocol envisages combat operations should follow puts both sequencing and containment before efficiency. The logic of sufficiency concerns the interpretation of distinction. However, proportionality is likewise efficiency defying. As established in section 3.1, proportionality contains a necessity condition. Therefore, more collateral damage cannot be traded against a gain in time or expenditure reduction.[76] Minimisation of time and costs only comes into play once there are several ways of achieving a military advantage which are equal in their humanitarian outlook.

What a belligerent is allowed to do according to the API is (1) attack objects that in no more than one causal step yield a military advantage (containment); (2) define this advantage in the light of, as a maximum, the goal of generic military victory (sequencing); and (3) choose the most efficient from among the ways of disabling the enemy that produces the least unintentional harm to civilians (proportionality). Given that the doctrine of EBOs implies the rejection of all three efficiency-defying propositions, it is no overstatement when military manuals call it 'a different approach for thinking about war'.[77]

The inclusion of an effects-based approach to targeting in US doctrine is quite recent and roughly coincides with the first appearance of the term 'war-sustaining' as part of the definition of military objectives in operational law doctrine. The Air Force's *Basic Doctrine* of 2003 describes EBOs as 'emerging'.[78] From then on virtually all doctrinal texts describe targeting as 'fundamentally effects based'.[79] Already in 2007, however, the US Army started to distance itself from EBOs. Since 2008, the Joint Forces Command has likewise eschewed the doctrine's

---

[76] UK doctrine permits an efficiency consideration in the determination of military necessity. 'Military necessity is now defined as "the principle whereby a belligerent has the right to apply any measures which are required to bring about the successful conclusion of a military operation and which are not forbidden by the laws of war" . . . namely the complete or partial submission of the enemy at the earliest possible moment with the minimum expenditure of life and resources' (UK Ministry of Defence (2005) §2.2).

[77] US Department of Defense (2003d) 41.　　[78] *Ibid.* 18.

[79] US Department of Defense (2006c/2011) vii.

terminology. Yet, the reason for this is not that EBOs ignore the boundary between genuinely military objectives and the rest of civilian society (containment) and between conduct of and resort to war (sequencing). Criticism centres on the allegation that the doctrine '[a]ssumes a level of unachievable predictability'.[80] Indeed Joint Forces Commander Mattis emphasised that while he rejected 'the more mechanistic aspects of EBO', he 'recognize[d] the value of operational variables, such as the political, military, economic, social . . . characteristics of the operating environment',[81] which the doctrine brings to a commander's attention. Moreover, the US Air Force continues to embrace EBOs and has since 2007 even extended their application.[82]

It is not surprising that the Air Force is the staunchest defender of EBOs. In the doctrine of strategic attack it has long embraced a vision of warfare that resembles EBOs. Effects-based targeting, it is said, merely takes strategic attack further.[83] Indeed, the military manual entitled *Air Warfare* of 2000 states that strategic attack is 'aimed directly at producing the strategic effect of enemy defeat, with no intermediate level effects on enemy forces involved'.[84] The doctrine document *Strategic Attack* of 2007 further elaborates that '[e]ffects upon fielded forces will generally be a by-product of achieving broader strategic objectives'.[85] The assumption underlying this recommendation to target with a view to achieving genuinely political effects is that 'very often [it] makes more sense to attack the person, nation, or organisation using the tool rather than the tool itself'.[86] Like EBOs, strategic attacks strive to achieve 'strategic, war-winning effects and objectives' 'as directly as possible'.[87] Like EBOs, strategic attacks endeavour to do so efficiently: 'producing the greatest effect for the least cost in blood and treasure'.[88] The Air Force credo is that '[i]f properly applied, strategic attack is the most efficient means of employing air and space power'.[89]

---

[80] US Department of Defense (2008b).   [81] *Ibid.*
[82] US Department of Defense (2011b) 19.
[83] US Department of Defense (2003d) 38.
[84] US Department of Defense (2000/2011) 7.
[85] US Department of Defense (2007b) 7.   [86] *Ibid.*, 4   [87] *Ibid.*   [88] *Ibid.*
[89] US Department of Defense (2004) 464.

4.3 The logic warfare ought to follow: sufficiency versus efficiency

The logic of efficiency

It is possible that the US once accepted the constraining force of the containment and sequencing commands, but changed its stance on Article 52(2) over time. Or the US may never have agreed with the logic of sufficiency, but failed to notice that it logically followed from the enthusiastically endorsed Article 52(2). After all, the historical interpretation in the previous chapter concluded that the delegations to the diplomatic conference did not deliberately choose the wording of paragraph 2 in order to forestall belligerents using political goals as a point of reference for the determination of progress in war. Nor does the qualification 'definite' denote a substantive agreement on the required degree of nexus between an object and military action. The logic of sufficiency emerges from a contextual reading of Article 52(2), the context being the Protocol's ambition to regulate the conduct of hostilities, first, independently of the resort to force and, second, accommodating equally military pragmatism and humanitarianism. Alternatively, it is possible that the US over time just put ever less emphasis on the separation of conduct and resort which allowed it to interpret the text more broadly.[90] The juxtaposition of the contextual interpretation of the API in the previous chapter with current US doctrine doubtlessly suggests that the US now rejects the commands implied by the logic of sufficiency.

The US is not the only state displaying implicit disagreement with the logic of sufficiency in its doctrinal take on the conduct of hostilities. Other members of the North Atlantic Treaty Organization (NATO) also embrace EBOs. Israel's 2008 Operation Cast Led likewise challenged the commands of containment and sequencing. The stated military goal of the air campaign was to end Hamas's ability to launch rocket attacks against Israel. The larger political goal of course was loosening Hamas's grip on the Gaza Strip. This overall political goal of the campaign rather than operational military success used as a point

---

[90] The official US position endorses the separation. Yet section 6.2 uncovers tendencies to dissolve the boundary between IHL and questions of resort in US air warfare.

of reference would have suggested that the large-scale destruction of government structures and public infrastructure was advantageous. A quest for ending Hamas's ability to threaten Israel with rockets would not explain, for instance, the notorious attack on a graduation ceremony of the police academy.

Scholarly debate likewise reveals signs of a fundamental disagreement about the logic warfare ought to follow. The controversy around kinetic psychological warfare against the civilian population can best be explained in terms of two alternative visions for the conduct of hostilities,[91] one based on the assumptions of sufficiency underlying the commands of containment and sequencing, the other emphasising efficiency like EBOs, shock and awe and strategic attack. Article 51(2) API, which contains the prohibition of '[a]cts or threats of violence the primary purpose of which is to spread terror among the civilian population', is the focal point of disagreement. At one end of the spectrum Marco Sassòli holds that the second sentence of the provision is redundant. After all, psychological warfare against the civilian population *per definitionem* creates first and foremost a psychological not a military advantage.[92] In stark contrast, eminent voices, specifically in the US military, exclude that same sentence from the customary standing of the provision.

The contention that '"undermining the government's political support" does offer a very "direct and concrete" military advantage'[93] seems plausible. The presupposition is that such psychological effects will end the war more quickly so that civilian morale is a very efficient targeting choice. However, the implication of this view is that the most immediate effect of a hostile action has no first-order connection to the competition between enemy militaries. A quicker end to the war, of course, has crucial military implications, but the nexus between such a terror-inducing attack and the war's ending is indirect (via pressure or the protests of a disaffected population). Moreover, in this reasoning the point of reference for the definition of advantage is not strictly

---

[91] Targeting *combatants*' will to fight with means not otherwise prohibited by IL is not part of this controversy about psychological warfare. After all, combatants' will to fight forms part of an enemy's 'military capabilities'. Problems with the law arise when the will of civilians – cronies, civilian leaders, the government at large or the morale of the general population – is targeted. Likewise International Humanitarian Law Research Initiative (2010) 110.

[92] Sassòli (1990) 397.   [93] Dunlap (2001b) 14.

speaking generic military victory. The idea, after all, is to achieve one's desired political end state *before* the enemy military is overcome, when the opposing regime is toppled by its own people. The belligerent in fact hopes not to have to gain military victory properly so-called at all.

Article 52(1) was drafted to prevent a repeat of the failed Second World War endeavour to bomb civilian populations into ceasing their support for their countries' war efforts. Targeting infrastructure in the hope that the distressed population will put pressure on the government, which is then deposed or at least softens up during negotiations – practised for instance during operations Allied Force and Desert Storm – counts on the same mechanism. Of course, it does not necessarily involve the same selection of targets. Neither during Desert Storm nor in the course of Allied Force did air crews ever deliberately and directly attack civilians, civilian residences or other uncontroversial civilian objects. Nevertheless, the mechanism in both cases is using military means to achieve a psychological effect in the hope of ending a war more quickly and achieving one's ultimate political goals more efficiently. The step of achieving with every attack a military advantage properly so-called is cut out.

General Charles Dunlap dismisses allegations of illegality with regard to such 'message targeting'[94] with the contention that '[t]hese are strikes aimed at bona fide military objectives ... whose intended effect is primarily psychological'.[95] But in the logic of the API, in order to establish that an object is a bona fide military target one has to show that its engagement contributes to the endeavour of overcoming the enemy military. Of course, the Clausewitzian imperative of overcoming an enemy's will to fight suggests that civilian morale is a highly valuable target of attack. By the same token, any attack almost regardless of the target ultimately has some implications for the competition between enemy militaries, specifically for the likely length at which it can be sustained. The examples of varying degrees of nexus introduced in section 3.2 demonstrate as much.

In reality there is no bright line that separates the civilian from the militarily relevant sphere. No eternal canon of objects whose engagement is sufficient for a competition between two militaries is available for belligerents to consult. I suggest that this is precisely what the definition of military objectives in the API added to the

---

[94] *Ibid.*, 20   [95] *Ibid.*, 14; also Hosmer (1996).

customary law of the time: the positive regime defining a legitimate target of attack requires the deliberate effort to draw such a line. Belligerents must identify the universe of objects whose destruction in the specific circumstances of the armed conflict yields in one causal step a genuine advantage in the pursuit of generic military victory. As already acknowledged, the proposition that in order to fight a war it is 'sufficient to disable the largest possible number of man',[96] and the notion that taking away from these men only the objects necessary to fight is sufficient, are not primarily descriptive assumptions. They are IHL's most fundamental regulative commands.

An interpretation of Article 52(2) that is not constrained by the two sufficiency commands of containment and sequencing generates a logic for the conduct of hostilities that allows for an emphasis on efficiency in hostilities. It is remarkable that the disagreement about which logic combat operations ought to follow, sufficiency or efficiency,[97] is not well understood either by scholars or military practitioners. The divide between proponents of sufficiency and efficiency is an unacknowledged one. I argue that many persistent interpretative debates in IHL, including the question about the permissibility of kinetic attacks on civilian morale and the controversy around war-sustaining objects, would be better understood and more easily resolved if the fundamental disagreement about the right logic for the conduct of hostilities were acknowledged and addressed. While treaty law squarely supports the logic of sufficiency, I have not yet established whether contemporary customary law envisages combat operations to be guided by an imperative of efficiency or by the commands of containment and sequencing based on the mentioned assumptions of sufficiency.

The impossibility of establishing the customary law of war

It is a rare combination for a legal regime to be laid down in a comprehensive and widely ratified treaty while the law in action in the same issue area is predominantly customary. The reason that this is true here is the minimal overlap between states that are party to the treaty and

---

[96] Declaration Renouncing the Use, in Time of War, of Explosive Projectiles under 400 Grams Weight of 29 November 1868 (St Petersburg Declaration), sentences 2 and 3.

[97] Both logics are defined in the appendix.

those that engage in the regulated activity.[98] How do we establish the customary definition of a legitimate target that binds those militarily active states that are not party to the API, including the US? The Protocol prescribes the logic of sufficiency. It reflects how its signatories believe states ought to behave as a matter of law and thus counts as a widely shared expression of *opinio juris*. If state practice reflected the logic of efficiency, as US military doctrine and its elaborations on operational law suggest it does, the central question in this attempt to shed light on the customary definition of a legitimate target of attack would be how much weight should be accorded to state practice and *opinio juris* respectively.

The question inspires disagreement. According to the traditional conception of IL all international obligations arise from the free will of states. In this reading state practice and customary law cannot fundamentally diverge over the long run. After all, practice is a manifestation of state consent. What at least theoretically is always a deviant practice to start with eventually inevitably develops legal relevance, notwithstanding contrary expressions of *opinio juris*.[99] The fact that the states which conduct contemporary warfare have mostly not become members of the API would create a presumption against the Protocol's customary standing. In this view, the commands of containment and sequencing would not constrain the belligerent following the customary definition of a legitimate target of attack. The latter could accord with the logic of efficiency.[100]

A more recent, some say progressive, approach to custom attributes more importance to evidence of a shared normative belief among states that a certain practice is required by law and that alternative courses of action are illegal.[101] This school of thought is more easily ready to disregard heterogeneous state practice and more quickly arrives at the conclusion that customary law has emerged or changed in the light of expressions of *opinio juris*.[102] Accordingly almost universal ratification

---

[98] Exceptions include the UK, the Russian Federation and Ethiopia.

[99] For instance, D'Amato (1971) 97f.

[100] This would, of course, raise the question whether the separation of IHL from questions of resort does not itself have customary standing thus impeding the logic of efficiency from being compatible with customary IHL, a question I bracket in this discussion.

[101] For this distinction see Roberts (2001).

[102] For instance, Simma and Alston (1988/89).

of the API, which is the result of a deliberate process of law-making, would be a strong indicator for the emergence of a customary definition of a legitimate target. That its implied logic is possibly not reflected in state practice would not necessarily obviate the emergence of custom. In this view, the strictures of the logic of sufficiency would define a legitimate target of attack under customary IL.

Some scholars hold that the traditional conception of custom as mostly based on state practice is particularly unsuited for IHL.[103] After all, given the prohibition on the use of force, states that end up in wars have in many cases already breached IL. Moreover, states' interests in war will often challenge or even contradict normative ideals about warfare. In the light of the high stakes associated with losing a war, belligerents are expected to consistently follow only their interests. Basing customary law largely on state practice would hence corrupt the normative integrity of IHL. Of course, advocates of the traditional conception of IL would respond that customary law is important precisely because there is no authority that *a priori* decides who is a delinquent and whose practice is fit to be a source of law. It is the prerogative of sovereign states to continuously refashion the consensus as to what is legally acceptable behaviour.

Yet in two areas of IL, disregard of practice and a singular reliance on *opinio juris* in fact account for the emergence of many bona fide customary rules: human rights law and international criminal law (ICL). Sassòli shows that human rights have expanded so rapidly and extensively because it is politically difficult for states to openly object to verbal expressions of *opinio juris* that accord with widely shared normative beliefs about the value of the human person.[104] Theodor Meron has observed that the International Criminal Tribunal for the Former Yugoslavia (ICTY) 'formally adhered to the traditional twin requirements for the formation of [customary law]. Yet in effect, ... without explicit acknowledgement, [the ICTY came] close to reliance on *opinio juris* or general principles of humanitarian law, distilled, in part, from the Geneva and Hague Conventions [italics mine]'.[105]

What IHL shares with human rights law and ICL is that it is harder for states to express purely strategic arguments that obviously privilege

---

[103] Among others, Meron (1987) 363; Meyrowitz (1981) 123; Sassòli (1990) 232.
[104] Sassòli (1990) 231, 234; likewise Spieker (1999) 217.   [105] Meron (1996) 239.

instrumental over principled considerations.[106] Of course, statements about how states 'believe' everyone should behave as a matter of law (*opinio juris*) do not necessarily express only normative beliefs about an ideal reality. As the negotiation records to the API have shown, states take their interests into account when making pronouncements about what behaviour they think law ought to demand. However, it is a distinctive characteristic of IHL that the activity it regulates is prohibited as a matter of law and highly problematic as a matter of morality. This places a high premium on issuing expressions of *opinio juris* that align more closely with humanitarian ideals than with instrumental considerations taking account of military imperatives in war.

While an overemphasis on state practice might undermine the integrity or credibility of customary IHL, as argued by proponents of a progressive approach to custom, overreliance on *opinio juris*, of course, risks creating law that reflects states' shared normative beliefs about war – their humanitarian ideals. Such a law would probably fail to take into consideration how states are prepared to actually behave as belligerents when their most vital interests are threatened. I have not yet investigated whether the logics of sufficiency and efficiency align with shared normative beliefs about war (mostly humanitarian considerations) and interests during war (often concerning military imperatives) respectively. However, it is telling that the US enthusiastically endorsed Article 52(2) API in the abstract, but when it came to establishing concrete guidelines for the behaviour of its troops, the evidently strong interest in waging war efficiently came to the fore.

The US interaction with the ICRC illustrates the clash between the traditional and the progressive approaches to customary law. The ICRC supports the view that the substance of the API reflects what states believe to be law. In this view the treaty embodies custom. By implication any divergent state practice is prima facie a violation of customary IHL, a view that the ICRC expressed in its comprehensive study on customary IHL of 2005.[107] The US relentless criticism of this study pits

---

[106] Scholars of IR argue that the legitimacy of norms that protect bodily integrity is accepted cross-culturally so that it is hard for states to voice opposition to them. See Keck and Sikkink (1998); Sikkink (2011).

[107] Henckaerts and Doswald-Beck (2005) xliii.

inconsistencies in state behaviour against the ICRC's systematic accumulation of expressions of *opinio juris*.[108]

One suggestion about how to overcome the dichotomy between the progressive and traditional approaches to custom, each of which always gives precedence to one element over the other, is the so-called sliding scale. According to this concept explicit and converging expressions of *opinio juris* weaken the requirements of frequency and uniformity of state practice. Widespread homogeneous state practice, in turn, reduces the need for expressions of *opinio juris*.[109] However, that leaves unanswered the question of what custom is if widespread and consistent expressions of *opinio juris* coincide with but contradict frequent and uniform state practice. For instance, hardly any state would affirm a right to torture, yet many engage in it, when they deem the stakes high enough.[110] The customary prohibition on torture is either iron clad or extremely weak, depending on whether one prioritises *opinio juris* or state practice. Such a divergence between *opinio juris* and state practice is likely in areas of international relations in which widely shared and well-internalised normative beliefs regularly contradict powerful situational imperatives, as is the case during war.

It is important to note here that I have not enquired into actual state *behaviour* yet. All that the previous section afforded was snapshots of a state's, namely the US, military and legal doctrine. Is it even correct to consider doctrine state practice or are the reviewed military manuals expressions of *opinio juris*? Like their appropriate respective weight, the definition of the two elements constituting customary law is subject to controversy. Anthony D'Amato, for instance, defines the two elements by distinguishing between what the state does (practice) and what the state says (*opinio juris*).[111] In this reading only actual behaviour counts as state practice and *opinio juris* are states' verbal acts, presumably including their military doctrine and operational law manuals. While an intuitively appealing approach, it can be but a starting point in the determination of custom. After all, not all behaviour counts as state practice. Behaviour which is accidental, habitual or due to comity, does not lock a state into a legal obligation. By the same token, jurists tend to argue that the denial of states that they use torture and/or the attempt to exclude certain interrogation techniques from the definition of torture

---

[108] See Bellinger and Haynes (2006).   [109] Kirgis (1987) 146.
[110] For instance, Waldron (2010b).   [111] D'Amato (1971) 49.

means that their behaviour does not count as a basis for new more permissive customary law on torture. It strengthens rather than weakens the customary prohibition on torture. Likewise, not all verbal acts of states that formulate an 'ought' are articulations of a belief about the requirements of *law*, in other words expressions of *opinio juris*.

Custom is defined as a 'practice accepted as law'.[112] That means it is a coincidence of expressed normative beliefs and similar behavioural patterns. In other words it is a convergence between the two elements of *opinio juris* and practice that is necessary for customary law to emerge. Accordingly the ICJ and the ICRC both maintain that one cannot establish the prevailing *opinio juris* and state practice separately because only practice undertaken *with* a corresponding *opinio juris* may form the basis for a legal obligation.[113] Both institutions therefore adhere to the approach of establishing '*opinio juris in* the practice of states [italics mine]'.[114] Practice can be both verbal as well as behavioural acts of states in this reading. The two types of acts count if, and only if, they also express an *opinio juris*. Of course, actual state behaviour is difficult to systematically evaluate, and an *opinio juris* potentially implied by behaviour is hard to discern. The ICJ's jurisprudence, like the ICRC's 2005 study on customary IHL, therefore focuses heavily on verbal practice.[115] The doctrine that *opinio juris* is best visible in state practice ends up as a nearly complete disregard of actual state behaviour and customary law that reflects states' verbal statements rather than behavioural patterns.

This practical problem aside, what does the ICJ's and ICRC's doctrine on customary law imply regarding IHL and the two logics for the conduct of hostilities? US military manuals qualify as verbal practice. Moreover they express a bottom line *opinio juris*: not every guideline they contain is a matter of law, but the behaviour they prescribe cannot be below the standard the US 'believes' IL demands. After all, it presumably does not instruct its troops to violate IL. As a source of customary law, military manuals hence suggest that targeting

---

[112] Article 38(1)b Statute of the ICJ (1945).

[113] To the contrary, the International Law Commission has issued lists of both verbal and behavioural acts that constitute state practice, suggesting that it can be evaluated separately from an enquiry into *opinio juris* (International Law Commission (1980) 34ff.).

[114] Henckaerts and Doswald-Beck (2005) xl. [115] Kelly (2000) 453.

according to the logic of efficiency is the standard required by IL. However, the negotiation record to the API likewise counts as a source of custom in the ICJ's view and the treaty itself has contributed to the emergence of custom. These instances of verbal practice require the legal definition of a legitimate target as envisaged by the logic of sufficiency. In the case of IHL, the notion that verbal and behavioural practice when accompanied by *opinio juris* are sources of custom merely displaces the controversy from the disagreement about which element is more important in the formation of custom to the question of whose practice and *opinio juris* are more important, those of belligerent states or those of the majority of the international community.

Like the previous two issues, this question is contested. The US Department of State in its rebuttal to the above-mentioned ICRC study on customary IHL all but demanded that the US should have more weight in the determination of custom. As a reason for this the correspondence pointed to the frequent US involvement in armed conflict.[116] The international legal doctrine of specially affected states indeed implies that certain states' practice is indispensable for the emergence of custom. As a matter of law some states do carry more weight in the formation of custom than others.[117] This, in turn, might mean that customary IHL can only develop in conformity with the practice of militarily active states, many of which have not ratified the Protocol, but implicitly embrace the logic of efficiency.

Against this understanding, the ICRC argues that '[a]lthough there may be specially affected States in certain areas of international humanitarian law, it is also true that all States have a legal interest in requiring respect for international humanitarian law by other States, even if they are not a party to the conflict'.[118] In addition, all states can suffer from means or methods of warfare deployed by other states, even if they tend not to practise the strategic offensive. This argument casts doubt on the notion that customary law could prescribe rules for and

---

[116] '[T]he Study ... tends to regard as equivalent the practice of States that have relatively little history of participation in armed conflict and the practice of States that have had a greater extent and depth of experience or that have otherwise had significant opportunities to develop a carefully considered military doctrine' (Bellinger and Haynes (2006) 2).

[117] *North Sea Continental Shelf Cases*, ICJ, Judgment on the Merits of 20 February 1969, ICJ Reports 1969, 43, §73f.

[118] Henckaerts and Doswald-Beck (2005) xix; also Danilenko (1993) 96.

confer permissions during the conduct of hostilities that conflict with the vision of how war ought to be waged that is embraced by an overwhelming majority of states with an acute interest in the regulation of warfare.

What these controversies suggest is that we cannot hope to establish customary law in war with any reliability. It is plausible that state practice, specifically behavioural patterns, reflects the situational imperatives that states tend to encounter in the area of regulation. According to the theory of IL developed in Chapter 2 those imperatives ground states' interests and in war they tend to track military imperatives. *Opinio juris*, specifically if enshrined in carefully drafted verbal statements, probably expresses more abstract, systemic imperatives or, in the terminology of this book, shared normative beliefs. In war those often concern humanitarian considerations. We require a convergence of *opinio juris* and practice for customary law to emerge. But humanitarian considerations tend to create imperatives for action that are diametrically opposed to those implied by military pragmatism.

In general, a convergence of normative beliefs about how one ought to behave and actual state behaviour is unlikely in areas in which shared abstract ideas about how we would ideally behave challenge situational imperatives. In addition, if some states engage in the regulated activity and thus often face those imperatives, and others do not, their perceived interests in this area differ. Yet it is in areas where shared normative beliefs and strong interests diverge, or areas in which various states perceive different imperatives as in their interest, that IL has its most important role to play. In fact, section 2.2 suggested that it is *only* when diverging reasons for action obtain that IL can make a difference. When all imperatives for action point in the same direction and all relevant actors share this perception, whether or not an actor resorts to IL in decision-making makes no counterfactual difference.[119]

We can only establish what customary law is with a reasonable degree of certainty if perceptions of utility (situational imperatives) and corresponding state practice converge with perceptions of appropriateness (abstract, systemic imperatives) expressed in *opinio*

---

[119] To recall, IL is a compromise between different imperatives for action. Its behavioural relevance depends on the fact that it provides a separate standard for evaluating actions, a standard that expresses a compromise between utility and appropriateness in a certain issue area.

juris. Then, however, we no longer require a compromise and strictly speaking the guidance of law. Either we do not need customary IL or we do not know what it is. In this case, we do not know what the customary definition of a legitimate target is.

This raises the question, of which law's effectiveness this book is testing when the next part turns to the empirical study of US air warfare. Due to the dilemma that in those areas in which we need IL the content of any customary law is inevitably highly contestable, most customary law that matters in contemporary international relations is also promulgated. After all, a law with several equally plausible diverging interpretations is neither particularly action guiding nor very useful in adjudicating claims about legitimacy. Security under law is so crucial to law's function in international relations that the twentieth century has seen a vast effort to promulgate customary law in multinational conventions. The API is one prominent example of this.

What can the theory of IL proposed in Chapter 2 make then of a rule of IL that exists both in custom and in positive law? Is such a law based on a compromise (positive law) or a convergence (customary law) between states' interests and their shared normative beliefs? Three alternatives are imaginable. First, progressive development: a positive rule acquires customary standing to bind non-parties because the promulgated compromise between interests and normative beliefs has served as a focal point for the general convergence of these motivational forces. Second, proper codification: well-established custom, the meaning of which is uncontroversial, is expressed in a treaty without alteration or clarification. In this area of international relations interests and shared normative beliefs converge so that IL, whether customary or positive, is unlikely to make a difference. Third, the grey area between codification and progressive development: a putative, controversial rule of customary law is expressed in a treaty, it is circumscribed by language and one of its many possible meanings is singled out and privileged to express one possible compromise between interests and shared normative beliefs. After the entry into force of the treaty can the customary standing of the chosen incarnation of the rule in the treaty be assumed? This may be highly desirable, but if non-parties contest the rule or display diverging practice, the need for a compromise is not met. The lines along which such a compromise is required are merely displaced from interests versus normative beliefs to parties versus non-parties.

The legal definition of a legitimate target evidently falls into this last category. The principle of proportionality (progressive development) and the imperative to distinguish (proper codification) are congruent in custom and positive law. Purposive and consequential indeterminacy, which are mostly connected to proportionality, therefore befall the positive and the customary definition of a legitimate target equally. The way in which belligerents are meant to distinguish (the interpretation of military advantage) has remained controversial, and custom cannot be assumed to be congruent with the promulgated definition of military objectives. That definition privileges an interpretation based on the logic of sufficiency. The semantic indeterminacy which is connected to the definition of military objectives thus specifically concerns the customary definition of a legitimate target of attack. As we cannot be sure that the customary principle of distinction is based on the logic of sufficiency, observing US decision-makers recur to IL when selecting targets means studying the application of Article 52(2) without assuming that decision-makers recognise the constraining influence of the containment and sequencing commands.[120]

---

[120] In its explanation of non-ratification the US cited reasons unrelated to the provisions defining a legitimate target of attack (Sofaer (1988)).

PART III

An empirical study of international law in war

'Daunting' is what a group of prominent IR scholars more than ten years ago considered the task of exploring whether compliance with law has 'a net effect' on behaviour.[1] The discipline has since largely failed to theorise about how law can emerge from underlying interests or normative beliefs. Studies that attempt to empirically disentangle the impact of these prior reasons for action and the influence of IL on behaviour are equally rare.[2] Part I addressed the theoretical desideratum and proposed a theory of how recourse to IL can afford a counterfactual added value; a theory of IL's behavioural relevance.[3] The following chapters test this theory and take on the redoubtable business of investigating whether, in fact, IHL has a counterfactual effect on target selection in US air warfare. Does the legal definition of a legitimate target of attack make a difference for how US military decision-makers define a legitimate target?[4]

In war it seems less likely than in other realms of international relations that law should be behaviourally relevant, so compelling is the intuition that states simply follow military imperatives and only draw on IL when it provides a legitimacy shield for the pursuit of their interests. Even if law made a difference, this net effect would also seem particularly elusive. Military decision-making is hidden from the public's eye and kept mostly out of its records. Actions in the chaos of combat are ripe with unintended consequences and outcomes are clouded by the proverbial fog. Yet the development of US air warfare is uniquely suited for investigating whether compliance with law has net effects on behaviour in combat operations. The extreme increase in the importance of law in military decision-making over a relatively short period of time practically invites a comparison between targets chosen without recourse to the legal definition of a legitimate target and those that US troops attacked with input of IHL.[5] The bombing of

---

[1] Goldstein *et al.* (2000); similar Abbott *et al.* (2000) 409.

[2] Exceptions include Lutz and Sikkink (2001); Sikkink (2011); Simmons (2009).

[3] For a definition of behavioural relevance see the appendix.

[4] Even though the US is not bound by the API, it regularly claims to apply the treaty's provisions that define a legitimate target of attack.

[5] In the following four chapters, I rely on a series of interviews with US military personnel. I conducted twenty-two semi-structured interviews with operators.

North Vietnam between 1965 and 1972 serves as a base line case as IL played a negligible role in shaping combat operations. The three campaigns – Operation Rolling Thunder (ORT), Operation Linebacker I (OLB I) and Operation Linebacker II (OLB II) – almost coincided with the beginning of the negotiations to the API. Moreover, as I argue below, the Vietnam experience paved the way for the institutional changes that initiated the subjection of US military operations to IL. The three campaigns the US conducted against North Vietnam are closest in time to the more legalised conflicts that the investigation focuses on. The bombing of Vietnam is, as a result, in technological and political terms most comparable to those later wars.[6] I contrast the three-time bombing of North Vietnam with the air war against Iraq in 1991, ODS, and the air campaign of the most recent major military US intervention abroad, OIF, in 2003.[7]

> Operators include pilots, joint terminal attack controllers and navigators. Twelve were deployed in 2003 during Operation Iraqi Freedom (OIF), three in 1991 during Operation Desert Storm (ODS), three over North Vietnam and four refrained from specifying their deployment. When quoting from any of these interviews, I refer to the interviewee by rank and deployment. In addition, I conducted eighteen elite interviews with Judge Advocate Generals (JAGs), intelligence analysts and commanders. With four exceptions, for which I was granted explicit permission, I likewise refrain from naming them, but refer to the interviews by numbers. The details of these eighteen elite interviews – date, place and the rank of the interviewee – and of the semi-structured interviews are listed in the bibliography.

[6] As opposed to, for instance, air operations during the Korean War or the Second World War.

[7] Certain instances of US air warfare between 1965 and 2003 are bracketed. One reason is that the analysis is restricted to major interstate armed conflicts that include a pre-planned air campaign. The US engagement in Grenada, for instance, falls below the threshold of scale and intensity that guides the case selection. In addition, the analysis excludes Operation Allied Force, in spite of its elaborate air campaign. It is not considered here because targeting, even targeting undertaken by US forces, was significantly influenced by constraints imposed by coalition partners (Lamb (2002) 13; also Cochrane (2001)). Even though both Iraq wars were likewise waged by coalitions, during these operations targeting was determined solely by the US (Battistella (2008) 6). Less obvious is the reason why Operation Enduring Freedom is bracketed. Without Operation Allied Force in the equation, the two instances of major US air warfare after the introduction of law into military operations were waged against the same country and the same regime: Iraq and the Baath Party under the leadership of Saddam Hussein. While the regime naturally changed in the twelve years between the two wars, the similarity of the two cases provides a high level of comparability. Afghanistan, on the other hand, presents a radically different country, regime and society. A comparison of two wars against Iraq and one against Afghanistan would highlight targeting differences that are unrelated to the point of enquiry: the role of law in shaping behaviour. It is not assumed that Vietnam and Iraq provided the same kinds of targets. The analysis accounts for the fact that Iraq was a more modern, industrialised society than Vietnam.

5 | The rise of international law in US air warfare

The task of this chapter is to describe the input of IL into decision-making about targeting in the three cases under investigation. In order to know what we are looking for we need a definition of what IL is. The theory of IL proposed in Chapter 2 derives the definition of IL from the way in which compliance with law can change behaviour. For the task at hand this is not a suitable approach to identifying IL because it hinges legality on what this part of the book wants to evidence and understand: the net effect of recourse to law on behaviour. For the purpose of grasping only the extent to which the US recurs to IL, I therefore rely on a thinner conception of IL, one that uses the form of norms to identify them as laws.

Section 1.3 discussed two alternative ways in which scholars of IR have attempted to define IL by its form: the liberal institutionalist concept of 'legalisation'[1] and a positivist approach that takes municipal law and its characteristics as a blueprint for the identification of IL. I choose 'legalisation' as a point of departure here, first and foremost because the parameters of this approach are based on observed developments in international relations rather than on domestic law. Second, unlike a positivist definition of law, 'legalisation' conceives of the subjection of decision-making to law as a matter of degree. The three proposed parameters – the precision of legal norms, the delegation of their interpretation and the obligation pull they exert[2] – provide 'identifiable dimensions of variation'.[3] They allow me to measure the extent to which actors follow their interests and normative beliefs in war via recourse to law.

---

[1] The inverted commas distinguish this specific theoretical approach to defining the legality of norms from the general phenomenon of subjection of an activity to regulation by law. It warrants stressing again that I never use the word legalisation to denote the legality of an activity.
[2] Goldstein et al. (2000).   [3] Abbott et al. (2000) 403.

The precision of the legal rules under investigation here – their increase in determinacy through promulgation as well as the fact that both the positive and customary definition of a legitimate target of attack still leave much to be desired when it comes to precision – was discussed at length in Part II. Here I focus on the two indicators for legalisation that describe direct entry points for IL into military decision-making. The first section outlines a gradual institutionalisation of recourse to the principles of distinction and proportionality in US combat operations. The second section focuses on decision-makers' sense of legal obligation and how it changes across the three cases under investigation.[4]

5.1 The institutionalisation of compliance

One indicator of the subjection of international relations to IL as conceived by 'legalisation' is 'that third parties [are] granted authority to implement, interpret and apply the rules; to resolve disputes and possibly to make further rules'.[5] Delegation of review in the area of IHL has increased considerably over time: from the rarely applied principle of universal jurisdiction for war crimes, to the creation of a never-deployed Fact Finding Commission, to the establishment of *ad hoc* tribunals and even an International Criminal Court. Yet the US has very successfully stayed on the margins of this trend. Given the virtual impossibility that US military personnel would ever stand before a tribunal other than a US military commission, it is unlikely that delegation as understood by proponents of 'legalisation' affects the definition of a legitimate target by US military personnel and hence the selection of objects for attack.

Definitely determinative of US conduct in war, on the other hand, is delegation of the application and interpretation of IHL before and during hostilities to a corps of JAGs that significantly gained in size and institutional standing over the period investigated. The institutionalisation of recourse to distinction and proportionality in warfare or, in other words, the entrenchment of professional legal argument in military decision-making, is arguably the most important pathway of IL

---

[4] How and why the original parameters of delegation and obligation are altered is addressed in the two sections below.
[5] Abbott *et al.* (2000) 401.

into decision-making in contemporary US wars. The following paragraphs illustrate how the degree of the institutionalisation of recourse to IL has radically risen over the period under investigation.

Target selection in Vietnam between 1965 and 1972

The record documenting the process of target selection during the US bombing of North Vietnam does hint at virtually no involvement of legal experts. In 1965, the Joint Chiefs of Staff had commissioned an initial '94-target' list for a possible air campaign against North Vietnam.[6] Once ORT started, the Seventh Air Force nominated targets mostly from this list. They were again reviewed by the Joint Chiefs and vetted by Secretary McNamara's civilian staff in the Department of Defense.[7] These reviews may have involved the Department's legal counsel, but also applied political and strategic considerations: namely the question of whether nominated targets might hamper or undermine the on-going negotiations with North Vietnam.[8] Targets once vetted were then sent to the White House. 'Johnson and his advisors chose the targets ... at the White House's weekly Tuesday luncheon'[9] without the input or even presence of legal counsel or JAGs.[10] The record is rather clear that with respect to the conduct of ORT the White House 'never sought advice with regard to US responsibilities and rights under the law of war'.[11]

Indeed President Johnson was notorious for generally eschewing expert advice from outside his inner circle.[12] He and Secretary McNamara 'maintained detailed tactical control of the missions'. Often Johnson did not even seek the opinion of the military commanders tasked with executing the war.[13] His successor's leadership style was even less conducive to giving legal counsel room for input. If at all President

---

[6] US Department of Defense (1971/2) 288.
[7] Gurney (1985) 142; Kattenberg (1982) 127; Parks (1982); Record (1998) 112; Smith (1994).
[8] The only commentator asserting that 'Secretary of Defense Robert S. McNamara ... referred it to his General Counsel for legal review' is Hays Parks. He does not provide his primary source (Parks (1982) 2f.). Other detailed discussions of the target selection process do not feature references to legal counsel. For instance, Kattenberg (1982) 220; Komer (1986) 52; Sharp (1968).
[9] Michael (2003) 4.   [10] Barrett (1997) 159.
[11] Parks (1982) 9; also Barrett (1997).
[12] Kattenberg (1982) 170f.; also Gibbons (1995).   [13] Caverley (2010/11).

Nixon sought advice not from individuals with specific expertise but from those whose personality, like his, was 'constructed on macho and toughness'.[14]

As a lesson from ORT, which was widely considered a strategic failure, the process of selecting targets and the responsibility for preparing attacks for OLB I partly shifted from the civilian and political staff of the government to the military commanders in the theatre.[15] This did not, however, prompt an involvement of deployed JAGs, who at the time solely focused on administrative and criminal law.[16] During OLB I and OLB II 'operational commanders selected targets for attack from the validated target list subject only to the guidance that the JCS [Joint Chiefs of Staff] be informed of target selections 24 hours prior to their strike'.[17] There is no indication that either the commanders themselves or the Joint Chiefs sought legal advice. Although targeting during ORT thus lay in different hands during the Linebacker operations, the institutional structures in place for target selection bear testimony to the virtual absence of professional legal input into decision-making both times.

None the less, it was the war in Vietnam that 'planted the seeds for an end to the almost exclusive focus of judge advocates on military justice and peacetime legal issues'.[18] After the public outrage over the My Lai massacre and the resulting courts-martial the Pentagon issued Directive 5100.77 in 1974. It tasked JAGs with 'ensuring that all US military operations complied strictly with the Law of War'.[19] The directive spelled out for the first time that JAGs were meant to advise commanders also on the legal implications of targeting choices. A new generation of JAGs was then trained in all aspects of strategic planning, operational design and execution, which previously were beyond the scope of a JAG's responsibilities.[20]

Target selection in Iraq in 1991 and 2003

The first time JAGs were included in a military operations centre was during Operation Just Cause in 1989.[21] Not two years later, 350

---

[14] Kattenberg (1982) 164.   [15] Smith (1994) 129.   [16] Dunlap (2001a).
[17] Parks (1983) 3.
[18] *History of the Judge Advocate General Corps*, www.carson.army.mil/LEGAL/History/.htm.
[19] *Ibid.*; US Department of Defense (1974/2006).   [20] See Dunlap (2001b) 16.
[21] *Ibid.* 6.; also Dunlap (2001a) 294.

attorneys and lawyers deployed with the allied troops to Iraq.[22] Though an unprecedented number at the time, it falls significantly short of the 2,200 JAGs, 350 civilian attorneys and 1,400 enlisted paralegals which, twelve years later, accompanied the troops into Iraq.[23] Besides their increased presence, a closer look at the process of pre-planned targeting during the two campaigns against Iraq suggests that the JAGs' actual influence was also considerably greater in 2003 than in 1991. This is visible at different stages of pre-planned air targeting: first, during early target planning, second, during concrete target development and, finally, during the execution of air strikes.

Target planning: in 1990, the contingency plan for regional conflict in south-west Asia, OPLAN 1002–90, provided the starting point for target planning. It was reviewed during Internal Look 90, an exercise of the United States Central Command and the Air Force Component Command. The exercise generated a first list of potential targets. However, as the situation in Iraq continued to evolve, existing plans and target lists seemed ever less adequate. This prompted General Norman Schwarzkopf, the head of Central Command, to ask the air staff's deputy director for war fighting, Colonel John Warden III, for input. Project Checkmate, Warden's planning cell in the Pentagon, devised the plan that has become known as 'Instant Thunder'. Colonel Warden recalls that no trained lawyers were involved in Project Checkmate, and nor were they consulted or asked to review the plan that was to guide the air campaign against Iraq.[24]

Target planning for OIF never had to start from scratch but could rely on the records of ODS. When this time an inventory of targets was created, '[e]very potential target was vetted by judge advocates for compliance with the Law of War before it got on the list, and then vetted again after it was complete'.[25] Furthermore early on, the US military created a no-strike list and – unprecedented in the history of US war planning – set up a phone number for United Nations (UN) agencies and non-governmental organisations to submit objects to be placed on the list and thus become immune from direct attack.[26] In parallel with these preparations the Combined Forces Command and Air Component Command together issued a targeting directive that

[22] *History of the Judge Advocate General Corps*, www.carson.army.mil/LEGAL/ History/.htm.
[23] *Ibid.*; also Blum (2001).   [24] Interview no. 1.   [25] Kahl (2007) 16.   [26] *Ibid.*

related military considerations specific to the Iraq theatre to obligations under IHL.[27] Contrary to ODS, the planning of air targeting during OIF was hence from the very beginning legally informed.

Target development: for ODS target development was undertaken by a planning cell in the Air Component Command, established on 20 August 1990 in Riyadh, which has become popularly known as the 'Black Hole'. Under the command of Brigadier General Buster Glosson, then Lieutenant Colonel David Deptula was placed in charge of translating target sets into so-called 'master attack plans', which featured for every day of the air campaign a list of individual targets with the parameters of the planned attack.[28] Now retired Lieutenant General Deptula recalls that lawyers did not routinely assist him, though they were at his disposal, if he needed to consult them.[29] Some commentators indicate that two JAGs were assigned to the Black Hole.[30] One of the JAGs, Major Heintzelman, counted among his responsibilities 'scrubbing' the master attack plan in the light of potential violations of the principles of distinction and proportionality.[31]

In 2003, J2, the intelligence division of the Pentagon, gathered extensive intelligence about each target on the initial list, including a computer-assisted collateral damage estimate.[32] The information was assembled in a folder and, unlike twelve years before, several JAGs were assigned the task of vetting the targets based on the information provided.[33] Intelligence specialists recall that target folders were often sent back by JAGs who felt that there was not enough information to clear or reject a target.[34] Corroborating this, JAGs recall that they frequently removed targets from the list.[35] The result of this process was a carefully vetted joint integrated prioritised target list. Every item on this list then went through a process of weaponeering and allocation, an attempt to mitigate as many anticipated unintended effects of an air

---

[27] Interview no. 15.   [28] Interview no. 10.   [29] *Ibid.*
[30] Lewis (2003) 489ff; Myrow (1996/7) 139.   [31] Lewis (2003) 498.
[32] Interview no. 15.
[33] Gordon and Martin (2005); Kahl (2007) 17f.; also Interviews nos. 8 and 13.
[34] Interview no. 15.   [35] Interviews nos. 7, 8, 12, 13, 14.

strike as possible.[36] In light of this new information every target was again legally reviewed and only then included in a master attack plan.[37]

Execution: in 1991, the execution of the air campaign followed the translation of master attack plans into so-called 'air tasking orders'. The latter were likewise drawn up in the Black Hole initially without legal input,[38] although JAGs were sometimes asked to look at completed tasking orders.[39] While in execution, air tasking orders were changed between 220 and 900 times.[40] Some of these changes are likely to have borne significance for the legality of the attacks. Whether these alterations were reviewed by the JAGs present was impossible to find out. However, in the absence of an institutionalised procedure for their consultation it would have been difficult for lawyers to even keep track of developments in target selection. The analogous role of intelligence officers corroborates that systematic legal review at this stage of the air campaign is unlikely to have been possible. In 1991, new stealth and precision capabilities suddenly afforded an unprecedented range of choice in the allocation of fire power from the air.[41] Military commanders later observed that lack of information turned out to be the limiting factor in the effectiveness of the air war as intelligence gathering could not keep up with the pace and possibilities of air targeting.[42]

To the contrary, in the twenty-first-century combined air operations centre several JAGs are on duty twenty-four hours a day. JAGs are present for both the development of air tasking orders as well as their execution. Even while already in the air a crew can consult the operations centre if unforeseen circumstances arise.[43] The air commander can communicate with the chain of command through a real-time chat, which includes the JAG on duty.[44] Some interviewed personnel suggested that the air crew was unlikely to directly interact with the JAG. However, air crews are aware and indeed emphasise that JAGs are part of the discussion that accompanies the air strike in the air operations

---

[36] Interview no. 2.   [37] Kahl (2007) 17f.; Interviews nos. 8 and 13.
[38] Interview no. 10.   [39] Lewis (2003) 499.   [40] *Ibid.* 498
[41] See Hallion (1992); Murray (1995).   [42] *Ibid.*; similar Cohen (1994) 199.
[43] Interview no. 13.
[44] Interview with US Air Force F-15E pilot of the rank of major deployed in OIF, 20 June 2008; interview with US Air Force B-1 pilot of the rank of major deployed in OIF, 19 June 2008; also Interview no. 13.

centre.[45] Although this step of pre-planned air targeting is often time sensitive, the entrenchment of legal considerations is allegedly optimised so that an *ad hoc* legally informed decision on a target, including a collateral damage estimate revised according to the changed situation, can be obtained in four to seven minutes.[46]

The picture that emerges for OIF is one of multiple institutionalised channels of communication. JAGs advised military planners and intelligence officers during target planning and target development. Commanders and operators consulted JAGs during target development and execution. In contrast, during ODS the influence of JAGs seems to have been haphazard and mostly limited to target development. What is striking about ODS is that even for that stage of pre-planned air targeting commentators differ quite considerably in their assessment of the influence of lawyers. The interview material suggests that in parts of the literature the role of lawyers in the air war of 1991 is slightly overstated. One plausible explanation is that the very deployment of JAGs into the centres of military decision-making was relatively innovative and thus amazed commentators at the time. It is mainly in comparison with the institutional setting and organisational culture of 2003, hence with hindsight, that the limitations of the JAG's role during ODS become evident.

5.2 The growing sense of legal obligation

Besides the consultation of legal experts during decision-making there is another pathway for IL into the definition of a legitimate target of attack in US air operations. Law may come to bear on decision-making processes and actors' motivations because those actors who select targets in war perceive themselves as under a legal obligation.[47] What does it mean for an actor to be under a legal obligation to act in a certain way?

---

[45] Interview with US Air Force B-1 pilot of the rank of lieutenant colonel deployed in OIF, 12 April 2011; interview with US Air Force joint terminal attack controller of the rank of colonel deployed in OIF, 11 April 2011.

[46] Interview no. 6; also Crawford (2010); Gordon and Martin (2005); several interviewees stressed that missions carried out by Special Forces were very unlikely to rise to the same standard of legal input. Similar McChrystal (2011) 66.

[47] Both military decision-makers and JAGs were adamant that JAGs only advise, and do not make decisions themselves.

Obligation is sometimes treated as an objective, discrete category, which measures the degree of 'bindingness' of a norm. In this view soft law at the lower end of the spectrum creates a weak legal obligation while *jus cogens* commands the highest possible degree. The notion that law pertains to the conduct of combat operations can be traced as far back as the Thirty Years War.[48] This does not mean that objectively the strength of legal obligations during hostilities has not changed since the seventeenth century. Section 4.1 outlined the historical evolution of the norms of proportionality and distinction from moral and religious imperatives largely without legal force, to codified soft law (Hague Rules of Aerial Warfare), and finally to 'intransgressible'[49] rules of customary and treaty law (the API). This development denotes a gradual increase in the strength of the obligation imposed by distinction and proportionality.

Over the period investigated here, however, changes in the perceived importance of distinction and proportionality in decision-making are not a function of an altered *de jure* status of the rules. Rather it is an increase in *de facto* relevance in the eyes of decision-makers that changed from 1965 to 2003. While *de jure* status and *de facto* relevance of a legal rule are certainly related, the latter can increase even while the former remains unchanged. The promulgation of the customary principles of distinction and proportionality in the API between the bombing of North Vietnam and the 1991 Gulf War did not change the strength of the obligations they impose – treaty law is not 'more binding' than customary law. However, promulgation probably did raise the profile of IHL and thereby the *de facto* relevance of law in war. In general, given the absence of enforcement, in IL a subjective sense of obligation *always* plays an important role for compliance irrespective of the *de jure* status of a rule. The variable 'legal obligation' is therefore not an objective, discrete variable but a continuous measure of decision-makers' subjective sense of obligation.

How can a sense of obligation be evidenced? The belief that a legal rule bears on one's behaviour implies the understanding that discussing courses of action only in terms of instrumental considerations is as

---

[48] Grotius (1625): 'I have advanced, that there is a common law among nations, which is valid alike for war and in war.'

[49] *Legality of the Threat or Use of Nuclear Weapons*, ICJ, Advisory Opinion of 8 July 1996, ICJ Reports 1996, §179.

inadequate as simply deliberating social or moral appropriateness. In David Kennedy's words '[y]ou are not speaking international law today if you seem to be expressing sovereign will or declaring what is just'.[50] Rather a sense of obligation implies decision-making 'in terms of the text, purpose, and history of the rules, their interpretation, admissible exceptions, applicability to classes of situations and particular facts'.[51] What we are looking for in the communication and discussions about target selection are arguments about utility or appropriateness made in terms of legality or with reference to IHL. A comparison suggests that decision-makers across the three cases of interest engage in markedly different discussions about target selection and display radically diverging attitudes towards IHL.

Interests, norms and recourse to law in North Vietnam

President Johnson's papers suggest that his foremost concern when making targeting choices was whether the bombing would in any way affect China's interests.[52] Whether air strikes could be interpreted by Russia or China as a signal that the US was abandoning peaceful coexistence was likewise determinative of target selection.[53] In addition, Johnson was set on preventing either of the two powers actively joining North Vietnam in the fight against the US, thereby undermining US military superiority. The aim of forestalling an escalation of the conflict in Indochina was thus a source of considerable restraint in the employment of air power.[54] This immediate imperative inspired, for instance, the establishment of an exclusion zone in the northern part of the Democratic Republic of Vietnam near its border with China.[55]

---

[50] Kennedy (2012)171; similar Abbott *et al.* (2000) 410.
[51] Abbott *et al.* (2000) 410; the analysis of targeting against North Vietnam relies largely on written sources as those are mostly in the public domain. In order to evidence the degree to which legal rules and justifications were invoked, I investigated statements by decision-makers in the records of the air campaigns against North Vietnam. In addition, I conducted three semi-structured interviews with US pilots deployed over North Vietnam (two Navy, one US Air Force) who corroborated the insights from the documents.
[52] Memo from Under-Secretary Ball to the President of 18 June 1965 quoted in Barrett (1997) 265; also Smith (1994) 129; Parks (1982) *passim.*
[53] Barrett (1997) 265.
[54] Likewise, Herring (1996) 5, 46; Jian (1995); Kaiser (2000) 439f.
[55] Clodfelter (2006) 67; Parks (1982) 13; Smith (1994) 130.

The second important consideration in President Johnson's definition of a legitimate target of attack and also a source of restraint was public opinion. Though US air strikes against the North were framed as in defence of the South against Northern aggression, the Johnson administration was keenly aware that using air power against an obviously inferior adversary would be problematic if it caused high numbers of civilian casualties.[56] Government records are replete with expressions of concern about how the American electorate at home and US allies in the free world would react to the bombing of North Vietnam.[57] In at times drastic language the president denounced the role of the media in making the war difficult by reporting on civilian casualties.[58] Not losing on the 'home front' was hence another immediate imperative, an instrumental consideration shaping Johnson's definition of a legitimate target of attack.

In the context of a discussion of American dependants remaining in North Vietnam at the outset of the bombing in 1965 the avoidance of collateral damage was also brought up as part of a decidedly more abstract imperative to protect human life in war.[59] In the choice of targets during ORT decision-makers thus invoked both instrumental considerations as well as to a lesser extent normative beliefs according to the theoretical framework developed in Part I. Interestingly the president and his advisers used language such as 'civilian casualties', 'discrimination' and 'legitimacy', but not 'laws of war', 'international law', 'customary law', 'Geneva Conventions' or 'Hague Conventions'.

Indications that President Johnson perceived IL as pertinent to his decisions about the conduct of hostilities in North Vietnam are absent

---

[56] Barrett (1997) 256; Caverley (2010/11); the US found it easier to place the responsibility for the humanitarian implications of the air war in South Vietnam on the local government. The lack of manifest obvious involvement of South Vietnam in the bombing of North Vietnam was considered a public relations rather than a legal problem. In the words of McGeorge Bundy, in the North US casualties were 'more visible to American feelings – than those sustained in the struggle in South Vietnam'. Quoted in Kahin (1987) 284; similar Pape (1996) 179; Smith (1994) 287.

[57] Barrett (1997) 289, 155; also Tilford (1988).

[58] The president in a meeting of 17 December 1965, quoted in Barrett (1997) 288; also meeting with Foreign Policy Advisory on Vietnam: President, Rusk, McNamara, Acheson, Ball, Raborn, Valentini of 16 May 1965, quoted in Barrett (1997) 159.

[59] Memo of Admiral Taylor to the President of 8 February 1965, quoted in Barrett (1997) 12f.

from the thoroughly documented and largely available records of his time in office. A memorandum from 1968 to the Secretaries of State and Defense and the Bureau of the Budget contains one of the very few explicit references to IL in the context of the US engagement in Vietnam. The president urged: the 'enemy has to believe' that in negotiations (not during combat operations) 'we will insist on an even-handed application of the rules of international law'.[60] This suggests that President Johnson, outside the realm of war, thought of IL as a potentially useful political instrument. UN resolutions were occasionally brought up in Cabinet meetings and in the president's discussions with his advisers, but solely in the context of legitimising the resort to force in the eyes of the world, never with regard to shaping combat operations.[61] Secretary McNamara in a memo summarised the determinants of US targeting choices during ORT. When reminding the president to take 'into account *all* considerations [italics mine]'[62] in his decisions about restrictions on bombing, he listed 'likelihood of success, risk of escalation, South Vietnamese reaction, domestic support, and so on',[63] but not legality.[64]

Where President Johnson most of the time simply did not seem to have had IL on his mind, his successor was explicitly dismissive of the notion that legal obligations could pertain to warfare. In the context of the legal inquest into the My Lai massacre and the sentencing of its main protagonist President Nixon is quoted as referring to the subjection of war to law as based on 'an obsolete idea that war is a game with rules'. He went on to say: 'we don't condone this [the massacre], but when men serve their country you cannot, during this crisis of war, follow this line [of prosecuting for war crimes] unless there's a direct breach of orders ... War is bad, so we've got to avoid more bad wars.'[65] Just like his predecessor during ORT, President Nixon, nevertheless, accorded a high priority to the goal of sparing civilians and not being seen to use air power indiscriminately during

---

[60] *Ibid.* 578; similar Parks (1982) 3.   [61] Barrett (1997) 42.

[62] Secretary McNamara in a Memo to the President 'Courses of Action in Vietnam 3 November 1965', quoted in *ibid.* 277.

[63] *Ibid.*

[64] References to IL are equally absent in official reports of the military leadership, for instance, in the report on the war by Ulysses S. Grant Sharp (1968).

[65] Quoted in Kimball (1998) 250.

OLB I and OLB II.[66] Crucially, this was always framed as an immediate imperative to safeguard US interests, rather than as a legal obligation – or, for that matter, a normative belief in the value of human life.

Hays Parks suggests that, contrary to ORT, the Linebacker operations were 'planned and executed with a conscious consideration of the law of war'.[67] He does not give evidence for when or how law played a part in decision-making or by whom legal standards were considered. Since the record does not hint at this consideration of the law either, it would appear that Parks's contention is the result of a retroactive assessment of the Linebacker operations in the light of IHL. In his view, the campaigns 'reflected accurate application of the law of war'.[68] Other commentators differentiate more explicitly between the role law actually played in shaping air strikes and the question of whether they conformed to IHL. The overall consensus is that IHL was not a salient factor in any of the three campaigns against North Vietnam. Not surprisingly many commentators find practices that violate the laws of war even as they stood at the time.[69]

As mentioned above, the main locus of decision-making about the selection of targets shifted between ORT and the Linebacker operations, which means that it is necessary to look for a sense of legal obligation not only among policy-makers but also among military personnel in the theatre. Though this study relies, as far as the Vietnam case is concerned, less on interviews and more on the abundant

---

[66] McAllister (2010/11) 101; similar Caverley (2010/11); Kimball (1998); Michael (2003) 10; Parks (1983) 4.

[67] Parks (1983) 5.

[68] *Ibid.* 5; it is noteworthy that Parks's interpretation of IHL errs on the side of military pragmatism. He opposes majority opinion with the view that a proportionality calculus does not 'include civilians injured or killed while working in a lawful target, such as an enemy power plant' (*ibid.* 11). This is reminiscent of the argument that civilians can be 'quasi-combatants', a notion laid to rest with the Geneva Conventions. He also mentions 'economic targets not directly associated with the military effort' among lawful targets whose engagement remained prohibited for political reasons during OBL I (*ibid.* 4). Needless to say any part of a country's infrastructure not directly associated with the military effort would not constitute a military objective according to the contextual interpretation of the API outlined in section 3.4.

[69] Among others, DeSaussure (1967); DeSaussure and Glasser (1975) 129, 139; Fall (1965); Firmage (1967); Green (1967); Krepon (1967); Meyrowitz (1994); Petrowski (1969) 485; Pickert (1967).

declassified records, participants in the air war against North Vietnam corroborated that JAGs were not visibly involved in the preparation of air strikes or the debriefing of pilots.[70] Interviewed veterans highlighted the importance of the rules of engagement and dismissed actual IL as irrelevant: 'These [the rules or engagement] were political constraints – the Geneva Conventions had nothing to do with it.'[71] This contention would present a puzzle today, as rules of engagement draw on and reference IL. They are, after all, drafted with considerable input from lawyers nowadays.[72] At the time, however, the Department of Defense

had sole responsibility for issuing the [rules of engagement] in Vietnam, pending any disapproval by the President. Secretary of Defense Robert McNamara tasked the [Joint Chiefs of Staff] to publish the rules and to send them to operational commanders.[73]

Those rules of engagement that are now in the public domain do not contain references to IHL.[74] While navigating complicated political restrictions that were widely perceived as cumbersome,[75] the military personnel involved in the US air wars against the Democratic Republic of Vietnam do not seem to have been guided by a sense of legal obligation.

Interests, norms and recourse to law in Iraq in 1991 and 2003

For the two Iraq wars I shift the focus of the investigation completely away from political decision-makers to military commanders and operators. Policy-makers' perceptions of whether legal obligations pertain to combat operations were simply less important for the conduct of the two wars against Iraq. They were virtually irrelevant for actual target selection.[76] In fact, ODS was the first US military mission in which the

---

[70] Interview with US Navy pilot deployed during the US engagement in Vietnam, 28 January 2009; also Interview no. 2.

[71] Interview no. 2; on the absence of legal knowledge among service members during the earlier air campaigns see also Fall (1965).

[72] Interview no. 15.   [73] Drake (1992).   [74] *Ibid.*

[75] For instance, Young (2009) 174; Parks emphasises the changes in the rules of engagement between ORT and the later Linebacker operations. He attributes the greater effectiveness of Nixon's war against North Vietnam to a 'combination of improved weapons, tactics, and rules of engagement' (Parks (1983) 6).

[76] There is one notorious exception. In 2003, under certain circumstances the Secretary of Defense had to approve targets. We will not know which criteria he used to make these decisions until the records of the George W. Bush administration are declassified.

theatre commander 'owned' the war plan. Partly as a result of the apparent problems of decentralised decision-making during the Vietnam War, an integrated Air Component Command was established to decide largely on its own how to wage the war from the air. The investigations of both wars against Iraq therefore focus on interviews with military personnel rather than on public statements of the respective Bush administrations.[77]

In exploring deployed personnel's sense of legal obligation I differentiate between operators, the proverbial 'trigger pullers' who are directly involved in applying force against the enemy, and other military decision-makers and planners in the targeting process, referred to as commanders. The few operators deployed in ODS that I was able to interview expressed puzzlement at the notion of obligations under IL pertaining to their conduct in war. This corroborates the tentative conclusion reached in the previous section that in 1991 JAGs were largely absent from the execution phase of air strikes. I therefore focus the search for a perception of legal obligation for ODS on commanders, but for OIF on operators as well as commanders.[78]

Retired Colonel Warden concedes that in the design of the air campaign meant to liberate Kuwait 'the law ha[d] some effect because it [was] pretty well internalised'.[79] However, he argues that 'the normative standard of the law is wrong, [because] it has developed with assumptions about what war is like, which are incorrect'.[80] He thus assigned a low priority to legal considerations when planning the air campaign for ODS.[81] The literature features a number of quotations

---

[77] Both President George H. W. Bush, on occasion of the war to liberate Kuwait in 1991, and his successor George W. Bush, in the lead-up to the 2003 invasion of Iraq, referenced IL in public statements (see for instance Roberts (1994)). Yet these communications were meant to shape public opinion. It is hence impossible to say whether these communications followed strategic considerations or were indicative of a sense of legal obligation. In order to evidence a sense of legal obligation the classified record of an administration, transcripts of closed meetings and the personal papers of the president would be required. Yet these documents are not yet available for either Bush administration.

[78] For more information about the interviews see the bibliography.

[79] Interview no. 1.   [80] *Ibid.*

[81] It is important to note that the air campaign that dominated ODS is not congruent with the Instant Thunder plan as envisaged by Colonel Warden. Nevertheless, the target sets proposed by Warden were the basis for what ended up on the master attack plans. See section 6.1; also Atkinson (1993) 63; Pape (1996) 228; Interview no. 10.

about target selection by now retired General Charles Horner, Air Component Commander at the time, which evoke the wording of the API.[82] While his statements suggest that Horner strove to meet the standards enshrined in the treaty, it is unclear whether this occurred out of a sense of legal obligation. Lieutenant General Deptula holds that when devising the master attack plans for ODS, a separate consideration of the law on his part was virtually superfluous. Before the doctrine became enshrined in official strategy documents, he followed EBOs rather than aiming at maximum destructiveness. He considered EBOs to be in 'lock-step' with legal obligations in general.[83] The notion that unprecedented technological capabilities, limited war aims and EBOs made the US prone to overfulfil any potential legal obligation anyway probably weakened commanders' sense of urgency to pay separate attention to IHL in 1991.

In contrast, JAGs who were involved in the war of 2003 describe decision-makers as receptive to, even eager for, legal input.[84] The notion that US warfare is not only technically, but also normatively superior compared with many other ways of waging war and that it is *per se* conducive to legality is still prevalent. However, complying with legal requirements is seen as anything but automatic or unproblematic nowadays.[85] While commanders do not expect ever to be sanctioned directly by virtue of IL, the rise of ICL has drawn attention to the fact that legal compliance is a complex, technical task requiring constant care and attention to detail.[86]

Operators deployed out of the combined air operations centre in Qatar stressed the importance of special instructions (referred to as 'spins') and rules of engagement over the Geneva Conventions. But contrary to their compatriots deployed in the air war against North Vietnam, nowadays operators are acutely aware that the rules of engagement and the spins reflect – and in the opinion of many they go beyond – the strictures imposed by IHL. After all, JAGs are involved in writing the rules of engagement and the spins.[87] Moreover, without exception, interviewed operators deployed in OIF attested to the comprehensiveness of their training in the laws of war. They stressed

---

[82] For instance, Atkinson (1993) 62f.; Roberts (1994) 150.
[83] Interview no. 10.   [84] Interview no. 13.   [85] Interview no. 11.
[86] *Ibid.*; Interview no. 13.   [87] Dunlap (2001b) 17.

the requirement to internalise beyond merely knowing the spins and rules of engagement.[88]

This sense of legal obligation is very robust. It seems, for instance, a minority view among US operators that reciprocity is a precondition for adherence to the law. Most interviewed pilots, joint terminal attack controllers and navigators unequivocally stated that US troops *always* strive for compliance with the laws of war, legal violations on the other side notwithstanding: 'What sets us apart is that we are observing of the law.'[89] It seems that in contemporary US air warfare legality is internalised as a crucial ingredient of mission success by operators. In fact, compliance with IL proved an integral part of the professional identity of most US military personnel interviewed.[90]

The difference between the sense of legal obligation displayed by commanders during ODS, on the one hand, and the interviewed military personnel who were deployed in 2003, on the other hand, evokes different stages in what Finnemore and Sikkink refer to as a norm's lifecycle.[91] The norm that 'law ought to be a major determinant of behaviour in air targeting' was only in the process of emergence at the time of ODS. Some rules crucial for targeting enshrined in the API, JAGs in the command centre and the very concept of legal argument on the battlefield were relatively new in 1991. Legality was one among several normative standards to refer to. To the contrary, the role of legal obligation in 2003 suggests the norm was at a stage at which actors adhere to it automatically and 'for reasons that relate to their identities'.[92] During OIF the norm that war ought to be waged in

---

[88] Interview with US Navy joint terminal attack controller of the rank of lieutenant colonel deployed in OIF, 11 April 2011; interview with US Air Force B-1 pilot in OIF, 12 April 2011; interview with US Air Force B-1 pilot of the rank of colonel deployed in OIF, 12 April 2011.

[89] Interview with US Air Force B-1 pilot of the rank of colonel deployed in OIF, 12 April 2011; likewise Kahl (2007) 8; Interview no. 18.

[90] The interviewees were almost all members of the US Air Force. The few exceptions are Navy personnel. This study makes no claim about the prevalence of a sense of legal obligation among members of other services. Several interviewees volunteered without being prompted that members of the United States Marine Corps and Special Forces such as Army Rangers display different attitudes to the laws of war.

[91] For the concept of a norm's lifecycle see Finnemore and Sikkink (1998); Sikkink (2011).

[92] Finnemore and Sikkink (1998) 902.

compliance with IHL had 'acquire[d] a taken-for-granted quality and [was then] no longer a matter of broad public debate'.[93] Finnemore and Sikkink describe the point where norms are followed because no one questions them and they are entrenched in institutional structures and agents' identities as the last stage of a norm's lifecycle.[94]

---

[93] *Ibid.*, 895.   [94] *Ibid.*; also Lutz and Sikkink (2001).

6 | *The changing logic of US air warfare*

This chapter seeks to establish whether and how target selection actually changed over the period under investigation. I do not enquire into the role of IL in determining what kinds of targets were selected for attack. In other words this chapter is not about the *legal* definition of a legitimate target. It examines what US decision-makers considered legitimate targets of attack and what they hence chose to bomb.[1] Did their conception of a legitimate target of attack develop between 1965 and 2003?

6.1 The definition of a legitimate target of attack in US air warfare

North Vietnam between 1965 and 1972

Between 13 February 1965 and 31 October 1968, the Johnson administration conducted a sustained air campaign against the Democratic Republic of Vietnam, dubbed Operation Rolling Thunder (ORT). The aim was to interrupt the flow of material and personnel from the North to the South, where it supported an insurgency against the US-backed government. After a pause in the bombing for roughly four years, the Nixon administration responded to a military offensive by the North against the South with OLB I. It lasted from 8 May to 22 October 1972. Following another much briefer interruption, President Nixon

---

[1] Legitimacy is not merely a matter of normative beliefs. Most people allow for instrumental considerations to play a role when actors make decisions about their behaviour. The use of the term 'legitimacy' denotes that rather than bringing to bear a preconceived normative, for instance moral, standard I enquire into the perception of a particular group of actors, here decision-makers involved in target selection. See also introduction, pp. 14f.

ordered the resumption of the air war on 15 December. An ultimatum the US had given the Democratic Republic of Vietnam to re-engage in peace negotiations had just passed. This latter phase of the air war is known as the Christmas Bombing or OLB II. What did the US target during these five years of waging war from the air against North Vietnam?

In 1964 the Joint Chiefs of Staff prepared a plan for a possible engagement of communist Vietnam from the air. It envisaged a concentrated and rapid destruction of ninety-four industrial, transportation and infrastructure targets.[2] Those included eighty-two fixed sites and twelve lines of communication, which were 'considered essential components of the North's war-making capacity'.[3] The stipulated objective of the bombing campaign was to destroy the North's military capabilities that supported the insurgency in the South.[4] While never officially implemented in full, as President Johnson opted for a more graduated approach, the ninety-four-target list continued to be the main source of targeting choices over the following four years. Very few of the targets initially selected were not also ultimately attacked. The first two objects engaged were an ammunitions depot and a Navy base.[5] The US Air Force and Navy subsequently targeted lines and means of transport, SAM-sites (launching pads for surface to air missiles) and airfields.[6] In the first half of 1966, the emphasis of the campaign shifted slightly to include oil-related objects.[7] The Hanoi petroleum oil and lubricant storage area was completely, its equivalent in Haiphong 80 per cent, destroyed.[8]

The so-called plan 'Rolling Thunder 52' interrupted this exclusive focus on the destruction of North Vietnam's military capabilities.[9] In November 1966, the Joint Chiefs suggested targeting power plants. This time their aim was 'to affect to a major degree both military and

---

[2] Michael (2003) 3; also Drake (1992).   [3] US Department of Defense (1967).
[4] Clodfelter (2006) 84f.; Pape suggests that different factions in the US government brought forward diverging strategies for the achievement of this goal. He stresses that these strategies were to some extent pursued in parallel and therefore cautions against the notion that targeting decisions during ORT can be interpreted as following one preconceived master plan (Pape (1996) 178).
[5] US Department of Defense (1971/2), vol. III, 284.   [6] Michael (2003) 11.
[7] Clodfelter (2006) 90ff.   [8] *Ibid.* 98, 128.
[9] US Department of Defense (1971/2), vol. III, 274; also Parks (1982) 2.

civilian support to the war effort'.[10] Mark Clodfelter emphasises the discontinuity in the intent of target planners: while previous plans were designed to erode capabilities 'Rolling Thunder 52 showed that they [the Joint Chiefs] had decided to attack North Vietnamese will directly'.[11] The plan was controversial and by 21 December, after only thirty-nine days, it was significantly curtailed. The campaign reverted back to focusing on military transport and compounds as well as industrial sites. At the end '[a]lmost 90% of Rolling Thunder's weight struck transportation related targets'.[12] Though many of them, for instance bridges and rail lines, also served civilian life, they all played a vital role in the unabated flow of men and materiel towards the South.

Was the only aim of these air strikes really to weaken the military capabilities of North Vietnam? Even after the abandonment of Rolling Thunder 52, some voices in the US government advocated targeting the will of the enemy directly rather than merely focusing on military capabilities.[13] However, President Johnson and the Chairman of the Joint Chiefs of Staff at the time, General Earle Wheeler, were both deeply ambivalent about directly attacking the enemy's morale.[14] In 1967, Wheeler effectively retracted that attacks on power plants during Rolling Thunder 52 were ever meant to weaken the will of the government or terrorise civilians in the North: 'The objective ... was not ... to turn the lights off in major population centres.' Attacks on power plants were 'designed to deprive the enemy of a basic power source needed to operate certain war-supporting facilities and industries'.[15] In a conversation with the president a year earlier Wheeler had qualified power plants as not 'recognized as a legitimate military target'.[16] Clodfelter stresses that even during the short-lived Rolling Thunder

---

[10] Clodfelter (2006) 102.

[11] *Ibid.*; Pape puts less emphasis than Clodfelter on the discontinuity between Rolling Thunder 52 and the rest of ORT. He highlights the focus on a new target set over the allegedly changed intent behind its engagement (Pape (1996) 185).

[12] Quoted in Clodfelter (2006) 134.

[13] Robert McNamara was one of the most consistent advocates of 'communicating with the bomb' (Young (2009) 163). Maxwell Taylor likewise argued in favour of using bombing 'to bring pressure on the will of the chiefs of the DRV [Democratic Republic of Vietnam]'. Quoted in Kahin (1987) 263.

[14] Clodfelter (2006) 102f.; Kahin (1987) 266.

[15] Chairman of the Joint Chiefs of Staff, Memorandum to the President of 5 May 1967, in US Department of Defense (1971/2), vol. IV, 152.

[16] Quoted in Clodfelter (2006) 103; legitimacy is not meant to refer to legality in this context, but to political acceptability.

52 Wheeler could advocate and justify attacks aimed at disrupting morale rather than eroding capabilities '[o]nly with supreme difficulty'.[17]

This reluctance to engage in bombing aimed directly at undermining morale explains why the brief official endorsement of this strategy, as part of Rolling Thunder 52, only afforded the military one additional target set: electrical power plants. The latter are dual-use objects that can also contribute to the military effort of a belligerent. Targets without direct relevance to the North Vietnamese ability to support the insurgency in the South, such as agriculture, political infrastructure or symbolic sites, were never part of ORT.[18] Admiral Ulysses Grant Sharp, Commander in Chief of the United States Pacific Command, stated that the goal of air strikes against the North to be the 'attrition of men, supplies, and equipment'.[19] The focus on capabilities rather than will to fight is also visible in the conception of progress during hostilities. The intelligence agencies in their assessment of the air strikes quantified the physical effects on enemy capabilities. In 1966, for instance, they reported the destruction of 4,600 trucks and fifteen locomotives, as well as a little over half of the country's power plants and major bridges.[20]

With the exception of Rolling Thunder 52, the four-year bombing of North Vietnam under the Johnson administration is an example of the use of air power in its interdiction function. For the purposes of this study interdiction missions are defined as air strikes that fulfil two criteria. First, they engage targets that fall in one of the following categories: (1) transport infrastructure used for military purposes, such as rail lines, trucks, trains and bridges; (2) industry used (*inter alia*) for genuine military purposes, such as weapons factories; (3) military forces, equipment and infrastructure, such as SAM-sites, compounds and bases. In other words, interdiction operations target uncontroversial or 'traditional' military objectives whose engagement generates a decrease in the enemy's military effectiveness in one causal

---

[17] *Ibid.* 107.   [18] Parks (1982) 2.

[19] US Department of Defense (1971/2), vol. IV, 109; also Clodfelter (2006); Drake (1992); Kapstein (2012) 140; Pape (1996) 194; Sharp (1968); even more so than Clodfelter and Drake, Pape and Kapstein stress the absence of attacks directly aimed at undermining civilian morale during ORT.

[20] Clodfelter (2006) 130, 134; also Drake (1992) 2; Kapstein (2012) 140; US Department of Defense (1971/2), vol. III.

step because these objects directly contribute to military action. Second, interdiction missions serve the aim of attrition. Attrition, according to the US Department of Defense, is '[t]he reduction of the effectiveness of a force caused by loss of personnel and materiel'.[21] Attrition hence denotes the intent to weaken the enemy's military capabilities, rather than other capabilities or morale.[22]

ORT caused significant damage in the Democratic Republic of Vietnam. Yet the campaign was widely recognised not to have undermined the regime's ability to fuel the insurgency in the South, mainly because the latter did not require very much materiel in order to be sustained.[23] Nevertheless, four years later, in May 1972, the Nixon administration likewise resorted to air strikes against the North with essentially the same operational objectives: Secretary of Defense Henry Kissinger stressed that OLB I aimed at the 'attrition of Northern military capabilities',[24] and would revolve around the interdiction of military transport towards the South.[25] This time some restrictions, for instance the prohibition on instant re-strike, were lifted and the exclusion zones melted away. In addition, newly available military technology enhanced the air campaign's destructiveness.[26] Compared to ORT, OLB I thus featured a largely unchanged intent (attrition) and

---

[21] US Department of Defense, *Military Doctrine Dictionary*, www.dtic.mil/doctrine/dod.

[22] According to the official definition of the US Department of Defense, interdiction operations are 'conducted to divert, disrupt, delay, or destroy the enemy's military potential before it can be brought to bear effectively against friendly forces, or to otherwise achieve objectives'. The definition of interdiction adopted here avoids a reference to the unclear concept of an enemy's 'military potential' and the obscure phrase 'otherwise achieve objectives'. The Pentagon also considers '[a]ir interdiction [to be] conducted at such distance from friendly forces that detailed integration of each air mission with the fire and movement of friendly forces is not required' (www.dtic.mil/doctrine/jel/doddict/data/a/00201.html). This excludes close air support (CAS) missions from interdiction. For the purpose of this analysis, interdiction operations include CAS. As the ground component is almost exclusively engaged in the attrition of enemy personnel and materiel, support of ground operations largely furthers this goal. The exception to this are those CAS missions that are called in by ground troops under fire, often referred to as 'troops in contact situations'. Their primary purpose is the defence of friendly forces. Interdiction hence includes all pre-planned support of ground forces (including very close support) but not assistance called in by troops in contact.

[23] Clodfelter (2006) 117; Lawrence (2008) 96.

[24] Michael (2003) 6; also Clodfelter (2006) 156.   [25] Clodfelter (2006) 156.

[26] *Ibid.*, 158, 173; also Parks (1983).

similar targets.[27] Yet it presented an increased intensity of effort; in Nixon's own words: 'we must go to the brink and destroy the enemy's war-making capacity. Johnson had lacked the will to do so; I have the will in spades.'[28] The insurgency in the South had morphed into a conventional war, which heightened its dependence on resupply. As a result, this time five months of air strikes made a difference. Though OLB I was thus more effective, it was likewise 'a pure case of interdiction bombing'.[29]

In contrast, the last phase of the air war against North Vietnam, the Christmas Bombing or OBL II, was not singularly geared towards attrition. As during ORT and OLB I, many of the fifty-nine targets struck formed an integral part of the North's ability to support the South: 'railroad yards and complexes accounted for 36 percent of the total sortie effort ... next were storage facilities such as warehouse complexes'.[30] This time, however, bombing also reached targets downtown in the population centres Hanoi and Haiphong. These air strikes did not further attrition. They were chosen with a view to weakening the leadership's will to fight and with the aim of 'inflict[ing] utmost civilian distress'.[31] Authors differ in their assessment of how much of the Christmas Bombing followed this genuinely changed intent.[32] Bomb damage was again assessed in physical terms rather than in 'distress imposed' or 'effects on North Vietnamese will to fight'. In light of the brevity of the campaign these physical effects

---

[27] Drake (1992); Pape (1996) 202.

[28] President Richard Nixon quoted in Kimball (1998) 315.

[29] Pape (1996) 199; also Clodfelter (2006) 156; it should be noted that Pape works with a slightly different conception of interdiction from Clodfelter and this study. He differentiates between military targets (65 per cent of OLB I), transport (32 per cent of OLB I) and industry targets (8 per cent of OLB I), which in the context of this investigation is unhelpful. Attacks on transport as well as industry targets can yield an immediate military advantage. If transport and industrial infrastructure directly contributes to the enemy's war effort, it constitutes a military and presumptively legitimate target. In fact, enemy railway lines are a classic object of attack during interdiction campaigns. Cement, explosives and chemical plants, which Pape considers 'industry targets', are likewise often part of the interdiction mission (Pape (1996) 182, 184).

[30] Michael (2003) 12; likewise Pape (1996) 202.   [31] Clodfelter (2006) 184.

[32] Pape unequivocally states that 'Linebacker II's purpose and target set largely paralleled those of Linebacker I' (Pape (1996) 201). In his view '[n]one of the available evidence suggests that civilian vulnerabilities contributed to the success of American coercion' during OLB II (Pape (1996) 209). For a different view see Clodfelter (2006) 184; Drake (1992).

were extensive.[33] After only eleven days, intelligence agencies reported *inter alia* '1600 military structures damaged or destroyed; 500 rail inter-dictions, 372 pieces of rolling stock damaged or destroyed; one fourth of the petroleum reserves destroyed; and 80 percent of the electrical power production destroyed'.[34]

To sum up, the destructiveness of the air campaigns against North Vietnam and their effectiveness with regard to undermining the North's ability to support the fighting in the South increased from ORT to OLB I and OLB II. Though the exclusion zone shrank and restrictions were lifted from 1965 to 1972, so that air strikes could reach many more targets in the later campaigns, the kind of targets struck remained largely the same: transportation used for military equipment and personnel, war-supporting industry, power plants, military compounds, oil-related targets and air defence structures.[35] In other words, all three bombing phases focused on uncontroversial military objectives whose destruction would directly yield a decrease in North Vietnam's military effectiveness. The intent behind their attack was the attrition of the North's military capabilities. Only ORT 52 and some air strikes during OLB II broke with this intent. They were meant to directly weaken the government's will and undermine the population's morale. With the exception of fifty days, the bombing of North Vietnam, which lasted altogether for four years and eighty days, thus presents a clear case of an interdiction campaign.

Iraq in 1991

On 16 January 1991, one day after the expiration of an ultimatum given to Iraq to withdraw its forces from Kuwait, an international coalition mandated by the UN under the leadership of the US launched a comprehensive air campaign. It focused on twelve sets of targets to be neutralised: (1) nuclear and biological facilities; (2) scud missile facilities; (3) military support production and research facilities; (4) lead-ership; (5) command, control and communication sites; (6) electrical power; (7) oil facilities; (8) railroads and bridges; (9) airfields; (10) naval and port facilities; (11) strategic air defences; and (12) Republican

---

[33] Drake (1992) 22; also Clark (2002).
[34] Clodfelter (2006) 194f.; Michael (2003) 12.
[35] Michael (2003) 12; Pape (1996) 201; likewise Clodfelter (1997).

Guards.[36] According to the data published in what is colloquially known as the *Gulf War Air Power Survey*,[37] circa 86 per cent of all air strikes focused on targets from sets (1), (2) and (9) to (12). These were objects at the heart of Iraq's ability to wage war in Kuwait.[38] Their engagement would not further any aim except for attrition.

This central role of interdiction operations is surprising. According to the then popular doctrinal teachings of the air campaign's main architect Colonel John Warden, fielded forces and military equipment were the least promising targets for air strikes. Warden rejected the notion that the enemy's military capabilities were necessarily an integral part of combat operations. He advocated the immediate and direct destruction of the enemy's true 'centres of gravity' instead.[39] In order of declining importance he considered those to be the enemy leadership, 'organic essentials', e.g. electrical power, infrastructure, populations and fielded forces.[40] Warden's thinking, in turn, was influenced by early air power advocates, who championed the independent use of air forces, and by the supporters of the emerging doctrine of EBOs. He hence took inspiration from a long line of thinking that suggested that rather than supporting the ground component, air forces should endeavour to win wars on their own. Warden was among those US planners who entertained the hope that the air war alone would persuade Iraq to retreat from Kuwait and that a ground war would not be necessary.[41]

Indeed, Instant Thunder was initially designed by Colonel Warden in accordance with these ideas. However, General Charles Horner, the head of the Air Force Component Command, and General Norman Schwarzkopf, the commander of Central Command (and thereby all coalition forces in Iraq), were both convinced that ultimately a ground campaign would be necessary. They therefore made sure that the interdiction of Iraqi military capabilities was included in the campaign plan.[42] In the end, the air war comprised both, the original targets of Instant Thunder as well as a large-scale effort to undermine Iraq's

---

[36] Lewis (2003) 488.   [37] US Department of Defense (1992).
[38] *Ibid.*, vol. II, Part II, 105ff.   [39] Warden (1989) 6, 117.
[40] Warden (1995) 43.
[41] US Department of Defense (1992), vol. II, Part I, 255.
[42] *Ibid.*, 265, 250, 277; also Shimko (2010) 58.

military capabilities in order to pave the way for ground combat.[43] This explains why ODS comprised 86 per cent interdiction missions.

If we recall that the bombing of Vietnam was a pure interdiction campaign, with the brief exceptions of Rolling Thunder 52 and parts of OLB II, US air targeting seems to have changed only slightly between Vietnam and Iraq. Yet a quantitative comparison between the air wars against North Vietnam and Iraq needs to account for one significant disanalogy: in both cases the source of the enemy's military power was outside the theatre of major ground warfare, where the US strove to effect a change, South Vietnam and Kuwait respectively. The engagement of Iraqi troops in Kuwait was planned and executed by the same coalition institutions that managed the bombing of targets in Iraq.[44] It is therefore included in the statistics provided for ODS. In contrast, air strikes in South Vietnam were not considered part of the war against North Vietnam. They were conducted 'under the cover' of supporting the South Vietnamese government. Targets were mostly nominated by local Vietnamese officials and were, at least *de jure*, authorised by the government of South Vietnam.[45] As a result, the study of US air targeting in Vietnam, undertaken above, solely analysed the bombing *outside* the area of major ground combat.

It is warranted then, at least for illustrative purposes, to compare ODS minus the engagement of Iraqi troops in Kuwait to the campaigns against North Vietnam. On one count based on the *Gulf War Air Power Survey* ODS consisted of 34,275 air strikes. According to the same data set 19,073 air strikes (55.6 per cent) were carried out in the Kuwait theatre of operations. It follows that 15,202 air strikes make up the part of ODS that can meaningfully be compared to the campaigns against North Vietnam. As mentioned above, 29,477 of all air strikes (86 per cent) were interdiction missions. Air operations in preparations or support of a ground war in Kuwait are considered interdiction

---

[43] Pape (1996) 219, 228.

[44] Cohen (1994) 2; US Department of Defense (1992), vol. II, Part I, 287.

[45] Sheehan describes how this fact considerably eased commanders' concern about civilian casualties (Sheehan (1988) 113). Air strikes in South Vietnam were also subject to much less scrutiny from Washington and followed different rules of engagement that put less emphasis on safeguarding noncombatant immunity. US Department of Defense (1971/2), vol. III, 274; similar Kahin (1987) 284; Sheehan (1988) 114.

missions according to the definition adopted here.[46] If we assume that all strikes against forces in Kuwait count as interdiction, 10,404 interdiction air strikes (29,477 minus 19,073) are left for Iraq proper. Out of the 15,202 air strikes which constitute the part of ODS that is analogous to the campaigns against North Vietnam, only circa 68 per cent thus fall in the category of interdiction – hence target sets (1), (2) and (9) to (11). In other words, if we take ODS minus the air operations in Kuwait, the relative weight of interdiction missions in US air operations decreases significantly compared to their role in North Vietnam. The use of air power in functions other than interdiction must have been a salient new feature of the 1991 air war against Iraq.

In which other ways was air power used then? Compared to the campaign plans for North Vietnam, ODS featured about double the number of target sets. This is mostly a result of greater differentiation among types of military structures. During the war against Vietnam targets from sets (3), (9), (10) and (12) would presumably all have fallen under 'military complexes'.[47] Target sets (6) electrical power, (7) oil facilities and (8) railroads and bridges comprise a range of dual-use objects that were, under slightly different denominations, also targeted during the Vietnam War era. As discussed above, the US then attacked dual-use objects almost entirely because of their role in North Vietnam's ability to support the insurgency in the South. They were chosen as targets mostly *in spite of* rather than because of their civilian functions. I therefore counted these attacks as interdiction operations.[48] What was the intent behind the engagement of dual-use structures in 1991? If it was attrition, we would have to add the air strikes falling under these three target sets to the 68 per cent interdiction missions counted so far. After all engagements of electrical power, oil facilities and bridges can under certain circumstances yield a genuinely military advantage in one causal step.

[46] This is unless they are called in by troops in contact, meaning under fire. During the first thirty-eight days of ODS, ground forces were not involved in the conflict. The air campaign was mostly over when the 100-hour-long ground war began. As a result, ODS does not feature air operations in troops in contact situations on a significant scale.

[47] US Department of Defense (1971/2), vol. IV, 109; in addition, North Vietnam simply did not have equivalents to target sets (1) nuclear and biological facilities and (2) scud missile facilities.

[48] As mentioned above, air strikes during Rolling Thunder 52 and some attacks during OLB II constitute an exception to this.

A closer look at statements from military planners of the bombing in 1991 reveals that the overriding intent behind the attacks on electrical power plants, oil facilities and bridges was to achieve results other than a direct decrease in Iraq's military effectiveness. Even though ousting Saddam Hussein was not an official campaign goal,[49] the air campaign strove to weaken the Baath Party regime in the eyes of a disaffected population.[50] According to reports from the *Washington Post*, some targets, namely electrical facilities, 'were chosen only secondarily to contribute to the military defeat of Baghdad's occupation army in Kuwait'[51] and 'were bombed primarily to create postwar leverage over Iraq'.[52] An unnamed Air Force planner was quoted as saying: 'Big picture, we wanted to let people know, "[g]et rid of this guy and we will be more than happy to assist in rebuilding ... Fix that, and we'll fix your electricity".'[53] As so often in the history of air power, in 1991, the regime proved politically much more resilient than US planners had expected.[54] Its collapse as a result of punishing air operations failed to materialise.[55]

What about the two remaining target sets (4) and (5)? Disabling command and control structures is an operational objective in virtually every war. However, attacks falling under target set (5) struck objects not considered during the air campaigns against the Democratic Republic of Vietnam. The coalition attacked 'communications assets such as the electrical, telephone exchanges, microwave relay towers, fibre optic cable nodes, bridges that carried communications cables and radio and television facilities'.[56] Of course, few of those objects were actually available in North Vietnam at the time. Despite the fact that these air strikes probably had an effect on Iraq's ability to continue

---

[49] Budiansky (2004) 414f.; Murray and Scales (2003) 10ff.; Shimko (2010) 58f. and 67; for a different view see Pape (1996) 215.

[50] Murray and Scales (2003) 10ff.; Shimko (2010) 67.   [51] Gellman (1991) A1.

[52] *Ibid.*   [53] *Ibid.*; similar US Department of Defense (1992), vol. II, Part I, 332.

[54] *Ibid.*, 330; for the argument that putting the civilian population under stress with bombing does historically not lead it to rise up and topple its leaders see Pape (1996); also Downes (2007).

[55] It should be noted that the subsequent uprisings among the Kurdish population in the north and the Shiites in the south, which in the absence of material outside support utterly failed at enormous costs to those involved, are sometimes associated with the weakening of the regime in the eyes of the population as a result of ODS (Murray and Scales (2003); Shimko (2010)).

[56] US Department of Defense (1992), vol. II, Part I, 66.

the occupation of Kuwait, the intent behind their engagement was, if not primarily to weaken enemy morale, then at least split between attrition and imposing distress by sowing confusion.

The one target set that does stand out as completely new in 1991 is (4) leadership. Attacks on leaders can, if they are part of the chain of command, generate a direct and genuine military advantage. Military leaders and some political leaders are therefore considered combatants/ military objectives and their command centres qualify as prima facie legitimate targets under IL.[57] Was the disruption of the chain of command the impetus behind leadership targeting in 1991? Under this target set the US attacked party headquarters, presidential palaces, government ministries and the headquarters of the secret police.[58] It is difficult to separate out the civilian from the military leadership in Iraq so that some of these air strikes may have been conducive to diminishing Iraq's military effectiveness. Yet the wide range of targets casts doubt over the interpretation that this was the only intent behind the selection of targets from set (4).

Moreover, if these air strikes did only serve to disrupt the chain of command, the very establishment of a separate target set would have been redundant. Any object or person whose engagement interferes with the chain of command is covered by target set (5), command and control. As mentioned, individuals who are part of the chain of command are combatants/military objectives and as such they are covered under target set (5). On the other hand, if the goal of these air strikes was to elicit a reaction on the part of the Iraqi elite to the demonstration that it would no longer be safe, let alone prosperous – providing it with an incentive for a 'premature' withdrawal from Kuwait[59] – then a separate target category did serve a purpose. The elite who would be the audience and objective of this 'message targeting' would comprise individual leaders who did not count as combatants and who would therefore not have been attacked under target set (5). Leadership targeting in ODS marks the beginning of a larger trend.

---

[57] The provisions that determine which persons can count as combatants or can be targeted because they directly participate in hostilities are not discussed separately here.

[58] Budiansky (2004) 414f.; Shimko (2010) 69.

[59] Shimko (2010) 61; also Murray and Scales (2003) 10; Pape (1996) 228.

Target set (4) was the least frequently attacked with only 0.6 per cent of all air strikes falling into this category. This stands in stark contrast to the importance of leadership targets twelve years later, as I will show below.

In conclusion, the air war in 1991 included a significant effort of traditional attrition.[60] However, overall interdiction was in relative terms less important during ODS than during the war against North Vietnam. A larger share of air strikes focused not on Iraq's military infrastructure properly so-called, but on dual-use economic and political infrastructure (14 per cent of all air strikes and 32 per cent of the air strikes outside the Kuwait theatre of operations). Dual-use objects can make an effective contribution to military action and attacks that aim to deny the enemy this contribution count as interdiction missions. However, considerable evidence suggests that the intent behind many of the air strikes on dual-use infrastructure in Iraq was at least in part to influence Saddam Hussein, his regime and ultimately also the Iraqi people. This impetus is most obvious in the establishment of leadership as a separate target set. While this kind of signalling or morale bombing had played a part during the campaigns against North Vietnam, it then remained a marginal phenomenon.[61]

The effects on civilian life of this systematic engagement of dual-use infrastructure in 1991 are subject to radically differing perceptions. Outside commentators deplored the humanitarian costs imposed by air strikes.[62] General Schwarzkopf, to the contrary, claimed to have '[c]ripple[d] Iraq's military system while leaving its agriculture and commerce intact and its population largely unharmed'.[63] Specifically in combination with the sanctions regime imposed on Iraq after the war, the destruction inflicted during ODS, in fact, constituted a devastating setback for the Iraqi people.[64]

---

[60] Shimko (2010) 61, 281.
[61] During ODS dual-use targets not only took a greater share of objects struck. US troops also attacked a wider range of structures than during the earlier campaigns against North Vietnam. This, however, is primarily attributable to the availability of these targets in the more industrialised Iraqi society and their absence in North Vietnam.
[62] Gellman (1991).
[63] Quoted in Roberts (1994) 155; similar UNICEF official quoted in al-Khahl (1991) 10.
[64] Downes (2008) 226f.; Graham (2004) 179; Zehfuss (2011) *passim*.

Iraq in 2003

On 19 March 2003, after an ultimatum given to Saddam Hussein and his sons to leave Iraq had expired, a US-led coalition started launching air strikes against 'targets of opportunity' at the outskirts of Baghdad.[65] In contrast to the previously discussed air campaigns, this time the ground war ran largely parallel to the air war and the theatres of operation were congruent.[66] As a result, OIF had to feature air power used in support of the ground component including CAS. The air war against North Vietnam had not comprised such missions, and ODS only to a very limited extent, given the brevity of the ground invasion. What does the parallel invasion mean for the comparison, specifically for the relative importance of interdiction? Missions in support of the ground component including CAS missions are considered interdiction missions because they are mostly meant to erode the adversary's military capabilities and are directed towards unconventional military objectives. The full-fledged invasion of Iraq in 2003 and the resulting need for extensive ground support hence meant that interdiction missions had to be overwhelmingly important during OIF.

However, according to data released by the Department of Defense in the report *Operation Iraqi Freedom – By the Numbers*, only 52 per cent of the available air power was initially allocated to the mission 'to support the ground component'. Of course, some interdiction missions do not serve the goal of supporting ground troops, for instance targeting of air defences. It is thus to be expected that the share of interdiction missions in OIF was higher than 52 per cent. According to the Department of Defense, 79 per cent of all aim points ultimately 'serviced' (15,592 in total) were considered part of the air forces' interdiction function.[67] A study by Carl Conetta states that 'somewhat

---

[65] Singal, Lim and Stephey (2003).

[66] As Rohde (2012) observes, the war in Iraq 'claimed 4,484 American lives, cost at least $700 billion, and lasted nearly nine years'. How many Iraqi lives were lost and wealth destroyed has yet to be calculated. Here I focus on a small part of this time period. The official end of major combat operations presented an important discontinuity, as the opponent of the US changed from a state military to a combination of sectarian armed groups, regime loyalists and foreign fighters. For an elaboration of this point see Shimko (2010) 24. The analysis here is limited to air strikes against Iraq between 19 March 2003 and 1 May 2003.

[67] US Department of Defense (2003b) 5.

less than 25 percent of the 15,592 aim points would have been devoted to purposes *other* than interdiction [italic mine]'.[68] It is therefore safe to say that around three-quarters of air strikes during OIF can be reckoned interdiction missions. Compared to ODS, in OIF the relative share of air strikes aiming at the attrition of Iraq's military capabilities had yet again declined *vis-à-vis* the use of air power in other ways. That is true in spite of the parallel large-scale ground invasion.[69]

Contrary to twelve years before, target development for OIF was not done according to target sets, but according to so-called 'desired mean points of impact' (DMPIs), which were categorised by the 'strategy-to-task mission' they would further if achieved.[70] While this provides added insight into the intent behind the use of air power, in many cases no information is available regarding the kinds of objects targeted. With regard to dual-use targets, Human Rights Watch, which otherwise credited the coalition with a general attempt to distinguish between civilian and military infrastructure, severely criticised the targeting of electrical power distribution and even more so of power generation facilities.[71] However, other commentators stress that, in contrast to twelve years before, the industrial and economic infrastructure of Iraq was largely spared, due to its utility for coalition forces in the impending occupation.[72] For this reason none of the bridges over the Euphrates was destroyed either.[73]

Rather than on economic infrastructure the emphasis of the campaign, particularly in the early days, was instead put on leadership, as well as command and control targets.[74] Fifty-five designated regime members were acknowledged targets. They were assembled on so-called 'personality identification playing cards'.[75] This most-wanted list included the Deputy Prime Minister, the Finance Minister, the Minister of the Interior, the Minister of Trade, the Minister for Higher Education/Scientific Research, the Presidential Secretary and

---

[68] Conetta (2003a) 8; this number likely excludes troops in contact situations.

[69] To recall, 86 per cent of air strikes during ODS were part of the interdiction mission. In a comparison with OIF it would not make sense to exclude from ODS air strikes against Iraqi forces in Kuwait, as was done for illustrative purposes in the comparison between ODS and the air campaigns against North Vietnam.

[70] US Department of Defense (2003b) 4.   [71] Human Rights Watch (2003) 6.

[72] Murray and Scales (2003) 170.   [73] *Ibid.*   [74] *Ibid.* 166.

[75] *Personality Identification Playing Cards*, www.defense.gov/news/Apr2003/pipc10042003.html.

several presidential advisers. While some of them wore uniforms, many did not fulfil military functions and their inclusion in the list seems to have been based on their roles in maintaining the Baath Party regime.[76] In addition, the US acknowledged air strikes on at least ten media installations,[77] on Baath Party headquarters and a communications centre.[78] For some media installations the US claimed that they were part of the chain of command, disseminating information to the troops. However, facilities that were targeted included non-state owned radio and television stations. This renders the explanation provided somewhat implausible.[79] A more likely motivation for the engagement was to undermine the information of the general population (sow confusion) and possibly the spread of propaganda.

Indeed, the second most important function of air power, after supporting the ground component, according to the distribution of DMPIs was 'the suppression of the regime's ability to command Iraqi forces and govern the State';[80] 1,799 DMPIs (9 per cent of all air strikes) were devoted to this aim. This strategy-to-task mission officially acknowledges the use of air power to directly achieve a genuinely political goal – undermining the regime's ability not only to command forces, but also to govern the state. Secretary of Defense Donald Rumsfeld elaborated in his first press briefing after the invasion that air strikes had been launched "on a scale that indicate[d] to Iraqis" that Saddam and his leadership were finished.[81] An important thrust of the air campaign, entirely separate from the attrition of military

---

[76] Interviews nos. 3, 4; the law in question concerns the definition of combatants and of persons directly participating in hostilities, rather than the distinction between military and civilian objects. Analysing the controversies surrounding the distinction between immune and non-immune persons would be beyond the scope of this chapter. It is nevertheless noteworthy that debates about how directly a person has to be connected to military operations in order to qualify as directly participating in hostilities and whether involvement in the political workings of a belligerent regime counts as directly participating, resemble the debates about the degree of nexus and the point of reference for the determination of a military advantage in the meaning of Article 52(2) API, discussed in Part II. Section 9.2 addresses some parallels and differences between distinction as far as objects are concerned and the differentiation between combatants and civilians.

[77] Human Rights Watch (2003) 6.   [78] Gordon and Trainor (2006) 212.

[79] Similar Human Rights Watch (2003) 6.

[80] US Department of Defense (2003b) 4f.; also Fontenot (2005).

[81] *Shock and Awe Campaign under Way*, www.cnn.com/2003/fyi/news/03/22/iraq. war.

capabilities, was hence the weakening of the political fabric of the Baath Party government for the ultimate purpose of regime change.[82]

The use of air power for regime change accords with the then fully institutionalised doctrine of EBOs. The popular doctrine of achieving rapid dominance, colloquially known as 'shock and awe',[83] incorporates the EBO thesis that military structures are probably not the enemy's centre of gravity. Yet shock and awe arguably takes this idea further. Achieving rapid dominance considers the civilian population an integral part of the audience to be shocked. It is worth recalling that in 1991 the aim of targeting the enemy's will by imposing distress on the civilian population had not been officially endorsed. In 2003 the acknowledged purpose of air power was 'not only to crush Iraqi troops', but the air assault against Baghdad was also 'supposed to make leaders lose control, so that those affiliated with the regime were starting to wonder where they stood', and in general 'to instil shock and awe'.[84] While killing Saddam Hussein was not an official mission in 1991, it commanded high priority in 2003. Just as Colonel Warden's ideas were not endorsed as the doctrinal basis of ODS, shock and awe was never officially adopted as the strategy behind OIF's air campaign.[85] Nevertheless, Secretary of Defense Donald Rumsfeld on several occasions expressed his agreement with the doctrine.[86]

Let me summarise the development of US air targeting over the three investigated air wars in terms of three trajectories of change: first, a decrease in the relative importance of interdiction operations. The three air campaigns against the Democratic Republic of Vietnam largely consisted of air strikes against transport infrastructure used for military purposes, attacks on military forces, equipment and infrastructure, war-supporting industry and power plants. These objects were targeted in order to further the attrition of North Vietnam's military capabilities. Interdiction continued to play a significant role in ODS and OIF.

---

[82] Similar Murray and Scales (2003) 167.   [83] Ullman and Wade (1996).

[84] *Effects-Based Operations Briefing of 19 March 2003*, www.defenselink.mil/transcripts/2003/t03202003_t0319effects.html; likewise Bowman (2003) 6: 'The invasion of Iraq was expected to begin with a 72–96 hour air offensive to paralyze the Iraqi command structure, and demoralize Iraqi resistance across the military-civilian spectrum.'

[85] Shimko (2010) 113; in addition, the architects of the doctrine argued that OIF 'did not bring the great shock and awe that [they] had envisaged'. Harlan Ullman quoted in Scarborough (2003); also Young (2009) 172.

[86] Also Shimko (2010) 144, 146.

None the less, its relative importance decreased in the two air campaigns against Iraq.

The second trajectory of change is the expansion in the range of dual-use objects that were made targets of attack over the period investigated. During the engagement of North Vietnam, even in the context of Rolling Thunder 52, dual-use targeting was limited to infrastructure, rail lines and bridges, war-supporting industry and power plants. ODS, in addition, included some leadership and command and control targets. Its most salient feature, however, was a much more systematic effort than in earlier wars to neutralise electrical and power generating facilities as well as war-supporting industry far from the theatre of ground operations. During OIF a wider range of Iraq's political leadership and its communications infrastructure, including media facilities, was disabled by air power than twelve years before.[87]

Dual-use targets can count as interdiction targets. However it is part of this second trend that the intent behind these kinds of attacks changed. Robert Pape stresses that during the war against North Vietnam most dual-use objects that the US attacked were targeted in spite of the civilian functions they performed.[88] To the contrary in 1991, the overriding intent behind attacks on five target sets was weakening the enemy's morale, i.e. coercing early withdrawal from Kuwait: (4) leadership, (5) command and control, (6) electrical power, (7) oil facilities and (8) railroads and bridges. During OIF the acknowledged goal, for instance behind attacks on communications infrastructure used by the government, was undermining the ability of the government to disseminate information/propaganda, hence achieving a psychological not a genuinely military advantage.

---

[87] As mentioned, some dual-use objects targeted in Iraq would not have been available in North Vietnam at the time. However, this is not true for all targets, for instance, the political infrastructure of the government.

[88] Pape (1996) 1990; this by no means implies that the US only conducted air strikes against North Vietnam that were in fact militarily advantageous. Pilots reported that technological limitations, bad weather and Vietnamese air defences meant that they often had not even a vague idea where their bomb load would land. The B-52 raids over North Vietnam's population centres during OLB II were almost incapable of meaningful discrimination. The point made here is that, with the exceptions mentioned, no deliberate attempt was made to target anything other than military capabilities narrowly defined.

The third trajectory of change is the emergence of air strikes without direct implications for the competition between enemy militaries. During OIF the immediate goal of some attacks was regime change, as suggested by the strategy-to-task mission to undermine the regime's ability to govern the state. Some objects targeted to this end did, unlike dual-use objects, lack any direct relevance for Iraq's military effort. The initial air assault comprised intensive targeting of leaders arguably not integrated into the chain of command, civilian political infrastructure and privately owned media facilities.[89] Even if we cannot establish what the intent behind these attacks was, they could not have yielded a genuine military advantage in one causal step.

6.2 The logic US air warfare follows: from sufficiency to efficiency

The role of political and military goals in target selection

The three wars investigated here occur in varying geopolitical contexts. They form part of different US grand strategies. While the air campaigns against North Vietnam are products of the Cold War, ODS can only be understood against the backdrop of the recent ending of this war. Freed from the rivalry with the Soviet Union, the US was not reluctant to assert its position as the only remaining great power even when urgent national interests were not immediately at stake. OIF, on the other hand, belongs in an international system irrevocably changed by 9/11. It forms part of a US grand strategy characterised by an all-consuming imperative to fight international terrorism. Not surprisingly, in the three cases under investigation, force, and specifically air power, was used in the pursuit of vastly different goals.[90] This raises a question: can the change in what was attacked described above not be exhaustively explained by these idiosyncrasies?[91]

---

[89] On the legality of attacking state-owned media facilities see ICTY (2000).
[90] Similar Record and Terrill (2004) 1; also Record (1998) 6.
[91] A variety of variables – besides input of IL for instance, developments in doctrine and military technology – change across the three cases and could potentially have encouraged the observed shifts in target selection. I return to their role in section 7.3. This section only focuses on the purpose of the use of force as a factor that potentially explains the observed changes in target selection.

A different way to characterise the evolution of US air warfare focuses not on three changes in what was attacked, but on why certain targets were selected. I have already investigated the intent behind the attack on dual-use targets in the previous section. Here I will systematically examine what kind of goal provided the immediate inspiration for *all* the different kinds of targeting choices observed and, in turn, what attacks were meant to achieve in the three cases. The analysis endeavours to show that, different goals notwithstanding, the changes in target selection described in the previous section constitute a salient trend in the development of US combat operations from the air.

I distinguish four types of goals at three different levels of abstraction that can spur the selection of a target.[92] The nomination of an object for attack can reflect concrete operational objectives or operational goals (OG). Examples include undermining a country's transport system or neutralising the adversary's air defences. Alternatively targets can be chosen with a view to achieving the overall military goals of a war, what I call 'generic military victory'.[93] I consider military goals those that can in theory be achieved with kinetic attacks on the 'battlefield' alone, such as ousting Iraq from Kuwait. Alternatively targeting choices can be directly motivated by political goals or the grand strategic goals of a belligerent. Political goals are those that even after a hypothetical complete destruction of the enemy's military capabilities would still require negotiations or an occupation of the defeated state in order to be secured, for instance regime change for the purpose democratisation. Alternatively political goals are also those that depend on a specific reaction of the enemy party, for instance concessions in on-going negotiations. Political goals of a war that are *not* specific to the country that is attacked, but serve US interests in a broader context or other parts of the world, are referred to as grand strategic goals (GSG). These are often reflected in the political goals of a war. I therefore treat them as on the same level of abstraction. A

---

[92] I avoid the common three-level break-up of military affairs into strategy, operations and tactics because the adjective 'strategic' is ambiguous. It sometimes refers to big-picture politics and sometimes to opportune courses of military action. I use the word strategy with the qualifier 'grand'. It hence denotes abstract political considerations.

[93] Operational goals are military goals short of generic military victory. For the introduction of the concept of a generic military victory see section 3.4; for a definition see the appendix.

differentiation is only necessary when targeting choices are directly inspired by political considerations that extrapolate from the conflict itself to other regions of the world or other conflicts. Yet those political considerations are not translated into concrete war aims.

The grand strategic context of ORT was characterised by the imperative to prevent what was considered the likely first step in a communist takeover of south-east Asia.[94] The US meant to demonstrate its credible commitment to containing the expansion of what it perceived as the Eastern bloc. The fall of South Vietnam was to be forestalled without provoking intervention by another great power.[95] These grand strategic imperatives are reflected in the overall goals of the campaign. One of them could have been achieved on the 'battlefield' alone: to undermine the North's support of the insurgency in the South with men and materiel.[96] The other two goals were political: first, weaken the will to fight in the North and gain concessions from its leadership during the on-going negotiations; second, boost the morale in the South and secure continued US influence over its government.[97] Indeed with ORT the Johnson administration 'carr[ied] out an essentially psychological campaign to convince Hanoi that the United States meant business'.[98] The two latter goals were not immediately tied to the North's military strength.

It is all the more remarkable then that the operational objectives developed for ORT placed such an obvious emphasis on the erosion of military capabilities. The two political goals were translated into genuinely military operational objectives: '(a) reducing North Vietnamese support of communist operations in Laos and South Vietnam, (b) limiting Vietnamese capabilities to take direct action against Laos and South Vietnam, and (c) impairing North Vietnam's capacity to continue as an industrially viable state'.[99] The military goal was concretised in the operational task to 'attrit [sic], harass, and

---

[94] Lawrence (2008) 48.   [95] US Department of Defense (1971/2), vol. III, 272.

[96] Drake (1992) 4.

[97] These two goals hence depended on a reaction by the enemy. All three goals were limited goals that did not necessitate an utter military defeat of the Democratic Republic of Vietnam. Similar Lawrence (2008) 98.

[98] US Department of Defense (1971/2), vol. III, 291.

[99] *Ibid.*, 277; note that this last military objective has a political dimension in that it could have been furthered by attacks on government facilities and infrastructure not related to the military capabilities of North Vietnam. Nevertheless, as adumbrated, the US did not deliberately target either.

interdict the [Democratic Republic of Vietnam] south of the 20 degrees'.[100] As outlined in detail in the previous section, until Rolling Thunder 52, and again after the end of its short shelf-life, the North was harassed by being 'attrited'.[101]

OLB I had the same grand strategic context and overall goals as ORT. Almost four years of bombing during ORT had brought into sharp relief that actually eliminating all military support of the insurgency was unlikely to be achieved. Compared to ORT, the two overall political goals hence further gained in importance over the military goal. Effecting the 'resumption of the peace talks by pressuring the North back to the bargaining table'[102] was now the primary US impetus. Some policy-makers also hoped that OLB I would persuade President Thieu of the Republic of Vietnam to accept an agreement, as he would witness that the US had done its utmost to exert pressure on the North.[103] In spite of this shift in relative importance among the three overall goals, they were again translated into operational objectives and precipitated similar targeting choices as before.

ORT and OLB I thus featured two distinct ways in which decision-makers chose targets. In both cases operational objectives that were military in nature most directly determined the choice of targets. Operational goals (OG) were either more concrete expressions of the overall military goal (MG) or translations of political goals (PG) into military tasks:

(1) GSG/PG → OG → target selection (TS)
(2) MG → OG → TS

In OLB II the goal of reducing the North's military support of the insurgency in the South took even more of a back seat. It appeared increasingly futile to militarily cripple the insurgency by bombing the North. Moreover, the Nixon administration was singularly focused on the peace negotiations in Paris.[104] While political and military goals were still translated via operational objectives into targeting choices, section 6.1 showed that some air strikes were meant to directly further the two political goals. In the selection of targets *per se* the difference between ORT and OLB I, on the one hand, and OLB II, on

---

[100] *Ibid.*, 342.   [101] *Ibid.*, 270; Komer (1986) 56.   [102] Michael (2003) 9.
[103] Kimball (1998) 209; Lawrence (2008) 158.   [104] Parks (1983) 11.

the other hand, is barely visible.[105] However, the direct translation of the political goals to change the parameters of the negotiations in Paris and undermine Northern morale into targeting choices is the distinctive subtext of the reasoning behind the selection of some targets during the Christmas Bombing. The campaign thus featured the same cognitive roadmaps to target selection as the previous two campaigns. However, targets were also chosen based on a shorter line of thinking connecting the overall political goals of the air campaign directly to target selection:

(1) GSG/PG → OG → TS
(2) MG → OG → TS
(3) GSG/PG → TS

The grand strategic context of the 1991 Gulf War emboldened the US to show that in a post-Cold War world it would wield its military might to prevent individual states from riding roughshod over the international order. One grand strategic goal was the assertion of the US position as the sole remaining great power and hegemon. Contrary to the campaign against North Vietnam, the official overall goals of ODS were all genuinely military: to destroy Iraq's capability to wage war; to destroy Iraq's chemical, biological and nuclear capabilities; and to liberate Kuwait City.[106] Given the military nature of these overall goals, operational objectives closely echoed them, while also expressing them on a lower level: the attrition of Iraq's war materiel, the gaining and maintaining air superiority, the interdiction of Iraq's supply lines to Kuwait, the weakening of the Republican Guards, the destroying of Iraq's weapons of mass destruction capabilities and liberating Kuwait.[107]

In order to achieve these ends the coalition could have simply destroyed Iraqi forces and thereby ousted them from Kuwait. While one streak of targeting choices was geared towards exactly that, some targets selected did not reflect these operational objectives or even the

---

[105] Being allowed to 'go downtown' for the first time brought structures within reach during OLB II that could previously not be attacked from the air. Yet, as mentioned, the kind of targets attacked did not change.

[106] According to Shimko official goals were '(1) removal of Iraqi forces from Kuwait, (2) restoration of Kuwait's sovereignty, (3) establishment of regional security and stability, and (4) protection of American lives' (Shimko (2010) 63).

[107] US Department of Defense (1992) vol. II, Part I, 328.

overall military goals. Instead they seem to have taken inspiration from the above-mentioned grand strategic goal of the US. The air campaign against targets in downtown Baghdad was not actually necessary for the achievement of any of the operational objectives or by presupposition military goals. It can only be explained by the desire to destabilise the regime and coerce early withdrawal (before the defeat of fielded forces) from Kuwait in order to make the victory quick and decisive. This in turn would demonstrate American superiority and the futility of challenging it militarily. The approach guiding bombing in ODS 'was not so much to match Iraqi power but to entirely overwhelm it ... [to] make the war short and victory certain'.[108] The two cognitive roadmaps to target selection in ODS were:

(1) MG → OG → TS
(2) GSG → TS

The grand strategic context of OIF was characterised by the vision of a largely neoconservative government that spreading freedom and democracy, if necessary by force, would keep America safe in the twenty-first century.[109] President George W. Bush outlined the overall goals behind the invasion of Iraq in 2003 to be threefold: 'to disarm Iraq, to free its people, and to defend the world from grave danger'.[110] The official overall war aims were more concrete:

1 A stable Iraq, with its territorial integrity intact and a broad-based government that renounces ... [weapons of mass destruction] development and use, and no longer supports terrorism or threatens its neighbors.
2 Success in Iraq leveraged to convince other countries to cease support to terrorists and to deny them access to ... [weapons of mass destruction].
3 Destabilize, isolate, and overthrow the Iraqi regime and provide support to a new, broad-based government.
4 Destroy Iraqi ... [weapons of mass destruction] capability and infrastructure.
5 Protect allies and US supporters from Iraqi threats and attacks.
6 Destroy terrorist networks in Iraq. Gather intelligence on global terrorism; detain terrorists and war criminals, and free individuals unjustly detained under the Iraqi regime.[111]

---

[108] Young (2009) 168.   [109] Woodward (2004).   [110] Singal *et al.* (2003).
[111] US Department of Defense (2003b) 4.

For the purposes of this investigation I treat goals (1) and (2) as mostly political.[112] Goal (3) is mixed and goals (4), (5) and (6) are genuinely military. Interestingly goal (6), though explicitly military, alludes to a grand strategic imperative, namely the fight against global terrorism (outside Iraq). As well as more elaborate than in previous campaigns, these ambitious overall goals hence differentiate less between the political and the military and even include explicit references to US interests outside Iraq.

The Department of Defense then listed ten operational objectives:

- Defeat or compel capitulation of Iraqi forces.
- Neutralize regime leadership.
- Neutralize Iraqi ... [tactical missile defence/weapons of mass destruction] delivery systems.
- Control ... [weapons of mass destruction] infrastructure.
- Ensure the territorial integrity of Iraq.
- Deploy and posture ... [combined forces command] forces for post-hostility operations, initiating humanitarian assistance operations for the Iraqi people, within capabilities.
- Set military conditions for provisional/permanent government to assume power.
- Maintain international and regional support.
- Neutralize Iraqi regime's ... [command and control] & security forces.
- Gain and maintain air, maritime and space supremacy.[113]

They largely concretise military goals and translate some of the political and mixed goals into operational objectives. Setting military conditions for a provisional/permanent government to assume power is a good example of such a translation of a political goal – namely to destabilise, isolate and overthrow the Iraqi regime and provide support to a new, broad-based government – into an operational objective. One could argue that maintaining international and regional support is not strictly speaking a military mission. However, it possibly refers to the need to avoid air strikes that would create disaffection in the audiences mentioned, for instance on religious structures used by the Iraqi military.

---

[112] In the sense that kinetic action on the battlefield alone could not even in theory achieve them. Goal (2) also contains an explicit reference to grand strategic goals.
[113] US Department of Defense (2003b) 4.

More remarkable than this potentially political operational objective is that, as indicated above, OIF featured strategy-to-task missions instead of target sets as the means to sort aim points into categories. They included:

- 'Maintain Air and Space Supremacy in the [Iraq Theatre of Operations]'
- 'Support the [Land Component] to achieve defeat or compel capitulation'
- 'Support the prevention of non-combatant forces from impeding [Combined Forces Component Operations]'
- 'Maintain Maritime Supremacy'
- 'Support [Combined Forces Component] to secure regional and international support'
- 'Conduct [Joint Reception, Staging, Onward Movement, and Integration Operations] . . . and maintain air posture'
- 'Continue suppression of Iraqi Regime's ability to command Iraqi forces & govern State'
- '. . . establish and operate secured airfields in Iraq'
- 'Support [Special Operations]'
- 'Suppress Iraqi . . . [tactical missile defence and weapons of mass destruction] delivery systems'
- '. . . support [Land Component] in neutralizing/controlling . . . [weapons of mass destruction] infrastructure & . . . [special support equipment]'[114]

Out of these eleven strategy-to-task missions, ten are broadly military, but one, which turned out to be the second most important, shows that overall goals had directly determined a strategy-to-task mission: the 'suppression of [the] Iraqi Regime's ability to command Iraqi forces & govern [the] State'. The first part of this mission merely repeats the overall military goal of the war without concretising it. The latter part could not possibly be accomplished with the destruction of military capabilities alone and restates the political goal of the war. OIF hence featured four different cognitive roadmaps to target selection. Operational objectives, which inspired strategy-to-task missions,

---

[114] *Ibid.*

reflected either overall military or political goals. But overall political and military goals also both directly precipitated attacks:

(1) MG → OG → TS
(2) GSG/PG → OG → TS
(3) GSG/PG → TS
(4) MG → TS

What this comparison shows is that the cognitive paths that lead up to the choice of military objectives for attack changed across the cases: the goal most immediately determinative of the selection of a target is more often a more abstract (read political) goal in the later wars. The mirror image of a cognitive path or roadmap to a targeting choice is the projected causal chain that the attack is meant to initiate. The more abstract the goal that most directly determines a targeting choice, the longer is the desired causal chain that is necessary before the attack generates a genuinely military advantage. For example, if the operational objective to disrupt command and control spurs the engagement of a telephone cable, then this desired impact materialises in one causal step. In comparison, if undermining the opposing belligerent's will to fight inspires the targeting of a privately owned media facility, the attacker counts on the materialisation of several causal steps as well as the absence of intervening agency to achieve this goal – the disruption of transmissions, decreased information/propaganda, increased confusion/doubts among the civilian population, decreased support of the war effort, etc.[115] As cognitive roadmaps between abstract political goals and targeting choices shorten, projected causal chains between kinetic impact and the genuinely military effect of attacks grow longer.

The argument presented here rests on the understanding that as a result of their specific sets of goals (grand strategic, political and military) different air campaigns are more or less conducive to interdiction or to targeting for political effect respectively. In both cases, North Vietnam and OIF, the US pursued ambitious political goals that could not have been secured with generic military victory alone. In both cases the US would have had to count on the assumption that generic military victory would in fact be sufficient for the

---

[115] See section 3.4 for a discussion of what it means to achieve a 'definite military advantage' according to Article 52(2) API.

achievement of its political goals. In both cases it would presumably have been more efficient to attack objects more closely related to the respective political goals than to destroy military capabilities. Yet for the most part the US did not stray from interdiction operations against the Democratic Republic of Vietnam. OIF, to the contrary, saw the selection of targets directly for the purpose of regime change.

ODS was much more amenable than either of the other two campaigns to being fought successfully with an exclusive focus on military capabilities. The absence of complex political goals meant that the US did not have to rely on the assumption that generic military victory would translate into political victory; generic military victory itself was the desired end-state. The observation that for the definition of a legitimate target, and hence the decision on what actually to attack, planners reached back to grand strategic goals makes the trend discovered all the more remarkable. Rather than explaining it away, awareness of the different goals of the examined wars brings into sharper relief that the definition of a legitimate target of attack as conceived by US decision-makers changed over the period under investigation.

The connection between objects and military operations and the definition of progress in war

Differences in the use of air power are commonly described in a number of dichotomies: limited versus total war, coercion versus destruction, and tactical versus strategic bombing. Can the observed change in US air targeting be described in terms of any of these categories?

The change definitely does not simply amount to a gradual decrease or increase in restraint. A comparison of ORT, OLB I and OLB II with US air strikes in Cambodia, Laos and South Vietnam at the same time suggests that the former three campaigns against North Vietnam were conducted with considerable restraint.[116] In 1991, increased international scrutiny and limited goals provided the incentive to exercise restraint in the use of air power against Iraq.[117] The imperative to avoid civilian casualties was equally strong in 2003. As a result, none of the air campaigns investigated amounts to total war or features systematic deliberate attacks on what US commanders considered

---

[116] Likewise Pape (1996) 209.   [117] Friedman and Friedman (1996) 393.

civilians or civilian structures. All campaigns without exception nevertheless took extremely high tolls on the civilian populations under attack. I will return to the question of the humanitarian consequences and the normative implications of the change in target selection between 1965 and 2003 in Part IV of the book. Here it is important to stress that the trends described do not in themselves indicate or result from fewer (or more) limitations on the use of air power. Nor do they prima facie decrease or increase the humanitarian costs of war.

The observed change does not simply equate with a shift from destruction to coercion or vice versa either. As pointed out, despite their operational emphasis on the destruction of military capabilities, all air campaigns against North Vietnam had a coercive impetus: to change the parameters of peace negotiations and to undermine the morale of the North's leadership and population. The same holds true for OIF. The US did not seek to utterly conquer Iraq, which would have been problematic with a view to post-war reconstruction and the minimal troop numbers deployed. Coercing the leadership to give up as early as possible was an important part of the military strategy. Similarly in 1991, destroying *all* Iraqi capabilities in Kuwait and completely interdicting their resupply may have been possible, but the US-led coalition endeavoured to compel early withdrawal from Kuwait none the less. The difference is that the US attempted to coerce North Vietnam mostly via destruction of its military capabilities. Only during OLB II did commanders also embrace the independent 'advantage' accruing from imposing distress on the civilian population. This trend continued during ODS where the weight of the effort further shifted away from capability destruction to a separate effort to pressure the regime directly. The partial emancipation of coercion from the attempt to weaken military capabilities is visible during OIF. Just as all the wars investigated here have a coercive dimension, so they all include the destruction of enemy military capabilities.

The wish to achieve political advantages directly with the use of air power is reminiscent of early air power theory,[118] which, for instance during the Second World War, inspired bombing that is often labelled 'strategic'. For two reasons, however, the change is not adequately described as a shift from so-called tactical to strategic bombing.

[118] Clodfelter (1997).

As far as pre-planned air strikes are concerned, operational objectives rather than tactical considerations presented the most concrete point of reference also during the campaigns against North Vietnam.[119] Second, the literature is inconsistent as to precisely what factor made Second World War bombing strategic: the independent use of air power or the political considerations that guided it.[120] If it is the former, all campaigns contain strategic as well as non-strategic air strikes. If we agreed to use strategic bombing to designate the use of air power directly for political gain we are closer to capturing the observed trends. Yet the term 'strategic bombing' is firmly associated with deliberate large-scale targeting of civilians from the air, for instance via area bombing and 'de-housing' of civilians. In opposition, the trends do not imply direct attacks on what are uncontested civilian objects, such as residential structures, hospitals or schools. To the contrary, the observed change goes hand in hand with an intensified effort to target precisely.

How can we best grasp the change positively? A relative decrease in interdiction, a change in intent behind dual-use targeting and the emergence of targets without immediate relevance to the competition between two militaries – the previous section described the common denominator of these three trajectories of change from 1965 to 2003 as a shortened cognitive roadmap and a lengthened projected causal chain in air targeting. A different way of expressing this is a lowering of the degree of nexus between objects chosen for attack and the competition between two enemy military forces, on the one hand, and a change in the point of reference used for the definition of progress in war towards including political war aims.

A decrease in interdiction missions means that fewer objects with a high degree of nexus to military operations (one causal step) are targeted and missions whose advantageousness is determined with regard to generic military victory are less dominant in combat

---

[119] This is not true for CAS that is called in by troops in contact. I do not count such missions as pre-planned.

[120] Moreover, as mentioned before, the term 'strategic' is used to designate the opportune course of action in military as well as political contexts. I understand the term here to mean politically prudent, which accords with the definition in US doctrinal documents. For a rejection of the notion that 'strategic targets' are a clearly defined category see also van Creveld quoted in Manea (2011).

operations. The changing intent behind the selection of dual-use objects as targets, namely the increased focus on undermining their civilian function, implies that generic military victory is more seldom the reference point for the determination of an object's value as a target of attack. The reference point for the selection of targets without immediate relevance to the competition between two militaries can be assumed to be something other than the goal of generic military victory. The three trends translate into more objects being targeted with a lower degree of nexus to military operations and progress more often being defined with regard to more abstract, more general points of reference.

It should be recalled that the logic of sufficiency[121] envisaged by the API prescribes that winning a war means overcoming an enemy militarily regardless of the ultimate political goal of the war. The point of reference for determining a military advantage is at maximum generic military victory (sequencing). A high degree of nexus between an object and the competition between militaries then determines what is considered a military objective and hence a prima facie legal target (containment). Those military objects are assumed to be sufficient for the achievement of generic military victory and the latter is premised as sufficient for the achievement of ultimate political or other goals behind the use of force. The change can hence be described as a loss in relative importance of the logic of sufficiency.

What takes its place? As section 4.3 outlined in detail, the logic of sufficiency competes with a logic that does not envision the maximal possible containment of warfare. The first command of the logic of efficiency[122] is selecting those targets that most efficiently contribute to victory. The pool of potential military objectives is wider due to the fact that a lower degree of nexus between objects and military operations qualifies objects as such. The pool of potential military objectives may also differ from war to war because the point of reference for the definition of progress is considerably more flexible than under the logic of sufficiency. The logic of efficiency envisions the war's desired political or other end-state as victory. The sequencing of warfare from the pursuit of politics is rejected and containment

---

[121] The logic is defined in the appendix.
[122] Both logics are defined in the appendix.

considerably weakened. The three observed trajectories of change in US targeting practices and the way in which they are connected to the three wars' respective political and military goals mean that over the period investigated we witness a shift in relative importance from the logic of sufficiency to the logic of efficiency in US air warfare.

7 | *The behavioural relevance of international law in US air warfare*

The two previous chapters described an increased subjection of US air warfare to IL and a rise in the relative importance of the logic of efficiency in target selection over the same time. Do these parallel developments suggest that IHL indeed makes a difference for behaviour in war? Based on the findings so far, can I claim that recourse to law has caused the observed change in what the US military considers a legitimate target and chooses to attack from the air?[1] One could interpret such a claim to imply the assertion of a law-like relationship between IL and the logic that combat operations follow: if belligerents comply with IL, warfare accords with the logic of efficiency. Yet the study of only US air warfare is clearly too limited in scope to warrant such a sweeping conclusion.[2] In addition, the finding of section 6.2 is not that warfare follows one logic at first, but abruptly switches to the other the moment IHL is allowed input into decision-making. The change in logics is gradual and in relative importance.

Of course, we can alternatively conceive of causality in probabilistic terms.[3] But the previous chapters alone would not warrant the corresponding conclusion either – that recourse to law in warfare increases the likelihood that the definition of a legitimate target of attack by decision-makers accords with the logic of efficiency, whether that likelihood is small or large in absolute terms. All that the study of US air warfare has so far shown is that a change in the role of law in war, on the one hand, and

---

[1] Understandings of causality differ and exhaustively discussing, or even just reviewing, them would be beyond the scope of this chapter; for insightful treatments of the topic see, among others, George and Bennett (2005); Klotz and Lynch (2007).

[2] In general, this deductive nomological model of causality is considered inapplicable to complex social phenomena, which, beyond the trivial, tend not to be governed by universal laws (Klotz and Lynch (2007) 14).

[3] For an application of a probabilistic understanding of causality to qualitative research in the social sciences see King, Keohane and Verba (1994).

a shift in the logic that combat operations follow, on the other hand, correlate in time. In order to move beyond a mere observation of parallel developments, I need to demonstrate that there is a plausible mechanism by which adherence to IL could have affected US military personnel's definition of a legitimate target in the observed way.

A connection between IL and the selection of objects for attack would have to lie in the decision-making process of commanders and operators on the battlefield.[4] In the following, I investigate this process in order to find out whether recourse to law influences the motivation behind and the intellectual effort involved in selecting targets for air strikes. In addition, I gauge whether the institutionalisation of recourse to law in decision-making systematically changes the way in which targets for air strikes are chosen. I rely on the theory of how IL works developed in Chapter 2, the analysis of the principles of proportionality and distinction undertaken in Chapters 3 and 4, and on interviews with commanders and operators in contemporary US air operations in order to establish whether the legal definition of a legitimate target makes a difference for how decision-makers in US air warfare define a legitimate target of attack.[5]

7.1 How international law works: the intellectual effect

Limited action guidance

Section 2.2 argued that law presents a compromise between immediate situational imperatives (interests) and more abstract systemic considerations (shared normative beliefs) for a particular area of international

---

[4] The method to be used then is process-tracing; see George and Bennett (2005) 147, 224; also Elster (1983) 23f.

[5] I refer to the proverbial 'trigger pullers' who are directly involved in engaging the enemy with force as operators in order to differentiate them from other decision-makers and planners in the targeting process, who are called commanders. I ignore politicians in this section as their influence over target selection has decreased in parallel to the subjection of US air warfare to considerations of IL. Quotations from operators are taken from semi-structured interviews with pilots, navigators and joint terminal attack controllers. In this section, which investigates the workings of law in combat operations, I refer only to ten interviews with operators who conducted missions that were directed from the combined air operations centre in Qatar since the invasion of Iraq in 2003. The numbers given are not meant to be read as quantitative evidence for the argument made. The material is used to illustrate a hypothesis, not to verify it statistically.

relations. Law then stipulates the behaviour an actor has to adopt in order for the outcome of her causal intervention into the world to align with this compromise between utility and appropriateness.[6] In Habermas's words, what specifically characterises law as a code for behaviour is that it 'is not only a symbolic system but an action system as well'.[7] While morality, for instance, usually limits itself to positing certain states of mind as right or wrong or prescribing general imperatives for behaviour, law specifies in detail which behaviour it requires. In general, the law's intellectual effect is that adherence to law makes it easier for a conscientious actor to make sure that right intent (abide by the law) leads to an acceptable outcome.

What is the specific intellectual effect of systematic recourse to the legal definition of a legitimate target in US air warfare? In order to establish that we have to revisit the question of the extent to which the legal definition of a legitimate target of attack guides action in war. What actions do belligerents have to take in order for their behaviour to conform to IHL? Section 3.2 suggested that the principle of distinction enshrined in Article 48 API demands that the intent to attack only military objectives be matched with the action of actually pointing one's weapon at an object that counts as such. That task requires two sorts of information: reliable intelligence regarding the object that is the intended target of attack and clarity about the definition of military objectives. In short, commanders and operators need knowledge of fact and knowledge of law in order to fulfil their obligation to distinguish under IHL.

Article 57(2)a(i) API specifies that the extent to which belligerents are obliged to acquire knowledge of fact during hostilities depends on feasibility; they have to 'do everything feasible to verify' that the object in question is indeed a military objective. Feasibility is context dependent. It is also to some extent a matter of perception. Usually, an important factor guiding an individual in fulfilling such a positive duty of care is an understanding of what would count as a lawful or unlawful outcome. If an actor considers it unfeasible to establish with a certain minimum likelihood that such an outcome will materialise, then it would be unreasonable to act because the duty of care cannot be fulfilled. Crucially, 'outcome' here refers to the status of the object that a weapon is pointed at, not the destruction that an attack causes.

---

[6] See section 2.1.   [7] Habermas (1996) 107.

Article 57(2)a(i) API demands verification that the object *targeted* is a military objective. It does not ask the belligerent to make sure that what is destroyed is actually the identified object.

Is even a complete absence of military objectives in the rubble not indicative of a violation of the principle of distinction? One could argue that Article 57(1) API, the duty to take constant care to spare the civilian population, implies an obligation to take steps to ensure that a weapon once fired also hits the chosen military objective rather than a civilian object. An attacker could, for example, investigate whether it is likely that the military objective will move or be blocked by a civilian object at the time of attack. The question of whether Article 57(1) indeed contains such a requirement of action is not particularly urgent for two reasons. First, many events or circumstances that might account for why an attack fails to hit the targeted military objective are genuinely unforeseeable. For instance, the movement of military objectives that actually can move (such as tanks) is often beyond the control or anticipation of the attacker even if he exercises constant care. Second, belligerents might wish they could target objects other than uncontroversial military objectives, hence the obligation to verify the status of the intended object of attack enshrined in Article 57(2). However, once belligerents have decided to target an object it is a safe assumption that they have an interest in also hitting it. Even without the urging of the law belligerents are therefore likely to pay attention to foreseeable events that might prevent an attack from engaging the intended military objective.[8]

What about knowledge of law? According to Article 83 API all combatants must be trained and aware of their legal obligations before they even deploy. Section 5.1 illustrated that nowadays the US largely complies with this obligation. Does being familiar with IHL mean that an individual knows whether any given object counts as a military objective and may be the target of an attack? The answer is different for positive

---

[8] Unintended, but foreseeable consequences of an attack concern the principle of proportionality. An attack that foreseeably misses its intended target is disproportionate if it therefore fails to yield a military advantage, but may be expected to create any civilian damage. The difficulty is that Article 51(5)b API treats expectations as binary. Either a military advantage is anticipated and collateral damage expected or they are not. The provision does not ask the belligerent to take into account the respective probabilities of their materialising. At what likelihood collateral damage counts as expected is as unclear as the probability at which a military advantage may reasonably be anticipated.

and for customary IL. The definition of military objectives in Article 52(2) interpreted contextually and thus in accordance with the logic of sufficiency[9] is fairly determinate and action guiding: it demands containment and sequencing.[10] Yet the US is not bound by the API; its military and legal doctrines do not acknowledge the strictures of the logic of sufficiency. Whether customary law requires targeting within those strictures cannot be established with any certainty.[11]

Article 52(2) has the status of customary law, but on its own, taken out of the context of the API, it leaves considerable room for interpretation. Section 3.2 demonstrated that the ordinary meaning and the purpose of the customary definition of military objectives (which reflect the wording of Article 52(2) API) do not definitively establish how closely related to combat operations an object has to be in order to be reckoned a military objective. Nor does such an approach set restrictions on the kind of first-order effects that an attack must generate in order to be legal. Given the semantic indeterminacy of the customary rule expressing Article 52(2) an individual faced with the task of choosing an object of attack needs to rely on her own judgement to define 'definite military advantage' and 'effective contribution to military action' and to determine whether they obtain in the case at hand. This in turn complicates decision-makers' task of deciding whether the feasibly attainable knowledge of fact is enough to verify the status of an object.

What about proportionality? Section 3.2 averred that the principle neither asks for attacks to have certain outcomes (consequential indeterminacy) nor guides the individual in how to weigh expected collateral damage and anticipated military progress (purposive indeterminacy). What does compliance with the principle of proportionality look like then? 'No tribunal to date has ever explicitly determined in a well articulated manner that disproportionate damage was caused when assessing an incident in which the disproportionate impact of the attack was not blatant or conspicuous.'[12] In addition, commanders interviewed acknowledged that even militarily trained individuals regularly have diverging opinions about what constitutes proportionate collateral damage.[13] If courts are unable to determine what a legal rule

---

[9] For a definition of the logic of sufficiency see the appendix.
[10] See section 3.4.   [11] See section 4.3.
[12] Fenrick (2004) 177; this state of affairs has not changed since 2004.
[13] Interviews nos. 1, 2, 4, 7, 9, 12, 13, 14, 15, 17.

implies for most situations that an individual will face in war and commanders disagree on more than just very difficult cases, it is safe to assume that most of the time a standard of reasonableness to guide a proportionality calculation eludes the individual attempting to bring her behaviour in line with the law. Many proportionality judgements will therefore amount to one (wo)man's internal and probably subjective musings about human life and military gain – a purely intellectual (rather than behavioural) effort ultimately unguided by law.[14]

But what about the parameters of this exercise in weighing up military gain and human life; can the attacker merely rely on her spontaneous collateral damage estimate or does she have an obligation to acquire a certain level of knowledge about the context of the attack? Surely making an effort to enquire into the projected side effects of an attack in order to form sound expectations is part of the obligation to take constant care to spare the civilian population enshrined in Article 57(1) API.[15] The wording 'may be expected' in Article 51(5)b, contrary to, for instance, 'what the commander expects', likewise suggests that it is the expectations of a reasonably well-informed person that counts. Does this imply that an attacker needs to make an active effort to gather information about the projected side effects of an attack?

The ICTY considers it 'necessary to examine whether a reasonably well-informed person in the circumstances of the actual perpetrator, making reasonable use of the information available to him or her, could have expected excessive civilian casualties to result from the attack'.[16] This interpretation of Article 57(1) does not add up to an obligation to

---

[14] Article 57(2)a(iii) enjoins belligerents to 'refrain from deciding to launch an attack which may be expected to cause [excessive] incidental loss of civilian life'. Article 57(2)b API further stipulates that once under way, 'an attack shall be cancelled or suspended if it becomes apparent that ... the attack may be expected to cause' excessive harm to civilians. The relevant time at which an actor has to evaluate information and make the proportionality assessment is hence not only before the attack, but also during its execution. That does not change the fact that the assessment itself remains subjective.

[15] The question of the implications for actions of Article 57(1) is much more urgent in the context of the principle of proportionality than regarding distinction. After all, belligerents do not necessarily have a natural interest in gathering information for their collateral damage estimate. In addition, many factors determining the likelihood and magnitude of collateral damage are under the control of the attacker, such as angle of attack, choice of weapon, time of attack, etc.

[16] *Prosecutor* v. *Galić*, ICTY, Judgment of the Trial Chamber of 5 December 2003, IT-98-29-T, §58.

actively gather information. Rather the duty of care can be considered fulfilled when the individual combatant pays attention to and does not ignore information that is already available to her. Of course, it is possible that failing to actively glean information about probable collateral damage constitutes a violation of IHL, but only disregard of information already available amounts to a criminal offence.

How far an actor has to go to gather information about the parameters of her proportionality calculus in order not to flout her duty to take constant care under IHL is not spelled out by the law. As mentioned above, in the case of distinction the outcome to be achieved through doing everything feasible is under customary law somewhat indeterminate (to achieve a definite military advantage). In contrast, for proportionality and hence for the attack as a whole, IHL does not ask the individual to look towards the probable outcome of her efforts. Section 3.2 explained that proportionality has to obtain regarding an actor's expectations, not the results of an attack (consequential indeterminacy). The law does not guide or restrict an individual's actions by requiring the specific amount of information that it would take to ensure with reasonable certainty that an attack resulted in a reasonable ratio of civilian casualties to military progress. Of course, as argued above, for most cases no such standard of reasonableness to judge either the results of an attack or for that matter an actor's expectations would be readily available anyway (purposive indeterminacy).

Article 57 contains two more obligations of conduct related to the principle of proportionality. Paragraph 2a(ii) tasks combatants with taking 'all feasible precautions in the choice of means and methods of attack with a view to avoiding, and in any event to minimizing, incidental loss of civilian life, injury to civilians and damage to civilian objects'. Paragraph 3 adds that 'when a choice is possible between several military objectives for obtaining a similar military advantage, the objective to be selected shall be that the attack on which may be expected to cause the least danger to civilian lives and to civilian objects'. In other words, an attack is not legal if an opportunity to further reduce expected collateral damage was missed. These two provisions allude to the condition of necessity that forms part of the proportionality principle in war.[17]

---

[17] See section 3.1, pp. 73f.

The principle of proportionality hence requires an effort in action through, for instance, choice of weapons or angle of attack, to minimise expected collateral damage and an effort to explore alternative targets to see whether they might have a more favourable proportionality calculus. What exactly does this duty of care imply? Does 'when a choice is possible' mean that a belligerent has to actively look for alternative targets or are individuals merely enjoined not to disregard a choice that presents itself during combat operations? Does 'minimizing incidental loss of life' require buying the most precise weapon available at the time? Again, the extent of the requisite effort to avoid civilian casualties depends on feasibility. But no matter how much action to mitigate expected collateral damage is deemed feasible, the question an individual faces is whether, based on the resulting information, she considers her expectations reasonably sound. The length to which she has to go to ascertain the necessity of an attack is not deducible from an understanding of what an adequate outcome of such an effort would look like.

In sum, the legal definition of a legitimate target requires individuals to take the following actions: (1) aim towards a bona fide military objective; (2) acquire some knowledge of fact about the objective to verify its status; (3) seek some information on the likely military advantage and collateral damage of the attack; (4) make an effort to mitigate collateral damage as much as possible; and (5) go some way towards exploring alternative courses of action. While this list is very comprehensive and the standards used (everything feasible and constant care) are extremely high, figuring out what action these obligations imply in any given situation is anything but straightforward. Tasks (1) and (2) are complicated because the compromise outcome an actor is meant to achieve when distinguishing is poorly defined under customary IHL (seek a military advantage). This problem also besets one-half of task (3). In addition, tasks (3), (4) and (5) leave it to the individual to determine which measures to acquire information constitute taking constant care and which actions to reduce collateral damage or verify the status of an object can reasonably be deemed feasible. Crucially, here the pressure to judge for oneself persists, whether an actor applies the customary or the positive definition of a legitimate target of attack.

Of course, all five tasks are much better guided by law than the intellectual task of figuring out whether a certain expected ratio between loss of human life and military gain is proportionate. When adhering to the principle of proportionality, the individual, not the law, determines the outcome that reflects an adequate compromise between immediate situational and more abstract, systemic imperatives. In all but the most extreme cases, no standard of reasonableness guides the belligerent in working out whether the projected outcome of an attack reflects such an acceptable compromise between utility and appropriateness. In war these normative standards frequently diverge, because the former often reflects the demands of military pragmatism and the latter tends to concern the protection of human life. The purposive indeterminacy of positive and customary IHL is not just a problem unto itself: it also means that tasks (3) to (5) cannot be fulfilled with a view to achieving reasonable certainty about whether the outcome of an attack complies with the law.

The focus on right intent

What is the significance of the fact that IHL does not fully live up to an actor's expectation of action guidance but nevertheless purports 'to relieve the individual of the burden to form her own judgements'[18] about whether or not a target can legitimately be attacked? Commanders could react to less than determinate law in two different ways. On the one hand, the combination of a rule coming in the guise of law, but providing insufficient action guidance, could leave a conscientious actor distressed and forced to think beyond the law. Commanders interviewed acknowledged that they did 'not often find answers in a treaty'.[19] They further confirmed that two militarily trained individuals in the same situation might well come to different conclusions regarding whether a given collateral damage estimate meant that an attack was permissible under the principle of proportionality.[20] Yet for the most part they did not voice concern over the law's limited action guidance.[21] On the other hand, confidence that abiding by law is enough in terms of doing the right thing – after all, this is what we expect the law to guarantee – combined with the fact that IHL does not actually prescribe very specific courses of action or outcomes to be achieved, might encourage commanders to simply follow immediate situational imperatives, i.e. their interests.

---

[18] Habermas (1996) 115.   [19] Interview no. 17.
[20] Interviews nos. 1, 2, 4, 7, 9, 12, 13, 14, 15, 17.
[21] *Ibid.*; similar Dunlap (2001b) 17.

Commanders interviewed seemed in good faith to attempt to do justice to their legal obligations. However, they expressed surprise at the notion that law might require them to articulate a military advantage separately from the political, moral or other aims of a war. Certainly the extra action guidance that the positive definition of a legitimate target, incorporating the principle of distinction based on the logic of sufficiency, provides is not brought to bear in US air warfare. In addition, a remarkable absence of a sense of individual responsibility regarding the immediate humanitarian and military consequences of attacks prevailed. A common narrative was that in war one cannot expect to control the consequences of one's decisions in the same way as during peacetime.[22] Doing the right thing means upholding a process that comprises several vetting stages and the systematic involvement of legal experts.[23] IL supports this notion by setting no standard for outcomes. It only requires the right state of mind first and an underspecified effort in action second. Commitment to a legal procedure expresses the former and is assumed to take care of the latter.[24]

While commanders are often far removed from the implications of their choices on the battlefield, operators are closer and do display a concern with the consequences of attacks. Asked what prevented them from just taking the easiest path to military advantage, eight out of ten operators interviewed first mentioned morality, religion, their personal integrity or a combination thereof. These answers often included statements that war is 'hell', 'nasty' and that 'inevitably innocent people get hurt'. Seven out of ten considered it a part of their own professional ethos not to harm civilians wantonly, while five further mentioned that it was specifically part of the American way of waging war to exercise restraint.[25] Only one of them also explicitly mentioned IHL as a source of restraint.

---

[22] Interviews nos. 2, 3, 5, 6, 7, 9, 10, 12, 13, 16.

[23] This process was described in detail in section 5.1.

[24] 'It is no question of personal morality; this is why you have the lawyer' (Interview no. 15). 'There is definitely a division of labour [between the lawyer and the military commander]' (Interview no. 17).

[25] The notion that professionalism in part hinges on adherence to the law appeared to serve as a means of delimitation from the enemy. Iraqi troops and later the insurgents were perceived as unprofessional rogues or even terrorists, who systematically flouted the rules of warfare.

Yet operators' behaviour is informed by law, not just because their actions tend to be approved by a chain of command that is replete with legal expertise. Many operators interviewed said that, rather than thinking of specific legal provisions or definitions, it was training, the rules of engagement, experience and intuition that guided their choices in the distribution of fire power. Of course, training and the rules of engagement are explicitly based on IL. Operators gather experience and form intuitions within an institutional environment that awards pride of place to adherence to law. Yet even though operators also emphasised the importance and comprehensiveness of their *legal* training, as mentioned above, they denied that law played a role in their decision-making. This suggests that learning about IHL does not provoke a conscious commitment on the part of operators to comply with law, for instance because they fear sanctions or come to believe in the legitimacy of IHL. Rather than via an intellectual effect, IL influences operators' behaviour through a subtle process of socialisation and acculturation.[26]

Asked where they would ultimately locate the responsibility for the damage they do with an attack, seven out of the ten operators asserted that it lay with the JAG who cleared the target. Six further mentioned the chain of command, and only three unambiguously assumed the main responsibility for dropping a bomb or mentioned the commander of the air crew as bearing it.[27] The targeting process accounts for the perception that JAGs bear the ultimate responsibility for an attack. Lawyers are extremely visible during the decision-making that leads up to an air strike. All targets are vetted and attacks are cleared before execution. The ability to communicate in real time with the combined air operations centre reduces to a minimum operators' need to make their own decisions.

When asked whether they trust this process to protect their integrity when doing their job, most operators said they did. They stressed that there was no need, and also very limited room, for them to think in terms of military advantage or proportionality when carrying out an air

---

[26] For the concept of acculturation see Goodman and Jinks (2009).

[27] Multiple answers to this question were possible. The salient finding is that operators appear to place more responsibility on the JAGs than commanders. Some fail to appreciate what commanders tend to emphasise: the JAG has merely an advisory role. Interestingly, operators without exception stated that in the case of air strikes called in by troops in contact, the ground commander 'buys the bomb' and assumes full responsibility.

strike. 'I [the pilot] am given a target folder with a collateral damage estimate already done and a suggestion of which weapon to use. I don't know the strategic goal of the campaign.'[28] Even though operators hence perceived the consequences of actions in combat as potentially problematic from a moral point of view, reliance on the legalised procedure considerably eased this concern. Operators demonstrated even more clearly than commanders that recourse to IL encouraged them to be satisfied with their intention to do the right thing if they had abided by the correct legal procedure.

The difference in perception between commanders and operators evokes a phenomenon of diffused responsibility often observed in bureaucratised processes, which has been dubbed 'the problem of many hands'.[29] The higher an actor is in the chain of command, the larger is the gap between her decision and the consequences of warfare, and the lower is therefore her sense of individual responsibility for outcomes. On the other hand, the closer an actor is to those outcomes, the less ability she has to shape decisions. 'Proportionality is out of our hands, all you have is a particular weapon; you drop it anyway.'[30] Commanders affirm that this restriction of operators' freedom of action is intended. 'A pilot is not supposed to question a target unless he has serious doubts. They don't get the big picture. The chain of command prevails over individual judgements.'[31] Even in the absence of institutionalised legal input, a chain of command would create a problem of many hands. However, it is IHL that allows conscientious actors at all levels to assume that being part of this bureaucratised process is enough for doing the right thing, enough to protect their integrity and do justice to their professionalism. Interviews with commanders and operators attested to this conviction. 'I am tasked with a mission and a weapon, someone else has taken legal and moral responsibility for it.'[32]

---

[28] Interview with US Air Force F-18 pilot of the rank of major deployed in OIF, 12 June 2008; not all operators interviewed were at ease with their lack of knowledge. Some said it was 'unnerving to not understand what they [were] up to; having to trust the chain of command'. Interview with US Air Force pilot deployed in OIF of the rank of major, 19 June 2008.

[29] Thompson (1980) 908.

[30] Interview with US Air Force pilot of the rank of major deployed in OIF, 12 June 2008.

[31] Interview no. 9.

[32] Interview with US Air Force F-15 pilot deployed in OIF of the rank of major, 20 June 2008.

In sum, interviews with commanders corroborated the hypothesis developed in Chapter 3: IHL does not provide definitive answers as to the permissibility of any one course of action in war. This is largely due to its semantic and consequential indeterminacy.[33] However, interviews also revealed that US military commanders none the less seek guidance from the law. Unsurprisingly they do so by consulting JAGs rather than by attempting to apply treaties or custom themselves. The salient intellectual effect of recourse to law(yers) is that it makes commanders less likely to determine the permissibility of their actions with a view to the actions' probable immediate consequences. Indeterminate IHL lends its authority to the notion that not safeguarding a certain humanitarian standard in the consequences of attacks is permissible. Even though the idea or narrative that it is enough to try because consequences in war escape control might exist independently of IHL, it is the latter that endows it with legitimacy.

The semantic indeterminacy of the customary principle of distinction and its resulting lack of action guidance mean that the definition of military objectives is wide open to targets being chosen with a view to what decision-makers perceive as in their interests. In the prevailing interpretation of Article 52(2) no particular degree of nexus to the competition between militaries is required and the first-order consequences of an attack can be advantageous with regard to any war goal, whether military, moral or political. The pool of potential military objectives is therefore vast. When choosing military objectives for attack from this pool, commanders reported that they recur to the overall aims of the war rather than to an abstract notion of generic military victory.[34] They bring their prior interests to bear. This natural tendency is promoted by IL because, as mentioned above, the legal definition of a legitimate target encourages decision-makers to look beyond the immediate consequences of their choices and actions and focus on what they mean to achieve in war. This arguably creates a bias in favour of a logic that hinges the legitimacy of targets on the big picture, like the logic of efficiency, rather than on small discrete steps in warfare, like the logic of sufficiency.

---

[33] Treaty law, contrary to customary IHL, in theory at least defines clearly where belligerents are allowed to aim their weapons.

[34] For a definition of generic military victory see the appendix.

The specific intellectual effect of the legal definition of a legitimate target thus seems to diverge from the intellectual effect of recourse to IL theorised in section 2.1. Recourse to IHL does not mean that operators' target selection generally yields a certain compromise outcome between utility and appropriateness. However, taking the indeterminacy of the legal definition of a legitimate target into account, it does work exactly as we would expect it to. After all, neither positive nor customary law prescribes such a specific compromise outcome as far as proportionality is concerned. Customary law, moreover, leaves the acceptable outcome of an effort in distinction underspecified. While semantic indeterminacy makes it possible that targets chosen in line with the logic of efficiency are not deviations from the law, consequential indeterminacy actually promotes the focus on overall political or moral goals in the selection of targets.

7.2 How international law works: the motivational effect

Section 2.1 stated that an actor's intent to apply the law is more clearly expressed in the outcome of action guided by law than is an actor's intent to act appropriately or morally correctly in the outcome of an action not guided by law. This is the justiciability of conduct that IL affords. That IL through justiciability provides a ready measure to assess the outcomes of action means that, other things being equal, following the law is more of an interest – an immediately instrumental course of action – than is acting in a socially appropriate or morally correct way in the absence of law. Besides an intellectual effect recourse to law can thus also have an impact on how actors perceive their reasons for action or motivations in a specific situation. Does recourse to IHL have a motivational effect in US air warfare? In order to answer this question we have to enquire into the extent to which the legal definition of a legitimate target of attack affords justiciability of the conduct of hostilities.

Limited justiciability

US commanders and operators have little reason to fear international criminal jurisprudence given the successful political effort to shield them from its jurisdictional reach. Although the US military's own justice system is a different matter, not every violation of IHL amounts to a war crime and states tend to prosecute their own only for the most egregious offences. First and foremost it is hence the institutional context that explains why nine out of the ten operators interviewed stated that concern for being later found to have broken the law played no role in the determination of their behaviour in combat. Eight of them spontaneously said that they did not know of an example of a legal sanctioning of a fellow airman related to the choice of a target of attack or a faulty proportionality judgement.[35] Commanders likewise stated that the prospect of criminal proceedings was so low that it did not affect their motivation to act one way or another.[36]

However, justiciability is not primarily a matter of court decisions and actual sanctions. A more important way in which IL can change an actor's perception of the motivational imperatives she faces is by providing her and the audience by which she wants her behaviour to be perceived as legitimate with a ready measure to assess her actions and to recognise when they fall short by looking at outcomes. Although they do not directly affect US combatants, the attempts of international adjudicative bodies to establish violations of proportionality and distinction *ex post facto* provide insight into the extent to which IHL offers such a measure.

Can a violation of the principle of proportionality be detected after an attack?[37] The Trial Chamber in the *Galić* case came closest to an actual discussion of what a disproportionate outcome might look like when discussing whether a fifty-fifty distribution of civilian and military

---

[35] Those who did know of an example mentioned the Canadian fratricide case of 2007. A disciplinary action was taken against pilots who had caused the death of friendly forces after firing on a target in spite of the command centre's refusal to clear it.

[36] Interviews nos. 2, 3, 4, 9, 16.

[37] The ICTY's statute contains a prohibition on 'wilfully causing great suffering or serious injury to body or health' of protected persons (*inter alia* civilians) in Article 2(c) and a proscription of causing 'extensive destruction and appropriation of property not justified by military necessity and carried out unlawfully and wantonly' in Article 2(d). These provisions reference Article 147 GC IV, which is sometimes considered a precursor to the principle of proportionality. However, the principle of proportionality arguably permits both the serious injury of civilians and extensive destruction of property, if those are caused in pursuit of a military advantage of enough significance. It follows that neither GC IV nor the ICTY's statute actually contains any reference to the principle of proportionality. Yet the customary standing of the principle of proportionality itself is widely recognised, even by non-parties to the API. Moreover, the case law extensively features the terms 'proportionate' and 'excessive'.

casualties would constitute a violation of the principle of proportionality.[38] It further hypothesised that 'an attack on a crowd of approximately 200 people, including numerous children, would be expected to cause' excessive loss of life.[39] At the end, however, the defendant was found guilty of directing an attack against civilians, which means violating the principle of distinction.

As mentioned above, no indictment for causing expected excessive civilian casualties has yet withstood appeal.[40] If courts are unable to do so, it is unlikely that either the decision-maker himself or his audience will readily recognise defiance of the principle of proportionality by looking at the civilian casualties and the military advantage that an attack produced. Not surprisingly, interviewees across the chain of command displayed a high level of certainty that 'it is nearly impossible to prove disproportionality'.[41] Due to its purposive and consequential indeterminacy the principle of proportionality fails to add to the 'weakly motivating forces of good reasons',[42] such as political or moral appropriateness, for not pursuing military progress without regard to humanitarian implications.

International criminal jurisprudence has been more successful in achieving and upholding indictments for unlawful attack based on violations of the principle of distinction.[43] As mentioned above, the principle of distinction does not require the destruction of specific objects, but the direction of attacks against them. The ICTY has nevertheless based convictions for failing to direct attacks against military

---

[38] *Prosecutor* v. *Galić*, ICTY, Judgment of the Trial Chamber of 5 December 2003, IT-98–29-T, §386.

[39] *Ibid.* §382.

[40] In the *Gotovina* case the Trial Chamber deemed '[f]iring twelve shells of 130 millimetres at Martić's apartment [which was accepted as a military objective] and an unknown number of shells of the same calibre at [another military objective] from a distance of approximately 25 kilometres, created a significant risk of a high number of civilian casualties and injuries, as well as of damage to civilian objects'. The Trial Chamber consider[d] that this risk was excessive in relation to the anticipated military advantage of 'firing' at these two military objectives (*Prosecutor* v. *Gotovina et al.*, ICTY, Judgment of the Trial Chamber of 15 April 2011, IT-06–90-T). The judgment was overturned on appeal. *Prosecutor* v. *Gotovina and Markač*, ICTY, Judgment of the Appeals Chamber of 16 November 2012, IT-06–90-A, §1910.

[41] Interview no. 15; see also Interview no. 16: 'People are not prosecuted because they wrongly apply the law.'

[42] Habermas (1996) 113.   [43] For an overview see Butler (2002); Fenrick (2004).

objectives on the outcome of attacks as a whole. In the *Milošević* case the judges found that 'due to its disproportionate and indiscriminate nature, it [the attack] was unlawfully directed against the civilian population'.[44] The ICTY repeatedly held that 'certain apparently disproportionate attacks may give rise to the inference that civilians were actually the object of attack'.[45] The tribunal also systematically used the duty of care according to Article 57 API to infer from belligerents' actions their intent to comply with or defy the principle of distinction:

[i]n order to determine whether the attack may be said to have been ... directed [against civilians], the following, inter alia, are to be considered: ... the extent to which the attacking force may be said to have complied or attempted to comply with the precautionary requirement of the laws of war.[46]

Does that not mean that the ICTY is after all providing combatants with a standard of reasonableness as to the length they have to go to in order to acquire knowledge of fact and a standard for the outcomes they have to achieve in war? Every application of Article 57 to a specific case indeed clarifies what reasonable people consider 'taking constant care' and 'doing everything feasible' in war. The same is not true for proportionality though. Chambers as well as the prosecution in several cases avoided evaluating behaviour in light of the principle. Even though they relied on proportionality to establish a violation of IL, they did not explicitly discuss how many civilian casualties in a specific context did or did not count as such.[47] In other instances, they denied even the

---

[44] *Prosecutor* v. *Milošević*, ICTY, Judgment of the Appeals Chamber of 12 November 2009, IT-98–29/1-A, §264.

[45] *Prosecutor* v. *Galić*, ICTY, Judgment of the Appeals Chamber of 30 November 2006, IT-98–29-A, §60; *Prosecutor* v. *Martić*, ICTY, Judgment of the Trial Chamber of 12 June 2007, IT-95–11-T, §69.

[46] *Prosecutor* v. *Galić*, ICTY, Judgment of the Appeals Chamber of 30 November 2006, IT-98–29-A, §142; also *Prosecutor* v. *Galić*, ICTY, Judgment of the Trial Chamber of 5 December 2003, IT-98–29-T, §58.

[47] *Prosecutor* v. *Gotovina et al.*, ICTY, Judgment of the Trial Chamber of 15 April 2011, IT-06–90-T, §1910–1911; the Appeals Chamber criticised that the Trial Chamber's finding of a disproportionate attack on the residence of Milan Martić 'was not based on a concrete assessment of comparative military advantage, and did not make any findings on resulting damages or casualties' (*Prosecutor* v. *Gotovina and Markač*, ICTY, Judgment of the Appeals Chamber of 16 November 2012, IT-06–90-A, §82). Judge Agius pointed out that the Appeals Chamber did not attempt to form a standard for foreseeable error or incidental harm either (*Prosecutor* v. *Gotovina and Markač*, ICTY, Dissenting Opinion of Judge Carme Agius of 16 November 2012, IT-06–90-A, §§12–14).

possibility that civilian deaths could have been incidental.[48] Extremely disproportionate outcomes of attacks can hence serve as an indicator that an attacker defied the principle of distinction. What it looks like to defy 'exclusively' the principle of proportionality remains in the dark. None the less it warrants emphasis that the ICTY set a (very low) standard of reasonableness suggesting that 'certain' extreme divergences between civilian casualties and military progress were 'manifestly' disproportionate.

The ICTY case law now offers a number of examples of what illegal attacks (those violating distinction) look like. Yet it is doubtful that combatants and the public therefore also recognise wrong intent and a violation of IL by looking at the outcomes of attacks. The ICTY's reliance on the standard of 'certain apparently disproportionate attacks' when ruling attacks to be in violation of the principle of distinction is properly question begging.[49] Moreover, without detailed investigations into precautions taken or eschewed, adherence to or defiance of the principle of distinction cannot be established with hindsight. To the general public the outcome of an attack guided by law no more or no less reflects the attacker's intent to abide by IHL than the outcome of an attack not guided by law manifests an actor's desire to act morally or in other ways appropriately. To the combatant, whose subjective ideas about proportionality guided the choice of a target in the first place, all that the actual outcome of an attack indicates is whether his expectations and projections were in fact accurate. The consequences of his actions do not provide any new evidence as to whether his efforts to gather knowledge of fact were sufficient. Nor do they settle whether a reasonable observer would consider the attack legal.[50]

---

[48] *Prosecutor* v. *Gotovina et al.*, ICTY, Judgment of the Trial Chamber of 15 April 2011, IT-06–90-T, §1899; *Prosecutor* v. *Popović et al.*, ICTY, Judgment of the Trial Chamber of 10 June 2010, IT-05–88-T, §775; likewise *Prosecutor* v. *Boškoski and Tarčulovski*, ICTY, Judgment of the Appeals Chamber of 19 May 2010, IT-04–82-A; in the appeal the defendant submitted that the Chamber had 'failed to consider what would constitute proportionate behaviour' (§39). However, the prosecution held that the civilian victims were clearly the object of the attack (§42) and the Appeals Chamber concurred (§46).

[49] For these attacks to be in violation of the law one would first have to prove that they actually violated the principle of proportionality.

[50] Unless the results qualify the attack as one of those 'certain manifestly disproportionate' ones, which itself is a rather vague category.

The unlawful attack cases before the ICTY mostly concern the targeting of uncontroversial civilian objects or utterly indiscriminate shelling.[51] After all, not all violations of IHL amount to war crimes and not all war crimes are grave enough to be subject to the jurisdiction of international adjudicative bodies.[52] So only the most egregious crimes even reach the ICTY.[53] The questions of whether an object was relevant enough to the military competition to warrant an attack and what the point of reference was to determine military advantage tend not to be in play. In other words, what would be more subtle violations of Article 52(2) (when it is read in the context of the API), and what may or may not be impermissible attacks under customary law,[54] would be unlikely to be subject to retroactive review even if the jurisdictional reach of international criminal jurisprudence were extended to grasp US military personnel. This means that we cannot rely on the 'judicial branch' of the international legal system to flesh out the correct interpretation of 'effective contribution to

---

[51] The judgments in the *Galić* case contain the most detailed elaborations on the crime of unlawful attack; however, they concern sniping and shelling, not aerial bombardment: *Prosecutor* v. *Galić*, ICTY, Judgment of the Trial Chamber of 5 December 2003, IT-98-29-T; *Prosecutor* v. *Galić*, ICTY, Judgment of the Appeals Chamber of 30 November 2006, IT-98-29-A, §142; also *Prosecutor* v. *Kunarac et al.*, ICTY, Judgment of the Appeals Chamber of 12 June 2002, IT-96-23 and IT-96-23/1-A; *Prosecutor* v. *Blaškić*, ICTY, Judgment of the Appeals Chamber of 24 July 2004, IT-95-14-A; *Prosecutor* v. *Kordić and Čerkez*, ICTY, Judgment of the Appeals Chamber of 17 December 2004, IT-95-14/2-A; *Prosecutor* v. *Milutinović et al.*, ICTY, Judgment of the Trial Chamber of 26 February 2009, IT-05-87-T.

[52] Article 1 ICTY statute confers the power on the tribunal to prosecute only 'serious violations of international humanitarian law'. The Rome Statute of the International Criminal Court of 1 July 2002 is even more explicit that not all violations of the principle of proportionality amount to war crimes. Under IHL all attacks anticipated to yield excessive results constitute a violation of Article 51 (4) API. To the contrary, Article 8(b) iv Rome Statute outlaws '[i]ntentionally launching an attack in the knowledge that such attack will cause incidental loss of life or injury to civilians or damage to civilian objects or widespread, long-term and severe damage to the natural environment which would be *clearly* excessive in relation to the concrete and direct overall military advantage anticipated [italics mine]'. Only attacks that generate *clearly* excessive rather than merely excessive results are criminalised. 'Clearly' does not refer to the possibility of anticipating the harm, but to the extent to which it is out of proportion with the military gain.

[53] Similar SáCouto and Cleary (2008).

[54] To recall, the discussion in section 4.3 proved unable to determine whether the definition of military objectives under customary IHL was constrained by the logic of sufficiency.

military action' and 'definite military advantage' under customary law either. Even if attacking objects with a low degree of nexus to military operations is indeed also illegal under customary law, it is unlikely to be criminal as well. Yet with very few exceptions it is criminal tribunals that interpret IHL or retroactively review behaviour in war.

One such exception is the Eritrea–Ethiopia Claims Commission, established pursuant to an agreement signed between the two states in December 2000.[55] Its award on Eritrea's claim number twenty-five delves into the interpretation of Article 52(2)'s definition of military objectives under customary law.[56] The case concerned the aerial bombardment of the Hirgigo power station in Eritrea. The Commission held that

the fact that the power station was of economic importance to Eritrea is evidence that damage to it, in the circumstances prevailing in late May 2000 when Ethiopia was trying to force Eritrea to agree to end the war, offered a definite advantage … The infliction of economic losses from attacks against military objectives is a lawful means of achieving a definite military advantage, and there can be few military advantages more evident than effective pressure to end an armed conflict.[57]

This directly contradicts the logic of sufficiency, specifically the command of containment, which requires the first-order effect of an attack to be genuinely military if it is meant to be legal and for the object in question to be a military objective. It is telling that the Commission did not qualify the immediate advantage yielded by the attack in question as 'military'. Of course, this arbitration is not enough to establish with certainty that targeting for other than immediate direct military advantage is indeed permissible under customary law. After all arbitration awards bind only the parties to the process. Nor does the Commission's finding necessarily render it easier for a combatant or his audience to infer intent from where a weapon is pointed.

To sum up, international adjudicative bodies with the capacity to investigate the facts and with detailed knowledge of the law can establish violations of the principle of distinction *ex post facto*. For three reasons this is true only for the most egregious violations: first,

---

[55] Agreement between the Government of the Federal Democratic Republic of Ethiopia and the Government of the State of Eritrea, Algiers, 12 December 2000.

[56] Neither Eritrea nor Ethiopia is a party to the API.

[57] Eritrea–Ethiopia Claims Commission (2005) Eritrea's claim no. 25, §121.

the divergence of illegality and criminality; second, the threshold of gravity that most adjudicative bodies observe; and third, the extra semantic indeterminacy of the customary definition of military objectives, which might mean that it is legal after all to attack objects with only an indirect or remote connection to military operations. Due to purposive indeterminacy, violations of 'exclusively' the principle of proportionality escape legal review even by proper courts and tribunals. To the military as well as the untrained observer the outcome of an attack in contemporary US air warfare is no more or less reflective of the attacker's intent than such an outcome would be if IHL were not available either to guide or to assess action in war. The purposive and semantic indeterminacy of the legal definition of a legitimate target (customary and positive) accounts for the extremely limited justiciability it affords.

The instrumental as the legitimate target

What about the motivational effect of the legal definition of a legitimate target then? Section 2.2 hypothesised that a lack of justiciability would weaken actors' motivation to recur to law, as 'doing the wrong thing' is not specifically visible in outcomes. However, the combination of a lack of justiciability with limited action guidance creates different incentives. The fact that IHL readily offers the label of legality while restricting belligerents' freedom of action only to a limited extent makes law an extremely attractive source of legitimacy. Indeed, IHL comes in the guise of law, which means that adherence may well be deemed sufficient for acting appropriately. Yet it creates very limited possibilities of being found in violation. IHL allows following the immediate requirements of the situation – interests or instrumental considerations – without being seen or perceiving oneself as neglecting more abstract systemic considerations. After all, the law bends to endorse many such interest-guided courses of action.

Commanders interviewed often emphasised the importance and indeed proximity of the JAG in military decision-making. Asked why they kept the JAG close, they stressed that it was a political or strategic necessity that the US wages war legally, if not legalistically. The term 'lawfare', coined by General Dunlap, aptly expresses the notion that legality is the inevitable normative framework for the assessment of conduct in war and that, for the sake of the support of public opinion, achieving victory legally is absolutely crucial.[58] '[M]ilitaries must adhere to the law of war – or at least create the perception of doing so – in order to preserve public and political support.'[59] The notion that involving legal expertise is an immediately pressing imperative guarantees recourse to law at least during the visible part of military operations. However, that the interest behind compliance is, first, availing the US conduct in war of IL's endorsement and, second, figuring out how to act, means that the indeterminacy of IHL is mostly appreciated rather than perceived as a problem.

The notion that IL is an 'easy' source of legitimacy rather than primarily a guide for action also influences the way in which IHL is brought to bear: 'You never ask a lawyer "can I?" you say what you want to do and ask for a way to do so legally.'[60] In turn, some JAGs see their role less as that of adjudicator and more as an advocate. They describe the US military as their 'client' whom the JAG enables to 'go about his business legally'.[61] An expectation and appreciation of indeterminacy also prevails in the interaction of JAGs with other military personnel. During target development for the invasion of 2003 intelligence analysts would resubmit a rejected target with a different label or under a new denomination if it was previously disqualified as a military objective.[62] This is not to suggest that these are somehow wrongful or sinister instances of professional conduct. In the absence of systematic enforcement IL relies for compliance on its convergence with interests. Presenting law as a 'useful tool in the commander's toolbox' is therefore an important task of the JAG.[63] However, that indeterminacy is appreciated means that the legal definition of a legitimate target is stretched to the maximum to endorse interest-guided targeting choices.

In conclusion, input of the legal definition of a legitimate target of attack into decision-making in air warfare influences the intellectual process and motivations involved in selecting targets in three ways. They each diverge from the theorised ideal in section 2.1. In line with the theory's predictions the divergence is explained by the law's threefold indeterminacy.

---

[58] See Dunlap (2008). [59] Canestaro (2004) 470. [60] Interview no. 1.
[61] Interview no. 8; also Interview no. 11: 'When you are a lawyer, you have to know the client's business; modern warfare is exceedingly complicated.' Also Interview no. 13: 'Our client is the institution, not an individual; the client deserves our best legal advice.'
[62] Interview no. 15. [63] Interview no. 17.

First, recourse to the principle of proportionality reinforces the notion that right intent and an unspecified effort in action are sufficient for acting rightly given IL's consequential indeterminacy. Both intent and action to do justice to proportionality are seen to be covered by the institutional involvement of lawyers in targeting decisions. The first intellectual effect of recourse to IHL in US air warfare is hence a focus on intentions – what one wants to achieve with the use of force – and a relative lack of attention paid to the immediate consequences of attacks. This creates a bias against the logic of sufficiency whose first imperative is that all attacks immediately achieve a genuinely military advantage.

Second, ideally the action guidance that law affords would make it easier for a conscientious actor to find a course of action that leads to an outcome that reflects a compromise between utility and appropriateness as enshrined in the law. Distinction is tied to the notion of achieving a military advantage, which in customary law is indeterminate. This means that actors have space to recur to their interests. Those tend to be derived from their goals in war when selecting targets for attack. Achieving those goals is much more immediately pressing than the abstract concept of a generic military victory that safeguards the equality of belligerents and upholds the distinction between *jus in bello* and *jus ad bellum*. The focus on overall – often political – goals in the choice of targets is the second intellectual effect specifically of the customary principle of distinction.

Third, the justiciability that IL affords is meant to provide that the instrumental course of action, the one that an actor perceives as in his immediate interest, is a course of action that leads to a compromise between interests (utility) and normative beliefs (appropriateness) as enshrined in the law. Yet the legal definition of a legitimate target of attack largely allows an actor simply to follow his interests and perceive this course of action as reflecting the compromise between utility and appropriateness endorsed by IHL. This is due to the law's purposive indeterminacy. This is the motivational effect of recourse to the indeterminate definition of a legitimate target of attack in both custom and treaty law: pursuit of utility is legitimated.

Are belligerents really free not to compromise at all? Or in other words, does this high degree of indeterminacy mean that IHL just endorses whatever the US is interested in targeting anyway? No, even the indeterminate legal definition of a legitimate target circumscribes somewhat what can count as a legitimate target. The previous chapters indicate that it does so in two ways. First, though IHL does not pos-itively specify the outcome to be achieved with an attack, the legal definition of a legitimate target of attack affords just enough justiciabil-ity to obviate the most extremely disproportionate outcomes as beyond the law. Although this does not quite add up to a standard of reason-ableness, in the sense of a yardstick applicable by most people to most cases, it means at least that there is no guarantee that an outcome in war will never be indicative of a violation of IL.

Second, while the legal definition of a legitimate target in treaty and custom does not very closely guide an individual's efforts by positively specifying how much is feasible, *not* taking any action to verify the status of an object and the necessity of an attack clearly constitutes a defiance of the law. In the words of the ICTY: belligerents are not permitted to act 'on the mere belief, unsupported by good evidence, that an object ... [is] a legitimate military objective'.[64] The process described in section 5.1 reflects many of the demands of Article 57 and the customary obligation to take precautions in attack. Even highly indeterminate IHL still resists interpretation on behalf of some instru-mental courses of action.

Treaty law properly applied – according to the argument presented in section 3.4 – would guide actors' efforts to distinguish between civilian objects and military objectives. However, the US technically applies customary law, and US military practices certainly feature air strikes that yield a genuinely military advantage only after more than one causal step. Here the semantic indeterminacy of customary law creates an opening for targeting according to belligerents' interests, which are naturally tied to the end-state sought with the use of force.

Yet even during OIF the air campaign did not comprise attacks separated by more than three causal steps from a genuine decrease in the enemy's military effectiveness.[65] This is true even though target selection was guided by the perceived imperative to connect air strikes to the political goals of regime change. The US, for instance, refrained from attacking symbolic and religious sites even though they might have weakened Iraqi morale more efficiently than undermining government propaganda by attacking media installations. Nor did the US target all

[64] *Prosecutor* v. *Galić*, ICTY, Prosecution Pre-trial Brief of 30 November 2001, IT-98–29-PT, §176.
[65] For examples see section 3.2.

categories of objects suggested by the doctrine of shock and awe, prominent US leaders' perception of the doctrine as both useful and appropriate notwithstanding.

In fact, a much more radical version of the logic of efficiency is imaginable: one that defies the principle of distinction as such and makes all parts of a belligerent society fair game.[66] If efficiency is the interest, the dominant, immediate situational imperative, why do US military decision-makers not go all out and select exactly those targets that promise the swiftest political victory? Is the restraining force of IHL at work here? After all, the customary definition of a legitimate target is in part promulgated. The absolute prohibition on targeting civilian objects and the notion that an attack has to achieve a *military* advantage at some point are not up for debate as they are unequivocally expressed in provisions of the API that are without a doubt recognised as of customary standing. Of course, the US might have other reasons to stick to a 'moderate' version of the logic of efficiency which expands the definition of military objectives within the penumbra of uncertainty of customary law, but respects absolute prohibitions. We need to take into account other influences and constraints on target selection in order to answer the question of why US military decision-makers limit themselves to the moderate version of the logic of efficiency. Why do they apparently perceive outright challenges to the principle of distinction as inappropriate even if those offer the most efficient path to political victory?

This chapter leaves another question open. Recourse to IHL inspires a focus on the overall goals of a war when defining progress in combat operations. But why do US decision-makers also put such an emphasis on achieving those goals as directly and quickly as possible? Endeavouring to achieve one's aims efficiently rather than inefficiently is simply rational and does not require further explanation. However, efficiency in war could mean different things, for instance, choosing the cheapest means available to get to the desired end-state or minimising collateral damage over political victory. The specific command that is part of the logic of efficiency is to attain the ultimate goals of a war as quickly and directly as possible, with the fewest air strikes possible. Neither simple rationality nor recourse to indeterminate IHL explains why that is the case.

---

[66] See the appendix for a succinct definition of both the moderate and the radical version of the logic of efficiency.

7.3 Other factors that influence which logic warfare follows

A focus on intent, a disregard for immediate consequences and the opportunity to consider many instrumental courses of action as also legitimate – the identified intellectual and motivational effects of recourse to indeterminate IHL – account for why decision-makers recur to their overall goals rather than to an abstract notion of generic military victory[67] when choosing targets. Recourse to the principle of proportionality leaves the point of reference for the definition of progress in war open to be filled with a belligerent's utilities. However, these effects of recourse to IL do not explain why the US uses the latitude afforded by indeterminate law to wage war efficiently in the specific way prescribed by the logic, meaning as quickly and with the fewest air strikes possible. Nor do we know why the US weakens the constraining force of the principle of distinction, but does not question it as such.[68] The exact logic that US air warfare follows requires further explanation.

The role of military technology and doctrine

Two important parameters for the conduct of hostilities change across the three historical cases examined in the previous two chapters. The technology used during combat operations progresses and the dominant military doctrine informing the conduct of hostilities varies over the period under investigation. I will ask two questions to gauge the potential role of military technology and doctrine respectively in determining the logic that combat operations follow. First, is the change that military technology and doctrine have respectively undergone linear and parallel to the gradual shift in the logic that US air warfare follows, as is the case with the increase in recourse to law? Second, is there a plausible mechanism by which the specific developments in technology and doctrine could have contributed to a higher number of air strikes following the logic of efficiency?[69]

---

[67] For a definition of generic military victory see the appendix.

[68] The appendix contains definitions of the moderate and the radical version of the logic of efficiency.

[69] For the purposes of the argument it is sufficient to identify the major trajectories of change in technology and doctrine. It would be beyond the scope of this chapter to exhaustively discuss in depth their respective developments. Several excellent accounts already exist; see Beier (2003); Biddle (2004); Clodfelter (2009); Davis (2003); Kagan (2006) 24ff.; Lambeth (1993).

Over the period investigated, the most pertinent change in military technology is the steady increase in the availability of precision-guided munitions.[70] They were first introduced into air warfare towards the end of the US engagement in North Vietnam, increasing the effectiveness and efficiency of air strikes in a few remarkable instances. The most notorious case is the Bien Hoa Bridge. Air strikes failed to completely destroy it in spite of numerous attempts until one well-placed attack with precision munitions brought it down. Yet the overall role of precision-guided munitions during the air campaigns against the Democratic Republic of Vietnam was marginal. Satellite-guided joint direct attack munitions made a noted appearance only during ODS. According to different estimates between 7 per cent and 10 per cent of all munitions dispensed from the air were precision guided in 1991.[71] In OIF this number rose to over 68 per cent.[72]

The gradual improvement in the precision of air strikes was accompanied by innovations in technology used for military command, control and communication (C3) as well as for and intelligence, surveillance and reconnaissance (ISR). As a result of improved C3 capabilities the so-called sensor to shooter cycle, the time between the identification of an object as a target and its engagement, shortened significantly over the period under investigation.[73] Timely and more reliable ISR meant that the US had better information about intended targets of attack. The first challenge in any attempt to engage, for instance, specific military leaders, military transport, camouflaged command posts or underground military bunkers is figuring out where exactly they are. While the likelihood that a bomb destroys what it is aimed at depends on precision, the likelihood that air strikes are aimed at the correct place in the first place depends on intelligence. Over the period under investigation gradual improvements in C3 and ISR capabilities hence heightened the chances that air strikes were aimed at what they were actually meant to engage.[74]

---

[70] For an account of the role of military technology during the war against Vietnam see Anderegg (2001); Kagan (2006) 24ff.

[71] Young (2009) 169; Zehfuss (2011) 559; Young holds that 40 per cent of the smart bombs nevertheless missed their targets. For a sceptical view on the import and effectiveness of precision-guided munitions in ODS see Lambeth (1993) 15ff.

[72] Conetta (2002) section 2; Human Rights Watch (2003) 16; Kahl (2007) 21; Wheeler (2004) 212; Wrage (2003) 27.

[73] Shimko (2010) 163, 215.

[74] I neglect to discuss the role of cyber warfare here. For an account of the role it played in 2003 see Arquilla (2012).

Even this very brief overview brings a twofold linear development in technological capabilities to the fore, which correlates in time with the shift from sufficiency to efficiency. Is there a plausible connection specifically between the ability to destroy military objects with increased precision and target selection with a view to efficiency? Did the ability to better and more quickly locate, identify and engage objects that form part of an enemy's society encourage belligerents to more often choose objects for attack that only indirectly contributed to the competition between enemy militaries, but whose engagement yielded a political or psychological advantage?

It is intuitively compelling that a focus on the direct achievement of political goals through air strikes should have gone hand in hand with the development of precision-guided munitions and improvements in intelligence gathering. After all, for the logic of efficiency to be implemented belligerents require the ability to target and also hit with some likelihood those structures that are identified as producing the desired political effects.[75] Targeting in line with the logic of efficiency would have hardly been possible without the advances military technology made between 1965 and the 1990s.[76] However, the same can be said for the logic of sufficiency. During the US engagement of North Vietnam the logic of sufficiency guided what the US *meant* to attack, not what air strikes actually destroyed. The great humanitarian calamities the air war caused, in spite of a general attempt to attack military targets, attest to the fact that air strikes did not often destroy (only) what they were meant to engage.[77] In other words, precision and C3/ISR capabilities are beneficial to the demands of both logics.

---

[75] Schaffer provides a detailed account of how during the Second World War parties on all sides attempted to bomb strategic targets and terrorise the civilian population in order to achieve quicker military progress. He demurs that at the time it 'was hard to locate a target area smaller than a city, and sometimes even that was too difficult'. As a result British long-range attacks on Germany were no more effective or efficient than German raids on Britain (Schaffer (2009) 34f.).

[76] Retired Lieutenant General Deptula emphasised that even during ODS technological capabilities and intelligence resources were the limiting factor in implementing EBOs (Interview no. 10).

[77] An estimated 52,000 North Vietnamese civilians and combatants died during ORT alone (Lawrence (2008) 99). Of course, in the South, where the US made virtually no effort to spare civilians, the effects of air power were even more devastating. For a chilling account see Sheehan (1988) 112.

Does the logic of efficiency not depend on modern technology to a greater degree than the logic of sufficiency? After all, the ability to precisely 'dose' the kinetic impact of a weapon is specifically important when air power is used to achieve political goals that depend on a reaction of the enemy belligerent. Moreover, if one cares about the second guiding principle of targeting, proportionality, less precision is required to destroy fielded forces than dual-use facilities or media installations which tend to be tucked away in or near population centres. In particular, leadership targeting, which epitomises warfare according to the logic of efficiency, chiefly depends on precision and on extremely timely and accurate intelligence. Even *with* modern technology, decapitation strikes during OIF produced no military advantage, only collateral damage.[78] Targeting according to the logic of efficiency without the requisite intelligence and precision capabilities is hence highly inefficient.[79]

On the other hand, if one does *not* accord priority to avoiding collateral damage, the reverse is true. Pape argues that 'advances in military technology have improved the effectiveness of [air strikes] ... against an opponent's military more than ... against an enemy's political and economic centres'.[80] The reason he gives is that civilian and dual-use objects are less fortified and more easily neutralised even if they are not directly hit. In contrast, hard targets such as missile silos or military bunkers need to be struck at specific points of impact in order to be affected. By the same token, many traditional military targets are purposely hidden, while dual-use objects and non-traditional targets whose engagement undermines civilian morale are often in plain sight. In this reading, precise information afforded by C3 and ISR capabilities is more vital to targeting according to the logic of sufficiency. Attrition of enemy military capabilities without precision-guided munitions and high levels of accurate intelligence might simply never be sufficient.

However, if we assume that causing collateral damage clashes with widely shared normative beliefs, then modern technology made targeting according to the logic of efficiency possible in a different way from the way in which it made it possible for air strikes to reflect the logic of

---

[78] Similar Zehfuss (2011) 549.

[79] See McChrystal (2011) for the argument that even in 2003 due to limited technological capacities 'information [that was] captured could not be exploited, analysed, or reacted to quickly enough – giving enemy targets time to flee'.

[80] Pape (1996) 213f.

sufficiency. Modern technology also made waging war in line with the logic of efficiency acceptable at all. Air strikes with Vietnam-era dumb bombs on privately owned media facilities, individual leaders hiding in downtown Baghdad, or electrical power plants would have been prime candidates to count as manifestly disproportionate attacks.[81] If anyone who cared about the infliction of civilian harm were watching, such attacks would have been prohibitively costly without precision-guided munitions and accurate intelligence.

In sum, before the invention and widespread use of smart weapons and modern information technology, both logics would have determined only what belligerents meant to attack, not what was actually hit.[82] The developments in military technology described made it possible to implement both logics in that the reasoning behind target selection would actually be reflected in the pattern of destruction caused by air strikes. The shrinking of the circular error probable afforded by modern technology brings this into sharp relief: since the Second World War the 'area at risk around the target has been reduced by a factor of 10,000 [italics omitted]'.[83] It is only in combination with another variable – the unacceptability of collateral damage – that modern technology is more important to the logic of efficiency than to its counterpart.[84]

What about military doctrine? As section 6.1 described, during the bombing of North Vietnam progress was measured in military objects destroyed and combatants killed. The doctrine of EBOs, which prescribes more complex measures for mission success, emerged only in the early 1990s. Though it left a mark on ODS, official military doctrine started to systematically recommend effects-based targeting only towards the end of the decade. ODS was furthermore informed by John Warden's influential book *The Air Campaign*, in which he argued that the enemy's military apparatus is the least promising kind of target. During OIF targeting was systematically effects based. In addition, the doctrine of shock and awe influenced decision-making. While it was conceived already in 1996, OIF was its moment of prominence. Shock and awe goes further in its focus on psychological effects and in

---

[81] In fact, decapitation attacks launched during OIF turned out to be manifestly disproportionate, precision munitions notwithstanding.

[82] Similar Thomas (2001) 89.   [83] Stone (2007) 140; Zehfuss (2011) 550.

[84] I will return to public attitudes about civilian casualties and their role in shaping combat operations in Chapter 8.

eschewing the destruction of military capabilities than either Warden's ideas or EBOs. Overall, doctrines that advocate the direct achievement of political goals with force and therefore the engagement of objects with a lower degree of nexus to the competition between enemy militaries, thus gained in prominence and became more radical from 1965 to 2003. In the period under investigation, doctrinal ideas that point in the same direction as the logic of efficiency came to the fore.

Is the logic of efficiency not itself simply a military doctrine? No. The logic of efficiency is a pattern of target selection observed in reality which is indicative of the reasoning behind the use of air power, a specific way of attempting to accommodate military and humanitarian imperatives in war. The definition of a legitimate target of attack in US air warfare is evidently influenced and informed by military doctrines. However, for two reasons the logic of efficiency, its manifestation in reality, is not the same as a military doctrine. First, it is imaginable that the logic of efficiency would have gained in importance without any of the above military doctrines coming to prominence at the same time. Though that is unlikely, military commanders may well ignore military doctrine and choose targets based on other considerations. In that case the observed targeting pattern that I designate as following a logic of efficiency would require an explanation other than doctrinal prescriptions. If we can imagine the existence of one phenomenon in the absence of another, they are certainly different, not the same.

Second, while there are dominant currents, it is never only one doctrine that influences military decision-makers at any given point in time. The reasoning manifest in the choice of targets that I refer to as the logic of efficiency unites ideas from different military doctrines. After all, EBOs, Warden's ideas, and shock and awe differ among themselves. Warden simply rejects the engagement of fielded forces as always the least efficient means to victory. EBOs, on the other hand, focus on whichever objects in the specific situation at hand promise the desired effects with a view to the intended end-state of a war. That end-state is often, but does not always have to be, political. While EBOs are primarily geared towards eliciting a reaction from the enemy leadership and influencing the adversary's 'system', the singular focus on and audience of shock and awe is the enemy's population. Just as these three concepts diverge, none is fully congruent with the logic of efficiency. The latter expresses their common denominator at a more abstract level: the overall goal of a war is the point of reference for the conception of progress, and military operations are not restricted to objects with a first-order connection to the competition between enemy militaries. Those targets are to be selected that promise the achievements of overall goals as quickly and directly as possible. Even though the logic of efficiency is therefore not a military doctrine itself, there seems to be a plausible connection between the development of military doctrine and the rise of the logic of efficiency.

Do changes in doctrine, then, explain changes in targeting? In section 4.2 the emergence of EBOs and shock and awe was taken to be an indicator of changing US practices that were later summarised as an increased relative importance of the logic of efficiency. Indeed, many military strategists describe doctrine as 'evolv[ing] from experience and from analysis of the continuing impact of new developments'.[85] In this view, military doctrine, rather than shaping the reality of warfare, is an outgrowth of changed geopolitical contexts or technological progress: military planners take account of emerging constraints on waging war and explore previously unavailable avenues to get to victory. In other words, the growing prominence of military doctrines that advocate efficiency is indicative of the emergence of a perceived interest in waging war efficiently. Of course, there is no reason to assume that doctrinal ideas are not also conceived at a theoretical level, as it were 'ahead of time', before new capabilities and constraints become evident.[86] In this case military doctrine does at least contribute to explaining where that imperative of efficiency in US air warfare comes from.

Whether and when specific doctrinal currents become the dominant framework for warfare certainly in part depends on the extent to which they respond to the demands of a changing reality. After all, EBOs and shock and awe are variations on earlier military doctrines that were under different guises en vogue before; section 4.2 mentioned strategic attack. Michael Sherry emphasises it is 'one of the oldest temptations of air power ... to regard it as serving less the needs of battle than the

---

[85] Worden (1998) 151; also Biddle (2004) 133, 206; Cooper (1997); Hallion (1997/98); Kagan (2006) 66; Sherry (1987) 358.

[86] Sherry holds that '[m]ore than any other modern weapon the bomber was imagined before it was invented' (Sherry (1987) 1). Similarly, Gray argues that for war in general 'practice le[ads] theory' (Gray (1999) 229). However the 'one environment ... for which theorists have been ... overprepared has been the air' (ibid., 230); similar Kagan (2006) 126.

opportunity to avoid it',[87] an imperative that is at the heart of *The Air Campaign*, EBOs as well as shock and awe. Indeed air commanders consider the belief that every allocation of force, every air strike, can immediately and directly achieve political effects to be 'the shibboleth of air power'.[88] This idea guided significant portions of air targeting on both sides during the First and Second World Wars.[89] Yet after the World Wars, doctrines advocating targeting directly for political effect re-emerged only in the 1980s and became dominant again in the 1990s.[90] As outlined above, they grew more radical in the quest for efficiency towards the end of this decade. This suggests that while currents in doctrinal thinking can influence actual air targeting, they certainly also respond to developing circumstances and changed perceived interests.

To sum up, the improvements in the precision of weapons and information technology for intelligence gathering and the re-emergence of doctrines that more and more explicitly advocate a focus on the direct achievement of political goals with air strikes correlate in time with the change in the logic US air warfare followed. Moreover, the developments in technology and doctrine, like the increased importance of IL described earlier, have plausible connections to the relative rise of targeting according to the logic of efficiency. Technology makes it possible, doctrine frames it as instrumental, and law endorses it as also appropriate.

Yet none of the three variables alone straightforwardly explains the relative rise of the logic of efficiency. Just as technology would have, and in fact did, also improve belligerents' ability to implement the logic of sufficiency,[91] other doctrines that would have endorsed other

---

[87] Sherry (1987) 358; likewise Canestaro (2004) 467; Gray (1999) 241; Lambeth (2000) 50; Sherry (2009) 185.

[88] Interviews nos. 10, 11.

[89] See Clodfelter (2008); Clodfelter (2009); Sherry (2009)176. The idea of circumventing the enemy's military forces and decapitating the adversary by exploiting a society's vulnerabilities emerged as early as 1918 in the guise of a theory of tank warfare (Kagan (2006) 106). German military doctrine between 1917 and 1945 likewise aspired to waging war in this way (*ibid.* 205).

[90] Kagan (2006) 112.

[91] After the war in Vietnam the Air Force developed the A-10, an airplane designed specifically to better support troops on the ground and conduct 'tactical missions' such as the destruction of individual tanks (Kagan (2006) 58f.). This suggests that technological developments often follow developments in the character of warfare.

logics might well have become prominent. Doctrine, like technological developments, to a certain extent follows the logic that warfare accords with rather than initiating it. By the same token, sections 7.1 and 7.2 showed why law encourages a focus on overall political goals and why customary law is indeterminate enough to endorse many targets prescribed by the logic of efficiency. It did not explain why the law is used to sanction targeting that aims to end the war with the fewest possible air strikes and as quickly as feasible. We still require an answer to the question of where this perceived interest in getting war over with quickly comes from.

The role of material and ideational change

What about larger changes in the international system over the period of interest? Did they influence what US decision-makers perceived as the instrumental and/or appropriate way to wage war? Across the three cases the most salient change in material circumstances is a rise in the preponderance of US military power and therefore superiority over its enemies. All three wars under investigation are fundamentally asymmetrical in that they were interventions by the US into the territory of another state, without involvement of or immediate danger to the US homeland.[92] While this was already true for the war in Vietnam, the US then had to fear the intervention of a peer competitor on behalf of the radically inferior enemy. Section 6.1 discussed the extent to which the desire to prevent a direct engagement of China or the Soviet Union affected the selection of targets in North Vietnam.[93] Iraq, on the other hand, had neither in 1991 nor in 2003 a powerful ally likely to intervene on its behalf. In general, US military superiority increased with the end of bipolarity.

---

[92] This does of course not mean that the claim of a threat to the US homeland, for instance, by weapons of mass destruction in 2003, was not drawn upon to raise the acceptability of the use of force. The point is that the conduct of hostilities never came close to actually spreading to US territory. Neither North Vietnam nor Iraq ever attempted to attack the Pentagon or other military installations on US territory, even though those were arguably legitimate targets of attack during the air war against North Vietnam and OIF respectively. The danger of retaliatory terrorist attacks, which is putatively raised during US involvements abroad, bears heavily on measures of homeland security, but not directly on the US conduct of wars abroad.

[93] See also Young (2009)162.

Since then the US has experienced a 'sequence of lopsided successes'[94] over its opponents. No other country now matches it in terms of resources devoted to intelligence gathering and military capabilities.[95] 'With twelve aircraft carriers and their accompanying task forces ranging the world's oceans, the only significant heavy airlift capacity and the only major stocks of precision-guided missiles and bombs, the US can defeat any opponent with only minimal losses.'[96] The 1991 Gulf War immediately became a paradigm case for easy military victory. Steven Biddle calculated that taking into account desertions and lack of weapons on the Iraqi side, the force on force ratio between the US and Iraq 'approached or exceeded 2:1 in combat manoeuvre strength and probably approached 3:1 in total personnel'.[97] While the US did not necessarily become more powerful between ODS and OIF, as outlined above, the technology at its disposal was even more advanced twelve years later.[98] In addition, Iraq's military strength arguably declined.[99] In 2003, the US conducted a full-fledged, militarily successful invasion with a rather light footprint in less than two months. A linear increase in asymmetry thus characterises the three wars investigated.

Asymmetry is particularly pronounced in air warfare. The war against Vietnam was the last in which the US encountered air to air combat. In the campaigns against Iraq the US not only prevented Iraqi planes from even taking off, it also rapidly neutralised enemy air defences and thus achieved uncontested air supremacy.[100] Such unilateral control of an important part of the battle space constitutes a

---

[94] Cohen (2004) 404.

[95] Jackson (2010) 242; also O'Hanlon (2009); Reus-Smit (2004c).

[96] Byers (2005) 150.

[97] On the gap in military capabilities between the US and Iraq in 1991 see Biddle (2004) 135f. Biddle also emphasises the role of better training, morale and superior strategy on the US side in keeping US casualties low and making victory quick (*ibid.* 147).

[98] *Ibid.* 201.

[99] The international sanctions regime stripped the Iraqi military of resources. (Kagan (2006) 330). As the country became ever poorer through the 1990s Saddam Hussein increasingly feared challenges from within. To prevent a coup supported by the military, most of the time only the Feddajin were allowed to train with life munitions (Atkinson (1993) 212, 448).

[100] Air supremacy is defined as '[t]hat degree of dominance in the air and space battle of one force over another which permits the conduct of operations by the former and its related land, sea, air and space forces at a given time and place without prohibitive interference by the opposing force' (US Department of Defense (2007e/2011) 40).

different kind of inequality between belligerents from the mere discrepancies in resources, technology and strategy which characterise virtually every war. Not least because of this guaranteed advantage the US has, over the course of the period of interest, come to increasingly rely on air power.[101] '[I]t is the distinctively American form of military intimidation.'[102]

What does asymmetry mean for how a war is fought? In combat operations conducted from a radically superior position the intervening party has a broader range of choices in the distribution of fire power. Freedom of action is particularly extensive in military operations from the air, not only because it is the part of the battlespace in which the US can count on reigning supreme. Compared to ground troops, air forces also literally have more room for manoeuvre. Attacks from this particular vantage point are therefore conducive to adaptation even while already in execution. Moreover, in distinction from an infantryman under fire, an airman even when threatened from the ground has the distance to weigh different courses of action and often even the option to entirely withdraw from immediate danger. Whatever is sought to accomplish with a pre-planned air strike, there are probably several ways of doing so.

Not unlike the rise in precision-guided munitions discussed above, these increased possibilities due to asymmetry could have been used to render targeting according to the logic of efficiency more efficient, just as they could have served to ensure the sufficiency of air strikes following the logic of sufficiency. Freedom of action makes possible, but does not necessarily lead to, the adoption of one particular logic of targeting.

It is noteworthy that more choice in the conduct of hostilities and better control of the battlespace due to asymmetry also create room for the consideration of legal obligations. The more different paths to a military advantage are militarily feasible, the higher the likelihood that one of them is also legal. By the same token, a radically superior belligerent may be more inclined to forgo the occasional military advantage in order to do justice to the law. However, asymmetry does not seem to be sufficient to explain increased recourse to IHL in US combat operations, it merely creates an opening for compliance.

---

[101] Belkin *et al.* (2002); Hosmer (2001).
[102] Cohen (1994) 3; also Clodfelter (2008).

Preponderance of US military power not only lowers the urgency of particular courses of action *during* war. On a very general level it is also true that the more powerful a state is the less likely is it that any given conflict becomes a matter of survival. From the perspective of Iraq the US interventions were wars of regime survival: that the Baath Party government was not threatened in 1991 became a certainty for the Iraqi government only in retrospect. From the point of view of the US and the coalitions it led, on the contrary, all three cases appear to have been wars of choice rather than of necessity or survival. Did the US resorts to force against North Vietnam and Iraq equally 'lack urgency'?

The Cold War made the use of force appear imperative in cases where the spread and possible encroachment of communism was concerned. The fall of the Soviet Union, of course, invalidated the notion that to counter a certain threat (communist expansion) war was presumed necessary and thus enjoyed automatic legitimacy in Western cabinets. Compared to the rhetoric around the escalating US involvement in North Vietnam, the government under George H. W. Bush portrayed the 1991 Gulf War far less in terms of an acute need for self-defence. Section 6.2 suggested that ODS was to the US a matter of protecting the international order and demonstrating its global pre-eminence. According to the terminology developed in section 2.1, the intervention in Vietnam was framed as demanded by immediate interests or utility, while collective self-defence on behalf of Kuwait was indicated by appropriateness.

However, 9/11 marked the emergence of a threat perceived equivalent to that of communism, so that the need to use force would again have appeared extremely pressing in cases concerning the threat of terrorist attacks. In fact, the premise of an absolute imperative to inhibit state support for international terrorism wherever it might be thought to appear is strikingly similar to the Cold War premise of an unquestioned exigency to contain communism in all its forms. The urgency of resort to force therefore does not decrease linearly across the three cases. From the perspective of the respective US administrations it declined from Vietnam to the first intervention in Iraq and increased again for the 2003 invasion.

At any point in time the 'US perspective' does not comprise only the administration's views. It arguably also includes public perceptions. The way in which the latter are formed changed from 1965 to 2003. America's engagement in Vietnam eventually came under scrutiny and then also faced public criticism. However, initially lack of knowledge and outright misinformation meant that the justification the government offered for the use of force (preventing south-east Asia from falling to communism and the collective self-defence of South Vietnam) was not questioned and nor was its urgency doubted. In 1965, 53 per cent of Americans thought that China was behind the attacks of the Vietcong on the government and its supporters in South Vietnam, 26 per cent blamed the North and only 7 per cent of Americans believed a civil war in the South had anything to do with the deteriorating security situation in the Republic of Vietnam.[103] When President Johnson first ordered the bombing of North Vietnam 67 per cent of Americans therefore favoured this course of action over passivity or withdrawal. The approval ratings of the president indeed climbed from 66 per cent to 69 per cent at the start of ORT.[104]

In the twenty-first century, it has not only proved significantly more difficult to frame one state as crucial in a certain threat scenario.[105] It is also a serious challenge to continuously present the use of force as without alternative and hence as warranting its costs in blood and treasure. The technological advances described above not only benefited military intelligence and communication. They also afforded the public a much more direct view on to the battlefield and increased the information available about faraway armed conflicts. The claim about a key role for Iraq in sponsoring international terrorism, in other words the narrative provided to construct urgency around the 2003 invasion, was from the outset in dispute. The war's ramifications for the Iraqi population and the toll it took on US forces were reported by journalists on the ground and made visible on YouTube. A constant stream of information was fed into the twenty-four-hour news cycle to reach Americans in their homes. The part of the US public that believed in a threat to the US from Iraqi weapons of mass destruction may have perceived the invasion as highly exigent. However, the utility and/or

---

[103] Fourteen per cent of them were not sure (Kahin (1987) 287).   [104] *Ibid.*

[105] It is virtually unimaginable that a US government could nowadays keep large-scale air raids on a country secret for a significant period of time, as the Nixon administration did with the bombing of Laos and Cambodia. While the Obama administration may initially have intended to keep the Central Intelligence Agency's drone programme under the radar, the level of academic and media enquiry, as well as the omnipresence of the subject in public discourse, suggests that any such endeavour must be considered a failure.

appropriateness of OIF was certainly from the start much more contested than either that of the US engagement in North Vietnam or ODS.

To recapitulate, in addition to the gradual rise in asymmetry, the
combination of two relevant trajectories of change potentially influenced
developments in US air warfare from 1965 to 2003. First, across the three
cases, combat operations became much more visible so that the opinion of
the American public increasingly mattered for the way war was waged.
Indeed, given the nature and the breadth of progress in communications
technology *global* public opinion likewise came to be relevant to the
conduct of hostilities. Second, partly as a result of this improvement in
public information, the perceived urgency of the three wars declined and/
or became contested. Whatever the public expects wars to look like, these
expectations presumably become stricter the less urgent a war appears.

What *does* it mean for the conduct of war that the public is watching?
Is there a reason why the American or a global audience would favour
warfare according to the logic of efficiency over sufficiency? In order to
answer this question we need to enquire into the substance of shared
ideas about war and shed light on whether they changed across the three
cases.[106] The implications of material changes – namely the improvement in communication technology and the increase in the preponderance of US military power – ultimately depend on the meaning
attributed to them by the relevant audience. I differentiate between the
US public and what I refer to as 'global public opinion' or the 'considered judgements of international society'[107] as two different relevant
audiences by whom the US strives to be seen as a legitimate actor.

The first tangible result of a change in shared beliefs about violence in
international relations in the twentieth century was arguably the formal
legal prohibition on the use of force in 1945. While outlawing war had
been a project in pacifist and feminist circles as well as among liberal
politicians and scholars for a while, it was only after two World Wars
that circumstances aligned to make it reality.[108] Spurred by the human

---

[106] Within the scope of this chapter such an enquiry necessarily stays at a very
general level.

[107] Section 8.2 discusses whether there is such a thing as a global public opinion and
addresses the concern of Western centricity.

[108] The Charter's less successful predecessors, the Pact of Paris and the Covenant of
the League of Nations (see bibliography for full names), were spectacularly
eclipsed by the outbreak of the Second World War. See Kritsiotis (2004) 50; also
Corten (2010).

suffering just witnessed, a majority of actors in the international community, including the major powers of the moment, were able to reach consensus on the establishment of a legal obstacle to the resort to force in international relations. Over the following decades this ideational change entailed the creation, elaboration and increased justiciability of a global human rights regime under IL. The end of the Cold War inspired a flurry of UN peacekeeping missions to ease the consequences of conflict and rebuild war-torn societies. Martha Finnemore and Kathryn Sikkink credit 'a long-term trend toward humanizing the "other", or "moral progress"'[109] with the revival of ICL and its institutionalisation in a number of adjudicative bodies in the 1990s. What is alternatively called the 'individualisation' or the 'humanisation' of general IL arguably reached a peak with the tentative qualification of state sovereignty for the sake of an emerging right to humanitarian intervention towards the end of the twentieth century.[110] At the heart of this ideational change lies what Theodor Meron calls the 'advent of a general distaste for the waste of human life'.[111] International relations at the turn of the century were characterised by a 'remarkable cross-cultural effectiveness ... [of] norms involving ... the prevention of bodily harm'.[112]

This humanisation of international relations linearly increased across the three wars under investigation as the ideational change favouring the preservation of individual life gathered pace. More frequent and comprehensive reporting on the human costs of war across the period not only meant that this ideational change became gradually more relevant to the conduct of war.[113] Changes in information technology may also have spurred 'greater intolerance for human suffering in times of war'.[114] A lack of perceived urgency of a specific war would have rendered it even more acute. All this explains the rising and now notorious casualty aversion specifically of Western societies. There seems almost universal agreement among scholars of IR that 'Western societies can now only fight wars which minimise human suffering'.[115]

---

[109] Finnemore and Sikkink (1998) 267; also Crawford (1993); Ray (1989).
[110] See, for instance, Morris (2006); Pattinson (2012); Roberts (2006); Shue (2006); Welsh (2006).
[111] Meron (2006) 6.   [112] Keck and Sikkink (1998).
[113] Byman, Waxman and Larson (1999) 59; Larson and Savych (2007) 208.
[114] Meron (2006) 6.
[115] Coker (2001) 2; likewise Beier (2003) 420; Farrell (2005) 179; McInnes (2002) 90; Owens (2003) 606; Rogers (2000); Zehfuss (2011) 552.

The 'zeitgeist that requires the reduction of human risk'[116] has been well documented to prevail in US society.[117] A project analysing various opinion polls discovered that among Americans the degree of casualty aversion chiefly depends on the public's beliefs about the appropriateness and/or utility of a specific war.[118] The contestation of both in the run up to the 2003 war against Iraq would have further augmented the casualty aversion of the US public. This corroborates the previously stated hypothesis that lack of urgency of resort heightens public expectations regarding the conduct of war. Empirical research also suggests that the American public displays a double standard in that it cares more about losses among its own troops than about enemy fatalities.[119] Crucially, however, these days, the plight of civilians in the countries under attack receives widespread media attention in the US as well. It by no means meets with indifference.[120] In countries not involved in the war, civilian casualties generate still more abhorrence than combatants' deaths, which with few exceptions do not tend to be individually reported outside combatants' countries of origin.

At first sight it is not clear why the ever closer scrutiny of a casualty-averse public and the intensification of this aversion should create a presumption in favour of either efficiency or sufficiency. I have not yet investigated whether warfare according to one of the logics creates fewer casualties and if so which one. However, on closer examination, a growing shared normative belief in the value of all human life provides an explanation for the emergence of an imperative to wage war efficiently in the way that the logic of efficiency suggests. The logic of sufficiency makes no claim at all to protect combatants' lives. In fact, it endows killing combatants with the legitimacy of a legally privileged course of action, an acceptable way to attain a military advantage. Of course, this is problematic first and foremost to those parts of the global public that care about the troops under attack from the US. However, as illustrated in Chapter 6, the logic of sufficiency favours attrition warfare. Not least the US experience in the Vietnam War fixed deeply in the collective American memory the association of drawn-out interdiction campaigns with large numbers of returning body bags.

---

[116] Zehfuss (2011) 546.   [117] For instance, Gelpi, Feaver and Reifler (2005).
[118] *Ibid.*   [119] Bacevich (1996); Butler (2004); Gregory (2004); Gregory (2006).
[120] Similar Larson and Savych (2007).

The logic of efficiency does, of course, likewise involve deliberate attacks on combatants. However, it lays a claim to the protection of human life that the logic of sufficiency does not make: minimising combatant and possibly even civilian losses by getting a war over with as quickly as possible, by reducing the number of air strikes it takes to end the war. That the logic of sufficiency protects civilians from the deliberate infliction of harm does not distinguish it from the moderate version of the logic of efficiency as manifest in contemporary US air warfare. After all, the US has never questioned the principle of distinction as such; it simply defines military objectives differently. The next chapter will discuss the normative implications of the two logics in much more depth. Here it suffices to note that at first sight the logic of efficiency enjoys an advantage over the logic of sufficiency in the eyes of a global public that abhors the waste of human life and an American public that is moreover anxious to protect US troops.

While it is hence plausible that casualty aversion means that in contemporary US air operations combatant deaths are no longer considered unproblematic and hostilities are kept as brief as possible, it is less clear why efficiency should be sought with regard to the achievement of the overall political goals of a war. Human suffering, at least the kind directly imposed by combat operations, presumably ends with one side achieving generic military victory.[121] Why then not simply focus on achieving the latter as quickly and directly as possible? Why focus on the desired political end-state? For an explanation we have to return to the prohibition on the use of force. This legal watershed rendered war a state of exception in need of a legal apology. If something is prima facie prohibited, unless it pursues one of a very small number of specific legitimising goals, those goals are naturally crucial – the more so the keener a belligerent is to uphold an aura of legitimacy.

The only legal apology available to a state unilaterally resorting to force is, of course, self-defence. However, over the last seventy-odd years the exercise of self-defence has very rarely meant that straightforward

---

[121] I do not mean to suggest that civilians and combatants in countries at war miraculously stop suffering once one side achieves generic military victory. However, that is unfortunately not necessarily the case when one side achieves the desired political end-state either. Generic military victory none the less marks the point at which the deliberate, legally sanctioned infliction of human suffering through direct physical violence ends. The repercussions of this violence tend to linger even past the point where one side also achieves their ultimate political aims.

defeat of an invading army. It is often a specific political end-state that affords the neutralisation of the threat that triggered the perceived need to resort to force from the point of view of the 'defender'. Achieving this political end-state which grounds a state's inherent right to self-defence exceptionally removes the stigma of aggression from the use of force. It is only natural that this source of legitimacy is kept at the forefront of combat operations. Every air strike that inflicts civilian casualties and/or puts troops at risk ought to also contribute to the achievement of the exceptional goals for which a state claims to rightfully deviate from the *Grundnorm* of peaceful international relations.

In this reading, the removal of war from the spectrum of regular international politics has paradoxically encouraged appeal in the conduct of combat operations to political aims. In the next chapter I return to the constant challenge this trend poses to the separation of *jus in bello* and *jus ad bellum*. Here it explains why a belligerent who has an interest in avoiding the reputational costs of being branded an aggressor is tempted to lend expression to the importance of its overall goals with every attack. NATO's Operation Allied Force in 1999 provides a striking example. The rationale behind so-called 'boutique bombing' was that the elite would get fed up with the war and put pressure on the leadership. Every air strike that put troops and civilians more at risk also inconvenienced Milošević and his cronies.

Asymmetry reduces the costs of waging war according to the logic of efficiency. Western casualty aversion and the internalisation of the prohibition on the use of force, against the backdrop of increased scrutiny by a better informed public, put a premium on doing so. What about the increased recourse to IHL? The US political establishment is notorious for the occasional assertion that US foreign policy is above IL.[122] Yet legalism is an important staple of American democracy.[123] Chapter 3 elaborated that what is legal can be deemed appropriate while also making allowances for the instrumental course of action in a certain situation. Arguments about utility as well as those about appropriateness can therefore generally be buttressed by showing that what is presented as in accordance with interests or shared normative beliefs is also legal. The necessity to demonstrate the legitimacy of war – to legally apologise for it – hence also created a strong

---

[122] Hurd (2007).
[123] Falk (1969) 220; also Garraway (2004); Keohane (2012a) *passim*.

incentive to enhance the acceptability of warfare with systematic, almost ostentatious recourse to law during the conduct of hostilities.

Is adherence to IHL more critical to securing support from the American public the more a war's appropriateness and/or utility are questioned? Do public doubts about a war's merits engender even more pressure to abide by IHL just as they apparently increase casualty aversion? Legally speaking, the level of adherence to IHL does not at all alter the legal status of the resort to force as such and vice versa. Whether decision-makers nevertheless hope that strict adherence to IHL compensates for a lack of perceived appropriateness, utility or legality of an invasion would be difficult to establish. After all, desiderata around the merits of any particular resort to force tend not to be openly admitted by those responsible for it or even those carrying it out.

For the general public this is a different matter. The separation of *jus in bello* and *jus ad bellum* is highly counterintuitive. It is therefore a relatively safe assumption that ordinary Americans, at least as far as non-legal experts are concerned, do not draw a clear distinction between their assessments of an armed conflict as such and the way in which it is conducted. As mentioned above, the analysis of a series of opinion polls revealed that Americans' tolerance for the human costs of combat operations is indeed chiefly determined by their perception of the 'rightness or wrongness' of the war in which these costs are incurred.[124] The reverse is likewise true. The anti-war movement of the 1960s, which gathered pace in lock-step with the casualty count, confirms what is ultimately a truism: Americans judge the legitimacy of a war in part based on how it is conducted.

Does that not mean that an American public that allegedly attaches importance to legalism should also demand the legality of *resort* to force? Nowadays it does. The year 2003 marked a '[w]atershed in the history of shared expectations regarding war'.[125] For the first time 'public opposition to the proposed invasion of Iraq ... was explicitly linked to the legal prohibition on the use of force'.[126] Adding diverging degrees of perceived urgency and improved information to the ever deeper internalisation of the legal prohibition on the use of force explains why pressure to abide by IHL mounted from the engagement in Vietnam through ODS to OIF. While the material changes in

---

[124] Gelpi *et al.* (2005) 7ff.   [125] Brunnée and Toope (2010) 287.
[126] *Ibid*. 277; likewise Jackson (2010) 219, 222.

technology and the distribution of power were necessary conditions for these developments, it is the changes in shared normative beliefs about violence in international relations that seem to explain both the progressive enhancement of the influence of IL on warfare and the boosted role of the logic of efficiency in the selection of targets.

7.4 What international law is: constitutive of legitimacy in war

The social construction of a legitimate target

Where does this leave us regarding the role of IHL in determining the definition of a legitimate target? That developments in shared normative beliefs may explain both the legalisation of warfare and its increasing accordance with the logic of efficiency raises the spectre of a spurious relationship between IHL and the definition of a legitimate target in US air warfare. Are the parallel changes in the role of law and the logic of warfare actually unrelated and both explained by developments in shared normative beliefs? No, sections 7.1 and 7.2 demonstrated that the change in target selection and the parallel subjection of combat operations to IL were not a mere coincidence. True, the semantic indeterminacy of IHL only creates an opening for the pursuit of temporal efficiency without accounting for it. But the previous sections also showed that looking beyond the immediate consequences of their choices and focusing on what they mean to ultimately achieve with the use of force is an intellectual effect of decision-makers' recurrence to purposively and consequentially indeterminate IHL. IL 'inspires' actors to tie the legitimacy of targets to the big picture rather than to small discrete steps in warfare, as the logic of sufficiency does.

The legal definition of a legitimate target as interpreted by US decision-makers promotes the infusion of combat operations with political and/or moral considerations. But so does the prohibition on the use of force. Moreover the increased casualty aversion explains the specific imperative of efficiency, to get the war over with quickly in order to stop risking the lives of combatants. These variables, the legal definition of a legitimate target, casualty aversion and the internalisation of the prohibition of the use of force (the latter two jointly constitute the ideational change described in the previous section) seem to be somehow jointly responsible for the change from sufficiency to efficiency. Yet, in this section I show that recourse to IHL relates to the definition of a legitimate target in US air warfare in a different way from the twofold ideational change described above. I start by summarising what the book has so far found out about the relationship between IHL and the definition of a legitimate target of attack by US military decision-makers.

How the intellectual and motivational effects of recourse to IHL play out is to a certain extent a function of belligerents' perceived interests and possibly their normative beliefs. The reason is that IL is epistemically dependent, which means that it does not provide a normative code or objective standard for guiding and evaluating action that is independent of appropriateness or utility. An actor's prior extra-legal conceptions of utility and appropriateness hence influence what IL means. For the interpretation of IHL those prior conceptions play a specifically significant role given the high degree of IHL's indeterminacy. The international public considers wars inappropriate inasmuch as they waste human life and do not pursue an exceptionally important political goal. US military decision-makers hence perceive keeping wars as short as possible as the instrumental course of action. The US perceives it as in its interest to wage war with the fewest possible air strikes, as briefly as possible and with a view to the direct achievement of political goals. This conception of utility underpins 'the US interpretation' of the provisions defining a legitimate target of attack, specifically the definition of military objectives. US military and legal doctrine do not accept the strictures of the logic of sufficiency, but advocate targeting in accordance with what I call the logic of efficiency.

In other words, the legal definition of a legitimate target of attack that US military decision-makers recur to in war cannot be grasped without the reasoning that I call the logic of efficiency. The legal definition of a legitimate target is not only epistemically, but also ontologically, dependent on the definition of a legitimate target of US decision-makers visible in contemporary air warfare. The variable that is supposed to explain why the definition of a legitimate target of attack in US air warfare accords with the logic of efficiency does not exist without the conception of a target that accords with the logic of efficiency by US decision-makers as the appropriate and instrumental, hence legitimate, target.

Is this not also true for the ideational change regarding violence in international relations? As mentioned above, the horrors of two World

Wars played midwife to the prohibition on the use of force.[127] The way wars are fought, including the logic they follow, thus feeds back into shared normative beliefs about the resort to force and the public's casualty aversion. The relationship between the twofold ideational change and the logic of warfare is not unidirectional, running from the former to the latter. Yet casualty aversion could have risen and the prohibition on the use of force could have been internalised without the understanding being held in anyone's mind that targeting according to the logic of efficiency was the appropriate and/or instrumental course of action. The ideational change and the logic of warfare interact with each other. However, the ideational change exists independently and its meaning can be established independently of the conception of a legitimate target as that target which follows the logic of efficiency by US decision-makers. As a result, we can conceive of the relationship as follows: the logic underlying the selection of targets shifted from sufficiency to efficiency upon the change in shared ideas about violence in international relations. The twofold ideational change is a cause of the relative increase in targeting according to the logic of efficiency.

If variable A (the legal definition of a legitimate target the meaning of which depends on the logic of efficiency) is ontologically and epistemically dependent on variable B (the definition of a legitimate target of attack in US air warfare), we cannot think of A as occurring and thereby causing B to transition from one state (accordance with the logic of sufficiency) to another (accordance with the logic of efficiency). We need to conceptualise how the legal definition (A) and the definition of a legitimate target of attack in US air warfare (B) relate to each other based on a snapshot of reality. In the air war of 2003, what US decision-makers defined as a legitimate target of attack can be described and categorised as following the logic of efficiency more often than sufficiency. Given the legal definition of a legitimate target, the legitimate target practised in 2003 came to have the properties associated with the logic of efficiency. Rather than asking for the causes of the change in logics we account for the properties of the definition of a legitimate target in contemporary US air warfare by reference to the properties of the legal definition of a legitimate target of attack (specifically its indeterminacy). We enquire into the constitution of a legitimate target of attack in US air warfare.

---

[127] Sherry (2009) 180.

Causal relations are sometimes referred to as transition theories because the variable that they explain exists in two different states, before and after the incidence of the cause. The logic of warfare transitions upon the incidence of changing collective ideas about violence in the international system. Some scholars understand this to mean not only that these collective ideas exist independently of the logic of warfare; they also precede the change in targeting in time. However, as adumbrated, the way wars are fought and shared normative beliefs about how they ought to be fought influence each other. The notion of a unidirectional causal chain between a change in the ideational structure of international relations and agents' changing behaviour is furthermore incompatible with a constructivist concept of the endogeneity of agency and structure. But what is the difference then between mutual constitution and mutual causation? As explained above, mutually constitutive variables are twin born or co-original. Yet interaction by causation between agency and structure can in theory be magnified to reveal one variable existing independently 'before' the other. As we try to explain how decision-makers define a legitimate target of attack in air warfare we have asked whether the cause can exist independently of the effect. An effect cannot exist independently of a cause, of course. Which one comes first depends on when we chose to look.

The factor I have neglected in this section so far is military doctrine. Clearly, doctrines, such as EBOs or shock and awe, which guide US military operations as the targeting shifts towards efficiency, are not independent of the real-world definition of a legitimate target in line with the logic of efficiency. The third section of this chapter outlined how in general doctrine is inspired by reality. This discussion even raised the question of whether the logic of efficiency could be considered to be at all separate from military doctrine. However, as the latter is also sometimes conceived in the abstract and real-world air targeting sometimes diverges from doctrinal recommendations, one cannot be reduced to the other. Like the legal definition of a legitimate target of attack, however, these doctrines do not exist independently of US decision-makers' perceptions of utility and appropriateness in war: perceptions that suggest the efficient is the legitimate target. They contribute to the constitution of certain targets as legitimate by endorsing the logic of efficiency as instrumental.

Constitution and variation

The discussion has revealed that the relationship between the ideational change, comprising increased casualty aversion and the internalisation of the prohibition on the use of force, and the logic of targeting is one of causal interaction. To the contrary, the legal definition of a legitimate target is constitutive of the definition of a legitimate target in US air warfare and vice versa. What we need to know now is whether constitutive factors make a difference as causes do? After all, the question is whether IHL has a counterfactual effect on US air warfare, i.e. whether it is behaviourally relevant.

Alexander Wendt argues that the 'effects of constitutive structures might be said to "vary" with their constituting conditions'.[128] For instance, if the US adhered to the less indeterminate positive definition of a legitimate target, the intellectual and motivational effect would be different: it would limit the quest for efficient air strikes to those that produce a genuinely military advantage in one causal step. While different logics of waging war are imaginable, the properties of the one that we currently observe can only be understood in virtue of the properties, and hence the intellectual and motivational effects, of customary IHL. In Wendt's words, '[w]hen constituting conditions vary, then so do their constitutive effects'.[129]

In fact, the effects of recourse to IL can theoretically vary widely because what the legal definition of a legitimate target means also depends on interpretation – the properties of the legal definition are partly assigned to it when actors interpret the law.[130] Within the conditions of possibility set by the indeterminate legal definition of a legitimate target of attack, different perceived utilities and normative beliefs can constitute a logic that could be different from the logic of efficiency. We know this because the logic of sufficiency is one such alternative. IHL sets the 'communicative framework in which actors debate issues of legitimate agency, purpose, and strategy' regarding the conduct of hostilities.[131] The precise effect of recourse to law depends on interpretation the more indeterminate the law is.

We can imagine that this customary definition of a legitimate target would become more important in US air warfare without the US defining

---

[128] Wendt (1998) 106.   [129] *Ibid.*   [130] Similar Kratochwil (2010).
[131] Reus-Smit (2004a) 23; also Risse (2000).

targets as legitimate in accordance with the logic of efficiency because decision-makers were guided by different perceptions of appropriateness and utility. Just like an altered legal definition of a legitimate target, an altered interpretation would imply different intellectual and motivational effects. In opposition, normative beliefs centring on casualty aversion and the prohibition on the use of force in international relations would not lead to a logic of warfare other than the one whose rise Part III has described. It seems that the 'effects' of constitutive factors vary *more* and in a less predictable fashion than the effects of causes.

To recall, the introduction cautioned that we can theorise in the abstract how IL can make a difference for behaviour, but what kind of difference it actually makes in any particular situation cannot be generalised or predicted. It needs to be observed in order to be assessed. The fact that prediction is one of the social sciences' most prized endeavours[132] goes some way towards explaining why constitutive factors are at times dismissed when it comes to grasping social phenomena. Another reason is the unquestioned acceptance in mainstream IR theory of the hermeneutic dichotomy between explaining and understanding. Explaining is to identify a phenomenon's causes and understanding that phenomenon is enquiring into its constitution. This distinction is often combined with the notion that understanding a phenomenon is a descriptive exercise rather than part of the hard theoretical work that is explaining and subsequently predicting social relations.[133] However, the categorisation of phenomena according to their properties does not merely describe them. Knowing how a social phenomenon such as the definition of a legitimate target is constituted has tremendous explanatory value.

By the same token, isolating the trigger or cause of a change helps us understand it. In the words of Friedrich Kratochwil: 'To have explained an action, is to have made it intelligible, having put it in a context, and shown that the attributions make sense according to intersubjectively shared standards.'[134] The example of the definition of a legitimate target of attack in US air warfare brings the equal explanatory value of causal and constitutive factors into sharp relief. While fear of a public opinion backlash if the war is bloody and drawn out might be the reason for why a commander puts the civilian leader's headquarters

---

[132] King, Keohane and Verba (1994) *passim*.   [133] *Ibid.*, 1.1.1.
[134] Kratochwil (2010).

on the priority target list (the cause), he does so *with* the reason that he sees himself as a professional, law-abiding commander, who focuses on producing the right kind of political effects while staying within the confines of the law (constitutive variable).

To conclude I return to the question of why the US refrains from attacking objects whose engagement promises the most direct achievement of overall political goals if their connection to military operations is remote. Why does US air warfare display the moderate, but not the radical, version of the logic of efficiency?[135] Chapter 6 suggested that the US only targets objects if the attack generates a genuinely military advantage in three or fewer causal steps. We can certainly imagine a public audience holding ideas that endorse total war as appropriate under certain circumstances. This would cause waging war according to the radical version of the logic of efficiency to be the instrumental course of action from the point of view of a closely watched great power and democracy. However, that is not the case. That the international public is increasingly averse to combatant deaths does not mean that the principle of noncombatant immunity is at all questioned or weakened. To the contrary, sensitivity to civilian deaths has increased with the general aversion to combatant casualties. Total war would be a highly inopportune course of action, contradicting the immediate imperative to maintain public support for the war and avoid reputational costs. Total war would hence objectively contradict considerations of utility. In addition, interviews suggested that US decision-makers clearly perceive direct attacks on uncontroversial civilian objects as illegal and inappropriate. After all, the (customary) legal definition of a legitimate target despite its considerable indeterminacy has certain unquestioned boundaries. It cannot be understood to endorse direct challenges to the principle of noncombatant immunity as a compromise between utility and appropriateness in war. The absolute prohibition on directly attacking civilians or civilian objects is promulgated in the API. There are hence causal as well as constitutive factors explaining why US decision-makers do not put the imperative of efficiency before the obligation to distinguish as such (radical logic of efficiency), but merely modify their interpretation of the definition of military objectives (moderate logic of efficiency).

---

[135] For definitions of the two versions of the logic of efficiency see the appendix.

The kind of question IR theorists have quarrelled about for decades is whether states would ever not wage total war because the legal definition of a legitimate target did not endorse it even though powerful causal forces favoured such a course of action as instrumental. Alternatively, with the same causal forces, but a different legal definition of a legitimate target, would we observe a different definition of a legitimate target in US air warfare? As mentioned, law in its creation, application and meaning depends on the prevailing perceptions of utility and appropriateness. It is therefore unlikely that legality will significantly diverge from these normative codes for an extended period of time. Interpretation, progressive development or disregard of the law would prevent that. Crucially Chapter 2 laid to rest the notion that therefore recourse to IL does not make a difference. IL does not provide a separate reason for action, it does not provide an independent normative standard, and it could not exist without the prior interests and shared normative beliefs that led to its creation. The difference it makes lies precisely in the (intellectual and motivational) effects of its mediating between utility and appropriateness. The outcome of this mediating depends on the law as well as utility and appropriateness. How much it depends on either is a function of the indeterminacy of the law. The instantiation of instrumental calculations or normative beliefs in IL has a counterfactual effect: IHL is behaviourally relevant in US air warfare.

PART IV

An evaluation of international law in war

8 | *The lack of normative success of international law in US air warfare*

Normatively evaluating IL is an exercise that is as dubious to mainstream legal positivists as it is to critical legal theorists. It presupposes that one assigns IL a substantive goal other than the provision of objective solutions to normative problems, a goal for which IL itself cannot account.[1] I hold that this is neither surprising nor problematic. The theory of IL proposed in Chapters 2 and 7 suggests that the role of law in society is to regulate social relations in accordance with a compromise between utility and appropriateness acceptable to that society. What that compromise looks like depends on the area of regulation and naturally differs across time and among societies. In other words, a standard for evaluating IL is necessarily historical-sociological in nature.[2] We hence have to ask what we expect IL to do in war and whether IHL does it in US air warfare. Contemporary US combat operations from the air are unprecedented and unmatched regarding the room afforded to legal considerations. If IL can render warfare normatively acceptable, this ability is probably on display in US air operations.

8.1 The logic warfare ought to follow: sufficiency versus efficiency

Judging international law by the consequences of war

Wars inevitably cause deaths and suffering on a large scale. Could we expect IHL to avoid killing in war, or at least to protect civilians against incidental death? If those were our normative expectations of what IHL should accomplish during US combat operations, law could not be normatively successful without *de facto* prohibiting any use of violence and thus warfare as such. If IHL is to do more than repeat the general

---

[1] Koskenniemi (2005) 6, 25.   [2] Likewise Reus-Smit (2003) 594.

prohibition on the use of force in international relations, which is already established by customary law and enshrined in Article 2(4) of the UNC, we should not expect it to have absolute humanitarian goals.[3] Section 2.2 showed that law is of necessity a compromise between appropriateness and utility. It needs to express an ideal of social coexistence rather than merely allowing actors to behave however they want to. Yet at the same time law cannot always prohibit actors from following immediate situational imperatives in order to meet a standard of maximum appropriateness either.[4] Law would be disregarded as an ultimately irrational institution. It follows that in order to fulfil the role of law in international relations, specifically in forcible state interactions, IHL needs to offer a compromise between humanitarian concerns (appropriateness) and immediate military imperatives (utility), however distasteful that may be.[5]

One such compromise would be to reduce killing in war as much as militarily possible. In fact, section 7.3 suggests that the international public increasingly objects to waste of human life in war, including the lives of combatants. However, IHL does not ask for the protection of combatants' lives at all. To the contrary, IHL acknowledges the utility of killing them, the military advantage that arises out of the attrition of enemy forces. IHL's only nod to humanitarianism concerning combatants is the proscription of unnecessary suffering. IHL does not try to reduce combatant casualties at all. On its own terms IHL's normative success is thus largely disconnected from the fate of combatants. I will raise the question of whether IHL *should* protect combatants' lives in the next section. Here it is safe to assume that in US air warfare IHL does not, at the expense of a military advantage (killing as many combatants as possible), accomplish a countervailing humanitarian

---

[3] For an in-depth discussion of this question see also Dill (2013).

[4] To recall, in the terminology of this book an actor perceives as in her interest courses of action that respond to the immediate imperatives of a specific situation. Her instrumental calculations determine and her strategic arguments express what is in an actor's interests. Following interests means pursuing utility. In opposition, extra-legal normative beliefs are imperatives for action that exist in spite of the immediate demands of a given situation. They may be related to an actor's conception of self, or other, her ideas about an ideal of coexistence, or her anticipation of future interactions. Principled considerations determine, aspirational arguments express, an actor's normative beliefs. Following them means that an actor seeks appropriateness.

[5] For a more detailed elaboration of this argument see Dill and Shue (2012).

goal (sparing as many combatants as possible) that it does not strive for. Even if recourse to IHL were correlated with fewer combatant deaths in US air warfare, that would be unlikely to be IHL's accomplishment. By the same token, if our expectations about IL's role in war comprise the reduction of *all* killing in war, including that of combatants, then even without an empirical enquiry we can assert that IHL is not normatively successful in US air warfare.

When it comes to the protection of civilians, the way in which IHL attempts to achieve a compromise between utility and appropriateness is the principle of proportionality.[6] Proportionality supposedly asks the belligerent to balance military imperatives and humanitarian considerations. The image of a balance has considerable appeal because it evokes a stable harmonious state. However, that is radically at odds with what it means to seek proportionality in war. Loss of human life and military gain are never in harmony: reasonable people disagree on all but the most extreme cases of excessive civilian casualties.[7] In addition, proportionality in war is not a stable state, but one that depends on the situation. After all, human life and military progress are not values that can either be expressed in terms of each other or translated into some common metric. I argued in section 3.1 that therefore any attack can only even aspire to being proportionate if the civilian casualties inflicted were among other things necessary, i.e. impossible to further reduce given the goal of achieving a certain independently legitimate military advantage.[8]

As far as the protection of civilians is concerned one measure of IHL's success could then be to ensure that the cumulative military gain during a war (one side must have achieved more than the other so that the former was able to overcome the latter) was attained with the fewest possible incidental civilian casualties overall. Of course, these are not really IHL's own terms because both positive and customary law only ask for decision-makers' expectations, not the results of attacks, to be proportionate. However, even if it were IHL's command that the collateral damage actually caused must have been necessary, it would be extremely difficult to plausibly argue and impossible to empirically establish that in any given war the same military outcome could or

---

[6] Any expected casualties among civilians must be proportionate to the independently justifiable military gain belligerents seek. See also section 3.1.
[7] See Chapter 3.2, pp. 84ff. and Chapter 7.1, pp. 200ff.   [8] See pp. 73f.

could not have been attained with fewer overall civilian casualties, had decision-makers recurred to law. Why not?

In 1991 the US attacked the Amiriyah bunker in downtown Baghdad. The air strike caused more than 400 civilian casualties, including scores of women, children and the elderly, who had sought shelter there.[9] Had the US known about the presence of civilians in the bunker, which the military brass vehemently denied,[10] the attack would have qualified as a war crime. Even without intelligence about the civilian use of the bunker the attack violated Article 57 API, and Human Rights Watch sharply criticised the US for failing to issue a warning, thereby embracing the likelihood of killing civilians.[11] Strict adherence to IHL by warning civilians of the impending attack would in all likelihood have reduced the number of civilian victims. For individual air strikes we can establish whether they caused more incidental deaths than necessary and whether adherence to IHL would have shrunk the casualty count, why not for a war overall?

In any war, there are presumably several different paths for one belligerent to overcome the other. IHL may well lead a belligerent down a path on which each independently legitimate attack causes only the necessary number of incidental civilian casualties. That does not mean that there may not have been an alternative path that would have resulted in overall fewer civilian victims. In addition, we cannot be sure that recourse to IHL never inspires air strikes that individually meet the requirement of necessary collateral damage, but that a belligerent would have refrained from carrying out had it not been for the endorsement of IL. To recall, section 7.1 found that one intellectual effect of recourse to IHL is to ease combatants' concern about the immediate humanitarian consequences of their actions.[12] Unless such an attack – an attack that a belligerent would not have carried out in the absence of law – renders unnecessary another attack with at least the same number

---

[9] For all intents and purposes a bunker is a shelter and vice versa. The question of legality hinges not on the designation of the structure, but on whether it is used by civilians or by military personnel.

[10] This is indeed unlikely given the military planners' focus on public relations and their awareness of the probable fall-out from such an event (Gordon and Trainor (2006) 326f.; US Department of Defense (1992) vol. II, Part I, 206). David Deptula, the master attack planner is quoted as reacting to the outcome of the attack with the words 'Boy, did we fuck up'; quoted in Atkinson (2003) 286.

[11] Human Rights Watch (1991) Chapter 3.   [12] See section 7.1, pp. 203ff.

of incidental civilian victims on the path to victory, IHL works to increase the cumulative collateral damage.

If we cannot know whether IHL reduces civilian casualties as much as possible, can we at least establish whether it reduces them at all compared to the same war fought without the input of IHL? A starting point for an assessment of IHL's normative success would then be an enquiry into whether increased recourse to IHL in decision-making across the three cases is correlated with fewer civilian war victims. However, the cumulative collateral damage caused by an air campaign is chiefly determined by the magnitude of the armed conflict. OIF pursued much more ambitious aims than ODS or the air campaigns against North Vietnam. Likewise, the technological and strategic capabilities of the attacker play a role in how much risk to civilians air strikes cause. These capabilities dramatically improved over the period investigated. In addition, the terrain, infrastructure and population density in the country under attack can be expected to make a difference for the degree of civilian suffering a war creates. These factors influence the risk of collateral damage possibly more immediately than target selection. Their variations make a comparison between the outcomes of the air campaigns against Vietnam and those against Iraq virtually meaningless.

But could we not simply account for variations in other factors when assessing whether the collateral damage in any given war was high or low? A comparison that is particularly tempting to draw is between the two wars the US fought against Iraq. Colin Kahl argues that it is remarkable that 'the number of civilians killed during the 2003 invasion was similar to that of the 1991 Persian Gulf War'.[13] After all, OIF was a full-fledged invasion. Is the fact that collateral damage did not significantly increase attributable to more systematic recourse to IHL in the selection of targets in 2003? As a general rule of thumb it is safe to assume that the additional precision technology employed in OIF reduced unintended casualties. At the same time, there is no reason to believe that war aims and technology cancel each other out so that similar numbers of civilian deaths must mean that the more widespread and systematic recourse to IHL during OIF failed to normatively improve warfare. We simply do not know how to weigh the impact of the attacker's capabilities, the conditions in the defending country and

---

[13] Kahl (2007) 11; similar Biddle (2004) 202; Conetta (2003a) 40.

the scale of military operations against the input of IHL when accounting for civilian victims of war.

Even if we could hold constant all these variables except for the degree of legal input into the selection of targets by the attacker, we could not isolate the influence of recourse to IHL on the outcome of a war. Military commentators stress that 'the enemy has a vote in the development of the battle'[14] and therefore presumably in how much collateral damage a specific selection of targets results in. Clodfelter holds that during ORT '[e]vacuations contributed to keeping the number of civilian casualties down'.[15] During OLB I and II, civilians were even more systematically relocated to the relative safety of the countryside. The regime in Iraq, to the contrary, arguably put less emphasis on the protection of its civilian population.[16] Of course, the 'attribution' of civilian casualties to actions either by the attacker or the defender is sometimes difficult and even more often controversial. In the case of the attack on the Amiriyah bunker the US alleged that the Iraqi government had callously put its own people at risk by inviting their presence in a bona fide military objective – the US claimed the bunker was used as a military command centre.[17] Iraq, to the contrary, emphasised that from the start of the war the bunker had served as a public shelter for civilians.[18]

Finally, even if we could account for variations in other factors and the actions of the defender, counting civilian victims of war beyond individual attacks is notoriously difficult. Over the course of the whole US engagement in Vietnam, which of course spans much more time than the air campaigns investigated here, estimates range from 2 million[19] to 4 million[20] civilian deaths. In absolute terms, civilian casualties were fewer in both wars against Iraq. However, precise numbers are likewise intensely contested. On one count the air war in 1991 caused a minimum of 110,000 civilian casualties.[21] Other estimates are one-tenth of

---

[14] Wynne (2010).   [15] Clodfelter (2006) 136, 195.   [16] Roscini (2005) 417.
[17] See Atkinson and Balz (1991); Gordon (1991) A17; Kahl (2006) 5; US Department of Defense (2010c) 11.
[18] Arkin (1997); Atkinson (1993) 285; the bombing of Amiriyah is a case of controversial rather than genuinely unclear attribution of civilian casualties.
[19] Mueller (1980) 507; Record (1998) 36f.; Tucker (1998) 453.
[20] Young (2009) 157.
[21] Clark (1992) 209; Clark's civilian casualty count challenges Kahl's assertion that ODS and OIF resulted in roughly the same amount of collateral damage. Clark's objectivity has on occasion been challenged.

that figure;[22] the Project on Defense Alternatives puts the civilian casualty count at 3,500.[23] The lowest figure is given by Human Rights Watch which counted between 2,500 and 3,000 civilian fatalities. The numbers for OIF likewise diverge. Iraq Body Count claims that 7,393 civilians died as a result of major combat operations.[24] The Project on Defense Alternatives estimates that 'only' 3,230–4,327 Iraqis perished during the US invasion.[25] Most endeavours to count victims of war do not factor in indirect collateral damage, namely civilian deaths due to the destruction of vital infrastructure, malnutrition, unexploded remnants of war, ensuing economic decline or civil war. Ultimately the conclusion is inescapable: we cannot judge IHL's normative success in US air warfare based on an empirical assessment of the respective wars' outcomes, no matter what expectations we have as to how the cumulative consequences of US combat operations would ideally look.

This chapter has so far considered the cases under investigation in light of six slightly different standards for assessing normative success of IHL based on the consequences of warfare: (1) avoid killing in war; (2) avoid civilian casualties; (3) reduce killing in war as much as possible; (4) reduce killing in war; (5) reduce civilian casualties as much as possible; and (6) reduce civilian casualties. Goals (1) and (2) would lead to utterly impracticable IHL that would probably accomplish nothing in the way of saving lives at all because it would be ignored. Like (1) and (2), standards (3) and (4) are not recognised as regulatory goals under current IHL. IHL does not demand that belligerents make an attempt to spare combatants' lives. However, unlike (1) and (2), we cannot reject (3) and (4) out of hand as being completely impracticable and therefore likely to have no effect at all. An empirical enquiry into whether IHL achieves goals that it does not set for itself in US air warfare is otiose. That is not to say that it is not a valid expectation to have of IHL that it reduce *all* killing in war either as much as possible or at all – an expectation the international public increasingly seems to have. Section 8.2 returns to the question of what exactly this expectation implies.

---

[22] Roberts (1994) 171; similar Daponte (1993), who counts 3,664 civilian fatalities.
[23] Conetta (2003a) 39.
[24] *Iraq Body Count Questions and Answers*, www.iraqbodycount.org.
[25] Conetta (2003a) 42; also Conetta (2003b).

Standard (5) is closest to the goal that IHL in fact attempts to achieve. It strives for the reduction of civilian casualties as much as possible in the expectations of decision-makers. On the assumption of a stable connection between expectations and outcomes of attacks this is the standard we could reasonably hold IHL to. The problem is that we have no way of knowing whether in US air warfare IHL achieves this goal or even the less demanding version (6) of reducing civilian casualties at all. A myriad of variables determine how many civilians die in any given war. Several of them do so more immediately than the selection of targets and by implication the guidance of law. The net humanitarian effect of IHL in US combat operations eludes us.

Judging international law by the distribution of harm

It is not feasible to judge the performance of IHL in the light of the humanitarian consequences of US air warfare. Yet we can evaluate the *way* in which IHL proposes to distribute harm in war and the way in which it attempts to accommodate both immediate situational (often military) and abstract systemic (often humanitarian) imperatives in US air warfare. As far as the side effects of warfare are concerned, the principle of proportionality seems to be without alternative as a way to strike a compromise between humanitarian and military concerns. However, Part II identified two different ways of distinguishing between targets, two alternative logics of distributing the permissible infliction of deliberate harm in war. Both claim to 'balance' utility and appropriateness, but in diverging ways. Can we decide which one is normatively preferable?

The logic of efficiency proposes to bring the infliction of harm and the pursuit of political goals together in the most efficient way possible. As from the beginning no absolute boundary impedes military action, the stronger party achieves its aims more quickly, thus ending the war sooner so that ultimately fewer people get hurt, or so the logic promises. The logic of sufficiency proposes to contain war in a military sphere that is only just sufficiently inclusive for a competition between two militaries to be carried out with a possibility of one side achieving military victory. As war is as much as possible and definitively contained fewer people get hurt, the logic claims. Both logics acknowledge that they regulate a normatively problematic and legally prohibited activity. One approach to dealing with the undesirability of war is to get it over quickly and achieve the supposedly legitimising goals to the use of force as directly as possible. The logic of efficiency is 'sharp wars are brief'. The alternative response to war's undesirability is to fence it in. The logic of sufficiency is 'contained wars are the least destructive'.

Of course, it is impossible to test whether 'the same war' results in more or fewer deaths (civilian or overall) depending on which logic guides target selection. Moreover, we do not know whether sharp wars are in fact brief enough to warrant their increased sharpness. In efficient wars, does enough of a society remain intact once one side has achieved its political goals to make up for the fact that fewer objects and persons enjoy immunity from the start? Nor do we know whether wars fought on an assumption of sufficiency are contained enough to warrant their increased length. In a contained war, does enough of a society remain immune from attack once sufficient objects and persons have been declared fair game to make up for the fact that this competition is likely to take longer? In other words, we can empirically establish neither whether either logic pans out nor which one produces 'better outcomes'. However, that does not affect our ability to compare those who are put in harm's way by the two logics.

An air campaign that follows the logic of efficiency would not involve the erosion of the military capabilities of the defender, including (wo)men in arms, to the same extent as one in accordance with the logic of sufficiency. The air campaign might also be shorter than one that avoids targets other than 'traditional' military objectives. Both features would mean fewer combatant deaths. At the same time, air strikes would more systematically engage the dual-use infrastructure relevant to the attacker's specific political goals. In addition, military operations would comprise attacks on objects more than one causal step away from the competition between enemy militaries. Both courses of action imply a more direct intervention into civilian life and therefore probably cause more collateral damage than attacking fielded forces and military equipment. It is plausible then that in a shift from the logic of sufficiency to the logic of efficiency we trade a decrease in combatant deaths for an increase in civilian deaths.[26]

---

[26] By 'combatants', I mean the integrated armed forces of a belligerent minus specifically protected persons in the meaning of Article 43 API. By civilian, I mean everyone else.

The extent of the trade-off between combatant and civilian deaths that is implied by a shift from the logic of sufficiency to the logic of efficiency naturally depends on how radically the latter is implemented. The logic of sufficiency provides a base line: combatants are allowed to die in large numbers and civilians only die as a side effect of intended attacks on military objectives. Military objectives are only those with a direct causal connection to the competition among militaries, including a limited range of dual-use objects. The attrition of unambiguous military capabilities implies a moderate risk of collateral damage. By contrast, if the logic of efficiency were applied in its radical form, those objects and persons would be directly targeted whose death or injury promised a quick achievement of the desired political end-state, regardless of their legal status. Depending on the political goals of the war that would probably include many persons we now consider civilians and objects deemed civilian. Attacks on the latter would heighten the risk of collateral damage. Compared to a classic war of interdiction, such an approach would presumably mean that fewer combatants died before one belligerent achieved its goals.

What about the 'moderate' version of the logic of efficiency that is manifest in contemporary US air warfare? It upholds the prohibition on directly targeting who and what is considered civilian. However, for two reasons, the logic none the less trades some combatant casualties for civilian ones. First, targeting in the light of efficiency considerations tends to mean that a wider range of dual-use targets are attacked. This bears a higher risk of collateral damage than attrition of enemy military capabilities. Second, while not turning away from the immunity of civilian objects or persons, the logic of efficiency broadens the category of military objective as far as objects are concerned within the large penumbra of uncertainty of customary IHL. Objects are legitimate targets on the basis of their contribution to achieving the war's political ends. As a result, some objects (media facilities, party headquarters) that according to the logic of sufficiency are considered civilian become targets of direct attack. That again raises the risk of collateral damage. In addition, it seems that the US 'brand' of the logic of efficiency broadens the definition of combatants to include civilian regime leaders, challenging established customary IHL. To the extent that the 'moderate' version of the logic of efficiency shortens the war, some combatants' lives are saved.

Empirical evidence bears out that the increase in the relative importance of the logic of efficiency in US air warfare *coincides* with a change in the ratio between combatant and civilian deaths to the detriment of the latter. The Project on Defense Alternatives argues that the 'portion of war fatalities that were civilian noncombatants may have been twice as great in OIF as in ODS: almost 30 percent in OIF versus almost 15 percent in Desert Storm'.[27] This finding is relatively robust as the civilian casualty numbers reported by the Project on Defense Alternatives are among the lowest for both wars. It is thus possible that both ratios are even higher. At the same time, it is unlikely that one is vastly too high due to an over-counting of civilian casualties. The number of combatant fatalities in both wars is much less controversial than the civilian casualty count.[28]

Yet if deaths among civilians are not a function of the attacker's choice of targets and hence the guidance of law alone, nor are casualties among combatants. In 1991 Iraqi troops lacked the skills necessary to defend themselves effectively.[29] Infantry troops, for instance, tended to rest and sleep in their tanks, which after a day in the heat of the desert presented extremely easy targets for infrared-equipped US munitions. Iraqi troops were even less prepared for combat twelve years later, a period during which Saddam Hussein, out of fear of internal opposition, had systematically stifled the general armed forces' training and sanctions had stripped the armed forces of much needed hardware.[30] As a result, the number of Iraqi combatants killed in 2003 was probably higher than would have been the case had the defending forces been better trained. This suggests that the deterioration of the ratio of civilian to combatant fatalities may have been even more significant. However, the main point is that other factors besides target selection influence the deadliness of a war for the defender's armed forces. Empirical verification of the hypothesis that the logic of efficiency *causes* higher civilian to combatant casualty ratios is therefore not possible.

If we nevertheless accept for its analytical plausibility the hypothesis that a shift in relative importance from the logic of sufficiency to the (moderate) logic of efficiency trades away the protection of some

---

[27] Conetta (2003a) 40.
[28] *Ibid.*: '13,000 fatalities in OIF versus approximately 26,500.'
[29] Atkinson (1993) 212, 448; Biddle (2004) 137ff.
[30] Atkinson (2004) 4f., 84; Conetta (2003a) 43.

civilians for the protection of some combatants, the question arises whether killing civilians is worse than killing combatants. Does the combatant/civilian distinction carry normative weight? One place to look for an explanation for why combatant deaths should be permitted while civilians enjoy immunity from direct attack is just-war theory. Conventional just-war theory holds that combatants as 'a class are set apart from the world of peaceful activity; they are trained to fight, provided with weapons, required to fight on command'.[31] According to Michael Walzer, a combatant has 'allowed himself to be made into a dangerous man'.[32] But are combatants under IHL in fact individuals who qualify as 'dangerous men'? Does IHL distinguish between combatants and civilians in accordance with differences in threat potential and consent?[33]

Combatants and civilians are jointly exhaustive and mutually exclusive categories. Every member of a belligerent society is part of one or the other. Crucially, which group an individual belongs to is not determined by her threat potential. Being a combatant means being a member of the organised armed forces; it is simply an assigned status.[34] Members of the organised armed forces far behind front lines or asleep in their barracks do not actually pose a threat to anyone. Incompetent or frightened cadets have not even the potential of doing so and are rather vulnerable. They remain combatants none the less. At the same time, a retired police sniper, notwithstanding considerable threat potential, would never rise to combatant status or lose his immunity from attack merely in virtue of his abilities. Overall there still may be a rough correlation between being a combatant and being potentially threatening to the enemy, but it does not seem to be the criterion according to which IHL actually draws the line.

Consent matters even less and if so only indirectly. Combatants and civilians cannot escape their status, but they can respectively gain or lose immunity from direct attack in virtue of their conduct. When

---

[31] Walzer (2006a) 144.   [32] *Ibid.*, 145.

[33] The next section will discuss whether threat potential/lack of vulnerability and consent to acquiring this potential could theoretically justify the radically decreased protection that the war convention affords combatants. The discussion here brackets this question.

[34] Not all members of the armed forces are combatants. Some, for instance the military clergy and medical personnel, are protected persons, i.e. immune from direct attack.

combatants are *hors de combat* because they have surrendered or are wounded, they are no longer legitimate targets. A civilian who chooses to directly participate in hostilities loses her immunity from deliberate attack. By withdrawing from combat she can regain it.[35] Civilians cannot unwittingly participate in hostilities, and they lose their immunity only when they intend to harm the adversary. However, IHL is agnostic as to whether combatants are voluntary professionals, conscripted forces or coerced by circumstances into giving up their immunity. In other words, combatants may not have consented to being made into more or less dangerous men at all.

The missing piece for explaining the distinction between civilians and combatants is the concept of sufficiency. It also makes sense of when civilians lose their immunity and when combatants gain it. IHL *posits* one class of people as all the targets of attack needed in order for the competition between two militaries to be carried out: the incorporated armed forces plus those persons that through their own actions prove willing to participate in this competition. As the assumption is that engaging this one class is sufficient for a military competition to be carried out with the possibility of generic military victory for one side to occur, every other object and person can be set aside as immune. Section 3.4 suggested that the split purpose of IHL means that it has to allow no more violence than is necessary (humanitarianism) and no less than is sufficient (military pragmatism) for the competition between enemies to be carried out. This turns out not to mean that IHL limits killing as much as militarily possible as far as the outcome of a war is concerned, as surmised above. It means allowing all killing of individuals whose engagement is necessary and sufficient while by implication prohibiting all intentional killing of individuals whose engagement is unnecessary.

Individual combatants may not in fact be threatening, but it is usually impossible for the attacker to tell. Combatants are the pool of people on which A can in good faith draw in its military effort, and overcoming them is therefore sufficient for B to achieve generic military victory – if indeed B can overcome A's military forces. It might be much more efficient to attack A's civilian leader rather than the lowly foot soldier, the nuclear scientist rather than the colonel, the retired police sniper

---

[35] The precise circumstances under which a civilian's actions override her status are subject to debate. See Akande (2010); Melzer (2009); Schmitt (2012).

rather than the newly recruited, ill-motivated conscript. By the same token, the first member of each pair might turn out to be less vulnerable or potentially more threatening. Yet IHL does not allow attacking them, because it assumes that in the competition between two militaries it is sufficient to engage the second member of each pair.[36] As far as persons are concerned, positive as well as customary IHL is crystal clear in requiring distinction to follow the logic of sufficiency.

Sufficiency fully explains the distinction between immune and non-immune persons in IHL, but does it lend it any normative weight so that we would 'prefer' combatant to civilian casualties? Section 7.3 suggested that in countries not involved in the armed conflict in question civilian casualties of war are even more abhorrent than combatant deaths, the raised sensitivity to the latter notwithstanding. If the normative success of law were purely a matter of perception, then IHL that imposes the logic of efficiency would be further from normative success than a law that commands containment and sequencing. But is this perception based on considered judgements or moral reasons? Why, if the choice is between killing combatants and killing civilians should we consider the latter even worse? I do not argue here that removing immunity from combatants can be morally justified. The question is investigated in the next section. Rather I ask whether there are moral reasons for why we should, all things considered, 'prefer' that combatants rather than civilians died in war – whether this is, as it were, less bad.

The association of being a civilian with vulnerability and innocence, in the sense of not posing a threat, may well contribute to the perception of civilian deaths as 'even worse'. Although these attributes were shown not to be present in every civilian and absent from every combatant, the very rough correlation between combatant status and threat potential/ ability to defend oneself cannot be dismissed as irrelevant in a moral enquiry either. There are two additional reasons why we should consider combatant deaths less bad than civilian victimisation that are often overlooked: security of expectations and minimal agency. Combatants know that they are legitimate targets even if they have not properly consented to the status. In addition, as a civilian it is only one's own conduct that can land oneself on the inside of the boundary around the sphere of deliberate military engagement, so civilians likewise have

---

[36] Unless the first member chooses to directly participate.

some agency in determining their fate. To the contrary, if we imagine a war fought in accordance with the radical logic of efficiency, then who will be targeted depends on the political goals the attacker pursues. In many cases efficiency considerations would suggest the intentional killing of certain civilians without any agency on their part or without their even seeing it coming.[37]

For instance, to reverse the annexation of the Falkland Islands by Argentina the logic of efficiency would have suggested a few direct attacks on high-value targets in downtown Buenos Aires. The military junta used the conflict to quell people's disaffection by arousing patriotic sentiment. Stirring popular opposition would arguably have been a more efficient means to end the war and regain control over the islands than engaging Argentina's armed forces at sea and from the air. Even if we use cases of legally relatively uncontroversial self-defence, an application of the radical logic of efficiency would thus suggest that civilians be targeted without any agency on their part and without their knowing that they were deemed legitimate targets.

It is an advantage of the logic of sufficiency that what happens to people is to some degree a result of their own choices and does not come as a surprise.[38] The flipside of the blanket permission to kill combatants is that for large numbers of civilians in every society, we generate security of expectations, and it is their *own* conduct that determines whether they remain immune from direct attack. By the same token, when belligerents determine who among their own citizens becomes a combatant they can take into consideration whom a society needs in order to continue to function during and after the war. When efficiency considerations determine who becomes a legitimate target of attack, the war cannot be contained in this way, and it is the attacker who determines who will be fair game. Minimal agency, relative security of expectations and a rough correlation of civilian status with

---

[37] I am grateful to Jonathan Parry for pointing out that this disadvantage of the logic of efficiency could theoretically be overcome if IHL made it an obligation for belligerents to announce their political goals and whom and what they considered legitimate targets accordingly. The practical relevance of this caveat, however, is extremely limited.

[38] Ideally IHL would require actual consent to becoming a member of the armed forces and thus a combatant. That IHL contains no such prescription is easily explained by the fact that how states recruit their defence forces is a case *par excellence* of what falls into the domestic jurisdiction of a state, aptly called the *domaine réservé* that is beyond the reach of IL.

vulnerability and the absence of threat all work together to suggest that the principle of noncombatant immunity carries moral weight and why we, all things considered, 'prefer' combatant to civilian deaths and, by implication, the logic of sufficiency over the logic of efficiency.

Besides this moral disadvantage of trading civilian for combatant protection the logic of efficiency is also inferior with a view to fulfilling the role of law in international relations in general and in war in particular. The logic of sufficiency draws a definitive line around the sphere of deliberate military engagement in any given war: only objects whose attack contributes in one causal step to the struggle for generic military victory between militaries are military objectives.[39] By contrast, there is, at least in theory, no limit to the kind of political goals that a belligerent might pursue with force and that would provide the point of reference for target selection. It follows that the logic of efficiency does not establish a definitive boundary around the class of persons or objects that can legitimately and intentionally be made casualties of a specific war. At some point in every war one side recognises that it will probably lose. That permissibility of actions in war is then a function of the scope and importance of that belligerent's political goals amounts to an invitation to escalate the latter in order to extend the former.

Of course, what kind of political goals a belligerent legally pursues with the use of force is a matter falling under the purview of *jus ad bellum*, the law regulating resort to force, not IHL. In the modern international system the prohibition on the use of force has taken the place of a (contested) list of just causes for war. The only legitimate aim of the unilateral use of force is now self-defence. Nevertheless, over sixty years of this system in operation have made abundantly clear that states pursue a wide range of political goals under that heading. Sometimes those strike us as illegal add-ons (regime change); at other times they reasonably concretise the reversal of an armed attack or the perceived immediate threat of it. One could argue that it is too much to ask of IHL that it hedge against escalating political ambitions and mission creep. Instead the law governing collective, preventive, pre-emptive and conventional self-defence should be specified and its application more effectively institutionalised. The argument has considerable merit.

---

[39] I am grateful to Cecile Fabre and Michael Gibb for drawing my attention to the fact that 'military' needs to be independently defined. The meaning of military cannot be explained in terms of the logic of sufficiency itself.

Significant institutional change in the international system would alter the ideal of normatively successful legal regulation of behaviour *in* war. Nevertheless, if it is to be normatively successful now, IHL needs to acknowledge the current realities of the international legal order. In the absence of systematic and effective adjudication of the resort to force, a non-escalatory logic of waging war is normatively preferable.

The comparison so far has focused on the logics' ways of distributing harm. But what about the way in which the two logics propose to compromise between utility and appropriateness in war? The logic of sufficiency's advantage here is coherence with other norms, namely that it supports the most important proposition of the international legal order: the use of force is not a normal tool of statecraft; it is not available as a legitimate means to pursue political goals. While on the surface affirming this injunction, the logic of efficiency lets the use of force for the pursuit of politics in through the back-door. It balances harm inflicted during war against the achievement of political goals, not military victory. The logic of efficiency carries the message that the pursuit of political goals with force can be the rational/cost-minimising thing to do. If the logic of efficiency came with the normative momentum of customary law, IL would suggest that pursuing political aims with force was also appropriate, if only that endeavour was efficient.[40]

One could interject here that the logic of sufficiency likewise allows states to achieve their political goals after winning an armed confrontation. The fact that the two pursuits – achievement of generic military victory and of political goals – are sequenced is merely an aesthetic advantage. I hold, in contrast, that the different stances on the connection between war and politics implicit in the two logics have significant implications: achieving a given political goal by force is easier if one directly attacks objects relevant to that goal. The logic of sufficiency, on the other hand, makes it difficult to win wars and rules out many political goals as unachievable with force in the first place. As in the modern international system war is not supposed to be easy, and belligerents have no right to have a shot at winning every war, the logic of sufficiency is the more appropriate framework for war's

---

[40] To recall, section 4.3 argued that it is impossible to establish with any certainty whether customary IHL allows targeting in accordance with the logic of efficiency or whether, like the API, it demands that belligerents follow the commands of containment and sequencing.

conduct.[41] Of course, the appeal to political goals during military operations also challenges the independence of *jus in bello* and *jus ad bellum*. Before we count undermining the independence principle as a disadvantage of the logic of efficiency in its own right, we first need to show that the separation serves a normative purpose. The next section will return to the question.

To conclude this comparison between logics we can summarise that the logic of efficiency even in the 'moderate' version that is manifest in US air warfare is normatively inferior to the logic of sufficiency on four counts. (1) The logic of sufficiency promises a better ratio of combatant to civilian deaths and the latter are found even worse than the former. This is true for moral reasons as well as according to public perception. (2) If an attacker chooses targets in accordance with the logic of sufficiency the defender has a modicum of agency and security of expectations about whom and what gets attacked. This, in turn, provides the possibility to protect individuals vital for a society's continued functioning. (3) The logic of efficiency makes the permissibility of conduct a function of a belligerent's overall goals. That provides an opening and indeed an invitation for broadening both one's goals and the sphere of legitimate military attack. The logic of efficiency makes for bad law. (4) The logic of efficiency undermines the normative fabric of the international system because it lends legitimacy to the direct pursuit of politics with force. The logic of sufficiency makes it difficult to win wars, rules out war as a useful instrument for the pursuit of many political goals, and acknowledges that no matter what we are trying to do with force and how efficiently we do it, war is an arduous, drawn-out catastrophe that cannot fully be redeemed.

8.2 The logic warfare ought to follow: sufficiency versus liability

The previous section gave moral reasons why combatant deaths are less bad than civilian victims of war, which to some extent explained the finding of section 7.3 that the international public, at least in countries not involved in a given war, differentiates between civilian and combatant casualties accordingly. The logic of efficiency trades the protection of some civilians against the protection of some combatants. That

---

[41] Section 9.2 discusses the implications of the logic of sufficiency for self-defence.

recourse to IHL in fact helps constitute the definition of a legitimate target as hinging on the efficient achievement of overall political goals in war therefore means that IHL is definitely normatively unsuccessful in contemporary US air warfare. After all, it could do better. This finding then to some extent explains the puzzle that originally inspired this book: air strikes conducted under the guidance of IHL and, as it turns out, in accordance with the logic of efficiency inspire academic criticism and popular outrage.

But does the previous section's finding also mean IHL would be normatively successful if it were able to vouchsafe that belligerents, who adhere to its strictures, wage war according to the logic of sufficiency? To recall, section 7.3 found that the relative decrease in targeting according to the logic of sufficiency was in part caused by the intensified public sensitivity to the waste of human life in war. Specifically, concern for the lives of combatants has gradually grown over the last sixty years; the resulting casualty aversion grounded the perceived utility of brief wars. So the logic of sufficiency likewise clashes with widely shared normative beliefs about warfare. However, contrary to what military strategists who advocate EBOs or shock and awe seem to believe, the logic of efficiency does not provide a solution to the modern belligerent's resulting problem of the high political and reputational costs associated with waging war. The reason is that concern for the protection of combatants has not weakened the stronger concern for the fate of civilians in war. The US reaction to the described ideational change in international relations of increasingly targeting according to the logic of efficiency turns out to be a mistake.

But if air warfare is perceived as legitimate neither when it accords with the logic of efficiency nor when it follows the commands of containment and sequencing, we have to enquire more closely what the shared normative beliefs that were outlined in section 7.3 and that caused the rise of the one and the decline of the other logic *actually* entail for the regulation of warfare. What logic would legal regulation have to impose on combat operations for them to be considered legitimate by an international public with an ever better view on to the battlefield?

Judging international law by the protection of individual rights

Imagine a scenario (1) in which (case A) a war that is fought according to the logic of sufficiency causes 10,000 combatant deaths and 2,000 civilian deaths. If (case B) it were fought according to the logic of efficiency it would cause 1,000 combatant deaths and 950 civilian deaths. The ratio of civilian to combatant deaths is much lower for case A, yet we would strongly prefer the war in which overall fewer civilians and fewer combatants die. Imagine the alternative scenario (2) in which (case A) the prognosis for the logic of sufficiency stays the same, but (case C) combat operations following the logic of efficiency would cause 2,000 combatant and 2,000 civilian casualties. The ratio changes, but we would presumably prefer case C and saving 8,000 combatants to having a better ratio between civilian and combatant casualties. Finally imagine scenario (3) in which case A again designates a war fought according to the logic of sufficiency, but this time (case D) waging the war in line with the logic of efficiency promises to cause 2,000 combatant and 3,000 civilian deaths. We have a choice between case A the loss of 12,000 and case D the loss of 5,000 lives. The previous section argued for a presumption against trading combatant for civilian deaths. But does this presumption hold when for each additional civilian casualty we could save eight combatants?[42] Waging war according to IHL interpreted based on the logic of sufficiency may well mean we 'choose' case A in scenario (3).

This chapter has so far uncovered that the ideational change manifest in a rising casualty aversion is comprised of two specific shared normative beliefs: the loss of combatants' lives in war is decreasingly acceptable and civilian casualties are still more abhorrent to large parts of the international public than combatant deaths. The former challenges the logic of sufficiency, the latter the logic of efficiency. The combination of these two beliefs might none the less suggest that things should after all stay as they are according to the legal situation: protection for civilians over protection for combatants. However, what the above scenarios bring into sharp relief is that the unapologetic and potentially limitless sacrifice of individuals (combatants) we otherwise know very little about, endorsed by the logic of sufficiency, clashes with widespread normative intuitions. This suggests that there is a third specific normative belief concretising the described ideational change that manifests

---

[42] Of course, the question is purely hypothetical because the previous section also showed that we cannot empirically connect the consequences of warfare to the targets chosen by the attacker and hence the logic underlying combat operations. The established analytical connection is between logics (target selection) and casualty *ratios*, not absolute casualty numbers.

itself as casualty aversion. Besides the fact that (1) combatants' lives are no longer considered dispensable, and that (2) civilian casualties are still considered 'even worse', (3) the sharp distinction between the two groups that IHL currently envisages seems inappropriate. Coming up with a ratio of how many saved combatants are worth a civilian life does not seem to be an appropriate solution. Given the combination of these three specific shared normative beliefs found, we need a different way of distinguishing altogether.

What do we expect IHL to do instead of demanding efficiency or imposing the structures of sufficiency? The normative ambitions of IL for the regulation of (peaceful) international relations in general certainly frame our expectations of what IHL should accomplish in war. An excursus into those ambitions and their recent development sheds light on the standard that the international society actually brings to bear when assessing IHL.

IL's normative ambitions were for a very long time extremely limited. International order traditionally rests on 'the minimal law necessary to enable state-societies to act as closed systems internally and to act as territory owners in relation to each other'.[43] According to this traditional understanding of IL, rather than promoting any positive understanding of international society, it delimits spheres of influence of states in order to preserve their integrity and continuity.[44] Law hence constrains state sovereignty only inasmuch as states bind themselves and to the extent that they consent to the application of a norm in their mutual relations. According to the so-called *Lotus dictum* rendered by the Permanent Court of International Justice '[t]he rules of law binding upon States . . . emanate from their own free will'.[45] What is not explicitly prohibited by such a consent-based rule is allowed.

In this context a legal norm very rarely achieves true universality, and IL remains fragmented. While IL thus fails to embody an autonomous ideal of how the international society ought to look,[46] this is true even more for domestic societies. IL has nothing to say about the internal affairs of states, their political organisation or the rights and duties of their citizens. It does not reach sub-state groups or individuals through

---

[43] Allott (1990) 324.   [44] Simma (1994) 230.
[45] *Case of the SS 'Lotus', France* v. *Turkey*, Permanent Court of International Justice, Judgment of 7 September 1927, File E.c. Docket XI Judgment no. 11 §16.
[46] Similar Koskenniemi (1991) 405.

the veil of state sovereignty. IL in this guise keeps expectations regarding the regulation of violence extremely low. Sovereign states are free to commandeer individuals to carry out their violent confrontations. And of course, sovereign equality means no state is qualified to sit in judgment on another, for instance to decide whether a war is fought for a legitimate reason. The use of force in the international realm is hence necessarily horizontal and legally symmetrical.[47]

IHL is quite clearly a relic of this 'traditional' IL. As adumbrated, it is agnostic about the ends to which states use force; it is cut off from moral and political considerations surrounding the use of force. Whether one side defends a possible ideal of international relations is irrelevant for who wins a war waged according to the logic of sufficiency. IHL does include many rules that are considered universal. However, their universality rests on their historical pedigree and is propped up by considerable indeterminacy; it does not arise from the notion that state consent is ever dispensable. The persistence of the US and other countries' objection to some norms and the fact that this objection is widely accepted, attests to that. Most importantly IHL allows the state a large margin of manoeuvre in forcibly pursuing a goal set by sovereign prerogative and permits the violation of individuals' right to life in this pursuit.

Yet, it is almost 'commonplace'[48] that over the last half century the emergence of a universal legal system has started to supersede this traditional network of bilateral relations. Legal concepts such as obligations *erga omnes*, *jus cogens* and a presumption against persistent objectors to the emergence of customary law bear testimony to the erosion, if not reversal, of the *Lotus dictum*.[49] Some norms of IL are considered binding in virtue of their important content rather than due to actual state consent. They can thus achieve true universality. The qualification of the role of state consent in IL has gone hand in hand with a revaluation of the role of the individual.[50] IL has consistently developed so as to consolidate the notion that the individual should be the main beneficiary of international legal regulation. While the state

---

[47] In fact, opposing belligerent states very rarely have equally valid legal or moral reasons for being in war with each other. IHL nevertheless treats them as equal because there is no non-political authority to objectively determine which side is, as it were, in the wrong.

[48] Cohen (2010).   [49] Similar Danilenko (1993) 357.

[50] See Allott (1990) 244; Dupuy (1986); Simma (1994) 247; Tomuschat (1993) 227.

remains the law's main addressee, consensus is ever wider that IL ought to be geared towards securing individual rights, a trend which is sometimes referred to as a humanisation of IL[51] or its individualisation.[52] The emergence of such a normative consensus has, in turn, created an opening for IL to be inscribed with a core set of shared basic norms, or a substantive ideal of international relations.[53]

Michael Bothe and Andreas Fischer-Lescano interpret the process of individualisation of IL and the reappraisal of the role of the state to mean that IL now 'restricts the sovereignty of the sovereigns' via certain truly universal non-abrogable norms.[54] IL, or so it is argued, is in a process of constitutionalisation.[55] What a constitution does is regulate through a web of overarching non-abrogable norms the fundamentals of social coexistence in a society in accordance with an agreed on normative ideal.[56] The development of IL over the last sixty years thus results in three interconnected changes: recognition of the individual as the main beneficiary of international legal regulation, qualification of the importance of state consent, and agreement on some universally accepted norms and hence an ideal of international coexistence. IHL lacks all three characteristics of modern IL.

This common ideal of an international society that jurists have diagnosed is likewise observed by scholars of IR. It is sometimes referred to as an increasing 'hegemony of ideas'[57] in the international system. Especially liberal scholars and some constructivists contend that 'if not politically, at least in terms of the cultural forms and in the construction of meaning, a world-civilization has been created'.[58] What legal scholars call the constitutionalisation of IL has in IR discourse found expressions like the waning of the Westphalian system,[59] a New World Order[60] or the arrival of a world society beyond merely an

---

[51] Meron (2006) 6, 9.
[52] See Harding (1999); Slaughter and Burke-White (2002).
[53] Similar Bogdandy (2006) 236; Eagleton (1939); Orakhelashvili (2006); Simma (1994) 233; Thürer (1996).
[54] Bothe and Fischer-Lescano (2002) 20.
[55] See Bryde (2003); Kumm (2004); Schilling (2005); Schreuer (1993); Weller (2002) 693ff.
[56] See Verdross (1926); also Fastenrath (1993); the notion that the compliance pull of a norm rests not on state consent but on its accordance with important values underlying the legal order as such, in turn, lies at the heart of true universality.
[57] Kratochwil (2010).   [58] *Ibid.*   [59] See McCormick (1993); Schreuer (1993).
[60] See Slaughter (2004).

international society.[61] At the heart of these developments, whatever they are called, is the notion that, if not its primary task, at least one major aim of IL is to secure individual rights. The rise of an increasingly justiciable international human rights regime is the epitome of the development of the international order over the last sixty years.[62]

It is noteworthy that the importance of these trends is contested, and they are often considered more superficial than the above outline would suggest. Even more importantly, this 'hegemony' of largely liberal ideas is extremely uneven across the world. Just as the terms 'international public' and 'shared normative expectations' used here are based in particular on observable commonalities between Western societies, the notion of a New World Order is rather Western-centric. This discussion by no means aims to veil the Western origin and liberal tendentiousness of these concepts or the contestation of individual rights in some parts of the world. However, as far as these trends describe IL Western centrism is less of a damning indictment than it is for many political concepts. Those norms that are described as subject to constitutionalisation here are at least *de jure* universally binding. As a result, and this is crucial for the argument of the book, even regimes that themselves violate individual rights and societies that may not have internalised them use the changed standards in IL as a means of political contestation and for rallying support when in conflict with liberal democracies. Afghanistan is an example *par excellence* of a country where the rootedness of individual rights in domestic culture and their application tends to be weak; yet the language of IL and human rights serves the government to articulate disaffection with the coalition forces. The relevance or purchase of these normative developments for the reality of interstate armed conflict is therefore beyond doubt.

Though IHL has not kept in lock-step with the development of general IL it has not remained insulated from these trends either. One result of the fact that the cavalier approach of IHL to individual rights has rendered it increasingly unpalatable is the encroachment of human rights law, the most immediate manifestation of an international order geared towards the individual, on to IHL's area of regulation.

---

[61] See Buzan (2004).

[62] I use the terms human rights and individual rights interchangeably. The former is widespread among jurists and scholars of IR; the latter is the preferred term of philosophers working on war. It is beyond the scope of the book to explore potential differences between the two concepts.

Traditionally IHL was considered *lex specialis* in relation to human rights, meaning that the latter ceased to apply in times of war.[63] However, this understanding no longer prevails. Though never fully illuminating how exactly the two branches of IL are meant to interact, the ICJ has solidified the understanding that human rights continue to be relevant in armed conflict and that IHL is merely for the time of hostilities superimposed over it.[64]

The most significant challenge to IHL's standard-setting authority stems from the practice of human rights bodies to adjudicate cases in the context of armed conflicts. The Inter-American Commission and Court on Human Rights have from their inception considered cases in the contexts of internal armed conflict, for instance, the civil war in El Salvador between 1980 and 1991. The Commission continues to apply IHL as *lex specialis* and frequently refers to the American Convention on Human Rights[65] in conjunction with Common Article 3 of the Geneva Conventions, even thought it is a body tasked with adjudicating human rights violations. In opposition, the Court rejects the doctrine of *lex specialis*, claiming that it lacks competence *ratione materiae* to apply IHL.[66] None the less the Court frequently refers to IHL. Based on the assumption of a 'complementarity'[67] between the two systems of law the Court uses provisions of IHL as interpretative tools to elucidate how certain human rights, such as the right to life, apply in situations of armed conflict.[68]

The European Court of Human Rights challenges the authority of IHL in yet another way. Like the Inter-American Court it unambiguously submitted that states party to the European Convention on

---

[63] See Garraway (2014).

[64] *Legality of the Threat or Use of Nuclear Weapons*, ICJ, Advisory Opinion of 8 July 1996, ICJ Report 5, 240, §25; see also Forowicz (2010) 314; Tomuschat makes the interesting point that many human rights treaties were probably drafted based on the conviction that they would cease to apply in war (Tomuschat (2002) 21).

[65] American Convention on Human Rights, 'Pact of San Jose', Costa Rica, 22 November 1969.

[66] Burgorgue-Larsen and Ùbeda de Torres (2011) 68ff.

[67] *Serrano de la Cruz Sisters* v. *El Salvador*, IACtHR, Preliminary Objections of 23 November 2004, Series C no. 120, §112.

[68] See, for instance, *Las Palmeras* v. *Colombia*, IACtHR, Preliminary Objections of 4 February 2000, Series C no. 67, §33; *Bámaca Velásquez* v. *Guatemala*, IACtHR, Judgment on the Merits of 25 November 2000, Series C no.70, §209.

Human Rights[69] 'owe' human rights to individuals in the *espace juridique* covered by the treaty as well as when they have effective control during an armed conflict.[70] At the same time, it has eschewed any explicit reference to the Geneva Conventions and the API, despite the overwhelming support for these instruments among its members.[71] The Court has investigated more than 280 cases of alleged human rights violations by Turkey against the Kurdish population in the north of the country, a situation that arguably reaches the threshold of an internal armed conflict.[72] In 2005, it rendered the first of 230 judgments, many of which found violations of the Convention in connection with the armed conflict between Russia and Chechnya.[73]

Based on its commitment to the understanding that human rights apply 'wherever a state exercises power, authority or jurisdiction over people'[74] the Court has also applied its legal instrument in situations of international armed conflict. In 2009, two rulings found violations of Articles 2, 3 and 5 of the European Convention on Human Rights during the Turkish invasion of northern Cyprus.[75] The air war by

---

[69] Full name Convention for the Protection of Human Rights and Fundamental Freedoms of 4 November 1950.

[70] *Bankovic and Others* v. *Belgium and 16 Other Contracting States*, EurCtHR, Court (Grand Chamber) Decision on Admissibility of 12 December 2001, EurCtHR Reports 2001–XII, no. 52207/99, §333.

[71] Forowicz (2010) 314.

[72] Landmark cases are, among others, *Özkan* v. *Turkey*, EurCtHR, Judgment (Merits) of 6 April 2004, no. 21689/93; *Ergi* v. *Turkey*, EurCtHR, Judgment (Merits and Just Satisfaction) of 28 July 1998, EurCtHR Reports 1998–IV, no. 23818/94; *Güleç* v. *Turkey*, EurCtHR, Judgment (Merits and Just Satisfaction) of 27 July 1998, EurCtHR Reports 1998–IV, no. 21593/93, §§63–64; *Loizidou* v. *Turkey*, EurCtHR, Judgment (Merits) of 18 December 1996, EurCtHR Reports 1996–VI, no. 15318/89; *Loizidou* v. *Turkey*, EurCtHR, Preliminary Objections of 23 March 1995, EurCtHR Reports 1995, no. 310.

[73] For instance, *Isayeva and Others* v. *Russia*, EurCtHR, Judgment (Merits and Just Satisfaction) of 24 February 2005, no.57950/00; 350 cases are still pending. In addition, three cases were brought by individuals against Bosnia-Herzegovina and two against Armenia in relation to the conflict with Azerbaijan over Nagorno-Karabakh.

[74] Meron (1995) 57; also Gross (2007) 1; Hampson (1992b) 119.

[75] *Varnava and Others* v. *Turkey*, EurCtHR, Judgment (Merits and Just Satisfaction) of 18 September 2009, no. 16064/90; *Andreou* v. *Turkey*, EurCtHR, Judgment (Merits and Satisfaction) of 27 October 2009, no. 45653/99; in the same context a case against Cyprus was ruled inadmissible: *Emin and Others* v. *Cyprus*, EurCtHR, Court (Fourth Section) Decision on Admissibility of 3 April 2012, no. 59623/08; and a case against both Cyprus and Turkey is still pending: *Güzelyurtlu*

NATO countries against the Federal Republic of Yugoslavia resulted in three applications, two declared inadmissible and one dismissed on grounds of merit. They none the less clarified the kind of jurisdictional link an individual must have to a belligerent state in order to have a claim against it.[76] With regard to Russia's 2008 invasion of Georgia more than 2,000 individuals have lodged applications with the Court.[77] In addition, an interstate dispute between the two countries is pending.[78] Georgia alleges indiscriminate and disproportionate attacks in Abkhazia and South Ossetia during the international armed conflict that is so far the only one that has ever incontestably been under the regulatory purview of the API. It remains to be seen whether the Court none the less continues to *de jure* rely solely on human rights law and thereby endorse the increasingly widespread notion that 'the long-standing separation of both systems may have outlived its usefulness'.[79]

To conclude, shared normative beliefs about violence in international relations, the evolution of general IL, the recent development of international relations and a trend in international adjudication all suggest that the touchstone of normative success of IL in the twenty-first century is the protection of individual rights. In order for warfare to meet with public approval IHL has to find a way to avoid the large-scale violation of individual rights in war.

The logic of liability and the distribution of harm

The notion that IL should protect individual rights, foremost among them the right to life, even in war presents a direct challenge to the distinction between combatants and civilians currently envisaged by

---

and Others v. *Cyprus and Turkey*, EurCtHR, Application to Institute Proceedings of 13 May 2009, no. 36925/07.

[76] See *Markovic and Others* v. *Italy*, EurCtHR, Judgment (Merits) of 14 December 2006, no. 1398/03, §100; *Bankovic and Others* v. *Belgium and 16 Other Contracting States*, EurCtHR, Court (Grand Chamber) Decision on Admissibility of 12 December 2001, EurCtHR Reports 2001–XII, no. 52207/99, §333; *Behrami and Behrami* v. *France* and *Saramati* v. *France, Germany and Norway*, EurCtHR, Court (Grand Chamber) Decision on Admissibility of 2 May 2007, no. 71412/01 and no. 78166/01.

[77] Tomuschat (2002) 23.

[78] *Georgia* v. *Russian Federation*, EurCtHR, Application to Institute Proceedings of 9 February 2009, no. 38263/08; *Georgia* v. *Russian Federation*, EurCtHR, Court (Fifth Section) Decision on Admissibility of 13 December 2011, no. 38263/08.

[79] Forowicz (2010) 320; Watkin (2004) 98, 34.

IHL. Section 8.1 suggested that the traditional justification of noncombatant immunity is based on combatants supposedly having consented to becoming 'dangerous men', but showed that this is a mistaken assumption. Combatants are not consistently more threatening to the enemy than civilians. Crucially, combatants cannot generally be deemed to have consented to their status either. But even if the correlation between combatants and threat potential and consent were perfect, from a perspective committed to individual rights a person who is threatening or has consented to military service cannot merely for those reasons be justifiably killed. The criticism that being a combatant does not amount to a forfeiture of one's right to life has been levelled against conventional just-war theory by a group of philosophers sometimes referred to as revisionist critics.[80] How do revisionist just-war theorists suggest that belligerents distinguish between persons who should be targeted and those who should remain immune from direct attack in war?

In liberal individual-rights affirming societies, without prior due process individuals may only be justifiably killed in self- (or other-) defence.[81] It is from this analogy that revisionist just war theorists have developed a list of conditions for when an individual is liable to potentially lethal attack by another in war. An individual is generally considered liable to be killed in self-defence only if she is (1) responsible for (2) contributing to (3) an unjustified threat, and (4) lethal attack is a proportionate and necessary response to the contribution.[82] Crucially, the first three conditions concern the conduct of the individual and her resulting moral status, not her membership in a group, for instance, the armed forces. In the words of Jeff McMahan: '[t]o say that a person is morally liable to being harmed in a certain way is to say that his own action has made it the case that to harm him in that way would not wrong him, or contravene his rights'.[83]

---

[80] The critique is mounted *inter alia* in Coady (2008); Fabre (2009); McMahan (2004a); McMahan (2009); McMahan (2010a); McMahan (2010b); McMahan (2011); McMahan (2012); Rodin (2002); Rodin (2008); Rodin (2011); Rodin (2012); Rodin and Sorabji (2005).

[81] I address a lesser evil justification for killing below.

[82] Lazar identifies as the common denominator of revisionist just war theorists that these four cumulative elements trigger liability to attack (Lazar (2012)).

[83] McMahan (2009) 11.

Revisionist just war theorists propose that this standard naturally also applies in war.[84] In this view, the inevitable harm caused in combat operations ought to be distributed according to neither sufficiency nor efficiency, but according to individual liability. If it were rigorously implemented, this logic of liability would ensure that warfare, as far as deliberate attacks are concerned, did not involve large-scale violations of individual rights. Given that the legitimacy of combat operations seems to hinge on protecting individual rights, the logic of liability has a much better chance than either the logic of sufficiency or efficiency of meeting with popular normative acceptance. The next logical step would then be to change IHL with the aim of imposing on combat operations the logic of liability and thus rendering IL normatively successful in the regulation of warfare. Currently IHL is not normatively successful in US air warfare, whether we make normative success a matter of an international public's expectations or whether we bring to bear an individual rights-based morality.

---

[84] McMahan (2004b); McMahan (2010b) 354.

9 | *The impossibility of normative success for international law in war*

The previous chapter arrived at the conclusion that the touchstone of normatively successful IL in war is the protection of individual rights and hence the imposition of what I refer to as the logic of liability. What would it look like if belligerents in combat operations acted accordingly by only attacking individuals liable to lethal attack?[1]

9.1 The limits of international law in war

The impracticability of warfare according to the logic of liability

Combatants who fight without a just cause or who resist a just attack contribute to an unjustified threat to the combatants on the other side and are hence liable to defensive harm (including deliberate attack).[2] By implication, if combatants use force in defence of a just cause, they do not forfeit their right to life and should remain immune.[3] The fact that the logic of liability abandons the independence of legitimate conduct in war from questions of resort creates numerous practical problems that have been widely discussed among just-war theorists.[4] What would the implications be for IL if a connection between legality of resort to force and conduct in war was officially acknowledged?

The only legal justification for resort to force without a mandate from the UN Security Council is self-defence.[5] On the assumption that only

---

[1] This chapter brackets the question whether and how individual rights violations stemming from incidental harm could be justified.

[2] McMahan (2009) 234; also Rodin (2008) 46.

[3] '[U]nless they lose rights for some reason other than acquiring combatant status, just combatants are innocent in the relevant sense' (McMahan (2006) 379; also Rodin (2008) 167; Rodin (2012) 1).

[4] For an overview see Rodin and Shue (2008) 7.

[5] The legal concept of self-defence is far from congruent with just-war theory's understanding of a just cause. However, in this section I only investigate the possibility of changing IHL without also challenging the prohibition on the use of

one side if any in every war acts in self-defence, IL would have to relinquish symmetry. It would have to allow one belligerent actions that were prohibited for the other. Belligerents often enter into wars because they mistakenly believe they are legally permitted to do so. Even if one side were aware that it was in want of a legal justification, the decision to nevertheless go to war suggests that the stakes are high. Moreover, such a deliberately unjust belligerent would probably lack scruples that could prevent it from using the law applicable to just belligerents. IL that is significantly less permissive for one side would then never be applied. The kind of asymmetry that the logic of efficiency entails – two opposing belligerents may attack different kinds of objects because they have diverging political goals – undermines the normative integrity of IL. The kind of asymmetry the logic of liability requires – law is consistently differentially permissive for opposing belligerents – undermines compliance with IL.

Deliberate disregard or misapplication of a law, even if probable and explicable, does not affect a law's validity. We might still be right to expect belligerents and presumably individual combatants to determine the legality of their cause before taking up arms. However, the question of whether a belligerent in fact has a right to self-defence is, even when approached in good faith, often difficult to answer. In order to attach legal significance to an individual's decision to fight allegedly without the legitimising claim of exercising self-defence, we would in fairness need to overcome fundamental epistemic uncertainties around self-defence. Jeff McMahan suggests that the establishment of an international court that in a timely and effective manner adjudicated questions of self-defence would mean that individuals could be expected to refuse to fight in a war that was declared illegal. They could be legally held to account if they did fight anyway.[6] In the absence of such a court McMahan acknowledges that '[a]t least at present, the law of war must diverge from the morality of war'.[7] Of course, this court would need to have features, such as universality and efficiency, that current international adjudicative bodies lack. In other words, unless international

---

force under general IL or engaging with a claimed right to humanitarian intervention. I hence assume that self-defence in accordance with Article 51 UNC is the only legal reason or 'just cause' for the unilateral resort to force. By implication, individuals fighting on behalf of a belligerent state unable to avail itself of that legal justification are what, for reasons of simplicity, I refer to as 'unjust combatants'. The state in question is an 'unjust belligerent'.

[6] McMahan (2008) 42; McMahan (2012).   [7] McMahan (2010b) 358.

relations undergo significant institutional change, IL must out of fairness to the individual stay independent of the legality of resort.

It may, in theory, be feasible for an international court to authoritatively determine in every war which side has a claim to self-defence so that combatants on one side could be sure that they were asked to contribute to an unjustified threat. However, even if that were the case, it would still be far-fetched to think that each of them actually contributed enough – either to the overall threat of waging an aggressive war or to individual battlefield encounters that threaten just combatants on the other side[8] – to render them liable to lethal attack.[9] In addition, besides the fact that individuals' causal connection to the overall war and/or individual threats might be indirect or slight, in many cases death, wounds or trauma would not be necessary and proportionate responses to their actions. In Seth Lazar's words: '[I]f the laws of war should mirror the liability view, then they must be not merely asymmetrical, but completely individuated both to the agent and to the specific act.'[10]

Of course, this is an extremely high standard – avoid rights violations completely. Could IL at least reduce them as much as possible? Indeed McMahan does not claim that a precise distribution of harm in accordance with each individual's liability is possible. He instead argues that as imposing harm is inevitable, small differences in liability among those we can target make all the difference and should determine who is harmed. In this context, Lazar has claimed that the logic of individual liability faces a dilemma 'borne out of the equally minimal responsibility of many combatants and noncombatants for the objectively unjustified threat posed by their belligerent state'.[11] If the threshold for liability to be killed is low enough to justify the intentional killings of a significant number of combatants on the unjust side, then many

---

[8] McMahan differentiates between combatants' contribution to the macro threat that is an unjust war and their contribution to threats on the battlefield which he refers to as micro threats (McMahan (2009) 725).

[9] This is not to say that combatants' deserts play a role in whether they may be attacked. We may believe that anyone who knowingly contributes to an unjustified threat is liable, however small that contribution may be. We might hence want to hold them to account. The question is, do we also think they are subject to the threatened person's right to potentially lethal self-defence? Without being able to discuss the matter exhaustively, I submit that liability to lethal attack for a very small contribution to an unjustified threat is at least contestable.

[10] Lazar (2010).   [11] *Ibid.* 210.

civilians lose their immunity from direct attack as well, because they can be expected to bear some responsibility for the initiation of the war. That combatants and civilians alike could be targeted would create a scenario Lazar conceives of as total war.[12] On the other hand, if the liability threshold was so high that it would preserve noncombatant immunity, not enough combatants would be legitimate targets of attack, it would be impossible to wage war and we would end up having to endorse pacifism.[13]

In my view, the fundamental problem does not lie with uncertainty about where to locate a threshold of liability to being killed. If it were at all possible to connect suffering harm in war to individual moral status, even imperfectly with a simple threshold of liability past which one can be attacked, it is not at all the case that we would end up with anything resembling total war. It would merely be a group of different people who were permitted to be intentionally killed (not combatants as such but all and only those civilians as well as those combatants above the threshold of liability). If such an imperfect version of the logic of liability could be implemented, there would be no reason to *also* uphold the principle of noncombatant immunity. The reason why McMahan is nevertheless reluctant to give up noncombatant immunity, and Lazar equates such a scenario with total war, is presumably that even an imperfect version of the logic of liability that merely directs all harm towards those liable to attack above a certain threshold is impossible to apply correctly. Identifying individuals' contributions would require the attacker to possess intelligence about the inner details of the adversary's society that warring states do not usually have.

Could we not ask each belligerent to designate those contributing above a certain threshold among its own citizens as liable, as the belligerents now designate some of them as combatants? It might then in theory be possible to attack individuals whose causal involvement in an unjustified threat was direct and significant. However, I have so far brushed over the requirement that individuals not merely unwittingly or accidentally, hence innocently, contribute to the threat, but that they do so responsibly. What does it mean to be responsible for one's contributions to an unjustified threat in such a way that one forfeits one's right to life? On a spectrum of liability, just above the innocent threat is the individual who voluntarily chooses to act in a way that foreseeably

---

[12] *Ibid.*, 188.   [13] *Ibid.*

contributes to a threat – what Lazar refers to as agent-responsibility.[14] We would still need a court adjudicating questions of resort to force in order to be able to assume that individuals on the side not fighting in self-defence, who chose to take up arms on behalf of their state none the less, are agent-responsible for contributing to an unjustified threat.

But would agent-responsibility be enough for people to forfeit their right to life? We still know nothing about individuals' motives for fighting or potential excuses.[15] In other words, the culpability of the individual still eludes us.[16] It seems odd to discount excuses as part of a way to regulate war that derives its appeal from the claim to be giving the individual her moral due. However, if we required a culpable contribution to the unjustified threat, then regardless of whom we tasked with applying the logic of individual liability in a given scenario, the agent would require near omniscience, rather than mere intelligence and good faith, to do so. The logic of individual liability, even if we accepted a threshold rather than a fully correct (individualised) distribution of harm, would inevitably be misapplied.

What if we stripped down the logic of individual liability even further? We could allocate harm according to individuals' (causal) contribution to the war effort without regard to the attending responsibility, even their knowledge of the facts.[17] This is very close to what the principle of noncombatant immunity and hence the logic of sufficiency in fact proposes to do. After all, it is in theory sufficient to engage an adversary's combatants and leave the civilians unharmed precisely because only the former are permitted to contribute directly to the fighting.[18] By the same token, this stripped-down version of the logic of liability would lose much of its original appeal over the logic of sufficiency and could hardly lay claim to avoiding large-scale violations of individual rights.

---

[14] Lazar (2009) 706.

[15] For an enquiry into potential excuses of unjust combatants see Lichtenberg (2008) 118.

[16] Some revisionists have lowered their standards from requiring culpability to ground liability to lethal attack to considering mere agent responsibility sufficient (for instance, McMahan (2011) 19). For a discussion of this trend among revisionist just-war theorists see Lazar (2009) 706–12.

[17] For instance, Fabre (2012) 76, 60 fn. 12, 72 fn. 21, 78 fn. 26.

[18] Of course, the required significance and immediacy of a contribution to hostilities might diverge depending on whether the sufficiency requirement/current IHL or the stripped-down liability standard is brought to bear.

Therefore individual liability is not a practicable criterion for distinction, and impracticable IL bears the great danger of being disregarded and missing the chance of making a difference in war. Section 8.1 has already discussed two hypothetical examples of IL that would be as impracticable as a law attempting to impose the logic of liability: IL that tries to avoid all killing (standard 1), and IL that avoids all civilian casualties (standard 2).[19] Contrary to these standards, though, IL with the ambition of either permitting only the killing of people who are liable to attack or reducing individual rights violations in war as much as possible by funnelling harm towards individuals liable above a certain threshold, bears considerable potential to make things worse. A law that attempts to avoid all killing is simply utopian, but does not lend itself as an apology for interest-guided behaviour that prioritises military imperatives over humanitarian considerations. After all, if law outlawed all killing any dead body would prima facie betray an actor's defiance of the law. On the other hand, given the obscurity of individuals' liability in the context of war, IL that licenses the killing of individuals that supposedly make a responsible contribution to the adversary's unjustified threat provides a ready apology for a wide range of attacks. Section 3.2 noted that apart from the elderly and children almost all members of a belligerent society can be construed as making a contribution to the war. The significance of this contribution and the responsibility borne for it are too contestable to provide any meaningful restriction on the infliction of harm.

Why IL cannot offer a connection between individual moral status and the distribution of deliberate harm that is deeper than the one offered by the principle of noncombatant immunity or the stripped-down version of the liability logic becomes particularly evident if we compare war to law enforcement in a domestic context. Imbued with the authority of the state's monopoly over the use of force, law enforcement is much more fundamentally asymmetrical than even the most uneven confrontation between states imaginable: arguably contemporary air warfare by Western coalitions against radically inferior adversaries under investigation here. Moreover, focused on a single individual or a manageable group of delinquents, law enforcement is geared towards the individual in the first place. War is fundamentally a physical confrontation between states, in which human beings are

---

[19] See p. 255.

conceived of as members of a collective (their state), rather than as individuals who are to be treated according to their own liability.

That the collective nature of war makes it impossible to give individuals their moral due is obvious and does not come as a surprise. Of course, human beings continue to exist during war as individuals with a moral status of their own, but in order for law to track that status at all and distribute harm accordingly, even if very imperfectly, it seems that we would have to make assumptions about the physical confrontation that place it outside the category of international armed conflict: a horizontal, violent and collective confrontation.

To recapitulate, IL cannot coherently channel harm in war towards the individuals liable to it. The contestability of individual liability invites bad-faith interpretations of IL so that wars waged according to the logic of liability may well involve more killing or rights violations than combat operations following another logic under the same circumstances. To the extent that a belligerent's assumptions about the enemy's individuals are systematically incorrect, which is likely, even a good faith attempt at following the logic of liability may involve as many or more violations of individual rights than combat operations waged according to the logic of sufficiency, in which at least civilians' rights are more likely to be respected. In addition, in the light of section 7.1's finding that the endorsement of IHL sometimes inspires air strikes a belligerent would not otherwise have carried out, it seems possible that following a law that attempts to impose the logic of liability could cause more harm or more violations of individual rights than not following law at all.[20]

The inability of international law to protect individual rights in war

Is there nothing more that IL can do for the reduction of individual rights violations in war? Pacifism is not a true solution even for the staunchest defender of human rights in international relations. After all, war may sometimes present the only means to prevent even more

---

[20] For reasons outlined in section 8.1 these claims about the consequences of waging war according to the logic of liability rest on analytical plausibility only and cannot be verified empirically.

violations of individual rights, for instance during a genocide.[21] This is also the intuition behind the widespread view that war, and by implication the killing of combatants, is sometimes morally justified, even though it infringes their rights. Of course, the notion that we can justifiably infringe some rights (during warfare) to avoid a greater violation of rights (for instance, genocide) raises the spectre of a consequentialist justification. Many revisionist just-war theorists would eschew the notion that the infringement of some individuals' rights to life, which the logic of sufficiency allows, can be justified by the achievement of a morally very important goal to which it contributes. David Rodin has forcefully argued that the rights violations inflicted in war present so-called *mala in se* and should therefore never be levelled out with consequentialist reasoning.[22]

But allowing a lesser-evil justification for war does not necessarily amount to trampling on individual rights for the purpose of maximising some other good. If we accept that war is only justified as the lesser evil when it preserves many individuals' rights while infringing some others', individual rights remain the 'touchstone' of the justification.[23] That in war many individuals' rights to life are at stake is generally considered a reason to doubt the validity of consequentialist justifications. Yet it can also be read as rendering consequences particularly important, specifically at the level of law. In Thomas Nagel's words, 'within the appropriate limits, public decisions will be justifiably more consequentialist than private ones. They will also have larger consequences to take into account.'[24]

Similarly Terry Nardin criticises the notion that public policies and by implication laws 'should be guided and judged by the same principles that govern individual conduct'.[25] He holds that the principles that guide public affairs are distinct from those guiding individual ethics. If any differentiation between private or individual morality and public policy or law is warranted, it is certainly that while the individual may not normally justify counteracting someone's right on the basis that the conduct contributes to a greater good, even if this were the

---

[21] For an exposition of this view see Shue (2008).   [22] Rodin (2011) 455, 460.

[23] I am grateful to Henry Shue for pointing this out to me. In such a scenario McMahan seems to waver, acknowledging that it is possible that 'infringing the rights of some to avert a greater evil to others' may be 'morally justified' (McMahan (2008) 23f.).

[24] Nagel (1979) 84.   [25] Nardin (2010).

overall better preservation of individual rights, it is a desirable feature of public policies and laws that they take into account the consequences of their systematic implementation for individual rights.

But can law ensure that killing in war is justified as the overall lesser evil? War does not seem to be a mechanism for distributing harms and goods in a normatively meaningful way even just between belligerent states, that is, according to some principle other than material strength subject to considerable chance. Not even if the regulation of conduct could draw on the relative justifiability of belligerents' respective causes? Perhaps this is where a stripped-down version of the logic of liability (that completely abstracts from responsibility and only looks at individuals' causal contribution to either a justified or an unjustified threat) still beats the logic of sufficiency, even though it approximates the principle of noncombatant immunity. Contrary to the logic of sufficiency, the stripped-down logic of liability remains asymmetrical and can, if it is respected, therefore 'guarantee' that the right side wins. After all, it would be vastly more permissive for the 'right side' than for the unjust belligerent.[26] Of course, here we run into the problem discussed above. Differentially permissive IHL is unlikely to be applied by the side deemed 'unjust'. But hypothetically, what would it look like if, rather than 'contributing individuals'/combatants on both sides, only those 'contributing individuals'/combatants were permitted to be attacked whose contribution was to an unjustified threat?

The absence of a claim to self-defence at *the level of the state* would imply that the individuals fighting on its behalf may inflict no harm at all, except perhaps in a very narrow set of self-defence situations that arise in individual battlefield encounters. In a physical confrontation under such a rule – all combatants on one side are legally required to hold still – the outcome would indeed reflect a difference in moral status between the belligerent states. However, as soon as the individuals on the unjust side do what this law demands – lay down their arms – they are not contributing to an unjustified threat anymore and therefore cease to be open to attack by the just side. The latter, as a result, very quickly, if compliance is instant immediately, runs out of legitimate targets for attack. Rather than regulating war, this imperfect version

---

[26] Of course, an actual guarantee is impossible. A very weak just belligerent might lose even with a head start provided by asymmetrical law.

of the logic of liability implies its prohibition. Like a law that requires two of the six standards for normative success discussed in section 8.1 (avoid all killing or avoid all civilian casualties)[27] a law that prescribed an asymmetrical logic of liability, however stripped down, would merely repeat the prohibition on the use of force, would probably be disregarded and would miss the opportunity to make any difference to the conduct of war at all.

Between the logics of sufficiency and efficiency, I was unable to establish which better limits harm overall. What about the protection of individual rights? As mentioned the logic of sufficiency protects civilians' right to life at least against direct attack at the price of not protecting any combatants' rights at all – not a great record. Whether and on what scale the logic of efficiency leads to the violation of individual rights is contingent on who and what counts as a legitimate target in the light of the goals a belligerent pursues – it is entirely unpredictable. Of course, neither logic *seeks* to regulate warfare with a view to preserving individual rights. But can we adjust the logics so that they are geared towards that normative standard?

From an efficiency point of view, persons and objects would be legitimate targets of attack if their military engagement led to the direct and quick achievement of the end-state that was determined to involve overall fewer infringements of individual rights: for instance, A defends itself against a tyrannical invader who violates its population's individual rights. The most efficient way to achieve this overall best end-state in terms of individual rights is for B to not inflict harm at all.[28] In other words, IHL would have to allow exactly those air strikes that mean that A wins as quickly as possible because that promises to minimise rights infringements overall.[29] While (the imperfect version of) the logic of liability transcends war as such, the logic of

---

[27] See p. 255.

[28] See Dill (2013) for the argument that it is often difficult/impossible to establish which side in a war needs to win for the overall best preservation of individual rights. The reason is that war often amounts to what I call an 'epistemically cloaked forced choice'.

[29] I bracket the question here of what such a logic would say if the fewest overall rights violations could be achieved by letting an illegal aggression stand because the aggressor was relatively benign and the defender too weak to win at all or without too much bloodshed. Would we forgo a state's right to territorial integrity and the society's right to self-determination for the sake of minimising individual rights violations overall? The so far relatively bloodless alleged

efficiency if applied asymmetrically unfailingly prohibits the use of any force by one side.

The conclusion is inescapable: the outcome of a physical confrontation does not necessarily, and not even probably, reflect the legal or moral standing of the belligerents as long as the law is symmetrical. It is only 'guaranteed' that the right side wins, if we allow IHL to be fundamentally asymmetrical. However, no matter how exactly we propose to get to the desired end-state, if that end-state is the avoidance of individual rights violations, an asymmetrical logic allows only one side if any to fight. In other words, IL cannot reliably bestow victory and defeat on states in accordance with whether they fight in favour of or against the overall preservation of individual rights. By implication, IL cannot vouchsafe that the infringement in war of the right to life of combatants, who are not individually liable to that fate, is justified as the lesser evil.

If we want to avoid IHL being ignored we cannot give up the symmetry between belligerents. If we want it not to serve as a ready apology for interest-guided behaviour, thus being potentially detrimental to the protection of individual rights, we cannot give up the principle of noncombatant immunity as the first rule of distinction. Within those parameters can we gear the logic of sufficiency, which fulfils both those criteria, towards the preservation of individual rights? Can combatant status be changed so that fewer people who are not liable to being killed are combatants and combatants are more often more liable than civilians? Of course, any added protection we offer combatants will benefit both 'just' and 'unjust' combatants. But sparing some individuals who might be liable to attack for the purpose of also sparing some who are not seems entirely appropriate as long as it does not render warfare impossible, thereby undermining any potential effectiveness of IL.

So far combatants are only shielded from unnecessary suffering and superfluous injuries. But would war really be impossible if we instituted a capture rather than kill criterion in IHL or a general least-harmful-means test? The issue is contested. The interpretative guidance on direct participation in hostilities issued by the ICRC suggested exactly this, stipulating that 'the kind and degree of force which is permissible against persons not entitled

invasion of Eastern Ukraine by the Russian Federation may well raise exactly this question.

to protection against direct attack must not exceed what is actually necessary to accomplish a legitimate military purpose in the prevailing circumstances'.[30] Another suggestion with a similar thrust is an 'actual threat' criterion. Only combatants who in the moment of the confrontation on the battlefield pose a direct threat are permissible targets for potentially lethal attack.[31]

Military practitioners have forcefully rejected the attempt to make direct attack conditional on necessity 1.[32] Of course, there are epistemic challenges to determining whether a combatant is in fact threatening. At the same time, the argument that the introduction of either a necessity threshold or a threat condition would make warfare impossible has not yet been made convincingly. In fact Gabriella Blum argues that it is the 'changing nature of wars and militaries [that] casts doubts on the necessity of killing all enemy combatants'.[33] Whether developments in military technology provide an opening for differentiating between combatants warrants more research. Certainly not interfering with the possibility of an armed competition between militaries proceeding is the requirement that individuals give actual, meaningful consent to becoming combatants and to fighting in a given war. If this were accompanied with an obligation on the part of a belligerent government to disclose necessary intelligence for combatants to make an informed choice about the reasons for a resort to war that they are asked to participate in, we would be one step closer to combatants actually being agent-responsible for their actions in war.

To conclude, the logic of sufficiency strengthened with a necessity, a threat and a consent requirement seems to be the best available compromise between appropriateness as it is perceived in the twenty-first century (based on an individual rights-based morality) and the basic military imperative of not making war impossible. That does not change the fact that no matter which logic it imposes IHL is unable to avoid large-scale violations of individual rights. It is therefore unlikely to ever be perceived as normatively successful. Even if an air strike

---

[30] Melzer (2009) 77–9.

[31] See Blum (2010) for an elaboration of this proposal.

[32] Schmitt (2010) 14 and 40; also Cohen and Shany (2007) 8f.; Green (2002) 444; for the explanation of different incarnations of the principle of necessity in IHL see section 3.1, pp. 79f.

[33] Blum (2010) 69.

kills individuals who were in fact liable to lethal attack, the international public is unlikely to be able to differentiate such attacks from the many air strikes that unavoidably kill individuals not liable to that fate.[34] From the point of view of the international public in the twenty-first century there are no truly legitimate targets of attack in war.

9.2 The potential of international law in war

IHL is not and cannot be normatively successful in war. The logic of sufficiency is the twenty-first-century belligerent's best bet to wage war with a view to quelling academic criticism and popular outrage. However, for that to be true we have to rule out that the logic of sufficiency is as impracticable as the logic of liability. We need to establish whether it is actually possible to wage war in accordance with the logic of sufficiency and whether IHL could be determinate enough to vouchsafe that belligerents who follow it wage war in line with the commands of sequencing and containment. Over the following paragraphs I will show that the logic of sufficiency is practicable in both respects.

The practicability of warfare according to the logic of sufficiency

I first investigate the validity of the assumption that generic military victory is sufficient to allow states to subsequently achieve their legitimate political/economic or other goals. This assumption underlies the command that belligerents ought to 'sequence'[35] the use of force and the pursuit of political goals. Given the blanket prohibition on the use of force in modern IL, there are no specific political goals that states may legitimately pursue with force and whose achievement is guaranteed after generic military victory. The exception to the prohibition on the use of force is self-defence, which is arguably a goal that states ought to be able to achieve with force. Eroding military capabilities, as the logic of sufficiency prescribes, is certainly conducive to repelling an armed

---

[34] Possible exceptions are prominent political or military leaders who have committed war crimes or acts of terrorism. They create the impression that a liability judgment without due process from afar is easy, after all.

[35] For definitions of sequencing, containment and the logic of sufficiency see the appendix.

attack. Generic military victory hence fulfils the need for self-defence in the meaning of Article 51 UNC.

If overcoming an enemy militarily and in fact achieving a generic military victory does *not* eliminate the threat that this enemy poses, it arguably did not call for (and thus legitimise) the use of force in the first place. In general, if generic military victory could not directly translate into the political goals an attacker attaches to self-defence, then these can be presumed to be add-ons to the claim of self-defence and to fall into the category of doing politics, for instance a specific outcome in negotiations, with force. Interviews with US military personnel reveal very little patience for the notion that combat operations should always be geared towards generic military victory, whatever ultimate goals a war might have. The prescriptive implications of the sequencing command are highly unpopular. Yet in the current international legal order, in which the only legitimate political goal in war is self-defence, the assumption that generic military victory is sufficient holds.

What about the assumption underlying the command of containment? To recall, it asserts that it is sufficient to engage combatants and those objects whose engagement directly (in one causal step) contributes to the goal of generic military victory. Crucially, the assumption does not presume to spell out what is sufficient to *win* a war. After all, only one side can win each war. What attacking combatants and military objectives narrowly defined are assumed to be sufficient for is a competition between enemy militaries and the possibility of one military overcoming the other and thus achieving a generic military victory. This sufficiency assumption expresses the agnosticism of IHL as to which side wins a war. After all, as mentioned, in the current international system there are no political goals whose pursuit with force is legally privileged.

Again self-defence is the exception, where this agnosticism seems inappropriate. It is easily possible to imagine a case in which it is *in*sufficient to attack an aggressor's combatants and military objectives narrowly defined to win a genuine war of self-defence. All we need for this scenario to become reality is a militarily strong aggressor and a weak defender who cannot overcome the aggressor's armed forces. Should the logic of sufficiency yield to the logic of efficiency in cases of self-defence? Is a defender allowed to fight the aggressor by targeting objects according to a broader interpretation of Article 52(2) or even target civilians?

As previously mentioned, almost all post-1945 wars were officially justified with a variation on the theme of self-defence. Allowing self-defence to trigger a different (less demanding) logic for the conduct of hostilities would further invite abuse of this already overstretched concept. If self-defence provided a waiver, the logic of sufficiency would never be applied. In fact, this is true for any set of rules that would be relaxed in cases of self-defence. The relaxed rules would end up being the only ones ever drawn upon.[36] What would guarantee that providing an exception for self-defence would not mean undermining the rule? Nothing short of an authoritative adjudication of questions of resort to force backed by enforcement powers – so not just a court as proposed by McMahan to decide which side is in the right, but also a police force that intervenes if the designated aggressor ignores the verdict. Only this would make it possible to reserve the permission to wage war exceptionally according to the logic of efficiency to cases of genuine self-defence.

However, I have come to this conclusion before; IHL needs to be effective in the imperfect, partially anarchic international legal order in which it currently operates. The best the international community can currently do to ensure that a state has a shot at truly and effectively winning a war in self-defence is to underwrite states' Article 51 right with a promise to intervene on their behalf if their own defensive action in accordance with the logic of sufficiency proves ineffective in overcoming an aggressor militarily.[37]

But the containment command faces a more fundamental challenge than the normative reservation that it may be too strict in cases of

---

[36] See also the above discussion of asymmetrical logics of warfare.
[37] The current legal situation regarding the role of the UN Security Council with regard to states' inherent right to self-defence is less than clear. Article 51 UNC reads: 'Nothing in the present Charter shall impair the inherent right of individual or collective self-defense if an armed attack occurs against a Member of the United Nations, until the Security Council has taken measures necessary to maintain international peace and security. Measures taken by Members in the exercise of this right of self-defense shall be immediately reported to the Security Council and shall not in any way affect the authority and responsibility of the Security Council under the present Charter to take at any time such action as it deems necessary in order to maintain or restore international peace and security.' While a state under armed attack presumably does not have to stop using force in self-defence as soon as the Council is seized of the matter, there is no legal assurance that the international community will actually restore peace and security or 'guarantee' a state's right to self-defence.

self-defence. Is there in reality a class of objects the engagement of which is sufficient even merely for the competition of two militaries to be carried out? Or rather, do we know what those objects are in order to consistently distinguish them from those that do not directly contribute to the competition among militaries? Beyond actual military equipment, such as tanks or grenade-launchers, there does not seem to be an eternal canon of objects that are relevant for military competitions everywhere. I submitted in section 4.3 that allegiance to the logic of sufficiency therefore amounts to *drawing* a line between objects the destruction of which directly impedes generic military victory and those that do not in a given war. The requirement that an attack has to generate a genuine military advantage in one causal step provides an effective guide for the application of Article 52(2) API. However, belligerents still have to make a good faith effort to sort objects into military versus civilian accordingly.

The ability of international law to impose the logic of sufficiency

The recognition that IHL relies on belligerents' good faith in applying the law gives us important clues as to how IHL would need to be changed in order to impose the logic of sufficiency. The obvious inference is that belligerents' incentives in war are important for the design of IHL. Assuming that a regime values the lives of its citizens and its resources in general, when belligerents designate their own persons and objects as legitimate targets, an imperative of sufficiency naturally obtains. That is, a belligerent must choose to include in its own forces enough of his people and objects to have a reasonable chance of military success, but not expose more than necessary to direct attack. To the contrary, on the same assumption that a regime values the lives of its citizens and its other resources, when it is asked to designate the *adversary's* objects and persons that are open to direct attack an imperative of efficiency naturally obtains.

IHL operationalises distinction among persons so that each belligerent allocates its *own* individuals to the two sides of the line between immunity and legitimate military engagement. In doing so, each belligerent gets a chance to protect certain segments of society. If A fights in good faith, A relies in military operations only on those of A's citizens designated as combatants. It follows that from the point of view of B, a military engagement of only A's designated combatants could in theory be sufficient for generic military victory. The fact that sufficiency considerations prevail when a belligerent designates its own combatants may be one explanation for why IHL as far as persons are concerned seems to be relatively successful in withstanding the imperative of efficiency that belligerents perceive in contemporary armed conflict.[38] In general, the category of combatant has not undergone the same linear expansion as that of military objective with regard to objects.

According to Article 52(2) API, an object can be a military objective in virtue of its nature, purpose, location or use. Nature is often inter-subjectively understood and relatively uncontroversial. If there is an eternal canon of military objectives across wars, it is those that are so by nature. It follows that there is a class of objects that presents itself as probably necessary and therefore legitimate to engage. A belligerent can in good faith rely on these objects in its own endeavour to achieve military victory. Yet whether an object in territory A is military by purpose or location, rather than nature, depends on B's perception, namely the anticipation of A's next moves. Theoretically each belligerent decides which objects become military objectives by its own use. In reality, however, use, like an object's purpose and location, is effectively determined by the adversary. IHL hence operationalises distinction among objects so that each belligerent has a considerable say in designating the universe of non-immune objects of the adversary. Three out of the four ways in which A's objects can become military objectives depend on B's perception. If both belligerents occasionally assume the role of attacker, an expectation of reciprocity can prevent A from perceiving too many of B's objects as military objectives. However, this is not the case in the asymmetrical wars investigated here. The US might have more trouble affirming that privately owned media facilities were military objectives when they spread propaganda if Fox News or MSNBC were in any danger of being attacked from the air.

As adumbrated, A designates A's citizens as either legitimate targets or immune civilians. However, in reality, during certain combat

---

[38] The other reason is that Article 43 API is more determinate than Article 52(2) API. There is no mistaking that the former demands distinction among persons in accordance with the logic of sufficiency.

operations B *does* get a say in allocating A's persons to either side of the distinction line. Where the defender is not a state's military force, especially in air warfare or where directly participating civilians are concerned, the line is effectively drawn by the attacker. In recent counter-insurgency operations one way in which the US distinguished among persons imitates the law defining military objects by identifying persons as legitimate targets in virtue of their gender, age and location (cumulatively). All 'military aged males' in certain areas are treated as legitimate targets of attack rather than protected civilians.[39]

Unlike certain US practices that challenge treaty law and stretch the customary definition of military objectives within its semantic indeterminacy, such as the attack on media facilities and political infrastructure, there is no arguing with the conclusion that treating all military-aged males as combatants is, like targeting civilian regime leaders, a misapplication of treaty as well as customary IL. If someone is not a combatant as identified by the defender, only her actual conduct, not her threat potential resulting from gender, age and location, can make her cross the line into the sphere of legitimate military engagement. In case of doubt a person is to be considered civilian.[40] The law defining a legitimate target of attack among persons is in theory determinate enough to defy an interpretation in light of efficiency considerations, even if it is applied by the attacker. In contrast, the customary law drawing the line between immune and non-immune objects with its contested point of reference for the determination of a military advantage and the unspecified degree of nexus between objects and military operations is too indeterminate to hold efficiency at bay when it is applied by the attacker.[41]

The second difference between the concretisation of distinction for objects and persons is that the line between combatants and civilians is drawn definitively *before* hostilities start.[42] With the exception of

---

[39] Bashir (2006).   [40] Article 50(1) API.

[41] The law was closer to distributing harm among objects in the same way as it does among persons (i.e. with a bright line drawn by the defender) when it regulated combat operations by declaring the immunity of undefended places. However, this is not an argument in favour of bringing Article 25 The Hague V on Neutral Powers and Persons and Article 1 The Hague IX back from desuetude. Modern industrialised societies are far too complex to isolate places as undefended. It is difficult enough to distinguish at the level of objects.

[42] The exception is direct participation in hostilities. Who among a society's civilians will choose to take up arms is not known in advance.

objects that are military by nature, the line between immune objects and those that are open to attack cannot be drawn in advance. As combat unfolds, the law explicitly allows an object to lose civilian immunity as a result of its use or location or as its military purpose becomes evident. This likewise plays into the hands of the efficiency imperative and against the containment command: during combat, at one point it will become obvious to one side that attacking only military objectives narrowly defined will not be sufficient to actually win. In this case the losing belligerent has a strong incentive to perceive more objects as military by purpose, location or use and include them in the category of military objectives.

It follows that one way to make it more likely that efficiency will not get the better of the determination of which objects are military objectives, I would think, would be to ask the defender to designate in advance facilities that will be used for military purposes, just as belligerents acknowledge in advance that some of their citizens are combatants and hence fair game. But what if hostilities radically change and a belligerent needs more than the initially designated objects to draw on in its on-going military effort? After all a belligerent can recruit more combatants if it turns out that it initially kept 'too many' citizens immune to successfully pursue the war. In the same way, any previously civilian object that starts to be useful in the war effort would need to be officially marked as such – just as combatants wear the uniform. If a belligerent used an object never designated as military to help the military effort, this would then be a breach of IHL, triggering an unprivileged legal status for those responsible,[43] and consequences comparable to those faced by noncombatants who directly participate in hostilities.[44] The point is that just as in the case of persons, it would only be in cases of a prior breach of IHL, hence in the exceptional rather than the regular case, that the 'perception' of the attacker mattered in the determination of the status of an object.

---

[43] This is already the case for a number of specifically protected objects.

[44] If intention to use an object militarily were acknowledged in advance and ruled out for all other objects, the categories of military objectives by location or purpose would be superfluous. In fact, during the drafting of Article 52(2) location and purpose were added to create the impression of exhaustiveness only when the word 'namely' between military objective and the following description was dropped (ORDC, vol. III, 208ff.).

Approximating the regime for the definition of objects that are military objectives to the legal regime that governs distinction among persons in this way would require a major change in the law. However, it is widely accepted that another codification conference, such as those in Geneva after the Second World War and in the 1970s, is extremely unlikely. A less intrusive way to render the definition of military objectives as far as objects are concerned better able to hold efficiency at bay would be to specify the required degree of nexus and the point of reference for the determination of a military advantage by reaffirming which logic the conduct of hostilities should follow. The past decade has seen a number of efforts to strengthen rules of IHL. Two such reinterpretative projects were mentioned in the previous chapters: the International Humanitarian Law Research Initiative's attempt to shed light on the application of IHL to air and missile warfare and the project by the ICRC to render the concept of direct participation in hostilities more determinate. Unfortunately, neither clarification effort works with, endorses or adheres to an explicit logic that the conduct of hostilities ought to follow.

Working from the premise of a prescribed logic in these interpretative efforts would bring into sharp relief the fault lines in the 'consensus' of the international community on how war ought to be waged. For instance, affirmation of the logic of sufficiency would lead to the acknowledgement that technology has made it possible to proportionately target objects and persons that are nevertheless off limits in virtue of the principle of distinction, such as civilian political leaders, some government structures and privately owned media facilities. Certain trends in military doctrine, such as EBOs and shock and awe, could be identified as challenging IHL. By the same token, an explicit endorsement of the logic of sufficiency would highlight that certain forms of psychological warfare, though they may bear little resemblance to Second World War terror-bombing, are, when the morale of the civilian population is targeted, illegal. Starting each clarification effort with an explicit endorsement of the logic that combat operations ought to follow could structure the currently decentralised effort to clarify IHL and ensure that the different interpretative projects end up creating a coherent legal framework.

In conclusion, the logic of sufficiency is practicable and IHL could be changed so that a belligerent would have to choose between fighting with the endorsement of IHL (customary or positive) and targeting according to the logic of efficiency. This section contains two suggestions about how to vouchsafe IHL's ability to largely guarantee that an actor who recurs to IHL ends up targeting according to the logic of sufficiency: (1) take belligerents' incentives seriously. If each belligerent designates its own persons and objects as legitimate targets or not, the logic of sufficiency prevails. If distinction is in the hands of the attacker, IHL has to be more determinate because it is up against a strong and natural imperative of efficiency. (2) Affirm the one causal step and the generic military victory requirements (the commands of containment and sequencing) and thus explicitly acknowledge that the conduct of hostilities has to follow the logic of sufficiency. The logic can then guide subsequent interpretation and clarification efforts. Only if there is basic agreement regarding the big picture – what do we want war that is comprehensively legalised to look like? – do efforts to clarify individual concepts not raise more interpretative controversies than they solve.

Conclusion

We can, I think, now tell the story of IL the book set out to explore. IL is a compromise between utility and appropriateness. It simultaneously depends on these normative codes for its meaning and on the corresponding reasons for action, i.e. interests and pre-legal normative beliefs, for its creation and for compliance. I call this the epistemic and the causal dependence of IL. At the same time, IL is irreducible to these variables. It has the potential to make a counterfactual difference for behaviour because compliance can have an intellectual and a motivational effect, which influence actors' beliefs about what is in their interests (utility) and how they ought to behave (appropriateness). Rather than an epiphenomenon of interests or non-legal norms, IL is thus a relevant variable in its own right for an explanation of how actors behave in international relations.

When compliance with IL leads to behaviour widely perceived as legitimate, IL is also normatively successful. This is less likely the more indeterminate a rule of IL is. But even a very determinate rule must, of course, also be determinate in the right way – the compromise between utility and appropriateness enshrined in it must correspond to international society's normative expectations of how such a compromise looks in its area of regulation. Customary IL, it turns out, is not a compromise between utility and appropriateness, but rests on a convergence between what various different actors tend to perceive as in their interest or required as a matter of norms in a certain situation. If actors' reasons for action in fact correspond with each other, instrumental and principled considerations suggest the same behaviour, customary IL is superfluous; if they do not, it is prohibitively indeterminate.

In addition to what I ambitiously refer to as a constructivist theory of IL, the book has uncovered an unacknowledged, but fundamental disagreement among lawyers as well as military practitioners about the right way (logic) of waging war. Specifically, how to strike a 'balance' between the often diverging imperatives of humanitarianism and military pragmatism during the selection of targets is contested. One way of accommodating them both is to contain military operations as much as possible by only allowing the engagement of objects and persons that are necessary and sufficient for a competition between enemy militaries to proceed. This logic of sufficiency also demands that states bracket their political goals during the conduct of hostilities so that warfare may be a competition between militaries rather than societies. The competing logic is 'sharp wars are brief'. This logic of efficiency requires selecting those targets whose engagement most quickly and directly leads to the achievement of a belligerent's desired political, moral or other goals. The dominant logic underlying US air warfare has changed over the last fifty years from sufficiency to efficiency. I suggest that this development is the effect of evolving shared normative beliefs about the use of force in international relations. In reaction to intensifying casualty aversion, specifically among Western societies, US military decision-makers perceive keeping wars brief as in their interest.

In parallel to this shift in logics the importance of recourse to IL in US command centres has risen dramatically. We can therefore draw a number of conclusions about IHL's role in US air operations and extrapolate to what we may generally expect IL to accomplish in the conduct of hostilities. IHL, as interpreted by military decision-making, proves constitutive of those decision-makers' shared belief that the legitimacy of a target hinges on the ability of its engagement to contribute directly to the quick achievement of an overall – often political – goal.[1] As it turns out, this is problematic because following the logic of efficiency trades the protection of civilians against increased security for combatants. Yet, general casualty aversion notwithstanding, civilian casualties are widely considered 'even worse' than fatalities among combatants by what I refer to as an 'international public'. The latter has emerged alongside the described ideational change. US military decision-makers' reaction to these evolving normative beliefs targeting according to the logic of efficiency violence and is therefore a mistake. Contemporary US air warfare

---

[1] While IL is a constitutive variable, the change in shared normative beliefs about combatant casualties in international relations is the main *cause* of the perceived utility and increased importance of the logic of efficiency and the altered definition of a legitimate target of attack.

meets with more rather than less academic criticism and popular outrage, despite compliance with IL.

IHL could force belligerents to choose between its endorsement and targeting according to the logic of efficiency if it were more determinate. It could 'impose' the logic of sufficiency on the conduct of military operations. However, even so, IL *cannot* render combat operations fully legitimate by either contemporary moral standards or this international public's shared normative expectations. Both increasingly centre on the protection of individual rights and would require warfare to follow a third logic, a logic of liability, which is impracticable.

The effectiveness of IL in war is, then, partial. IL makes a counterfactual difference when it is complied with (I call this behavioural relevance), but it does not and cannot render war normatively acceptable in the twenty-first century (normative success). This explains the puzzle that inspired this book in the first place: intense condemnation of US military operations for the humanitarian costs they inflict coincides with widespread commendation for their comprehensive subjection to IHL. The story of IL, IL's inability to render warfare normatively acceptable and the unacknowledged divide over how to wage war in the twenty-first century have important implications for constructivist IR theory, for the legal regulation of war and for the practice of war. They also invite further research on these subjects.

Social construction: collective decision-making and international law's story

Compliance with IHL is more decentralised than is the case for most regimes of IL, which are complied with (or not) through legislative action or a government's foreign policy choices.[2] In contrast, it is individual commanders and operators who recur to IHL for action guidance or for a source of legitimacy. It is for their intellectual process and motivation that IL makes a difference. Are the motivational and the intellectual effects, and hence the proposed theory of IL's behavioural relevance, limited to legal regimes that are implemented in this atypical way?

---

[2] I am grateful to Kathryn Sikkink for drawing my attention to this specificity of IHL.

Ultimately all IL is recurred to, interpreted and implemented by individuals. There is no reason why a clearly outlined course of action should not make it easier for a political leader to adjust state behaviour so that it accords with the compromise between utility and appropriateness enshrined in IL (intellectual effect), if compliance with IL or acting appropriately is indeed the goal. By the same token, the pertinence of IL may well render the legal option the instrumental course of action for a state/government facing a foreign policy choice (motivational effect). Compliance with IL will then depend on the state's perceived national interest and on the shared normative beliefs related to a society's, a government's and individual politicians' identity (causal dependence). Prevailing understandings of utility will shape how IL is interpreted (epistemic dependence). Therefore, in principle there is no reason why the scope conditions of this theory should be limited to specific regimes of IL that require not only state officials, but many and diverse other individuals, to share in compliance.

None the less, compliance with general IL is probably often a collective process, while adherence to IHL is, at least outside the command centre, an individual choice. By the same token, the interpretation of IHL and deliberation about behaviour in war under the guidance of IHL often amount to one (wo)man musing about human life and military gain. The question of how the cognitive and motivational effects of IL play out in collective decision-making, which may be drawn out much longer and involve communicative deliberation, invites further research. In addition, the structures within which political and military actors come to a decision differ. Bureaucracies with entrenched legalism can through socialisation and acculturation effect almost automatic compliance. I have only in passing touched on non-deliberate adherence to IL, but focused instead on the role of individual agency and deliberate decision-making. But structures of course provide the medium for non-deliberate as well as deliberate recurrence to IL. The interplay of different ideational structures and the cognitive and motivational effects of recourse to IL requires further exploration.

International law: indeterminacy and the rule of law in war

IHL could do better in war than it currently does. This book proposes two kinds of adjustments for the laws of war. First, given the finding that the logic of sufficiency is the best IHL can do, but is by far not good enough, IHL needs to be changed as much as possible with a view to honouring the shared normative belief that combatants are not a collective without individual moral or legal rights, readily dispensable in the pursuit of political goals with force. The three additional requirements for the legality of attacks against combatants contemplated in section 8.2 are: a least-harmful-means test (what I describe as a necessity 1 standard in section 3.1), actual immediate threat and actual meaningful consent to assuming the role of combatant in a given war. All three suggestions are vulnerable to the criticism that they complicate warfare. It is the task of further research to explore to what extent ideational change in international relations and the resulting normative pressures none the less render these changes the instrumental course of action in war. That they are appropriate is beyond doubt.

Second, in the light of the finding that the logic of sufficiency is preferable to the logic of efficiency, IHL needs to be changed to prevent belligerents on the strategic offensive from bending to the pressure of keeping a war brief at the cost of keeping it contained. Both proposed measures to render IHL able to underwrite the logic of sufficiency imply limiting the indeterminacy of the definition of a legitimate target of attack, specifically under customary IL. In general, determinacy is important for legal effectiveness. Section 2.2 suggested that indeterminacy renders less predictable what kind of intellectual and motivational effect adherence to a particular law generates. An indeterminate legal rule's interpretation yields further to the interests and normative beliefs that the compliant agent pursues via recourse to IL. If normative success amounts to IL's ability to regulate an issue area in line with an agreed on compromise between utility and appropriateness in that issue area, then any indeterminacy is problematic and the less of it a law has, the better.

A substantive definition of normative success of IL – impose the agreed on compromise between utility and appropriateness – creates a prima facie case against indeterminacy. However, is achieving specified outcomes the be-all and end-all of legal regulation? If we abstract from the substantive goals of legal regulation, an alternative measure for normative success of IL that is valid across different issue areas is a state referred to as the rule of law. While definitions of the rule of law differ, at its core is the task of protecting the individual as a moral agent from the arbitrary power of the state,[3] in that the individual is aware what precisely is expected of her and what she can be held to account for in every situation of her life.[4] Given the centrality of security of expectations to the rule of law, many of the formal characteristics we generally associate with it likewise hinge on determinacy: they include clarity, concreteness and the public availability of laws.[5] There does not seem to be a conflict between the substantive and the formal purpose of international law: the less indeterminacy, the better.

While individual security of expectations is important for moral agency, it has been argued that 'ordinary people are urging something other than the formal elements ... when they clamour for the Rule of Law'.[6] Jeremy Waldron maintains that 'law is a mode of governing people that treats them with respect, as though they had a view or perspective of their own to present in the application of the norm to their conduct'.[7] While formal features, such as absence of vagueness and public availability of law, provide the backdrop for this 'dignitarian aspect'[8] of legal regulation, it is validated in legal procedures that recognise the individual as a reason-endowed being, procedures that give the individual a forum for the expression of her views. In this reading, deliberation in the creation of law, discretion in its application and fair adjudication by competent judges are as integral to the rule of law as individual security of expectations and acceptable outcomes.[9]

It seems that regarding individual moral agency, the relationship between the formal and the procedural aspect of the rule of law is dialectical: agreement on what the law is and the parameters of how it changes (formal security) are a condition for any deliberation about law (procedural openness). However, too much certainty regarding what the law is and how it can be changed (formal security) limits or even stifles deliberation (procedural openness). Only open-ended

---

[3] Being a full moral agent refers to the ability of an individual to make decisions and act in line with a generally accepted normative code and, as a result, fully 'bear the related moral burdens of duty and blame for specific acts and outcomes'. For a discussion of moral agency from an IR theory perspective see Erskine (2010).

[4] Chesterman (2008); Fuller (1969) 162; Nardin (2008); Raz (1979) 214.

[5] Formal characteristics of the rule of law closely resemble the eight criteria that Brunnée and Toope advance as forming the basis of interactional IL. See section 1.3; Brunnée and Toope (2011b) 68; also Fuller (1969).

[6] Waldron (2010c) 5.   [7] *Ibid.* 14.   [8] *Ibid.*, 17.   [9] Waldron (2011b) 5.

deliberation does justice to the fact that law is ultimately fully man-made. Accepting law as the product of choices by reason-endowed individuals requires not closing the channels that funnel human reason into law. If these channels are too wide open, however, we are no longer ruled by law but by men. This tension between formal security and procedural openness underlying the rule of law draws attention to the fact that maximising determinacy bears a cost. In Jeremy Waldron's words, it obstructs 'thoughtfulness'.[10]

This raises two questions. First, would rendering IHL more deter-minate undermine the dignitarian aspect of IHL and thus the rule of law in war? Second, in a normative evaluation of law, how much weight is carried by the procedural aspect of the rule of law compared to the ability of law to guarantee a specific agreed-on substantive outcome? Rather than generating a specific outcome, should law perhaps endeavour to ensure that enough human reason finds its way into the application of law so that regulation by law does justice to the capacity of human thoughtfulness in a complex and changing reality without giving way to arbitrariness? I hold that the answers to these two questions depend on each other. When we come up with a substantive standard for our expectations about what a specific legal regime can do, understanding that indeterminacy is a double-edged sword with regard to the rule of law is crucial. If we want to preserve more room for individual judgement, outcomes are necessa-rily less predictable. If we make law dense and unyielding, we forgo human reason as a resource to fine-tune prescribed rules in a complex reality.

What about the case at hand? When it comes to combat operations we do not actually have that much 'faith ... in [individuals'] ability to think about and interpret the bearing of a whole array of norms and precedents to their conduct'.[11] I broached the argument in Chapter 3 and Chapter 7. War is an area where, even if we assume a good faith attempt, reasonable notions of right, wrong or excessive diverge considerably and understandably as often the life of the individual making the judgement is on the line. In addition, actors regularly act under extreme time pressure and/or without the most basic information. Section 4.1's investigation of the negotiation records for the API

---

[10] *Ibid.*   [11] Waldron (2010c) 19.

suggested that this is precisely the vision of limited individual agency that underlies IHL. Moreover, interviews suggested that it is a widespread narrative that the individual cannot be held to account for his actions in war in the way he is held to account in peace. The reason is the perception that non-contingent characteristics of war would make that fundamentally unfair.[12] In this reading, not much is lost when we impose determinate IHL that stifles individuals' judgement in war.

Given our limited faith in human reason in the circumstances of war, the existing degree of procedural insecurity of IHL is puzzling. On the one hand, IHL's limitations of agency suggest that we cannot expect more of the individual combatant than wanting the right thing, suggesting that we cannot even ask very much in terms of attempting to *do* the right thing.[13] On the other hand, the application of IHL is impossible without extensive value judgements on the part of individual agents. Recalling the drafting history of the API, the use of standards such as 'excessive' and 'feasible' in crucial places was deliberate, with a view to limiting individuals' responsibility for outcomes. But vague standard-like rules also afford less action guidance; or rather they impose a much higher cognitive burden on the conscientious individual if they are to guide action.[14] It is a fundamental misconception that indeterminate legal obligations do justice to individuals in situations in which their moral agency is strained. This misconception is the birth defect of the API.

That we do not expect the individual to employ the same standard of care in war, that we do not punish negligence in combat and that we do not think individuals own the results of their actions in the way they do in peacetime has historically made for weak review procedures. However, now ICL has started to deliver procedures that shine a light on whether an individual has in a certain situation made a reasonable value judgement. For now the reach and substantive scope of international criminal jurisprudence are extremely limited.[15] IHL's indeterminacy, specifically the principle of proportionality's consequential and purposive indeterminacy, none the less limits ICL's elaboration in case law. Section 7.2 suggested that, in turn, international jurisprudence challenges the limitations to agency under IHL. The rise of ICL thus brings into sharp relief the reality that recognising the individual as

---

[12] See section 7.2.   [13] See section 3.2.   [14] Waldron (2010a) 8.
[15] See section 7.2.

a full moral agent, specifically in morally difficult situations, requires a certain degree of determinacy from the law that IHL does not possess. Treating the individual seriously as an 'active centre of intelligence' or striving for the rule of law in war adds a reason to render IHL more determinate, rather than providing an argument against it. In the case of IHL we do not have to decide between achieving a certain outcome and preserving the rule of law, including its dignitarian aspect: both would be enhanced by less indeterminacy.

US bombing and the dilemma of violence in a semi-constitutionalised order

Warfare inevitably marks the breakdown of peaceful interstate relations and the violation of individual rights on a large scale. At the same time, the use of force by states against states is sometimes the only available means to maintain order or protect human life. The book has demonstrated that IHL cannot reconcile non-pacifist foreign policies with liberal human rights-centred conceptions of appropriateness. It cannot solve the twenty-first-century dilemma around the use of force in the international system. If we accept, first, that safeguarding individual rights is a moral standard applicable in international relations and the touchstone of successful IL; second, that it is impossible to avoid large scale violations of individual rights in war; and third, that the international order requires a mechanism for the legitimate use of violence in order to be sustainable, we need to find forcible alternatives to war.

Does the notorious targeted killing of individuals often with unmanned aerial vehicles, a regular practice of the current US administration, constitute such an alternative? Like targeting according to the logic of efficiency, the attacks colloquially referred to as 'drone strikes' radically decrease the risk to the attacker's troops. In addition, they seem to avoid enemy combatants perishing in the thousands as they would do in war. The reputational costs associated with the deaths of combatants became evident when on 2 March 1991, shortly before the end of ODS, the US killed scores of Iraqi troops on Highway 80 between Kuwait and Basra. The legality of the attacks depended on whether the Iraqi troops were withdrawing (illegal) or merely retreating (legal), and on whether they had violated a prior ceasefire agreement, as the commanding general alleged.[16] These subtleties were of little importance to the media, which broadcast gruelling images of smoking tanks and charred bodies. Seen in this light it appears to make sense to kill the 'high-value' person rather than to wage war against the country and its men in arms. Targeted killings, even more so than EBOs or shock and awe, are the epitome of the logic of efficiency. They are born out of the perceived pressures to minimise risk to friendly and to an extent also to foreign troops – the same pressures that initiated the rise of efficiency considerations in US air warfare.

Can the investigation of the logic of efficiency here thus shed light on the normative implications of targeted killings, which are highly contested – and vice versa? It proved impossible to establish whether the logic of efficiency creates more collateral damage than warfare following the logic of sufficiency. Such a counterfactual argument should be easier with regard to individual drone attacks. But what do we compare them to? All-out war fought according to the logic of sufficiency against Somalia, Yemen and Pakistan? Then, of course, targeted killings probably save both combatants and civilians. However, in the counterfactual scenario in which the option of targeted killings is unavailable, these wars are extremely unlikely to take place – due to their material but also their reputational costs. Do we or should we not instead compare the casualty count of drone strikes to alternative measures of diplomacy, development aid and law enforcement operations? Even more so than EBOs or shock and awe, targeted killings lower the threshold for the use of force, by *supposedly* circumventing ideational and legal obstacles to using force in international relations – obstacles that were hard won and painfully erected over the last sixty years.

Section 8.1 demonstrated that to follow the logic of efficiency means trading away some protection of civilians for increased protection of combatants. That is certainly true for drone strikes as well. After all they are framed to make warfare against a country's military forces unnecessary, while their harmful side effects on civilians persist and continue to make headlines.[17] The analysis here showed that this

---

[16] For a thorough retelling of the events leading up to what is sometimes referred to as the 'Turkey Shoot' see Hersh (2000).

[17] See, for example, International Human Rights and Conflict Resolution Clinic (Stanford Law School) and Global Justice Clinic (NYU Law School) (2012); Human Rights Watch (2013).

trade is at odds with lingering beliefs about civilian casualties being 'even worse' than combatant deaths. This suggests that, like targeting according to the logic of efficiency during all-out war, the policy of targeted killings is a misguided reaction by military and political decision-makers to the normative pressures of contemporary international society. If technology is meant to solve the twenty-first-century belligerent's problem of widespread reproof and a loss of legitimacy, it needs to address the fact that the deaths of individuals as a side effect of military operations are never unproblematic and only contestably legitimate.[18]

The book does not hide the appeal that the logic of efficiency has at first glance. After all, we would badly want defensive wars to be efficient. By the same token, in a scenario in which the legitimacy of the use of force as such is beyond doubt – for instance, against a small ruling elite committing genocide against an ethnic minority – targeted killings or what could simply be referred to as assassinations, might be the solution to the dilemma that while war is morally costly so is pacifism. For that to be the case, though, the use of unmanned aerial vehicles and the legal 'permission to assassinate' would need to be regulated and institutionalised, an endeavour for which it is hard to imagine, let alone establish, the requisite international structures. Perhaps nothing short of a world government[19] could control and properly administer legalised targeted killings. In that case, however, this world government would presumably also be able to instead apprehend the individual in question by means of international law enforcement in order to subject him or her to legal due process. Similarly, only radical institutional change in international relations would mean that the logic of efficiency reserved for defensive wars did not undermine the legal regulation of warfare as such. Even more than the logic of efficiency, targeted killings fail to fulfil their promise of improving the normative implications of the justified use of force.

Normative beliefs shared across the international society that increasingly demand giving the individual her moral due are far ahead of this society's institutional structures, which are still largely

---

[18] This insight raises a question regarding the future usefulness of air power that is beyond the scope of this conclusion.

[19] A concept that is not only largely utopian, but also raises formidable normative challenges.

geared towards the rights of sovereign states. IL may be in a process of constitutionalisation, but for that process not to generate perverse results such as targeted killings and the rise of the logic of efficiency in air warfare, institution building needs to stay in lock-step with ideational change. This means that future research on violence in the international system urgently requires a joint effort of ethicists, jurists and social scientists.

Bibliography

Secondary sources

Aaken, Anna van (2006) To do Away with International Law? Some Limits to 'The Limits of International Law', 17 *European Journal of International Law* 289.

Abbott, Kenneth W. (1989) Modern International Relations Theory: A Prospectus for International Lawyers, 14 *Yale Journal of International Law* 2.

(2004/5) Toward a Richer Institutionalism for International Law and Policy, 1 *Journal of International Law and International Relations* 9.

Abbott, Kenneth W., Robert O. Keohane, Andrew Moravcsik, Anne-Marie Slaughter and Duncan Snidal (2000) The Concept of Legalization, 54 *International Organisation* 401.

Abbott, Kenneth W. and Duncan Snidal (2000) Hard and Soft Law in International Governance, 54 *International Organization* 421.

(2002) Values and Interests: International Legalization in the Fight Against Corruption, 31 *Journal of Legal Studies* S141.

(2012) Law, Legalization, and Politics: An Agenda for the next Generation of IR/IL Scholars, in Jeffrey L. Dunoff and Mark A. Pollack, eds., *Interdisciplinary Perspectives on International Law and International Relations: The State of the Art*, Cambridge University Press.

Abi-Saab, George (1984) The Specificities of Humanitarian Law, in Christophe Swinarski, ed., *Studies and Essays on International Humanitarian Law and Red Cross Principles in Honour of Jean Pictet*, Berlin: Springer Verlag.

Adler, Emanuel (1997) Imagined (Security) Communities: Cognitive Regions in International Relations, 26 *Millennium* 1.

(2005) *Communitarian International Relations: The Epistemic Foundations of International Relations*, New York: Routledge.

Adler, Emanuel and Vincent Pouliot, eds. (2011) *International Practices*, Cambridge University Press.

Akande, Dapo (2010) Clearing the Fog of War? The ICRC's Interpretive Guidance on Direct Participation in Hostilities, 59 *International and Comparative Law Quarterly* 180.

Akehurst, Michael (1977) Custom as a Source of International Law, 47 *British Yearbook of International Law* 1.

al-Khahl, Samir (1991) Iraq and its Future, *New York Review of Books*, 11 April 1991.

Allott, Philip (1990) *Eunomia: New World Order for a New World*, Oxford University Press.

(2001) The Emerging Universal Legal System, 3 *International Law Forum du Droit International* 12.

Alter, Karen (2000) 'Regime Design Matters: Designing International Legal Systems for Maximum or Minimum Effectiveness', Paper presented at the 41st ISA Conference Los Angeles.

Altman, Andrew (2012) Introduction, in Claire Finkelstein, Jens David Ohlin and Andrew Altman, eds., *Targeted Killings: Law and Morality in an Asymmetrical World*, Oxford University Press.

Anderegg, Clarence R. (2001) *Sierra Hotel: Flying Air Force Fighters in the Decade After Vietnam*, Air Force History and Museums Program.

Archer, Margaret S. (1982) Morphogenesis versus Structuration: On Combining Structure and Action, 33 *British Journal of Sociology* 455.

Arkin, William N. (1997) Baghdad: The Urban Sanctuary in Desert Storm? *Airpower Journal* Spring.

Arquilla, John (2012) Cyberwar is Already Upon Us, *Foreign Policy* March/April.

Ashley, Richard K. (1986) The Poverty of Neorealism, in Robert O. Keohane, ed., *Neorealism and its Critics*, New York NY: Columbia University Press.

Atkinson, Rick (1993) *Crusade: The Untold Story of the Persian Gulf War*, Boston NA: Houghton Mifflin Company.

(2004) *In the Company of Soldiers: A Chronicle of Combat in Iraq*, New York: Henry Holt and Co.

Atkinson, Rick and Dan Balz (1991) Bomb Strike Kills Scores of Civilians in Building Called Military Bunker by US, Shelter by Iraq, *Washington Post*, 14 February 1991.

Austin, John (1832/1995) *The Province of Jurisprudence Determined*, Cambridge University Press.

(1879) *Lectures on Jurisprudence or the Philosophy of Law*, London: Campbell (reprinted by Thoemmes Press in 2002).

Ayson, Robert (2011) *The Changing Character of Warfare*, Cambridge University Press.

Bacevich, Andrew J. (1996) Just War: Morality and High Technology, 45 *The National Interest* 37–47; reprinted (1998) Just War in a New Era of Military Affairs, in Elliott Abrams, ed., *Close Calls: Intervention, Terrorism, Missile Defense and 'Just War' Today*, Lanham MD: Rowman and Littlefield.

Barnett, Michael and Kathryn Sikkink (2010) From International Relations to Global Society, in Christian Reus-Smit and Duncan Snidal, eds., *The Oxford Handbook of International Relations*, New York NY: Oxford University Press.

Barrett, David M. ed. (1997) *Lyndon B. Johnson's Vietnam Papers: A Documentary Collection*, College Station TX: Texas A&M University Press.

Bashir, Martin (2006) 'Rules of Engagement: "Kill all Military-Aged-Males"', www.truth-out.org/article/rules-engagement-kill-all-military-age-males (last accessed 29 March 2011).

Battistella, Dario (2008) *The Return of the States of War: A Theoretical Analysis of Operation Iraqi Freedom*, Colchester: ECPR Press.

Bederman, David (2006) *International Law Frameworks*, New York: Foundation Press.

Beier, Marshall J. (2003) Discriminating Tastes: Smart Bombs, Non Combatants and Notions of Legitimacy in Warfare, 34 *Security Dialogue* 413.

Belkin, Aaron, Michael Clark, Gigi Gokcek, Robert Hinckley, Tom Knecht and Eric Patterson (2002) When Is Strategic Bombing Effective? Domestic Legitimacy and Aerial Denial, 11 *Security Studies* 51.

Bellavia, David with John R. Bruning (2008) *House to House: An Epic Memoir of War*, New York: Free Press.

Bellinger, John, III and William J. Hayes II (2006) 'US Initial Reactions to ICRC Study on Customary International Law', www.state.gov/s/l/2006/98860.htm (last accessed 16 June 2011).

Belt, Walter Stuart (2000) Missiles over Kosovo: Emergence, Lex Lata of a Customary Norm Requiring the Use of Precision Munitions in Urban Areas, 47 *Naval Law Review* 115.

Bergen, Peter and Katherine Tiedemann (2011) Washington's Phantom War, 90 *Foreign Affairs* 4.

Berman, Paul Schiff (2005) Book Review: Seeing Beyond the Limits of International Law, 84 *Texas Law Review* 1256.

Besson, Samantha (2011) Sovereignty, International Law and Democracy, 22 *European Journal of International Law* 373.

Besson, Samantha and John Tasioulas, eds. (2010) *The Philosophy of International Law*, Oxford University Press.

Best, Geoffrey (1983) *Humanity in Warfare: The Modern History of the International Law of Armed Conflict*, New York: Routledge.

(1997) *War and Law Since 1945*, Oxford University Press.

Biddle, Stephen (2004) *Military Power: Explaining Victory and Defeat in Modern Battle*, Princeton University Press.

Biddle, Tami Davis (2002) *Rhetoric and Reality in Air Warfare: The Evolution of British and American Ideas about Strategic Bombing, 1914–1945*, Princeton University Press.

Blum, Gabriella (2010) The Dispensable Life of Soldiers, 2 *Journal of Legal Analysis* 1, 69.

Blum, Vanessa (2001) Jag Goes to War, *Legal Times*, 15 November 2011, www.law.com (last accessed 12 November 2008).

Bogdandy, Armin von (2006) Constitutionalism in International Law: Comment on a Proposal from Germany, 47 *Harvard International Law Journal* 223.

Bork, Robert H. (1989/90) The Limits of 'International Law', 18 *National Interest* 3.

Bothe, Michael (2001) The Protection of the Civilian Population and NATO Bombing on Yugoslavia: Comments on a Report to the Prosecutor of the ICTY, 12 *European Journal of International Law* 531.

Bothe, Michael and Andreas Fischer-Lescano (2002) Protego et Obligo: Afghanistan and the Paradox of Sovereignty, 3 *German Law Journal* 1.

Bothe, Michael, Karl J. Partsch and Waldemar A. Solf, eds. (1982) *New Rules for Victims of Armed Conflicts: Commentary on the Two 1977 Protocols Additional to the Geneva Conventions of 1949*, Dordrecht: Martinus Nijhoff Publishers.

Bowman, Steve (2003) *Iraq: US Military Operations*, Washington DC: Congressional Research Service Report to Congress.

Brunnée, Jutta and Stephen J. Toope (2000) International Law and Constructivism: Elements of an Interactional Theory of International Law, 39 *Columbia Journal of Transnational Law* 19.

(2010) *Legitimacy and Legality in International Law: An Interactional Account*, Cambridge University Press.

(2011a) International Legal Practice, in Emmanuel Adler and Vincent Pouliot, eds., *International Practices*, Cambridge University Press.

(2011b) Interactional International Law: An Introduction in Symposium on *Legitimacy and Legality in International Law: An Interactional Account* by Jutta Brunnée and Stephen J. Toope, 3 *International Theory* 307.

(2011c) History, Mystery, and Mastery, Symposium on *Legitimacy and Legality in International Law: An Interactional Account* by Jutta Brunnée and Stephen J. Toope, 3 *International Theory* 348.

Bryde, Brunn-Otto (2003) Konstitutionalisierung des Völkerrechts und Internationalisierung des Verfassungsrechts, 42 *Der Staat* 61.

Budiansky, Stephen (2004) *Air Power: The Men, Machines, and Ideas that Revolutionized War from Kitty Hawk to Iraq*, New York: Penguin Books.

Bull, Hedley (1977) *The Anarchical Society*, Hong Kong: Macmillan.

(1995) Society and Anarchy in International Relations, in James Der Derian, ed., *International Theory: Critical Investigations*, Hong Kong: Palgrave Macmillan.

Burgorgue-Larsen, Laurence and Amaya Ùbeda de Torres (2011) *The Inter-American Court of Human Rights: Case Law and Commentary*, Oxford University Press.

Butler, Judith (2004) *Precarious Life: The Powers of Mourning and Violence*, New York: Verso.

Butler, Richard J. (2002) Modern War, Modern Law, and Army Doctrine: Are We in Step for the 21st Century? 32 *Parameters* 45.

Buzan, Barry (2004) *From International to World Society*, Cambridge University Press.

(2007) *People, States and Fear*, Colchester: ECPR Press.

Byers, Michael (1999) *Custom, Power and the Power of Rules: International Relations and Customary International Law*, Cambridge University Press.

(2005) *War Law: Understanding International Law and Armed Conflict*, London: Atlantic Books.

(2010) International Law, in Christian Reus-Smit and Duncan Snidal, eds., *The Oxford Handbook of International Relations*, New York NY: Oxford University Press.

Byers, Michael, ed. (2000) *The Role of Law in International Politics: Essays in International Relations and International Law*, Oxford University Press.

Byman, Daniel, Matthew C. Waxman and Eric V. Larson (1999) *Air Power as a Coercive Instrument*, Santa Monica CA: RAND Corporation.

Canestaro, Nathan (2004) Legal and Policy Constraints on the Conduct of Aerial Precision Warfare, 37 *Vanderbilt Journal of Transnational Law* 431.

Carnahan, Burrus (1998) Lincoln, Lieber and the Laws of War: The Origins and Limits of the Principle of Military Necessity, 92 *American Journal of International Law* 213.

Carr, Edward Hallet (1946) *The Twenty Years' Crisis, 1919–1939: An Introduction to the Study of International Relations*, London: Macmillan.

Caverley, Jonathan D. (2010/11) Explaining US Military Strategy in Vietnam: Thinking Clearly about Causation, 35 *International Security* 124.

Centre for Law and Military Operations (2004) *Legal Lessons Learned from Afghanistan and Iraq*. Vol. I: *Major Combat Operations (11 September 2001–1 May 2003)*, Charlottesville VA: The Judge Advocate General's Legal Center and School.

Chatham House (2011) 'Summary of the International Law Discussion Group', Meeting held at Chatham House 21 February 2011, www. chathamhouse.org.uk/files/18899_il210211summary.pdf (last accessed 17 March 2011).

Chayes, Abram (1972) An Inquiry into the Workings of Arms Control Agreements, 85 *Harvard Law Review* 905.

(1974) *The Cuban Missile Crisis: International Crises and the Role of Law*, New York: Oxford University Press.

Chayes, Abram and Antonia Handler Chayes (1993) On Compliance, 47 *International Organization* 176.

(1995) *The New Sovereignty: Compliance with International Regulatory Agreements*, Cambridge MA: Harvard University Press.

Chesterman, Simon (2008) An International Rule of Law? 52 *American Journal of Comparative Law* 2.

Chinkin, Christine M. (1989) The Challenge of Soft Law: Development and Change in International Law, 38 *International and Comparative Law Quarterly* 850.

Clark, Gregory S. (2002) *Linebacker II: Achieving Strategic Surprise*, Naval War College Newport RI: Naval War College.

Clark, Ramsey (1992) *The Fire this Time: US War Crimes in the Gulf*, New York: Thunder's Mouth Press.

Clodfelter, Mark (1997) Molding Air Power Convictions: Development and Legacy of William Mitchell's Strategic Thought, in Phillip S. Melinger, ed., *The Paths of Heaven: The Evolution of Air Power Theory*, Maxwell AL: Air University Press.

(2006) *The Limits of Air Power: The American Bombing of North Vietnam*, Lincoln NE: University of Nebraska Press.

(2008) A Strategy Based on Faith: The Enduring Appeal of Progressive American Airpower, 49 *Joint Force Quarterly* 24.

(2009) Back from the Future: The Impact of Change on Airpower in the Decades Ahead, *Strategic Studies Quarterly* Fall 104.

Coady, Tony C. H. J. (2008) The Status of Combatants, in David Rodin and Henry Shue, eds., *Just and Unjust Warriors: The Moral and Legal Status of Soldiers*, Oxford University Press.

Coates, Anthony (2008) Is the Independent Application of *Jus in Bello* the Way to Limit War? in David Rodin and Henry Shue, eds., *Just and Unjust Warriors: The Moral and Legal Status of Soldiers*, Oxford University Press.

Cochrane, Kathryn (2001) *Kosovo Targeting – a Bureaucratic and Legal Nightmare: The Implications for US/Australian Interoperability*, Fairbairn: Royal Australian Aerospace Centre.

Coe, Robert A. and Michael N. Schmitt (1997) Fighter Ops for Shoe Clerks, 42 *Air Force Law Review* 49.

Cohen, Amichai and Yuval Shany (2007) *A Development of Modest Proportions: The Application of the Principle of Proportionality in the Israeli Supreme Court Judgement on the Lawfulness of Targeted*

Killings, International Law Forum, The Hebrew University of Jerusalem, Research Paper no. 5–07.

Cohen, Eliot (1994) The Mystique of US Air Power, 73 *Foreign Affairs* 109.

(1995) The Meaning and Future of Air Power, 39 *Orbis* 189.

(2004) Change and Transformation in Military Affairs, 27 *Journal of Strategic Studies* 404.

Cohen, Jean (2010) Sovereignty in the Context of Globalization: A Constitutionalist Pluralist Perspective, in Samantha Besson and John Tasioulas, eds., *The Philosophy of International Law*, Oxford University Press.

Coker, Christopher (2001) *Humane Warfare*, London: Routledge.

Colgan, Jeff D., Robert O. Keohane and Thijs Van de Graaf (2012) Punctuated Equilibrium in the Energy Regime Complex, 7 *The Review of International Organizations* 117.

Conetta, Carl (2002) *Operation Enduring Freedom: Why a Higher Rate of Civilian Bombing Casualties*, Project on Defense Alternatives, Briefing Report no. 13.

(2003a) *The Wages of War: Iraqi Combatant and Noncombatant Fatalities in the 2003 Conflict*, Project on Defense Alternatives, Research Monograph no. 8.

(2003b) *Catastrophic Interdiction: Air Power and the Collapse of the Iraqi Field Army in 2003*, Project on Defense Alternatives, Briefing Memo no. 30.

Cooper, Jeffrey R. (1997) Another View of the Revolution in Military Affairs, in John Arquilla and David Ronfeldt, eds., *In Athena's Camp: Preparing for Conflict in the Information Age*, Santa Monica CA: RAND.

Cordesman, Anthony H. (2003) *The Evolving Ethical, Moral, and Legal Dilemmas of the Iraq War*, Washington DC: Centre for Strategic and International Studies.

Corten, Olivier (2010) *The Law Against War: The Prohibition on the Use of Force in Contemporary International Law*, Oxford and Portland RI: Hart.

Crawford, Emily (2010) *The Treatment of Combatants and Insurgents Under the Law of Armed Conflict*, Oxford University Press.

Crawford, James and Martti Koskenniemi (2012) Introduction, in James Crawford and Martti Koskenniemi, eds., *The Cambridge Companion to International Law*, Cambridge University Press.

Crawford, Neta C. (1993) Decolonization as an International Norm: The Evolution of Practices, Norms and Beliefs, in Laura W. Reed and Carl Kaysen, eds., *Emerging Norms of Justified Intervention*, Cambridge MA: American Academy of Arts and Sciences.

(2007) Individual and Collective Moral Responsibility for Systemic Military Atrocity, 15 *The Journal of Political Philosophy* 187.

(2010) *Bugsplat: US Standing Rules of Engagement, International Humanitarian Law, Military Necessity, and Non-Combatant Immunity*, Washington DC: United States Institute of Peace.

Cummins, Robert (1983) *The Nature of Psychological Explanation*, Cambridge MA: Massachusetts Institute of Technology Press.

D'Amato, Anthony (1971) *The Concept of Custom in International Law*, Ithaca NY: Cornell University Press.

Danilenko, Gennady (1993) *Law-Making in the International Community*, Dordrecht: Martinus Nijhoff.

Daponte, Beth Osborne (1993) A Case Study in Estimating Casualties from War and Its Aftermath: The 1991 Persian Gulf War, 3 *Medicine & Global Survival* 2.

Davis, Mike (2003) War-Mart: Revolution in Warfare Slouches Toward Baghdad – It's All in the Network, *San Francisco Chronicle*, 9 March 2003, D1.

Davis, Nancy (1984) The Doctrine of Double Effect: Problems of Interpretation, 65 *Pacific Philosophical Quarterly* 107.

DeSaussure, Hamilton (1967) The Laws of Air Warfare: Are There Any? in Richard A. Falk, ed., *The Vietnam War and International Law*, Princeton University Press.

DeSaussure, Hamilton and Robert Glasser (1975) Methods and Means of Warfare: Air Warfare-Christmas 1972, in Peter D. Trooboff and Arthur J. Goldberg, eds., *Law and Responsibility in Warfare: The Vietnam Experience*, Chapel Hill NC: University of North Carolina Press.

Dill, Janina (2013) Should International Law Ensure the Moral Acceptability of War? 26 *The Leiden Journal of International Law* 2.

Dill, Janina and Henry Shue (2012) Limiting Killing in War: Military Necessity and the St Petersburg Assumption, 26 *Ethics and International Affairs* 311.

Dinstein, Yoram (2002) Legitimate Military Objectives Under the Current Jus in Bello, in Andru E. Wall, ed., *Legal and Ethical Lessons of NATO's Kosovo Campaign*, Newport RI: Naval War College.

(2005) *War Aggression and Self-Defence*, Cambridge University Press.

(2010) *The Conduct of Hostilities Under the Law of International Armed Conflict*, Cambridge University Press.

Donelly, Jack (2010) The Ethics of Realism, in Christian Reus-Smit and Duncan Snidal, eds., *The Oxford Handbook of International Relations*, New York NY: Oxford University Press.

Doty, Rosanne Lynne (1997) Aporia: A Critical Examination of the Agent-structure Problematique in International Relations Theory, 3 *European Journal of International Relations* 365.

Dougherty, Bernard and Noelle Quénivet (2003) Has Armed Conflict in Iraq Shown once more the Growing Dissension Regarding the Definition of a Legitimate Target? What and Who can be Lawfully Targeted? 4 *Humanitäres Völkerrecht* 188.

Downes, Alexander B. (2007) Restraint or Propellant? Democracy and Civilian Fatalities in Interstate Wars, 51 *Journal of Conflict Resolution* 872.

(2008) *Targeting Civilians in War*, Ithaca NY: Cornell University Press.

Downs, George W., David M. Rocke and Peter N. Barsoom (1996) Is the Good News About Compliance Good News About Cooperation? 50 *International Organisation* 379.

Drake, Ricky (1992) *The Rules of Aerial Defeat: The Impact of Aerial Rules of Engagement on Operations in North Vietnam 1965–1968*, Maxwell AL: School of Advanced Airpower Studies Air University.

Dunlap, Charles J., Jr (1999) Technology: Recomplicating Moral Life for the Nation's Defenders, 29 *Parameters* 24.

(2000a) Kosovo, Casualty Aversion, and the American Military Ethos: A Perspective, 10 *Air Force Journal of Legal Studies* 95.

(2000b) The End of Innocence: Rethinking Noncombatancy in the Post-Kosovo Era, 14 *Strategic Review* 9.

(2001a) The Revolution in Military Legal Affairs. Air Force Legal Professionals in the 21st Century, 51 *Air Force Law Review* 293.

(2001b) 'Law and Military Interventions: Preserving Humanitarian Values in 21st Century Conflicts', www.duke.edu/~pfeaver/dunlap.pdf (last accessed 16 August 2009).

(2008) Lawfare Today, 3 *Yale Journal of International Affairs* 146.

Dunoff, Jeffrey L. (2011) What is the Purpose of International Law? 3 *International Theory* 326.

Dunoff, Jeffrey L. and Mark A. Pollack (2012a) International Law and International Relations. Introducing an Interdisciplinary Dialogue, in Jeffrey L. Dunoff and Mark A. Pollack, eds., *Interdisciplinary Perspectives on International Law and International Relations: The State of the Art*, Cambridge University Press.

(2012b) Reviewing Two Decades of IL/IR Scholarship. What We've Learned, What's Next, in Jeffrey L. Dunoff and Mark A. Pollack, eds., *Interdisciplinary Perspectives on International Law and International Relations: The State of the Art*, Cambridge University Press.

Dupuy, René-Jean (1986) *La Communauté Internationale Entre Mythe et l'Histoire*, Paris: Economica.

Eagleton, Chy de (1939) International Law and 'Public Order', 33 *American Journal of International Law* 3.

Elster, Jon (1983) *Studies in Rationality and Social Change: Explaining Technical Change*, Cambridge University Press.

(1989) *The Cement of Society: A Study of Social Order*, Cambridge University Press.

Engle, Eric Allen (2009) The History of the General Principle of Proportionality: An Overview, 13 *Willamette Journal of International Law and Dispute Resolution* 149.

Epping, Volker (2007) Confronting New Challenges: International Humanitarian Law and Knut Ipsen, in Wolff Heintschel von Heinegg and Volker Epping, eds., *International Humanitarian Law Facing New Challenges. Symposium in Honor of Knut Ipsen*, Berlin and Heidelberg: Springer.

Eritrea–Ethiopia Claims Commission (2005) 'Partial Award Western Front, Aerial Bombardment and Related Claims'. Eritrea's Claims 1, 3, 5, 9–13, 14, 21, 25 and 26, www.pca-cpa.org/upload/files/FINAL%20ER%20 FRONT%20CLAIMS.pdf (last accessed 25 May 2011).

Erskine, Tony (2010) Locating Responsibility: The Problem of Moral Agency in International Relations, in Christian Reus-Smit and Duncan Snidal, eds., *Oxford Handbook of International Relations*, Oxford University Press.

Fabre, Cécile (2009) Guns, Food, and Liability to Attack in War, 120 *Ethics* 36.

(2012) *Cosmopolitan War*, Oxford University Press.

Faiez, Rahim (2012) Afghanistan: NATO Airstrikes Killed 8 Civilians, *The Huffington Post*, 27 May 2012, www.huffingtonpost.com/2012/ 05/27/afghanistan-nato-airstikes-civilans_n_1548672/html   (last accessed 19 January 2012).

Falk, Richard (1969) Six Legal Dimensions of the United States Involvement in the Vietnam War, in Richard Falk, ed., *The Vietnam War and International Law*, Princeton University Press.

Fall, Bernard B. (1965) 'Vietnam Blitz', *New Republic*, 9 October 1965, 17.

Farrell, Henry and Martha Finnemore (2009) Ontology, Methodology and Causation in the American School of International Political Economy, 16 *Review of International Political Economy* 58.

Farrell, Stephen (2008) Iraqis Protest Deadly Raid by I.S. on Village, *New York Times*, 20 September 2008.

Farrell, Theo (2005) *The Norms of War: Cultural Beliefs and Modern Conflict*, Boulder CO: Lynne Rienner.

Fastenrath, Ulrich (1993) Relative Normativity in International Law, 4 *European Journal of International Law* 305.

Fearon, James and Alexander Wendt (2002) Rationalism v. Constructivism: A Sceptical View, in Walter Carlsnaes, Thomas Risse and Beth A. Simmons, eds., *Handbook of International Relations*, London: Sage.

Fehl, Caroline (2004) Explaining the International Criminal Court: A 'Practice Test' for Rationalist and Constructivist Approaches, 10 *European Journal of International Relations* 357.

Fenrick, William J. (2004) The Prosecution of Unlawful Attack Cases Before the ICTY, 7 *Yearbook of International Humanitarian Law* 153.

(2009) Applying the Targeting Rules to Practical Situations: Proportionality and Military Objectives, 27 *Windsor Year Book of Access to Justice* 271.

Fichtelberg, Aaron (2008) *Law at the Vanishing Point: A Philosophical Analysis of International Law*, Surrey: Ashgate.

Fick, Nathaniel (2005) *One Bullet Away: The Making of a Marine Officer*, New York: Houghton Mifflin.

Fidler, David P. (1996) Challenging the Classical Concept of Custom: Perspectives on the Future of Customary International Law, 39 *German Yearbook of International Law* 198.

Finnemore, Martha (1999/2000) Are Legal Norms Distinctive? 36 *New York University Journal of International Law and Politics* 699.

Finnemore, Martha and Kathryn Sikkink (1998) International Norm Dynamics and Political Change, 52 *International Organization* 887.

(2001) Taking Stock: The Constructivist Research Program in International Relations and Comparative Politics, 4 *Annual Review of Politic Science* 391.

Finnemore, Martha and Stephen J. Toope (2001) Alternatives to 'Legalization': Richer Views of Law and Politics, 55 *International Organization* 743.

Firmage, Edwin Brown (1967) The Law and the Indochina War, in Richard A. Falk, ed., *The Vietnam War and International Law*, Princeton University Press.

Fitzgerald, Mary C. (2003) A Noncontact, Contact War: What Iraqi Freedom Showed Russia and China, 141 *Armed Forces Journal* 26.

Fletcher, George P. and Jens David Ohlin (2008) *Defending Humanity: When Force is Justified and Why*, Oxford University Press.

Fontenot, Gregory (2005) *On Point: The United States Army in Operation Iraqi Freedom*, Annapolis MD: First Naval Institute Press.

Forowicz, Magdalena (2010) *The Reception of International Law in the European Court of Human Rights*, Oxford University Press.

Franck, Thomas M. (1990) *The Power of Legitimacy Among Nations*, Oxford University Press.

(1992) Legitimacy in the International System, in Martti Koskenniemi, ed., *International Law*, Aldershot: Ashgate.

(1995) *Fairness in International Law and Institutions*, Oxford University Press.

(2006) The Power of Legitimacy and the Legitimacy of Power: International Law in an Age of Power Disequilibrium, 100 *American Journal of International Law* 88.

Friedland, Martin L. ed. (1989) *Sanctions and Rewards in the Legal System: A Multidisciplinary Approach*, Toronto University Press.

Friedman, George and Meredith Friedman (1996) *The Future of War: Power, Technology and American World Dominance in the Twenty-First Century*, New York: Crown Publishers.

Fuller, Lon L. (1958) Positivism and Fidelity to Law: A Reply to Professor Hart, 71 *Harvard Law Review* 630.

(1969) *The Morality of Law*, New Haven CT: Yale University Press.

Gardam, Judith Gail (1993) Proportionality and Force in International Law, 87 *American Journal of International Law* 391.

Gardner, John (2001) Legal Positivism. 5½ Myths, 46 *American Journal of Jurisprudence* 199.

Garraway, Charles (2004) Interoperability and the Atlantic Divide: A Bridge over Troubled Waters, 34 *Israel Yearbook on Human Rights* 105.

(2014) The Law Applies But What Law? in Matthew Evangelista and Henry Shue, eds., *The American Way of Bombing: How Legal and Ethical Norms Change*, Ithaca NY: Cornell University Press.

Gasser, Hans-Peter (1993) *International Humanitarian Law: An Introduction*, Bem and Geneva: Henry Dunant Institute/Paul Haupt Publisher.

Gellman, Barton (1991) Allied Air War Struck Broadly in Iraq: Officials Acknowledge Strategy Went beyond Purely Military Targets, *The Washington Post*, 23 June 1991, A1.

Gelpi, Christopher, Peter D. Feaver and Jason Reifler (2005) 'Casualty Sensitivity and the War in Iraq', http://people.duke.edu/~gelpi/iraq.casualties.pdf (last accessed 26 August 2013).

George, Alexander L. and Andrew Bennett (2005) *Case Studies and Theory Development in the Social Sciences*, Cambridge MA: Massachusetts Institute of Technology Press.

Gibbons, William Konrad (1995) *The US Government and the Vietnam War: Executive and Legislative Roles and Relationship. Part IV July 1965– January 1968*, Princeton University Press.

Giddens, Anthony (1984) *The Constitution of Society: Outline of the Theory of Structuration*, Oakland CA: University of California Press.

Goldsmith, Jack L. and Eric A. Posner (2005) *The Limits of International Law*, Oxford University Press.

Goldstein, Judith, Miles Kahler, Robert O. Keohane and Anne-Marie Slaughter (2000) Introduction: Legalization and World Politics, 54 *International Organization* 385.

Goldstein, Judith and Robert O. Keohane (1993) *Ideas in Foreign Policy*, Ithaca NY: Cornell University Press.

Goldstein, Judith and Lisa L. Martin (2000) Legalization, Trade Liberalization, and Domestic Politics: A Cautionary Note, 54 *International Organization* 603.

Goodman, Ryan and Derek Jinks (2004) How to Influence States: Socialization and International Human Rights Law, 54 *Duke Law Journal* 621.

(2005) International Law and State Socialization. Empirical, Conceptual, and Normative Challenges, 54 *Duke Law Journal* 102.

(2008) Incomplete Internalization and Compliance with Human Rights Law, 19 *European Journal of International Law* 725.

(2009) Acculturation and International Human Rights Law: Toward a more Complete Theoretical Model, 20 *European Journal of International Law* 443.

Gordon, Michael R. (1991) US Calls Target a Command Center, *New York Times*, 14 February 1991.

Gordon, Michael R. and Bernard E. Trainor (2006) *Cobra II: The Inside Story of the Invasion and Occupation of Iraq*, New York: Pantheon Books.

Gordon, Robert W. (1982) Critical Legal Histories, 36 *Stanford Law Review* 125.

Gordon, Steven C. and Douglas D. Martin (2005) Modelling and Simulation for Collateral Damage Estimation in Combat, 309 *Proceedings of the International Society for Optical Engineering* 5805.

Graham, Stephen (2004) Postmortem City: Towards an Urban Geopolitics, 8 *City* 165.

Gray, Colin S. (1999) *Modern Strategy*, Oxford University Press.

(2006) *Another Bloody Century. Future Warfare*, Phoenix Paperbacks.

Grayling, A. C. (2006) *Among the Dead Cities. The History and Moral Legacy of the WWII Bombing of Civilians in Germany and Japan*, New York NY: Walker Publishing Company.

Green, Leslie C. (1967) Aftermath of Vietnam: War Law and the Soldier, in Richard A. Falk, ed., *The Vietnam War and International Law*, Princeton University Press.

(2002) The 'Unified Use of Force Rule' and the Law of Armed Conflict: A Reply to Professor Martin, 65 *Saskatchewan Law Review* 427.

(2003) 'Legal Positivism', in *Stanford Encyclopaedia of Jurisprudence*, http://plato.stanford.edu/entries/legal-positivism/ (last accessed 04 October 2012).

Greenspan, Morris L. (1959) *The Modern Law of Land Warfare*, Oakland CA: University of California Press.

Gregory, Derek (2004) *The Colonial Present. Afghanistan, Palestine, Iraq*, Oxford: Blackwell.

(2006) 'In Another Time-zone, the Bombs fall Unsafely ... '. Targets, Civilians and Late-modern War, 9 *Arab World Geographer* 88.

Grieco, Joseph M. (1988a) Anarchy and the Limits of Cooperation. A Realist Critique of the Newest Liberal Institutionalism, 42 *International Organization* 485.

(1988b) Realist Theory and the Problem of International Cooperation. Analysis with an Amended Prisoner's Dilemma Model, 50 *The Journal of Politics* 600.

Gross, Aeyal M. (2007) Human Proportions: Are Human Rights the Emperor's New Clothes of the International Law of Occupation? 18 *European Journal of International Law* 1.

Gross, Michael L. (2009) *Moral Dilemmas of Modern War. Torture, Assassination, and Blackmail in an Age of Asymmetric Conflict*, Cambridge University Press.

Grotius, Hugo translated by Francis W. Kelsey (1625) *De Jure Belli ac Pacis*, Oxford: Clarendon Press.

Guirola, Amos N. (2012a) The Importance of Criteria-based Reasoning in Targeted Killing Decisions, in Claire Finkelstein, Jens David Ohlin and Andrew Altman, eds., *Targeted Killings: Law and Morality in an Asymmetrical World*, Oxford University Press.

(2012b) Determining a Legitimate Target: The Dilemma of the Decision-Maker, 47 *Texas International Law Journal* 135.

Gurney, Gene (1985) *Vietnam: The War in the Air: A Pictorial History of the US Air Forces in the Vietnam War. Air Force, Army, Navy, and Marines*, New York: Crown Publishing Group.

Guzman, Andrew T. (2002) A Compliance-Based Theory of International Law, 9 *California Law Review* 1823.

Haas, Peter M. (1992) Epistemic Communities and International Policy Coordination, 46 *International Organization* 35.

Habermas, Jürgen (1996) *Between Facts and Norms: Contributions to a Discourse Theory*, Cambridge: Polity Press.

(1998) *Rationality and Religion: Essays on Reason, God and Modernity*. Cambridge MA: Massachusetts Institute of Technology Press.

Hallion, Richard P. (1992) *Storm over Iraq: Air Power and the Gulf War*, Washington DC: Smithsonian Institution Press.

(1998) Airpower and the Changing Nature of Warfare, 17 *Joint Forces Quarterly* 39.

Hampson, Françoise J. (1992a) Proportionality and Necessity in the Gulf Conflict, 86 *Proceedings for the American Society of International Law* 45.

(1992b) Using the International Human Rights Machinery to Enforce the International Law of Armed Conflict, 31 *Revue de Droit Militaire et de Droit de la Guerre* 119.

(1993) Means and Methods of Warfare in the Conflict in the Gulf, in Peter Rowe, ed., *The Gulf War 1990–1991 in International and English Law*, London: Routledge.

(2010) The Principle of Proportionality in the Law of Armed Conflict, in Sarah Perrigo and Jim Whitman, eds., *The Geneva Conventions Under Assault*, London: Pluto Press.

Harding, Christopher (1999) The Significance of Westphalia: An Archaeology of the International Legal Order, in Christopher Harding, ed., *Renegotiating Westphalia*, Dordrecht: Martinus Nijhoff Publishers.

Hart, H. L. A. (1958) Positivism and the Separation of Law and Morals, 71 *Harvard Law Review* 539.

(1997) *The Concept of Law*, Oxford University Press.

Hartigan, Richard Shelly (1982) *The Forgotten Victim. A History of the Civilian*, Chicago IL: Precedent Publishing.

Hathaway Oona A. and Harold Hongju Koh (2005) *Foundations of International Law and Politics*, New York: Foundation Press.

Heintschel v. Heinegg, Wolf (2003) Der Irak-Krieg und Ius in Bello, 41 *Archiv des Völkerrechts* 272.

Henckaerts, Jean-Marie and Louise Doswald-Beck, eds. (2005) *Customary International Humanitarian Law*, vol. I, Cambridge University Press.

Henkin, Louis (1979) *How Nations Behave: Law and Foreign Policy*, New York NY: Council on Foreign Relations.

Henkin, Louis, Richard Crawford Pugh, Oscar Schachter and Hans Smit (1993) *International Law*, Eagan MN: West Publishing.

Herol, Marc W. (2009) 'Unworthy' Afghan Bodies: 'Smarter' US Weapons Kill More Innocents, in Stephen J. Rockel and Rick Halpern, eds., *Inventing Collateral Damage: Civilian Casualties, War, and Empire*, Toronto: Between the Lines Press.

Herring, George (1996) *America's Longest War. The United States and Vietnam 1950–1975*, New York: John Wiley and Sons.

Hersh Seymour (2000) 'Overwhelming Force: What Happened in the Final Days of the Gulf War?', *The New Yorker*, 22 May 2000, 49.

Hopf, Ted (1998) The Promise of Constructivism in International Relations Theory, 23 *International Security* 171.

Hosmer, Stephen T. (1996) *Psychological Effects of US Air Operations in Four Wars 1941–1991: Lessons for US Commanders*, Santa Monica CA: RAND Corporation.

(2001) *Why Milosevic Decided to Settle when he did*, Santa Monica CA: RAND Corporation.

Hull, Isabel V. (2005) *Absolute Destruction: Military Culture and the Practices of War in Imperial Germany*, Ithaca NY: Cornell University Press.

Human Rights Watch (1991) *Needless Deaths in the Gulf War: Civilian Casualties During the Air Campaign and Violations of the Laws of War*, A Middle East Report, New York NY: Human Rights Watch.

(2003) *Off Target: The Conduct of the War and Civilian Casualties in Iraq*, A Middle East Report, New York NY: Human Rights Watch.

(2013) *Between a Drone and AlQaida: The Civilian Cost of US Targeted Killings in Yemen*, New York NY: Human Rights War.

Hurd, Ian (2007) Breaking and Making Norms: American Revisionism and Crises of Legitimacy, 44 *International Politics* 194.

(2010) Constructivism, in Christian Reus-Smit and Duncan Snidal, eds., *The Oxford Handbook of International Relations*, New York NY: Oxford University Press.

Hurka, Thomas (2005) Proportionality in the Morality of War, 33 *Philosophy and Public Affairs* 34.

(2008) Proportionality and Necessity, in Larry May, ed., *War: Essays in Political Philosophy*, Cambridge University Press.

Hurrell, Andrew (2002) Norms and Ethics in International Relations, in Walter Carlsnaes, Thomas Risse and Beth A. Simmons, eds., *Handbook of International Relations*, London: Sage.

International Committee of the Red Cross (1978) 'Official Records of the Diplomatic Conference on the Reaffirmation and Development of International Humanitarian Law Applicable in Armed Conflicts/ Conférence diplomatique sur la réaffirmation et le développement du droit international humanitaire applicable dans les conflits armés' (1974–7), Vols. I–XIV, Geneva, www.loc.gov/rr/frd/Military_Law/RC-dipl-conference-records.html (last accessed 4 October 2012).

(2009) 'ICRC Georgia Opinion Survey 2009', www.icrc.org/Web/eng/siteeng0.nsf/htmlall/views-from-field-report-240609/$File/Our-World-Views-from-Georgia-I-ICRC.pdf 9 (last accessed 14 July 2009).

International Criminal Tribunal for the Former Yugoslavia (ICTY) (2000) 'Final Report to the Prosecutor by the Committee Established to Review the NATO Bombing Campaign Against the Federal Republic of Yugoslavia' of 8 June 2000, www.icty.org/sid/10052 (last accessed 4 October 2012).

International Humanitarian Law Research Initiative (2009) 'Manual on International Law Applicable to Air and Missile Warfare', Program on Humanitarian Policy and Conflict Research at Harvard University, www.ihlresearch.org/amw/aboutmanual.php (last accessed 4 October 2012).

(2010) 'Commentary on the HPCR Manual on International Law Applicable to Air and Missile Warfare', Program on Humanitarian Policy and Conflict Research at Harvard University, www.ihlresearch. org/amw/aboutmanual.php (last accessed 4 October 2012).

International Human Rights and Conflict Resolution Clinic (Stanford Law School) and Global Justice Clinic (NYU Law School) (2012) 'Living Under Drones. Death, Injury, and Trauma to Civilians for US Drone Practices in Pakistan', www.livingunderdrones.org/report/ (last accessed 14 December 2013).

International Institute of Humanitarian Law (2006) 'The Manual on the Law of Non-International Armed Conflict, San Remo', www.dur.ac. uk/resources/law/NIACManualIYBHR15th.pdf (last accessed 20 May 2011).

International Law Commission (1980) Draft Articles on State Responsibility, 'Yearbook of the International Law Commission II', UN Doc. A/CH.4/ SER.A/1980/Add.1, http://untreaty.un.org/ilc/publications/yearbooks/ Ybkvolumes(e)/ILC_1980_v2_p1_e.pdf (last accessed 4 October 2012).

(2000) 'Final Report of the Committee on the Formation of Customary (General) International Law, Statement of Principles Applicable to the Formation of General Customary Law', Report of the Sixty-Ninth Conference, http://untreaty.un.org/ilc/reports/2011/english/annex.pdf (last accessed 4 October 2012).

Jackson, Robert (2010) *The Global Covenant*, Oxford University Press.

Janis, Mark Weston (2004) *The American Tradition of IL: Great Expectations 1789–1974*, Oxford University Press.

Jian, Chen (1995) China's Involvement in the Vietnam War 1964–69, 142 *China Quarterly* 366.

Jochnick, Chris af and Roger Normand (1994) The Legitimation of Violence: A Critical History of the Laws of War, 35 *Harvard International Law Journal* 49.

Kagan, Frederick W. (2006) *Finding the Target: The Transformation of American Military Technology*, New York and London: Encounter Books.

Kahin, George McT. (1987) *Intervention: How America Became Involved in Vietnam*, Garden City: Anchor Books.

Kahl, Colin H. (2006) How We Fight, 85 *Foreign Affairs* 83.

(2007) In the Crossfire or the Crosshairs? Norms, Civilian Casualties and US Conduct in Iraq, 32 *International Security* 7.

Kahler, Miles (2000) Conclusion: Causes and Consequences of Legalization, 54 *International Organization* 661.

Kaiser, David E. (2000) *American Tragedy: Kennedy, Johnson and the Origins of the Vietnam War*, Cambridge MA: Harvard University Press.

Kalshoven, Frits (1991) Noncombatant Persons, in Horace B. Robertson Jr, ed., *The Law of Naval Operations*, Newport RI: Naval War College Press.

Kant, Immanuel trans. by H. J. Paton (1956) *Groundwork of the Metaphysic of Morals*, New York and London: Harper Torchbooks.

Kapstein, Ethan B. (2012) Measuring Progress in Modern Warfare, 54 *Survival* 137.

Kattenberg, Paul M. (1982) *The Vietnam Trauma in American Foreign Policy 1945–75*, New Brunswick NJ: Transaction Books.

Keck, Margaret and Kathryn Sikkink (1998) *Activists Beyond Borders: Advocacy Networks in International Politics*, Ithaca NY: Cornell University Press.

Keeva, Steven (1991) Lawyers in the War Room, 77 *American Bar Association Journal* 52.

Kelly, Patrick J. (2000) The Twilight of Customary International Law, 40 *Virginia Journal of International Law* 450.

Kelsen, Hans trans. from the second German edition by Max Knight (1967) *Pure Theory of Law*, Oakland CA: University of California Press.

Kennedy, David (1987) *International Legal Structures*, Baden-Baden: Nomos.

(2006) *Of Law and War*, Princeton University Press.

(2012) Lawfare and Warfare, in James Crawford and Martti Koskenniemi, eds., *The Cambridge Companion to International Law*, Cambridge University Press.

Keohane, Robert O. (1989) Neoliberal Institutionalism: A Perspective on World Politics, in Robert O. Keohane *International Institutions and State Power*, Boulder CO: Westview.

(1997) International Relations and International Law: Two Optics, 38 *Harvard International Law Journal* 487.

(2000) Ideas Part Way Down, 26 *Review of International Studies* 125.

(2002) Rational Choice Theory and International Law: Insights and Limitations, 31 *Journal of Legal Studies* 307.

(2009a) Discordant Cooperation Reinventing Globalization to Reduce Gender Inequality, in Debora Satz and Robert Reich, eds., *Towards a Humanist Justice: The Political Philosophy of Susan Muller Okin*, Oxford University Press.

(2009b) 'Social Norms and Agency in World Politics', www.nyustraus. org/fellows/documents/RobertKeohane.pdf (last accessed 15 January 2011).

(2009c) The Old IPE and the New, 16 *Review of International Political Economy* 34.

(2012a) Twenty Years of Institutional Liberalism, 26 *International Relations* 2.

(2012b) Hegemony and After: What Can Be Said About the Future of American Global Leadership? 91 *Foreign Affairs* 4.

Kimball, Jeffrey (1998) *Nixon's Vietnam War*, Lawrence KS: University Press of Kansas.

King, Gary, Robert O. Keohane and Sidney Verba (1994) *Designing Social Inquiry: Scientific Inference in Qualitative Research*, Princeton University Press.

Kingsbury, Benedict (1997/8) The Concept of Compliance as a Function of Competing Conceptions of International Law, 19 *Michigan Journal of International Law* 345.

Kirgis, Frederic L., Jr (1987) Custom on a Sliding Scale, 81 *American Journal of International Law* 146.

Klabbers, Jan (2004/5) The Relative Autonomy of International Law or the Forgotten Politics of Interdisciplinarity, 1 *Journal of International Law and International Relations* 35.

Klotz, Audie and Cecilia Lynch (2007) *Strategies for Research in Constructivist International Relations*, Armonk NY and London: Sharpe.

Koh, Harold Hongju (1997) Review Essay: Why Do Nations Obey International Law? 106 *The Yale Law Journal* 2599.

Komer, Robert W. (1986) *Bureaucracy at War: US Performance in the Vietnam Conflict*, Boulder CO: Westview Press.

Koskenniemi, Martti (1990) The Politics of International Law, 1 *European Journal of International Law* 4.

(1991) The Future of Statehood, 32 *Harvard International Law Journal* 397.

(2000) Carl Schmitt, Hans Morgenthau, and the Image of Law in International Relations, in Michael Byers, ed., *The Role of Law in International Politics: Essays in International Relations and International Law*, Oxford University Press.

(2005) *From Apology to Utopia: The Structure of International Legal Argument*, Cambridge University Press.

(2011) The Mystery of Legal Obligation, Symposium on *Legitimacy and Legality in International Law: An Interactional Account* by Jutta Brunnée and Stephen J. Toope, 3 *International Theory* 319.

(2012a) Law, Teleology and International Relations: An Essay in Counterdisciplinarity, 26 *International Relations* 3.

(2012b) International Law in the World of Ideas, in James Crawford and Martti Koskenniemi, eds., *The Cambridge Companion to International Law*, Cambridge University Press.

Kramer, Michael and Michael N. Schmitt (2008) Lawyers on Horseback? Thoughts on Judge Advocates and Civil-Military Relations, 55 *University of California Los Angeles Law Review* 1407.

Krasner, Stephen D. (1983) Structural Causes and Regime Consequences: Regimes as Intervening Variables, in Stephen Krasner, ed., *International Regimes*, Ithaca NY: Cornell University Press.

(1999) *Organized Hypocrisy*, Princeton University Press.

(2010) Sociological Approaches, in Christian Reus-Smit and Duncan Snidal, eds., *The Oxford Handbook of International Relations*, New York NY: Oxford University Press.

Kratochwil, Friedrich V. (1989) *Rules, Norms and Decisions: On the Conditions of Practical and Legal Reasoning in International Relations and Domestic Society*, Cambridge University Press.

(2000) How Do Norms Matter? in Michael Byers, ed., *The Role of Law in International Politics: Essays in International Relations and International Law*, Oxford University Press.

Krepon, Michael (1967) Weapons Potentially Inhumane: The Case of Cluster Bombs, in Richard A. Falk, ed., *The Vietnam War and International Law*, Princeton University Press.

Kritsiotis, Dino (2004) When States Use Armed Force, in Christian Reus-Smit, ed., *The Politics of International Law*, New York NY: Cambridge University Press.

Kumm, Mattias (2004) The Legitimacy of International Law: A Constitutionalist Framework of Analysis, 15 *European Journal of International Law* 907.

Kutz, Christopher (2008) Fearful Symmetry, in David Rodin and Henry Shue, eds., *Just and Unjust Warriors: The Moral and Legal Status of Soldiers*, Oxford University Press.

Kydd, Andrew H. (2010) Methodological Individualism and Rational Choice, in Christian Reus-Smit and Duncan Snidal, eds., *The Oxford Handbook of International Relations*, New York NY: Oxford University Press.

Lamb, Michael W., Sr (2002) *Operation Allied Force: Golden Nuggets for Future Campaigns*, Maxwell AL: Air War College Maxwell Paper no. 27.

Lambeth, Benjamin S. (1993) *Achieving Air Supremacy in Operation Desert Storm*, Santa Monica CA: RAND Corporation.

(2000) *The Transformation of American Air Power*, Santa Monica CA: RAND Corporation.

Larson, Eric V. and Bogdan Savych (2007) *Misfortunes of War: Press and Public Reactions to Civilian Deaths in Wartime*, Santa Monica CA: RAND Corporation.

Lauterpacht, Hersch (1952) The Problem of the Revision of the Law of War, 360 *British Yearbook of International Law* 382.

Lawrence, Mark A. (2008) *The Vietnam War: A Concise International History*, Oxford University Press.

Lazar, Seth (2009) Responsibility, Risk, and Killing in Self-Defense, 119 *Ethics* 699.

(2010) The Responsibility Dilemma for Killing in War: A Review Essay, 38 *Philosophy and Public Affairs* 180.

(2011) War, in Hugh Lafollette, ed., *International Encyclopaedia of Ethics*, Oxford: Wiley-Blackwell.

(2012) The Morality and Law of War, in Andrei Marmor, ed., *Routledge Companion to Philosophy of Law*, London: Routledge.

Legro, Jeffrey (2005) *Rethinking the World: Great Power Strategies and International Order*, Ithaca NY: Cornell University Press.

Lewis, Michael (2003) The Law of Aerial Bombardment in the 1991 Gulf War, 97 *American Journal of International Law* 481.

Lichtenberg, Judith (2008) How to Judge Soldiers Whose Cause is Unjust, in David Rodin and Henry Shue, eds., *Just and Unjust Warriors: The Moral and Legal Status of Soldiers*, Oxford University Press.

Luban, David (1988) *Lawyers and Justice: An Ethical Study*, Princeton University Press.

Lukacs, Martin (2006) Pulitzer-winning Investigative Journalist Seymour Hersh Slams Bush at McGill Address, *The McGill Daily*, 31 October 2006.

Lutz, Ellen L. and Kathryn Sikkink (2000) International Human Rights Law and Practice in Latin America, 54 *International Organization* 633.

(2001) The Justice Cascade: The Evolution and Impact of Foreign Human Rights Trials in Latin America, 2 *Chicago Journal of International Law* 1.

Manea, Octavian (2011) The Age of Airpower: An Interview with Martin van Creveld, *Small Wars Journal*, 26 June 2011, 1.

Margalit, Avishai and Michael Walzer (2009) Israel: Civilians and Combatants, *New York Review of Books* 56, 14 May 2009, 21.

Martin, Francisco F. (2002) The Unified Use of Force Rule Revisited: The Penetration of the Law of Armed Conflict by Human Rights Law, 65 *Saskatchewan Law Review* 406.

Massing, Michael (2007) Iraq: The Hidden Human Cost, *New York Review of Books*, 20 December 2007, 82.

Matheson, Michael J. (1987) Session One: The United States Position on the Relationship of Customary International Law to the 1977 Protocols Additional to the Geneva Conventions, 2 *American University Journal of International Law and Polity* 419.

Mattern, Janice Bially (2011) A Practice Theory of Emotion for International Relations, in Emanuel Adler and Vincent Pouliot, eds., *International Practices*, Cambridge University Press.

Maxwell, Mark 'Max' (2012) Rebutting the Civilian Presumption: Playing Whack-A-Mole Without a Mallet? in Claire Finkelstein, Jens David Ohlin and Andrew Altman, eds., *Targeted Killings. Law and Morality in an Asymmetrical World*, Oxford University Press.

McAllister, James (2010/11) Who Lost Vietnam? Soldiers, Civilians, and US Military Strategy, 35 *International Security* 95.

McChrystal, Stanley A. (2011) Becoming the Enemy, 185 *Foreign Policy* 66.

McClatchy, Shah (2010) 'Pakistanis Protest Civilian Deaths in US Drone Attacks', www.mcclatchydc.com/2010/12/10/105104/pakistanis-protest-civilian-deaths.html?utm_source=twitterfeed&utm_medium=twitter&utm_term=news (last accessed 4 September 2012).

McCormick, Neil (1993) Beyond the Sovereign State? 56 *The Modern Law Review* 1.

McCormack, Timothy L. H. and Helen Durham (2009) Aerial Bombardment of Civilians: The Current International Legal Framework, in Yuki Tanaka and Marilyn B. Young, eds., *Bombing Civilians: A Twentieth-century History*, New Haven CT: The New Press.

McInnes, Colin (2002) *Spectator-sport War: The West and Contemporary Conflict*, Boulder CO: Lynne Rienner.

McKeogh, Colm (2002) *Innocent Civilians: The Morality of Killing in War*, Basingstoke: Palgrave Macmillan.

McMahan, Jeff (1994) Revising the Doctrine of Double Effect, 11 *Journal of Applied Philosophy* 201.

(2004a) The Ethics of Killing in War, 114 *Ethics* 693.

(2004b) War as Self-Defense, 18 *Ethics and International Affairs* 75.

(2006) The Moral Equality of Combatants, 14 *Journal of Political Philosophy* 377.

(2008) The Morality of War and the Law of War, in David Rodin and Henry Shue, eds., *Just and Unjust Warriors: The Moral and Legal Status of Soldiers*, Oxford University Press.

(2009) *Killing in War*, Oxford University Press.

(2010a) Laws of War, in Samantha Besson and John Tasioulas, eds., *The Philosophy of International Law*, Oxford University Press.

(2010b) The Just Distribution of Harm Between Combatants and Noncombatants, 38 *Philosophy and Public Affairs* 343.

(2011) Duty, Obedience, Desert, and Proportionality in War: A Response, 122 *Ethics* 1.

(2012) The Prevention of Unjust Wars, in Yitzhak Benbji and Naomi Sussman, eds., *Reading Walzer*, London: Routledge.

Mearsheimer, John J. (1995) A Realist Reply, 20 *International Security* 82.

(2001) *The Tragedy of Great Power Politics*, London and New York NY: W. W. Norton and Company.

Mégret, Frédéric (2011) War and the Vanished Battlefield, 9 *Loyola University Chicago International Law Review* 131.

(2012) International Law as Law, in James Crawford and Martti Koskenniemi, eds., *The Cambridge Companion to International Law*, Cambridge University Press.

Melson, David A. (2009) Targeting War-Sustaining Capability at Sea: Compatibility with Additional Protocol I, *The Army Lawyer* 44.

Melzer, Nils (2009) 'Interpretive Guidance on the Notion of Direct Participation in Hostilities Under International Humanitarian Law', www.icrc.org/eng/assets/files/other/icrc_002_0990.pdf (last accessed 4 October 2012).

(2012) Bolstering the Protection of Civilians in Armed Conflict, in Antonio Cassese, ed., *Realizing Utopia: The Future of International Law*, Oxford University Press.

Mercer, Jonathan (2005) Rationality and Psychology in International Politics, 59 *International Organization* 77.

Meron, Theodor (1987) The Geneva Conventions as Customary Law, 81 *American Journal of International Law* 348.

(1995) Extraterritoriality of Human Rights Treaties, 89 *American Journal of International Law* 1.

(1996) The Continuing Role of Custom in the Formation of International Humanitarian Law, 90 *American Journal of International Law* 238.

(2006) *The Humanization of International Law*, Dordrecht: Martinus Nijhoff Publishers.

Meyer, Jeanne M. (2001) Tearing Down the Façade: A Critical Look at the Current Law on Targeting the Will of the Enemy and Air Force Doctrine, *Air Force Law Review* 143.

Meyrowitz, Henry (1981) Le Bombardement Stratégique d'Après le Protocole Additionnel I aux Conventions de Genève, 41 *Zeitschrift für ausländisches öffentliches Recht und Völkerrecht* 1.

(1994) The Principle of Superfluous Injury and Unnecessary Suffering, 229 *International Review of the Red Cross* 98.

Michael, Philip S. (2003) *The Strategic Significance of Linebacker II: Political, Military and Beyond*, Carlisle PA: United States Army War College.

Moravcsik, Andrew (2010) New Liberalism, in Christian Reus-Smit and Duncan Snidal, eds., *Oxford Handbook of International Relations*, New York NY: Oxford University Press.

(2012) Liberal Theories of International Law, in Jeffrey L. Dunoff and Mark A. Pollack, eds., *Interdisciplinary Perspectives on International Law and International Relations: The State of the Art*, Cambridge University Press.

Morgenthau, Hans J. (1948) *Politics Among Nations: The Struggle for Power and Peace*, Columbus OH: McGraw-Hill.

Morris, Nicholas (2006) Humanitarian Intervention in the Balkans, in Jennifer M. Welsh, ed., *Humanitarian Intervention and International Society*, New York NY: Oxford University Press.

Mueller, John E. (1980) The Search for the 'Breaking Point' in Vietnam: The Statistics of a Deadly Quarrel, 4 *International Studies Quarterly* 497.

Murray, Williamson (1995) *Air War in the Persian Gulf*, Baltimore MD: Nautical & Aviation Publishing Company of America.

Murray, Williamson and Robert H. Scales (2003) *The Iraq War: A Military History*, Cambridge MA: Harvard University Press.

Myrow, Stephen A. (1996/7) Waging War on the Advice of Counsel: The Role of Operational Law in the Gulf War, 7 *US Air Force Academy Jounal of Legal Studies* 131.

Nagel, Thomas (1979) *Mortal Questions*, Cambridge University Press.

Nardin, Terry (2008) Theorizing the International Rule of Law, 34 *Review of International Studies* 385.

   (2010) International Ethics, in Christian Reus-Smit and Duncan Snidal, eds., *The Oxford Handbook of International Relations*, New York NY: Oxford University Press.

Neff, Stephen C. (2005) *War and the Law of Nations: A General History*, Cambridge University Press.

Nye, Joseph S. (2010) International Relations: The Relevance of Theory to Practice, in Christian Reus-Smit and Duncan Snidal, eds., *The Oxford Handbook of International Relations*, New York NY: Oxford University Press.

Obradovic, Konstantin (1997) The Prohibition of Reprisals in Protocol I: Greater Protection for War Victims, 320 *International Review of the Red Cross* 520.

O'Connell, Mary Ellen (2008) *The Power and Purpose of International Law*, Oxford University Press.

O'Hanlon, Michael (2009) *Budgeting for Hard Power*, Washington DC: Brookings Institution Press.

Ohlin, Jens David (2012) Targeting Co-belligerents, in Claire Finkelstein, Jens David Ohlin and Andrew Altman, eds., *Targeted Killings. Law and Morality in an Asymmetrical World*, Oxford University Press.

Onuf, Nicholas G. (1989) *World of our Making: Rules and Rule in Social Theory and International Relations*, Columbia SC: University of South Carolina Press.

Orakhelashvili, Alexander (2006) State Immunity and International Public Order Revisited, 49 *German Yearbook of International Law* 327.

Owens, Patricia (2003) Accidents don't just Happen: The Liberal Politics of High-technology 'Humanitarian' War, 32 *Millennium Journal of International Studies* 595.

Pape, Robert A. (1996) *Bombing to Win: Air Power and Coercion in War*, Ithaca NY: Cornell University Press.

Parks, Hays W. (1982) Rolling Thunder and the Law of War, 33 *Air University Review* 2.

(1983) Linebacker and the Law of War, 34 *Air University Review* 2.

(1990) Air War and the Law of War, 32 *Air Force Law Review* 2.

(1991/2) The Gulf War: A Practitioner's View, 10 *Dickinson Journal of International Law* 393.

Pattinson, James (2012) *Humanitarian Intervention and the Responsibility to Protect*, Oxford University Press.

Petrowski, Lawrence C. (1996) Law and Conduct of the Vietnam War, in *The Vietnam War and International Law*, Richard A. Falk, ed., Princeton University Press.

Pickert, Perry L. (1967) American Attitudes Toward International Law as Reflected in the Pentagon Papers, in Richard A. Falk, ed., *The Vietnam War and International Law*, Princeton University Press.

Pictet, Jean (1952) *Commentary I: Geneva Convention for the Amelioration of the Condition of the Wounded and Sick Armed Forces in the Field*, Geneva: International Committee of the Red Cross.

Pilloud, Claude, Yves Sandoz, Christophe Swinarski and Bruno Zimmermann, eds. (1987) *Commentary on the Additional Protocols of 8 June 1977 to the Geneva Conventions of 12 August 1949*, Norwell MA: Martinus Nijhoff Publishers.

Primoratz, Igor (2007) *Civilian Immunity in War*, Oxford University Press.

Pufendorf, Samuel ed. James Tully (1991) *On the Duty of Man and Citizen According to Natural Law*, Cambridge University Press.

Raski, Marcus and Devin West (2008) *Collateral Damage: A US Strategy in War?* Washington DC: Institute for Policy Studies.

Rasulov, Akbar (2006) Review. From Apology to Utopia: The Structure of International Legal Argument, 16 *Law and Politics Book Review* 583.

Ratner, Steven (1999/00) Does International Law Matter in Preventing Ethnic Conflict? 32 *New York University Journal of International Law and Politics* 591.

(2002) Jus ad Bellum and Jus in Bello After September 11, 96 *American Journal of International Law* 905.

Raustiala, Kal and Anne-Marie Slaughter (2002) International Law, International Relations and Compliance, in Walter Carlsnaes, Thomas Risse and Beth A. Simmons, eds., *Handbook of International Relations*, London: Sage.

Ray, James L. (1989) The Abolition of Slavery and the End of International War, 43 *International Organization* 405.

Raz, Joseph (1979) *The Authority of Law: Essays on Law and Morality*, Oxford: Clarendon Press.

Record, Jeffrey (1998) *The Wrong War: Why We Lost in Vietnam*, Annapolis MD: Naval Institute Press.

Record, Jeffrey and W. Andrew Terrill (2004) *Iraq and Vietnam. Differences, Similarities and Insights*, Newport RI: Strategic Studies Institute US Army War College.

Reus-Smit, Christian (1996) *The Constructivist Turn: Critical Theory After the End of the Cold War*, Australian National University, Department of International Relations, Working Paper no. 4.

(1999) *The Moral Purpose of the State: Culture Social Identity, and Institutional Rationality in International Relations*, Princeton University Press.

(2003) Politics and International Legal Obligation, 9 *European Journal of International Relations* 591.

(2004a) *The Politics of International Law*, in Christian Reus-Smit, ed., *The Politics of International Law*, New York NY: Cambridge University Press.

(2004b) Society, Power and Ethics, in Christian Reus-Smit, ed., *The Politics of International Law*, New York NY: Cambridge University Press.

(2004c) *American Power and World Order*, Cambridge: Polity Press.

(2008) Constructivism and the Structure of Ethical Reasoning, in Richard Price, ed., *Moral Limit and Possibility in World Politics*, New York NY: Cambridge University Press.

(2011) Obligation Through Practice: Symposium on *Legitimacy and Legality in International Law: An Interactional Account* by Jutta Brunnée and Stephen J. Toope, 3 *International Theory* 339.

(2013) *Individual Rights and the Making of the International System*, Cambridge University Press.

Reus-Smit, Christian and Ian Clark (2007) Resolving International Crises of Legitimacy, 44 *International Politics* 2.

Reus-Smit, Christian and Duncan Snidal (2010) Between Utopia and Reality: The Practical Discourses of International Relations, in Christian Reus-Smit and Duncan Snidal, eds., *The Oxford Handbook of International Relations*, New York NY: Oxford University Press.

Richardson, James L. (2010) The Ethics of Neoliberal Institutionalism, in Christian Reus-Smit and Duncan Snidal, eds., *The Oxford Handbook of International Relations*, New York NY: Oxford University Press.

Ricks, Thomas E. (2002) Target Approval Delays Cost Air Force Key Hits, 1 *Journal of Military Ethics* 109.

Risse, Thomas (2000) 'Let's Argue!' Communicative Action in World Politics, 54 *International Organization* 1.

Roat, John Carl (2000) *The Making of US Navy Seals. Class-29*, Toronto and New York: Random House.

Roberts, Adam (1994) The Laws of War in the 1990–91 Gulf Conflict, 18 *International Security* 134.

(2003) Law and the Use of Force After Iraq, 45 *Survival* 31.

(2006) The United Nations and Humanitarian Intervention, in Jennifer M. Welsh, ed., *Humanitarian Intervention and International Society*, New York NY: Oxford University Press.

Roberts, Adam and Richard Guelff, eds. (2002) *Documents on the Laws of War*, Oxford University Press.

Roberts, Anthea Elizabeth (2001) Traditional and Modern Approaches to Customary International Law: A Reconciliation, 95 *American Journal of International Law* 756.

Robertson, Horace B., Jr (1997/98) The Principle of the Military Objective in the Law of Armed Conflict, 8 *US Air Force Academy Journal of Legal Studies* 35.

Rockel, Stephen J. (2009) Collateral Damage: A Comparative History, in Stephen J. Rockel and Rick Halpern, eds., *Inventing Collateral Damage: Civilian Casualties, War, and Empire*, Toronto: Between the Lines Press.

Rodin, David (2002) *War and Self-Defense*, Oxford University Press.

(2008) The Moral Inequality of Soldiers: Why Jus in Bello Assymetry is Half Right, in David Rodin and Henry Shue, eds., *Just and Unjust Warrior: The Moral and Legal Status of Soldiers*, Oxford University Press.

(2011) Law and Morality in War, in Hew Strachan and Sibylle Scheipers, eds., *The Changing Character of War*, Oxford University Press.

(2012) *War Proportionality and Double Effect*, in Yitzhak Benbji and Naomi Sussman, eds., *Reading Walzer*, London: Routledge.

Rodin, David and Henry Shue, eds. (2008) *Just and Unjust Warriors: The Moral and Legal Status of Soldiers*, Oxford University Press.

Rodin, David and Richard Sorabji (2005) *The Ethics of War: Shared Problems in Different Traditions*, Surrey: Ashgate.

Rogers, A. P. V. (2000) Zero Casualty Warfare, 837 *International Review of the Red Cross* 165.

(2004) *Law on the Battlefield*, Manchester University Press.

Rohde, David (2012) The Obama Doctrine: Obama's Secret Wars, 192 *Foreign Policy* 64.

Roscini, Marco (2005) Targeting and Contemporary Aerial Bombardment, 54 *International and Comparative Law Quarterly* 411.

Rose, Gideon (1998) Neoclassical Realism and Theories of Foreign Policy, 51 *World Politics* 144.

SáCouto, Susana and Katherine Cleary (2008) The Gravity Threshold of the International Criminal Court, 23 *American University International Law Review* 807.

Salopek, Paul (2012) Collateral Damage: Obama's Secret Wars, March/April *Foreign Policy*.

Sandholtz, Wayne and Alexander Stone Sweet (2004) Law, Politics, and International Governance, in Christian Reus-Smit, ed., *The Politics of International Law*, New York NY: Cambridge University Press.

Sassòli, Marco (1990) *Bedeutung einer Kodifikation für das allgemeine Völkerrecht mit besonderer Betrachtung der Regeln zum Schutz der Zivilbevölkerung vor den Auswirkungen von Feindseligkeiten*, Basel: Helbing & Lichtenhahn.

(2005) Targeting: The Scope and Utility of the Concept of 'Military Objectives' for the Protection of Civilians in Contemporary Armed Conflicts, in David Wippman and Matthew Evangelista, eds., *New Wars, New Laws? Applying the Laws of War in 21st Century Conflicts*, Ardsley NY: Transnational Publishers.

Scarborough, Rowan (2003) US Air Attack Found Lacking in 'Shock and Awe', *Washington Times*, 31 March 2003.

Schaffer, Ronald (2009) The Bombing Campaigns in World War II: The European Theatre, in Yuki Tanaka and Marilyn B. Young, eds., *Bombing Civilians: A Twentieth-century History*, New York: The New Press.

Schilling, Theodor (2005) *On the Constitutionalization of General International Law*, European University Institute, Jean Monnet Working Paper 06/05.

Schmitt, Michael N. (1992) The Confluence of Law and Morality: Thoughts on Just War, 3 *US Air Force Academy Journal of Legal Studies* 91.

(1997/8) Book Review: Law on the Battlefield, 8 *US Air Force Academy Journal of Legal Studies* 255.

(1998) Bellum Americanum: The US View of Twenty-First Century War and its Possible Implications for the Law of Armed Conflict, 19 *Michigan Journal of International Law* 1051.

(2002) *Ethics and Military Force: The Jus in Bello*, Carnegie Council on Ethics and International Affairs, www.michaelschmitt.org/Publications (last accessed 17 August 2009).

(2003) Armed Conflict and Law in this Century, 30 *Human Rights* 3.

(2004) Targeting and Humanitarian Law: Current Issues, 34 *Israel Yearbook on Human Rights* 59.

(2006a) Fault Lines in the Law of Attack, in Susan Breau and Agnieszka Jachec-Neale, eds., *Testing the Boundaries of International Humanitarian Law*, London: British Institute of International and Comparative Law.

(2006b) Effects-Based Operations and the Law of Aerial Warfare, 5 *Washington University Global Studies Law Review* 265.

(2007) 21st Century Conflict: Can the Law Survive? 8 *Melbourne Journal of International Law* 443.

(2008) Asymmetrical Warfare and International Humanitarian Law, 62 *Air Force Law Review* 1.

(2010) The Interpretive Guidance on the Notion of Direct Participation in Hostilities. A Critical Analysis, 1 *Harvard National Security Journal* 5.

(2012) Military Necessity and Humanity in International Humanitarian Law. Preserving the Delicate Balance, 50 *Virginia Journal of International Law* 759.

Scholz, John T. (1984) Voluntary Compliance and Regular Enforcement, 6 *Law and Policy* 385.

Schreuer, Christoph (1993) The Waning of the Sovereign State: Towards a New Paradigm for International Law, 4 *European Journal of International Law* 447.

Schweller, Randall L. (1998) *Deadly Imbalances: Tripolarity and Hitler's Strategy of World Conquest*, New York NY: Columbia University Press.

Shanker, Thom (2008) Air Force Plans Altered Role in Iraq, *New York Times*, 29 July 2008.

Shapiro, Scott J. (2006) What is the Internal Point of View? 75 *Fordham Law Review* 1157.

Sharp, Ulysses S. G. (1968) *Report on Air and Naval Campaigns Against North Vietnam and Pacific Command-wide Support of the War June 1964 – July 1968*, Washington DC: US Government Printing Office.

Shaw, Martin (2005) *The New Western Way of War: Risk-Transfer War and its Crisis in Iraq*, Cambridge: Polity Press.

Sheehan, Neil (1988) *A Bright Shining Lie: John Paul Vann and America in Vietnam*, New York: Random House.

(2009) The United States and Strategic Bombing: From Prophecy to Memory, in Yuki Tanaka and Marlyin B. Young, eds., *Bombing Civilians: A Twentieth-century History*, New York: The New Press.

Sherry, Michael (1987) *The Rise of American Air Power: The Creation of Armageddon*, New Haven CT: Yale University Press.

Shimko, Keith L. (2010) *The Iraq Wars and America's Revolution*, Cambridge University Press.

Shue, Henry (2003) War, in Hugh LaFollette, ed., *Oxford Handbook of Practical Ethics*, Oxford University Press (reprinted in 2005, in: Matthew Evangelista, ed., *Peace Studies: Critical Concepts in Political Science*, New York NY: Routledge).

(2006) Limiting Sovereignty, in Jennifer M. Welsh, ed., *Humanitarian Intervention and International Society*, New York NY: Oxford University Press.

(2008) Do We Need 'A Morality of War'? in David Rodin and Henry Shue, eds., *Just and Unjust Warriors: The Moral and Legal Status of Soldiers*, Oxford University Press.

(2010) Laws of War, in Samantha Besson and John Tasioulas, eds., *The Philosophy of International Law*, Oxford University Press.

(2011) Target-selection Norms, Torture Norms, and Growing US Permissiveness, in Hew Strachan and Sibylle Scheipers, eds., *The Changing Character of War*, Oxford University Press.

Shue, Henry and David Wippman (2002) Limiting Attacks on Dual-Use Facilities Performing Indispensable Functions, 35 *Cornell International Law Journal* 559.

Sikkink, Kathryn (1998) Transnational Politics, International Relations Theory, and Human Rights, 31 *Political Science and Politics* 516.

(2011) *The Justice Cascade: How Human Rights Prosecutions are Changing World Politics*, London and New York NY: W.W. Norton and Company.

Simma, Bruno (1994) From Bilateralism to Community Interest in International Law, 250 *Collected Courses of The Hague Academy of International Law* 217.

Simma, Bruno and Philip Alston (1988/9) The Sources of Human Rights Law: Custom, *Jus Cogens* and General Principles, 12 *Australia Yearbook of International Law* 82.

Simma, Bruno and Andreas L. Paulus (1998) The 'International Community': Facing the Challenge of Globalization, 9 *European Journal of International Law* 266.

Simmons, Beth A. (1998) Compliance with International Agreements, 1 *Annual Review of Political Science* 75.

(2009) *Mobilizing for Human Rights. International Law in Domestic Politics*, Cambridge University Press.

Simpson, Gerry (2010) The Ethics of new Liberalism, in Christian Reus-Smit and Duncan Snidal, eds., *The Oxford Handbook of International Relations*, New York NY: Oxford University Press.

Singal, Jesse, Christine Lim and M. J. Stephey (2003) Shock and Awe, *Time*, www.time.com/time/2007/iraq/1.html (last accessed 20 January 2011).

Slaughter, Anne-Marie (2004) *A New World Order*, Princeton University Press.

Slaughter, Anne-Marie and William Burke-White (2002) An International Constitutional Moment, 43 *Harvard International Law Journal* 1.

Slaughter, Anne-Marie, Andrew S. Tuliumello and Stephan Wood (1998) International Law and International Relations Theory: A New Generation of Interdisciplinary Scholarship, 92 *American Journal of International Law* 3.

Slaughter-Burley, Anne-Marie (1993) International Law and International Relations Theory: A Dual Agenda, 87 *American Journal of International Law* 205.

Sloane, Robert D. (2010) Review of Law at the Vanishing Point: A Philosophical Analysis of International Law by Aaron Fichtelberg, 104 *American Journal of International Law* 549.

Smith, John T. (1994) *The Strategic Bombing Campaign in North Vietnam 1965–1968*, Surrey: Air Research Publications.

Sofaer, Abraham D. (1988) AGORA: The US Decisions Not to Ratify Protocol I to the Geneva Conventions on the Protection of War Victims (Cont'd), 82 *American Journal of International Law* 784.

Sorell, Tom (2003) Morality and Emergency, 103 *Proceedings of the Aristotelian Society, New Series* 21.

Spieker, Heike (1999) Die Bedeutung der ad hoc-Tribunale bei der Errichtung des ständigen Internationalen Strafgerichtshofs: einige völkerrechtliche Aspekte, 12 *Informationsschritten Humanitäres* 4, 216.

Stein, Arthur A. (2010) Neoliberal Institutionalism, in Christian Reus-Smit and Duncan Snidal, eds., *Oxford Handbook of International Relations*, Oxford University Press.

Stone, John (2007) Technology and the Problem of Civilian Casualties in War, in Brian Rapperts, ed., *Technology and Security. Governing Threats in the New Millennium*, Basingstoke: Palgrave.

Swaine, Edward T. (2002) Rational Custom, 52 *Duke Law Journal* 559.

Tavernise, Sabrina and Andrew W. Lehren (2010) A Grim Portrait of Civilian Deaths in Iraq, *New York Times*, 23 October 2010, A1

Thomas, Ward (2001) *The Ethics of Destruction: Norms and Force in International Relations*, Ithaca NY: Cornell University Press.

Thompson, Alexander (2012) Coercive Enforcement in International Law, in Jeffrey L. Dunoff and Mark A. Pollack, eds., *Interdisciplinary Perspectives on International Law and International Relations: The State of the Art*, Cambridge University Press.

Thompson, Dennis F. (1980) Moral Responsibility of Public Officials: The Problem of Many Hands, 74 *American Political Science Review* 905.

Thürer, Daniel (1996) Das Selbstbestimmungsrecht der Völker und die Anerkennung neuer Staaten, in Hanspeter Neuhold and Bruno Simma, eds., *Neues Europäisches Völkerrecht nach dem Ende des Ost-West-Konfliktes?* Baden-Baden: Nomos.

Tilford, Earl H. (1988) *Setup: What the Air Force Did in Vietnam and Why*, Maxwell AL: Air University Press.

Tomuschat, Christian (1993) Obligations Arising for States Without or Against Their Will, 241 *Collected Courses of The Hague Academy of International Law* 195.

(2002) Common Values and the Place of the Charter in Europe, 14 *European Review of Public Law* 159.

(2010) Human Rights and International Humanitarian Law, 21 *European Journal of International Law* 15.

Trimble, Phillip R. (1986) A Revisionist View of Customary International Law, 33 *UCLA Law Review* 665.

Trubek, David M., Patrick Cottrell and Mark Nance (2005) *'Soft Law,' 'Hard Law,' and European Integration. Toward a Theory of Hybridity*, http://eucenter.wisc.edu/OMC/Papers/EUC/trubeketal.pdf (last accessed 12 February 2011).

Tucker, Spencer C., ed. (1998) *Encyclopaedia of the Vietnam War: A Political, Social, and Military History*, Oxford University Press.

Tyler, Tom R. (2006) *Why People Obey the Law*, Princeton University Press.

Uhler, Oscar M. and Henry Coursier (1958) *Commentary on Geneva Convention IV Relative to the Protection of Civilian Persons in Time of War*, Geneva: International Committee of the Red Cross.

UK, Ministry of Defence (2005) *The Manual of the Law of Armed Conflict*, Oxford University Press.

Ullman, Harland and James P. Wade Jr (1996) *Shock and Awe: Achieving Rapid Dominance*, Washington DC: National Defense University Institute for National Strategic Studies.

Uppsala Conflict Data Project (2009) *Code Book*, www.prio.no/sptrans/ 1423485763/Codebook_UCDP_PRIO Armed Conflict Dataset v4_2009.pdf (last accessed 13 July 2009).

US Department of Defense (1957/1976) The Joint Chiefs of Staff, *The Law of Land Warfare*, Field Manual 27–10 of 15 July (revised 1976).

(1967) The Joint Chiefs of Staff, *Air Operations Against North Vietnam and Laos, Target Study – North Vietnam*.

(1971/2) *The Pentagon Papers: The Defense Department History of United States Decision Making on Vietnam*, 'Senator Gravel Edition', Boston MA: Beacon Press.

(1974/2006) *Department of Defense Law of War Programme*, Directive 5100.77 of 5 November 1974 (last reissued as US Department of Defense Directive 2311.01E of 9 May 2006).

(1976) Department of the Air Force, *International Law: The Conduct of Armed Conflict and Air Operations*, Air Force Pamphlet 110–31.

(1989) Army Judge Advocate General's Legal Center & School, International and Operational Law Department, *The Commander's Handbook on the Law of Naval Operations*.

(1992) *Conduct of the Persian Gulf War*, Final Report to Congress of April.

(1995) Army Judge Advocate General's Legal Center & School, International and Operational Law Department, *The Commander's Handbook on the Law of Naval Operations.*

(1997) Air Land Sea Application Centre, *The Joint Targeting Process and Procedures for Targeting Time-Critical Targets*, Field Manual 90–36 of 25 July.

(1998) Department of the Air Force, *Intelligence Targeting Guide*, Air Force Pamphlet 14–210 of 1 February.

(2000/11) Department of the Air Force, *Air Warfare*, Doctrine Document 2–1 of 22 January 2000 (last changed 28 July).

(2002a) Army Judge Advocate General's Legal Center & School, International and Operational Law Department, *Operational Law Handbook.*

(2002b) The Joint Chiefs of Staff, *Joint Doctrine for Targeting*, Joint Publication 3–60 of 17 January.

(2003a) Army Judge Advocate General's Legal Center & School, International and Operational Law Department, *Operational Law Handbook.*

(2003b) Assessment and Analysis Division, 'Operation Iraqi Freedom – By the Numbers', www.globalsecurity.org/military/library/report/2003/uscen taf_oif_report_30apr2003.pf (last accessed 12 January 2011).

(2003c) *Military Commission Instruction* no. 2 of 30 April.

(2003d) Department of the Air Force, *Basic Doctrine*, Doctrine Document 1 of 17 November.

(2004) Army Judge Advocate General's Legal Center & School, International and Operational Law Department, *Operational Law Handbook.*

(2006a) Army Judge Advocate General's Legal Center & School, International and Operational Law Department, *The Military Commander and the Law.*

(2006b) Army Judge Advocate General's Legal Center & School, International and Operational Law Department, *Operational Law Handbook.*

(2006c/2011) Department of the Air Force, *Targeting*, Doctrine Document 3–60 of 8 June (last changed 28 July 2011).

(2007a) Army Judge Advocate General's Legal Center & School, International and Operational Law Department, *Operational Law Handbook.*

(2007b) Department of the Air Force, *Strategic Attack*, Air Force Doctrine Document 2–1.2 of 12 June.

(2007c) Joint Forces Command, *Joint Fires and Targeting Handbook* of 19 October.

(2007d/2011) The Joint Chiefs of Staff, *Joint Targeting*, Joint Publication 3–60 of 13 April (last changed 28 July 2011).

(2007e/2011) *Air Force Glossary*, Air Force Doctrine Document 1–2 of 11 January 2007 (last changed 28 July 2011).

(2008a) Army Judge Advocate General's Legal Center & School, International and Operational Law Department, *The Military Commander and the Law*.

(2008b) Joint Forces Command, *Memorandum for Joint Forces Command*, 14 August.

(2008c) Army Judge Advocate General's Legal Center & School, International and Operational Law Department, *Operational Law Handbook*.

(2010a) The Joint Chiefs of Staff, *Joint Operations*, Joint Publication 3–0 of March.

(2010b) Department of the Army, *The Targeting Process*, Field Manual 3–6 of November.

(2010c) Army Judge Advocate General's Legal Center & School, International and Operational Law Department, *Operational Law Handbook*.

(2011a) Army Judge Advocate General's Legal Center & School, International and Operational Law Department, *Operational Law Handbook*.

(2011b) Department of the Air Force, *Basic Doctrine, Organization, and Command*, Doctrine Document 1 of 14 October.

(2012) Army Judge Advocate General's Legal Center & School, International and Operational Law Department, *Operational Law Handbook*.

US Department of State (1965) Under-Secretary George Wildman Ball, *Keeping the Power of Decision in the South Viet-Nam Crisis*, Memo to the President 18 June.

Verdross, Alfred (1926) *Die Verfassung der Völkerrechtsgemeinschaft*, Vienna and Berlin: Springer.

Vitoria, Francisco ed. Ernest Nys (1995) *De Indis et De jure Belli Relectiones*, Gretzville NY: W. S. Hein.

von Stein, Jana (2012) The Engines of Compliance, in Jeffrey L. Dunoff and Mark A. Pollack, eds., *Interdisciplinary Perspectives on International Law and International Relations: The State of the Art*, Cambridge University Press.

Waldron, Jeremy (2010a) *Vagueness and the Guidance of Action*, New York University, Public Law and Legal Theory Working Papers, Paper 10–81.

(2010b) *Torture, Terrorism and Trade-Offs*, Oxford University Press.

(2010c) *The Rule of Law and the Importance of Procedure*, New York University Public Law and Legal Theory Working Papers, Paper 10–73.

(2011a) *Thoughtfulness and the Rule of Law*, New York University, Public Law and Legal Theory Working Papers, Paper 11–1.

(2011b) Are Sovereigns Entitled to the Benefit of the International Rule of Law? 22 *European Journal of International Law* 315.

Waltz, Kenneth N. (1979) *Theory of International Politics*, Columbus OH: McGraw-Hill.

Walzer, Michael (2004) *Arguing About War*, New Haven CT: Yale University Press.

(2006) *Just and Unjust Wars: A Moral Argument with Historical Illustrations*, New York: Basic Books.

Warden, John A., III (1989) *The Air Campaign. Planning for Combat*, Washington DC and London: Brassey's.

(1995) The Enemy as a System, 9 *Airpower Journal* 43.

Warner, Daniel (1998) The Nuclear Weapons Decision by the International Court of Justice: Locating the Raison Behind Raison d'Etat, 27 *Millennium* 299.

Watkin, Kenneth (2004) Controlling the Use of Force: A Role for Human Rights Norms in Contemporary Armed Conflict, 98 *American Journal of International Law* 1.

(2005) Canada/United States Military Interoperability and Humanitarian Law Issues, 15 *Duke Journal of Comparative and International Law* 281.

Weber, Max (1949) 'Objectivity' in Social Science and Social Policy, in Edward A. Shils and Henry A. Finch, eds., *Max Weber on the Methodology of the Social Sciences*, Glencoe IL: Free Press.

Welch, David A. (1993) *Justice and the Genesis of War*, Cambridge University Press.

Weller, Marc (2002) Undoing the Global Constitution: UN Security Council Action on the International Criminal Court, 78 *International Affairs* 693.

Welsh, Jennifer M. (2006) Conclusion: The Evolution of Humanitarian Intervention in International Society, in Jennifer M. Welsh, ed., *Humanitarian Intervention and International Society*, New York NY: Oxford University Press.

Wendt, Alexander (1992) Anarchy is What States Make of it: The Social Construction of Power Politics, 46 *International Organization* 391.

(1995) Constructing International Politics, 20 *International Security* 71.

(1998) On Constitution and Causation in International Relations, 24 *Review of International Studies* 101.

(1999) *Social Theory of International Politics*, Cambridge University Press.

(2000) On the Via Media: A Response to the Critics, 26 *Review of International Studies* 165.

Wenger, Etienne (1998) *Communities of Practice: Learning, Meaning, and Identity*, Cambridge University Press.

Wheeler, Nicholas (2004) The Kosovo Bombing Campaign, in Christian Reus-Smit, ed., *The Politics of International Law*, New York NY: Cambridge University Press.

White House, Office of the Press Secretary (1987) Letter of Transmittal to the Senate of the United States of 29 January (reprinted in 81 *American Journal of International Law* 910).

Wohlforth, William C. (2010) Realism, in Christian Reus-Smit and Duncan Snidal, eds., *The Oxford Handbook of International Relations*, New York NY: Oxford University Press.

Woodward, Bob (2004) *Plan of Attack*, London: Pocket Books.

Worden, Mike (1998) *Rise of the Fighter Generals: The Problem of Air Force Leadership*, Maxwell AL: Air University Press.

Wrage, Stephen (2003) Precision Air Power in the Second Gulf War, 19 *Defence and Security Analysis* 277.

Wright, Evan (2005) *Generation Kill: Devil Dogs, Iceman, Captain America, and the New Face of American War*, London: Transworld Publications.

Wynne, Michael W. (2010) '"Re-norming" the Asymmetric Advantage in Air Dominance. "Going to War with the Air Force you Have". Second Line of Defense', www.sldinfo.com/?p=11968 (last accessed 17 February 2010).

Young, Marilyn B. (2009) Bombing Civilians from the Twentieth to the Twenty-first Century, in Yuki Tanaka and Marilyn B. Young, eds., *Bombing Civilians: A Twentieth-century History*, New York and London: The New Press.

Young, Oran (1979) *Compliance and Public Authority*, Baltimore MD: Johns Hopkins University Press.

(1989) *International Cooperation: Building Regimes for Natural Resources and the Environment*, Ithaca NY: Cornell University Press.

Zehfuss, Maja (2011) Targeting: Precision and the Production of Ethics, 17 *European Journal of International Relations* 543.

Zoepf, Katherine and Sam Dagher (2008) For Family in Iraq, Drop in Deaths is not Enough, *New York Times*, 3 November 2008.

Interviews

Eighteen interviews were conducted with commanders, JAGs and intelligence analysts. They are listed below. With five exceptions I refrain from naming the interviewees in accordance with their wishes.

Interview no. 1 with ret. Colonel John A. Warden III, 12 June 2008, Command and Staff College Shrivenham UK.

Interview no. 2 with US Air Force Colonel, 24 June 2008, US Air Force Headquarters Arlington Virginia.

Interview no. 3 with US Air Force Major, 26 June 2008, US Air Force Intelligence Analysis Agency Arlington Virginia.

Interview no. 4 with US Air Force Colonel, 26 June 2008, US Air Force Intelligence Analysis Agency Arlington Virginia.

Interview no. 5 with US Air Force Major, 26 June 2008, US Air Force Intelligence Analysis Agency Arlington Virginia.

Interview no. 6 with ret. US Air Force Colonel, 26 June 2008, US Air Force Intelligence Analysis Agency Arlington Virginia.

Interview no. 7 with US Air Force Major and JAG, 27 June 2008, US Air Force Operations and International Law Division Arlington Virginia.

Interview no. 8 with ret. US Air Force and JAG, JAG, 27 June 2008, US Air Force Operations and International Law Division Arlington Virginia.

Interview no. 9 with US Air Force Colonel, 27 June 2008, US Air Force Office of the General Counsel Arlington Virginia.

Interview no. 10 with Lieutenant General David A. Deptula, US Air Force's deputy chief of staff for intelligence, surveillance and reconnaissance, 1 June 2008, US Air Force Headquarters Arlington Virginia.

Interview no. 11 with US Air Force Major General Charles Dunlap, Deputy Judge Advocate General, 2 July 2008, US Air Force Department of the Judge Advocate General Arlington Virginia.

Interview no. 12 with US Air Force colonel and JAG, 28 July 2008, US Air Force Operations and International Law Division Arlington Virginia.

Interview no. 13 with US Air Force colonel and JAG, 28 July 2008, US Air Force Operations and International Law Division Arlington Virginia.

Interview no. 14 with res. US Air Force colonel and JAG, 28 July 2008, US Air Force Operations and International Law Division Arlington Virginia.

Interview no. 15 with Marc Garlasco, Senior Intelligence Analyst covering Iraq in 2003, 1 August 2008, New York NY.

Interview no. 16 with US Army colonel and JAG, 5 August 2008, US Army Office of the Judge Advocate General, Washington DC.

Interview no. 17 with US Army colonel and JAG, 5 August 2008, US Army Office of the Judge Advocate General, Washington DC.

Interview no. 18 with retired US Navy Admiral Leon A. Edney, 2 February 2009 (over the phone).

Twenty-two semi-structured interviews were conducted with pilots, joint terminal attack controllers and navigators. Twelve of them were deployed in OIF, three of them were deployed in ODS, three were deployed over North

Vietnam and four did not specify their deployment. Most of them did not wish to be named. When quoting from specific interviews I, therefore, refer to operators by rank and deployment.

USN captain (unspecified deployment), 8 May 2008

USAF F-18 pilot of the rank of major deployed in OIF, 12 June 2008

USAF F-14 pilot of the rank of major deployed in OIF, 18 June 2008

USAF B-1 pilot of the rank of major deployed in OIF, 19 June 2008

USMC F-16C pilot of the rank of major deployed in OIF, 20 June 2008

USAF F-15E pilot of the rank of major deployed in OIF and OAF, 20 June 2008

USAF F-15 pilot of the rank of major deployed in OIF, 20 June 2008

USAF F-15 pilot of the rank of captain deployed in OIF, 24 June 2008

USAF F-4 pilot of the rank of colonel deployed during ORT, 24 June 2008

USAF major (unspecified deployment), 24 June 2008

USAF colonel deployed in OIF, 28 July 2008

USAF joint terminal attack controller of the rank of major deployed in OIF, 28 July 2008

USAF (now) retired colonel deployed in ODS, 29 July 2008

USAF (now) retired colonel deployed in ODS, 31 July 2008

USAF (now) retired colonel deployed in ODS, 31 July 2008

USN pilot deployed during the US engagement in Vietnam (unspecified rank). 28 January 2009

USN pilot deployed during ORT (unspecified rank), 28 January 2009

USAF navigator (unspecified rank and deployment), 28 January 2009

USN joint terminal attack controller of the rank of lieutenant colonel deployed in OIF, 11 April 2011

USAF F-16 pilot of the rank of lieutenant colonel deployed in OIF, 11 April 2011

USAF B-1 pilot of the rank of colonel deployed in OIF, 12 April 2011

USAF predator operator (unspecified rank and deployment), 12 April 2011

Appendix

Behavioural relevance of IL

IL is behaviourally relevant if recourse to law makes a counter-factual difference for behaviour. This means that adherence to IL has an effect on behaviour beyond what interests and non-legal normative beliefs would have led an actor to do anyway. The agent in question would have acted differently had she merely followed her normative beliefs and/or interests without considering IL.

Causal dependence of IL

In the international realm, actors create IL and comply with it if this serves their prior interests and/or accords with their extra-legal normative beliefs. IL does not provide an independent reason for action.

Containment command

When choosing targets for attack A has to engage objects and persons in B that contribute in *one causal step* to the competition between A's and B's military forces. This is deemed sufficient for this competition to proceed and for one side to achieve generic military victory.

Contingent indeterminacy

No matter how specific a legal prescription is, there are always cases for which it is unclear whether a legal rule applies. The extent of this 'penumbra of uncertainty' is contingent on the architecture of a legal regime and the language used. Contingent indeterminacy explains how far a rule of IL bends to endorse the interpreting actor's prior interests or extra-legal normative beliefs.

Epistemic dependence of IL

Given IL's structural indeterminacy (see below), what it means always to a certain extent depends on the interpreter's conception of utility and appropriateness. IL does not provide a normative code for guiding action or an objective standard for evaluating behaviour that is independent of utility or appropriateness.

Generic military victory

Overcoming the enemy's military through attrition of military capabilities and fielded forces, regardless of the political, moral or other non-military context of a war and without regard to the ultimately desired end-state.

Intellectual effect of IL

As IL is more action guiding than much of morality or social norms, recourse to IL makes it easier for the actor to determine how to behave. It also makes it more likely that the consequences of the actor's behaviour reflect the compromise between utility and appropriateness that the international society has enshrined in IL and therefore deems legitimate.

Interest

Reasons for action that emerge as urgent, direct imperatives in a given situation and which promise relatively close gratification.

Logic of efficiency (moderate)

A wages war according to the logic of efficiency (moderate) if those objects and persons in B are targeted whose engagement is expected to reduce B's military capabilities *in three or fewer causal steps* and yield an immediate advantage in light of A's overall political, moral or other goals. Progress in war is defined in light of the political, moral or other end-state that A seeks with the use of force.

Logic of efficiency (radical)

A wages war according to the logic of efficiency (radical) if those objects and persons in B are targeted whose engagement promises the quickest and most direct achievement of A's overall political, moral or other goals. The principle of distinction is ignored.

Logic of liability

A wages war according to the logic of liability if those persons are targeted who (1) responsibly contribute to B's unjustified threat, (2) whose engagement is necessary to avert the threat they pose and (3) whose engagement is proportionate to their contribution to B's unjustified threat.

Logic of sufficiency

A wages war according to the logic of sufficiency if only those objects and persons in B are targeted whose engagement is expected to reduce *in one causal step* B's military capabilities and yield a genuine advantage for A in the competition between A's and B's militaries. Progress in war is defined with a view to the achievement of generic military victory. A's political, moral or other goals do not bear on which objects or persons are targeted.

Motivational effect of IL

As the intellectual effect of IL makes it more likely that the consequences of an actor's behaviour betray her intent to comply with or defy the law, acting appropriately, in this case adhering to IL, is more of an interest (as defined above) and less of a norm (as defined below) than acting appropriately would be in the absence of IL.

Norm

Imperatives for action that arise in spite of the demands of the situation. They can be related to an actor's concept of self, to anticipated developments, or her ideas as to how a society works or ought to work.

Normative success of IL

Normatively successful IL vouchsafes that an actor recurring to it will behave in a way that meets an extra-legal normative standard. One important such standard is whether behaviour generated *inter alia* by behavioural relevance of IL is perceived as legitimate. If the touchstone of normative success is perceived legitimacy, we have to identify the audience whose reflective approval IL seeks.

Ontological dependence of IL

IL as a reason for action or motivational force does not exist independently of interests and norms. IL as a normative code or standard does not exist independently of utility and appropriateness.

Sequencing command

A may only strive for generic military victory during the conduct of hostilities. A has to act as if generic military victory is sufficient for the achievement of A's political, moral or other goals.

Structural indeterminacy

IL depends for its existence and for its meaning on prior motivational forces (interests and normative beliefs) and the normative standards they imply (utility and appropriateness). The meaning of a rule of IL can therefore not be determined independently of the interpreting agent's perception of utility and appropriateness. This indeterminacy is 'a structural property' of all IL.

Index

CAMBRIDGE STUDIES IN INTERNATIONAL
RELATIONS